Sikhism and History

Sikhism and History

Edited by
Pashaura Singh
N. Gerald Barrier

OXFORD
UNIVERSITY PRESS

OXFORD
UNIVERSITY PRESS

YMCA Library Building, Jai Singh Road, New Delhi 110 001

Oxford University Press is a department of the University of Oxford. It furthers the
University's objective of excellence in research, scholarship, and education
by publishing worldwide in

Oxford   New York

Auckland Bangkok Buenos Aires Cape Town   Chennai
Dar es Salaam Delhi Hong Kong Istanbul Karachi Kolkata
Kuala Lumpur Madrid Melbourne Mexico City Mumbai Nairobi
São Paulo Shanghai Taipei Tokyo Toronto

Oxford is a registered trademark of Oxford University Press
in the UK and in certain other countries

Published in India
By Oxford University Press, New Delhi

© Oxford University Press, 2004

The moral rights of the author have been asserted
Database right Oxford University Press (maker)

First published 2004

All rights reserved. No part of this publication may be reproduced,
stored in a retrieval system, or transmitted, in any form or by any means,
without the prior permission in writing of Oxford University Press,
or as expressly permitted by law, or under terms agreed with the appropriate
reprographics rights organization. Enquiries concerning reproduction
outside the scope of the above should be sent to the Rights Department,
Oxford University Press, at the address above

You must not circulate this book in any other binding or cover
and you must impose this same condition on any acquiror

ISBN 0 19 566708 5

Typeset by Le Studio Graphique, New Delhi 110 029
Printed in India at Sai Printopack Pvt. Ltd., New Delhi 110 020
Published by Manzar Khan, Oxford University Press
YMCA Library Building, Jai Singh Road, New Delhi 110 001

**Library
University of Texas
at San Antonio**

Prepared under the auspices of
The Sikh Studies Program,
University of Michigan
In honour of
Professor W.H. McLeod

Contents

Acknowledgments

The Michigan Sikh Studies Program and the Department of Asian Languages and Cultures, University of Michigan, Ann Arbor, provided generous financial support for the September 2001 international conference on which this book is based. The Sikh Studies Association gave assistance in organizing the event and helped with publicity. Members of the Ann Arbor and Detroit area Sikh community also assisted greatly with hospitality and other necessary arrangements for conference, and their generous donations are sincerely appreciated.

The editors wish to thank Professor Donald S. Lopez, Chair, Department of Asian Languages and Cultures (ALC), for his help with last-minute details of the Conference Program. Professor Shirley Neuman, Dean of the College of Literature, Science and the Arts, showed special interest in this conference, and we thank her for her support and participation in the inaugural session. We are grateful to Jennifer Eshelman, ALC Department Administrator, and Karen Munson, ALC Secretary, for making excellent arrangements during the conference. Dr Virinder Singh Grewal, Dr Satnam Singh Bhugra, Dr Jaswant Singh, Dr Amrik Singh Chatha, Dr Jaswinder Kaur Chatha, Dr Trilochan Singh, Chain Singh Sandhu, Baldev Singh Dhaliwal and Raman Kaur have contributed energetically in many ways to build the new programme in Sikh studies at the University of Michigan. Their selfless and untiring support is much appreciated. Maninderpal Singh and Manpreet Kaur volunteered many hours in preparing materials for the conference. A number of students of Michigan Sikh Study Circle (MSSC) assisted in various ways. We thank all of them for their timely help.

The complete list of the participants, invited speakers, and respondents is given at the end of the volume. The first part of the introduction, putting the conference into perspective by highlighting Professor W.H. McLeod's contribution in the field of Sikh studies, is by Pashaura Singh and the second part, dealing with the interpretive discussion of various essays, by N. Gerald Barrier. Although the essays are well documented and discuss certain sensitive issues in a scholarly fashion, the interpretations are the responsibility of the authors and do not necessarily reflect the viewpoint of the editors, the sponsors of the conference, the University of Michigan, or the publishers. We welcome suggestions and constructive criticism that may be incorporated into a revised edition.

PASHAURA SINGH
N. GERALD BARRIER

Section One

Introduction–I
The Contribution of Professor W.H. McLeod
in the Field of Sikh Studies

Pashaura Singh

I

This volume grows out of an international conference on Sikh studies hosted by the Program in Sikh Studies and the Department of Asian Languages and Cultures between September 27–29, 2001 at the University of Michigan, Ann Arbor. The conference theme was: 'Sikhism in the Light of History'. Sikhism is the newest of the world religions, with origins not in a distant prehistory that can never be fully recovered, but in a period of rich historical sources. As a consequence, scholars of Sikhism are able to explore issues of scriptural authority, social history, gender, diaspora, and national and religious identity from perspectives that scholars of other religions often lack. Indeed, the Michigan conference was able to explore some of the consequences of Sikhism's appearance in the light of history—for scholars of Sikhism, for scholars of religion, and for scholars of history.

In the plenary session of the conference on Thursday, September 27, 2001 at Michigan Union, Donald S. Lopez, Chair of the Department of Asian Languages and Cultures, acted as the moderator and welcomed the scholars of Sikh studies who had come from four continents. Welcoming the conference participants, Dean Shirley Neuman of the College of Literature, Science and the Arts made the following opening remarks:

In 1999 the Regents of the University of Michigan approved the establishment of the Tara Singh and Balwant Kaur Chattha and Gurbaksh Singh and Kirpal Kaur

Brar Sikh Studies Professorship. The Chair and Professorship is to be tenured in the Department of Asian Languages and Cultures in the College of Literature, Science and the Arts. The Professorships in the College are endowed by many kinds of donors with different motives. But for me, the stories behind these endowed Professorships that always move me the most are those in which a great many members of a community work together, each contributing what they can to realize their shared goal of a Professorship. Such community activity speaks to a desire to preserve a cultural heritage and respectful recognition that one of the best ways of doing so is through the teaching and scholarship that characterize a great university such as the University of Michigan. This Chair in Sikh Studies is a consequence of such a desire and such recognition. And, it is also the consequence of a great deal of hard work, dedication and generosity by many members of the Sikh Studies Association.

Providing the location of Sikh studies in the field of South Asian studies that form an integral part of the University of Michigan's academic focus on area studies, the Dean further noted:

The Chair has been established at a timely moment ... Our decision to make the study of India a priority in this initiative recognizes the importance of its cultures and religions and the history of great civilizations and of its great and emerging strengths in the community of twenty-first century nations. The Sikh Studies Chair is crucial part of that initiative.

In her closing remarks, Dean Shirley Neuman made the following observations on the scholarly activities of the Sikh Studies Program:

Over the past two years the endowment provided by the Sikh Studies Association has given us the opportunity to promote understanding of the Sikh tradition in several ways. This distinguished gathering here of scholars of Sikhism from around the world is one of those very fine opportunities. Beginning this evening, for the next two days, you will together present and discuss 'state of art' scholarship about Sikh tradition from the perspectives of many disciplines, including religious studies, literary studies, history, gender studies, sociology and anthropology. The work that you will present and the work that you will do here over the next two days is crucial to the continuing development of Sikh studies as a scholarly discipline. And, as the events of the last two weeks have all too sadly shown, your work is also crucial in bringing a more informed understanding of the Sikh tradition to the American people. Your task then over the next two days is a large one. But there is also an occasion for this gathering that is purely joyous. And, that is to honour the life and work of Professor Hew McLeod. I have met Professor McLeod only once before this evening. But in that hour I learnt more about Sikh studies than I have in my entire previous life. He is a wonderful scholar of Sikhism and a wonderful spokesperson for the scholarship of this tradition. I am delighted to welcome him back to Ann

Arbor and to this conference. And, most of all, I am honoured and I am pleased to inaugurate this conference on 'Sikhism in the Light of History' and to welcome each and every one of you to it.[1]

The inaugural function celebrated the lifetime achievement of W.H. McLeod, an eminent historian who has made a seminal contribution in the field of Sikh studies. The Sikh Studies Program of the University of Michigan acknowledged his contribution by presenting him a plaque with the following inscription: 'The University of Michigan Sikh Studies Program honours William Hewat McLeod with a Lifetime Achievement Award for his distinguished contribution to the field of Sikh Studies.' Donald S. Lopez and Pashaura Singh represented the University of Michigan, while Virinder Singh Grewal, Satnam Singh Bhugra, Jaswant Singh, Amrik Singh Chattha, Jaswinder Kaur Chattha, Raman Kaur, Baldev Singh Dhaliwal, and Chain Singh Sandhu gave the honour on behalf of the Sikh Studies Association.

As a leading Western scholar of Sikh religion and history, W.H. (Hew) McLeod has single-handedly introduced, nourished and advanced the field of Sikh studies over the last four decades. On a number of occasions, he has represented the Sikhs and Sikhism to both academic and popular audiences in the English-speaking world. He appeared as an expert witness in the court-hearing of the 'Royal Canadian Mounted Police (RCMP) Turban Case' in Calgary, Alberta in 1994. Thanks to Professor McLeod, the Canadian Sikhs scored a major victory in this case and won the right to wear turbans as part of their dress as RCMP officers. In 1999 he appeared for Canadian Human Rights Commission in a hearing involving Sikh *kirpans* ('miniature swords') carried on aircraft.

Let me give a brief biographical sketch of Hew McLeod. He was born on 2 August, 1932 in Feilding, a town in the North Island of New Zealand, near which his father had a sheep farm. He attended secondary school at Nelson College in the South Island town of Nelson. While at school, he decided to abandon his intention to be a farmer, and instead chose to be a teacher at school. He went from school to the University of Otago as an undergraduate and did a BA and an MA in History. He followed those degrees with three years at the Knox College Theological Hall. Soon after entering the University of Otago as an undergraduate Hew was greatly attracted by the Student Christian Movement (SCM). The SCM was certainly a Christian movement, but everything in the Christian faith was open to question. Nothing was sacrosanct. Belonging to the SCM not only provided him with continuing contact with the Church, but it also permitted him to freely express and accept any religious doubts. This was an emphasis that Hew greatly appreciated, though it did serve to keep him in the Church rather longer than would otherwise have been the case.

Hew McLeod and his wife Margaret travelled to India in 1958 and stayed there altogether for nine years. His first five years (1958–1963) were spent learning the Punjabi and Hindi languages and teaching in the Christian Boys' Higher Secondary School in Kharar (near Chandigarh). After that he did a PhD in London under the guidance of Professor A.L. Basham. The focus of his doctoral thesis was on 'The Life and Doctrine of Guru Nanak', a work which was published by Clarendon Press in 1968 at Oxford in the revised form under the new title of *Guru Nanak and the Sikh Religion*. Having received his PhD degree in 1965, Hew McLeod returned to India for four years as Lecturer in Punjab History at Baring Union Christian College, Batala (1965–9). Then he returned to New Zealand and joined the History Department at University of Otago, Dunedin, where he retired as Professor of History in 1997. He acquired a DLit degree from the University of London in 1990 for his outstanding work in the field and was elected a Fellow of the Royal Society of New Zealand (FRSNZ) in 1999. The Royal Society of New Zealand consists primarily of scientists, but a small number of others get in on the grounds that they are social scientists.

In addition to a distinguished teaching and research career at the University of Otago in New Zealand, Hew McLeod has held fellowships and teaching positions at numerous UK and North American institutions, including Oxford and the University of Toronto. He won the Smuts Memorial Fellowship in Commonwealth Studies at University of Cambridge in 1969–70 and Leverhulme Visiting Fellowship in Pre-Colonial History at the University of Sussex in 1970–1. In 1986 he was the Canadian Commonwealth Fellow at the Centre for Religious Studies, University of Toronto, when he introduced the study of the Sikh tradition to the North American academic mainstream. This was the crucial time when, after the events of 1984, the Sikhs had become the focus of worldwide attention.

Not surprisingly, Hew McLeod was chosen from an international pool of scholars to deliver the nationwide lectures on the history of religions in 1986 sponsored by the American Council of Learned Societies. This was indeed a rare distinction that no other scholar of Sikhism, and few other scholars of South Asian studies, had ever achieved. This was not only an honour for Hew McLeod, but also an indication that the study of the Sikh tradition had finally achieved its rightful place in the Western academic establishment. During this tour of hectic lecture series Hew suffered a severe stroke on February 2, 1987 at New York that prevented him attending an international conference on 'Sikh History and Religion in the Twentieth Century' on February 13–15, 1987 at the University of Toronto.

The constant support of Margaret McLeod was crucial to her husband's dramatic recovery from the stroke. In less than a year and a half, Hew McLeod resumed his writing, editing, teaching, chairing his department at the University of Otago, and in September 1988 returned to Toronto as visiting professor of Sikh history and religion, serving for five years at the University of Toronto (1988–92). These years coincided with my preparation for the PhD degree and I had the rare privilege to have him as my supervisor. Arguably the foremost academic in the field of Sikh studies, Professor McLeod taught me skills of scientific inquiry. Passing muster with this meticulous scholar was a highlight of my professional life. He guided me with gentle care and much sternness.

In his first communication with me after setting my paper for comprehensive examination, Hew McLeod wrote to me from New Zealand on 28 February 1989:

I have just dispatched your examination paper to Ron Sweet. I am writing to you to say that you must not answer the questions in a particular way merely because you think that I shall approve of the answers. You are not going to be marked down because you disagree with me. You will be marked down only if you fail to give adequate reasons for your opinion (where opinion is called for) and I am well aware that there is more than one opinion available on several subjects. Answer truly and truthfully, and do so with reasons, and you will receive full credit for your answers, even if they disagree with my own.[2]

Thus right from the beginning Professor McLeod allowed me to even have disagreements with his own views and encouraged me to become my own person. That is what I cherish the most from my experience with him. I still remember the day when it was heavily snowing in Toronto. During the class I had expressed the desire to see his forthcoming book from Columbia University. In that cold and heavy snow he walked to my apartment and knocked at the door. When I opened the door he offered me the galley proofs of his book. This is the compassionate side of a man who has always cared for his students. As a footnote, it gives me further satisfaction that I was the first Sikh to receive a PhD degree in 1991 with specialization in the area of Sikh studies from a Canadian university.

After retiring from the University of Otago, Hew McLeod held a visiting fellowship at Balliol College, Oxford, in 1997–8. In 2000 he received a grant from the Rockefeller Foundation that enabled him to pursue his research in the quiet surroundings of Bellagio on Lake Como in North Italy. Hew McLeod is the author of fifteen books, four edited translations, two edited volumes, three booklets and more than seventy articles published in academic journals and books. A complete list of his publications is given as an appendix to this introduction. The Clarendon Press published many of his early works at Oxford. His works have been received with much enthusiasm and global critical acclaim.

In fact, the academic issues raised by Hew McLeod have drawn a great many polemic responses from traditional Sikh scholars that have generated more heat than light for the last three decades. He has been the target of a determined campaign launched by a particular group of Sikh scholars who have challenged his motives to undermine the Sikh faith. It is no wonder that he frequently justifies his academic approach with a 'concern for sympathetic understanding'. The following section actually deals with this issue in detail. Let us listen to Hew McLeod's own voice in the first person from an article on 'Methodology and Belief'. This is taken from a short paper sent by him to a Sikh conference held at Birmingham in September 1998.

II

I am a historian (or rather I attempt to be one) and all my work is built upon the need for historical evidence. I am not primarily concerned with theology, although as we shall see shortly it is altogether impossible to analyse the material which interests me without becoming distinctly and deeply involved in concerns which properly concern the theologian. My field is accurately described as religious history or as the history of a particular religion, namely the Sikh religion. However, one must never ignore the fundamental fact that it is History which I study and seek to understand. This means that the methodology which I use is emphatically historical. It may be a dated methodology, but it remains one that is specifically historical.

The first of the two key periods during which I learnt and absorbed this methodology was during the mid-fifties while I was doing my undergraduate work in the University of Otago in Dunedin, New Zealand. This foundation was considerably enlarged by the years which I spent at the School of Oriental and African Studies in London during the mid-sixties. The result of these two periods was that I emerged as an explicitly western historian. For this I make no apology. The western historical method may embody shortcomings and weaknesses, but personally I hold these to be minor. The fact is I am a western historian and proud of it.

What characterizes a western historian? To my mind the characteristic which stands above all others is the quest for evidence. The work of a western historian must involve a considerable amount of time spent on the slow, patient, and (for many) monotonous search for evidence. This does not mean searching in places which reveal only evidence which will suit a pre-formed view of the subject. It does not involve the suppression of inconvenient evidence either. Most assuredly it does not. From the evidence which emerges, the historian must seek to frame a pattern for the course of events of any particular period, one which takes into full account the testimony of all the evidence which has been uncovered.

This, of course, is a counsel of perfection. It assumes that western historians will bring to their analysis minds free from all influence and will consequently be able to determine a thoroughly unbiased interpretation. But no historian is like this. No historian is unbiased, and, although some may be relatively free from such influences, none is completely immune.

The answer to this problem must be to encourage all historians to be as fair and unbiased as they possibly can be. They must know that they will never succeed completely in this respect, but the greater the effort put into it, the more likely they are to reach sound conclusions.

But here one encounters a deeper and much more intractable problem. How is one to decide what is fair and unprejudiced? The western historian may answer that an appeal to rationalism will determine the issue. The West lives in the glow of the Enlightenment and of the scientific revolution, and everything should accordingly adhere to the principles of rationalism. Let it accord with scientific precepts, and let it be plainly and honestly reasonable.

This implies that the western approach to all such issues is the only sound one. It amounts in fact to truth, or so the proponents of this view will assert or assume. Are they correct? Some will emphatically deny this, insisting that there are spiritual or 'eastern' interpretations which allow for a much wider concept of truth. Westerners may deny that this is so, and the progressive decline of religion in the West would seem to support their view. Opponents will answer that with the educational system firmly under their control it is little wonder that their view marches forward, gathering all within its sway. And so the debate continues, although in the West at least there appears to be little doubt who is winning.

This does not necessarily mean that the western view is right. For me, however, it would appear to be the correct interpretation. I was born into a society which, by and large, accepted the Enlightenment and the scientific revolution; and I was certainly educated in accordance with their principles. This means that I am unashamedly western in my viewpoint, and when it came to acquiring a knowledge of historical method the western path was the way I followed. I was trained as a western historian, and for all the problems of bias which still remain it is as a western historian that I shall continue to work.

And so it is as a western historian that I approach Sikh history. I found my way to Sikh history by one of those paths which can lead a person in the most surprising of directions. I grew up as an undergraduate in a New Zealand in the days when New Zealand was one of the wealthiest countries on earth, and I felt it was my bounden duty to share what we had at home with other less fortunate peoples. This meant going to one of their countries and (so I imagined) making myself useful. It also answered the need for overseas travel which even then was a strong motive for young New Zealanders.

At that time, in the late fifties, almost the only New Zealand organizations which offered this kind of opportunity were the churches. I belonged to a Presbyterian church in Dunedin and I believed that I was a devout if somewhat doubting Christian. Employment with a religious mission was therefore no problem and so I applied to my own church for an overseas job. I was given a job teaching English in the Punjab.

Arriving in the Punjab I soon became aware that I was not well fitted for the task to which I had been appointed. Local teachers taught English as well as I did, and some of them could do it conspicuously better. While continuing the work for which I had been appointed I therefore turned back to what was my real interest, namely History. I began casting around for what might be rewarding and very soon decided that Sikh history was the lively subject for one living in the Punjab. I read at some length into the subject and then when I was due for leave I entered the School of Oriental and African Studies in London. From this period in the mid-sixties there eventually emerged my first book *Guru Nanak and the Sikh Religion*.

During this period two influences were brought to bear upon my work. The first was the awareness that Sikh history could not possibly be studied without an intimate knowledge of Sikh religion. The two are inextricably intertwined, and one cannot understand one without also understanding the other. The Penguin book entitled *Sikhism* is the result of this realization.

The second influence was the awareness (not yet faced) that I did not believe what the Christian message taught. This came to light in early 1966 after we had returned to the Punjab, when both my wife and I simultaneously opened our inner thoughts to each other and discovered that we were both unbelievers. I had never really believed, instead convincing myself that I ought to believe and that therefore I was a believer. Now, however, I could face the fact that I was not one and for both of us the experience was exhilarating to say the least. Since then my wife has called herself an agnostic and I have usually termed myself an atheist. Perhaps a softer word would be more appropriate, for one must be aware that the words 'atheism' and 'atheist' have a distinctly pejorative meaning for many people. 'Unbeliever' is such a word. For the last thirty-two years my personal philosophy has been that of an unbeliever and emphatically it continues to be so. I do not believe in a God and therefore I am an unbeliever.

This conviction does not mean that I am unable to appreciate other points of view or philosophies which their adherents term religious or spiritual. Although they may believe that I am disqualified from understanding such convictions I would hold that this is at most only partially correct. My perspective is from an essentially detached position as well as that of a former believer. I believe that it is one which enables me to view others with understanding and to pose questions which should be regarded as sympathetic. Whether they will be regarded as sympathetic is, of course, another question. This is an area in which I have been conspicuously unsuccessful—but I keep on trying.

Appendix
W.H. McLeod's Publications

For the benefit of students and researchers it will be quite useful to provide the updated list of McLeod's publications:

1. BOOKS

1.1 Books published

Guru Nanak and the Sikh Religion. Oxford: the Clarendon Press (1968). First Indian ed., rev. New Delhi: OUP (1976). Third impression 1988. Oxford India Paperbacks 1996, 1998. xii, p. 259. Reprinted as a part of the omnibus volume *Sikhs and Sikhism* (New Delhi: OUP, 2000).

The Evolution of the Sikh Community. New Delhi: OUP (1975). Oxford: the Clarendon Press (1976). viii, p. 119. Oxford India Paperbacks 1996, 1998. xi, p. 127. Reprinted as a part of the omnibus volume *Sikhs and Sikhism* (New Delhi: OUP, 2000).

Early Sikh Tradition. A Study of the Janam-sakhis. Oxford: the Clarendon Press (1980). xiv, p. 317. Reprinted as a part of the omnibus volume *Sikhs and Sikhism* (New Delhi: OUP, 2000).

Punjabis in New Zealand: A History of Punjabi Migration, 1890–1940. Amritsar: Guru Nanak Dev University (1986). Illus, maps. iv, p. 199.

The Sikhs: History, Religion, and Society. New York: Columbia University Press (1989). ix, p. 161.

Who is a Sikh? The Problem of Sikh Identity. Oxford: the Clarendon Press (1989). New Delhi: OUP (1989). x, p. 140. Reprinted as a part of the omnibus volume *Sikhs and Sikhism* (New Delhi: OUP, 2000), second printing of Indian edition (New Delhi: OUP, 2003).

Popular Sikh Art. A selection of bazaar posters with accompanying text. New Delhi: OUP (1991). Illustrated. xi, p. 139.

Punjab to Aotearoa: Migration and Settlement of Punjabis in New Zealand 1890–1990. With S.S. Bhullar. Hamilton: New Zealand Indian Association Country Section (Inc.) (1992). Illustrated p. 177.

Historical Dictionary of Sikhism. Lanham, Md., and London: Scarecrow Press (1995), New Delhi: OUP (2002, Indian edition). p. 323.

Sikhism. London: Penguin Books (1997). p. 334.

Gandhi and Indian Independence. With Richard Webb. Auckland: Macmillans (1998). p. 108.

Sikhs and Sikhism. Omnibus volume containing reprints of *Guru Nanak and the Sikh Religion, Early Sikh Tradition, The Evolution of the Sikh Community,* and *Who is a Sikh?,* all originally published by the Clarendon Press, Oxford, and Oxford University Press, New Delhi. New Delhi: Oxford University Press (1999). p. 259+317+127+140.

Exploring Sikhism: Aspects of Sikh Identity, Culture, and Thought. Collected articles. New Delhi: Oxford University Press (2000). p. 288.

Sikhs of the Khalsa: A History of the Khalsa Rahit. New Delhi: Oxford University Press (2003). p. 482.

Discovering the Sikhs: Autobiography of a Historian. Delhi: Permanent Black (2004).

1.2 *Edited translations (translations by W.H. McLeod)*

The B40 Janam-sakhi. An English translation with introduction and annotations of the India Office Library Gurmukhi manuscript *Panj. B40*, a janam-sakhi of Guru Nanak compiled in AD 1733 by Daya Ram Abrol. Amritsar: Guru Nanak Dev University (1980). xiv, 32, p. 271.

Textual Sources for the Study of Sikhism. Manchester: Manchester University Press (1984). Chicago: University of Chicago Press (1990). x, p. 166.

The Chaupa Singh Rahit-nama. The rahit-nama attributed to Chaupa Singh Chhibbar and the associated prose rahit-nama attributed to Nand Lal. Gurmukhi text and English translation with introduction and notes. Dunedin: University of Otago Press (1987). p. 260.

1.3 *Translation into Punjabi of work published in English*

Guru Nanak de udesh. Punjabi translation of Part V of *Guru Nanak and the Sikh Religion.* Translator: Mohan Jit Singh. Amritsar: Guru Nanak Dev University (1974). p. 115.

1.4 *Published work edited*

Henry Steinbach, *The Punjaub* (1st ed. London, 1846) 2nd edition, with introduction by W.H. McLeod. Karachi: Oxford University Press (Oxford in Asia Historical Reprints) (1976). xxxiv, p. 183.

1.5 *Edited volumes*

The Sants: Studies in a Devotional Tradition of India. Ed. Karine Schomer and W.H. McLeod. Berkeley: Berkeley Religious Studies Series; Delhi: Motilal Banarsidass (1987).

Sikh History and Religion in the Twentieth Century. Ed. Joseph T. O'Connell, Milton Israel, Willard G. Oxtoby, W.H. McLeod, and J.S. Grewal. Toronto: University of Toronto Centre for South Asian Studies (1988).

2. BOOKLETS

The Sikhs of the Punjab. A text for use in secondary schools. First NZ edition published by Graphic Educational Publications, Auckland (1968). Second

NZ edition by Whitcombe & Tombs, Auckland (1970). Indian edition by Lyall, Ludhiana (1969). UK edition by Oriel Press, Newcastle-on-Tyne (1970). p. 32.

The Way of the Sikh. For children 10–12 years. Amersham, UK: Hulton Educational Publications (1975 and four reprints). p. 60.

A List of Punjabi Immigrants in New Zealand 1890–1939. Hamilton, Country Section of the Central Indian Association (1984). Illustrated. p. 82.

3. BOOKLET-LENGTH TRANSLATIONS

The Life of Guru Nanak according to Bhai Gurdas. Trans. with brief introduction and notes of Bhai Gurdas's *Var* 1, stanzas 23–45, and *Var* 11, stanzas 13–14. *The Panjab Past and Present* III.1 and 2 (1969), 32–44.

The Mahima Prakas Varatak: A History of the Ten Gurus. Trans. with introduction and notes of the portion dealing with Guru Nanak. *The Panjab Past and Present* III.1 and 2 (1969), 54–87.

4. ARTICLES

4.1 *Articles published*

Guru Nanak and Kabir. *Proceedings of the Punjab History Conference* (1966 for 1965), pp. 87–92.

Procedures in analysing the sources for the life of Guru Nanak. *Journal of Indian History* XLV:1 (April 1967), pp. 207–27.

The teachings of Guru Nanak. *The Sikh Review* XVI:172 (Nov. 1967), pp. 9–14.

The influence of Islam upon the thought of Guru Nanak. *Sikhism and Indian Society: Transactions of the Indian Institute of Advanced Study* IV (1967), pp. 292–308. Slightly revised version reprinted in *History of Religions* VII.4 (May 1968), pp. 302–16. Reprinted in *Exploring Sikhism* (New Delhi: OUP, 2000), pp. 3–18.

The Miharban Janam-sakhi: an examination of the *gost* form with special reference to Pothi Hariji and Pothi Chaturbhuj of the Miharban Janam-sakhi. Introductory essay in the Khalsa College edition of *The Miharban Janam-sakhi*, vol. II. Amritsar: Khalsa College (1969), i–xii.

Sabad da sidhant: Guru Nanak ji te Kabir di tulana. *Alochana* (1969). In Punjabi. Reprinted in *Pahili Patasahi Sri Guru Nanak Dev ji.* Ed. Pritam Singh. Ludhiana: Panjabi Sahit Akademi (1969), pp. 332–8.

Guru Nanak and the Impact of Modern Scientific Thought. *The Sikh Review* XVIII: 196 (December 1969–January 1970), pp. 85–91.

Hakikat rah mukam Raje Sivanabh ki: an account of the Way to the Abode of Raja Sivanabh, being an examination of a prose passage appended to many manuscript copies of the Adi Granth. *Proceedings of the Punjab History Conference 1969*, 4 (1970), pp. 96–105.

The janam-sakhis as sources of Punjab history, *Proceedings of the Punjab History Conference 1969*, 4 (1970), pp. 109–21.

Sikhism. *Man and his Gods: Encyclopedia of the World's Religions*. Ed. Geoffrey Parrinder. London: Hamlyn (1971), pp. 210–21. Repr. in *World Religions from Ancient History to the Present*. Ed. Geoffrey Parrinder. New York: Facts on File (1983), pp. 250–61.

The Nanak of Faith and the Nanak of History. *History and Contemporary India*. Ed. J.C.B. Webster. Bombay: Asia Publishing House (1971), pp. 46–56. Reprinted in *Exploring Sikhism* (New Delhi: OUP, 2000), pp. 37–46.

Sikhism. *Expository Times*, 83: 12 (Sept 1972), pp. 356–9.

The Kukas: a millenarian sect of the Punjab. *W.P. Morrell: A Tribute*. Ed. G.A. Wood and P.S. O'Connor. Dunedin: University of Otago Press (1973), pp. 85–103. Reprinted in *The Panjab Past and Present* XIII: 1 (April, 1979), pp. 164–87. Reprinted in *Exploring Sikhism* (New Delhi: OUP, 2000), pp. 189–215.

Pitfalls for the writer of History. Proceedings of a Weekend School, Dunedin, 2–3 October 1971. Dunedin: New Zealand Library Association, Otago Branch (1973), B1–17.

Inter-linear inscriptions in Sri Lanka. *South Asia* 3 (August 1973), pp. 105–6.

Ethical standards in world religions: the Sikhs. *Expository Times* 85: 8 (1974), pp. 233–7. Repr. in *The Sikh Courier* 7: 5 (Spring 1975), pp. 4–9.

Ahluwalias and Ramgarhias: two Sikh castes. *South Asia* 4 (October, 1974), pp. 78–90. Reprinted in *Exploring Sikhism* (New Delhi: OUP, 2000), pp. 216–34.

Nanak. *Encyclopaedia Britannica* (1974), pp. 821–2. Reprinted.

Sikhism. *A Cultural History of India*. Ed. A.L. Basham. Oxford: the Clarendon Press (1975), pp. 294–302. Repr. *Man's Religious Quest*. Ed. Whitfield Foy. London: Croom Helm in association with the Open University (1978), pp. 287–97.

Colonel Steinbach and the Sikhs. *The Panjab Past and Present* IX.2 (October, 1975), pp. 291–8.

The significance of Baba Farid as a symbol of human brotherhood. *The Journal of Religious Studies*, V.1 & 2 (Spring–Autumn, 1974), pp. 225–37.

Religious tolerance in Sikh scriptural writings. *Guru Tegh Bahadur*. Ed. G.S. Talib. Patiala: Punjabi University, (1976), pp. 228–42.

Trade and investment in sixteenth and seventeenth century Punjab: the testimony of the Sikh devotional literature, *Essays in Honour of Doctor Ganda Singh*. Ed. Harbans Singh and N.G. Barrier. Patiala: Punjabi University (1976), pp. 81–91.

Punjabis in New Zealand. *NZASIAN* 4 (1977), pp. 13–21.

Mangal Singh of Otorohanga. *Art of Living* III: 4 (April, 1976), pp. 9–10, 43. Repr. in *The Sikh Sansar* 6: 1 (March, 1977), pp. 16–17.

On the word panth: a problem of terminology and definition. *Contributions to Indian Sociology* 12: 2 (1979), pp. 287–95. Reprinted in *Exploring Sikhism* (New Delhi: OUP, 2000), pp. 139–48.

The Sikh Scriptures: some issues. *Sikh Studies: Comparative Perspectives on a Changing Tradition*. Ed. Mark Juergensmeyer and N. Gerald Barrier. Berkeley: Berkeley Religious Studies Series (1979), pp. 97–111.

The Sikhs of the South Pacific. *Sikh Studies: Comparative Perspectives on a Changing Tradition*. Ed. Mark Juergensmeyer and N. Gerald Barrier. Berkeley: Berkeley Religious Studies Series (1979), pp. 143–58.

The question of semantics. *Rituals and Sacraments in Indian Religions*. Ed. Clarence O. McMullen. Delhi: ISPCK (1979), pp. 9–15.

The Sikhs and the Maoris. *The Panjab Past and Present* XV.1 (April 1981), pp. 232–3.

The Punjabi community in New Zealand. *Indians in New Zealand*. Ed. Kapil N. Tiwari. Wellington: Price Milburn (1980), pp. 113–21. Reprinted as 'The Sikhs and Sikhism in New Zealand' in *The Panjab Past and Present*, XVI-II (Oct 1982), pp. 407–16.

Kabir, Nanak, and the early Sikh Panth. *Religious Change and Cultural Domination*. Ed. David N. Lorenzen. Mexico City: El Colegio de Mexico, 1981, pp. 173–91. Reprinted in *Exploring Sikhism* (New Delhi: OUP, 2000), pp. 19–36. Spanish edition: *Cambio religiso y dominacion cultural*. Mexico City: El Colegio de Mexico, 1982, pp. 191–209.

The problem of the Panjabi rahit-namas. S.N. Mukherjee *India: History and Thought. Essays in Honour of A.L. Basham*. Calcutta: Subarnarekha (1982), pp. 103–26. Reprinted in *Exploring Sikhism* (New Delhi: OUP, 2000), pp. 103–25.

Sikhism entries in *The Penguin Dictionary of Religions*. Ed. J. Hinnells. London: Allen Lane (1983). Forty entries on Sikhism. Repr. in *The Facts on File Dictionary of Religions*. New York: Facts on File (1984).

The Khalsa Rahit: the Sikh identity defined. *Identity Issues and World Religions*. Selected Proceedings of the Fifteenth Congress of the International Association for the History of Religions. Ed. Victor C. Hayes. Bedford Park, SA: The Australian Association for the Study of Religions at the South Australian College of Advanced Education (1986), pp. 104–9. Reprinted in *Exploring Sikhism* (New Delhi: OUP, 2000), pp. 126–35.

The development of the Sikh Panth. *The Sants: Studies in a Devotional Tradition of India*. Ed. Karine Schomer and W.H. McLeod. Berkeley: Berkeley Religious Studies Series; Delhi: Motilal Banarsidass (1987), pp. 229–49. Reprinted in *Exploring Sikhism* (New Delhi: OUP, 2000), pp. 49–69.

The meaning of 'Sant' in Sikh usage. *The Sants: Studies in a Devotional Tradition of India*. Ed. Karine Schomer and W.H. McLeod. Berkeley: Berkeley Religious Studies Series; Delhi: Motilal Banarsidass (1987), pp. 251–63. Reprinted in *Exploring Sikhism* (New Delhi: OUP, 2000), pp. 149–61.

The Sikhs: crisis and identity in a religious tradition. *Harvard Divinity Bulletin* XVII: 2 (January–May, 1987), pp. 7–9.

Editors' introduction in *Sikh History and Religion in the Twentieth Century*. Ed. Joseph T. O'Connell, Milton Israel, Willard G. Oxtoby, W.H. McLeod, and J.S. Grewal. Toronto: University of Toronto Centre for South Asian Studies (1988), pp. 9–15.

A Sikh theology for modern times. *Sikh History and Religion in the Twentieth Century*. Ed. Joseph T. O'Connell, Milton Israel, Willard G. Oxtoby, W.H. McLeod, and J.S. Grewal. Toronto: University of Toronto Centre for South Asian Studies (1988), pp. 32–43.

History: 'an academic amusement'. *Studies in Orientology: Essays in Memory of Professor A.L. Basham*. S.K. Maity, Upendra Thakur, and A.K. Narain. Agra: Y.K. Publishers (1988), pp. 90–4.

Articles in *The Encyclopedia of Asian History*. Ed. in Chief Ainslie T. Embree. New York: Asia Society of New York and Charles Scribner's Sons. London: Collier Macmillan (1988). Articles on Sikhs and Sikhism: Nanak, Ranjit Singh, Akali Dal, Tara Singh, and Fateh Singh.

The first forty years of Sikh migration: problems and some possible solutions. *The Sikh Diaspora: Migration and Experiences beyond the Punjab.* Ed. N.G. Barrier and V.A. Dusenbery. Delhi: Chanakya Publications; Columbia, Mo: South Asia Publications (1989), pp. 29–48. Repr. in *Studies in Sikhism and Comparative Religion* VIII: 1 (April 1989), pp. 130–41. Reprinted in *Exploring Sikhism* (New Delhi: OUP, 2000), pp. 237–53.

Teaching History to Undergraduates in India: a trans-Indian view. *On Being a Teacher.* Ed. Amrik Singh. New Delhi: Konark Publishers (1990), pp. 190–204.

The role of Sikh doctrine and tradition in the current Punjab crisis. *Religious Movements and Social Identity.* Ed. Bardwell L. Smith. Vol. 4 of *Boeings and Bullock-carts: Studies in Change and Continuity in Indian Civilization. Essays in Honour of K. Ishwaran.* Delhi: Chanakya Publications (1990), pp. 96–116.

The contribution of the Singh Sabha Movement to the interpretation of Sikh history and religion. *Religious Studies in Dialogue: Essays in Honour of Albert C. Moore.* Ed. Maurice Andrew, Peter Matheson and Simon Rae. Dunedin: Faculty of Theology, University of Otago (1991), pp. 143–151. Reprinted in *Exploring Sikhism* (New Delhi: OUP, 2000), pp. 91–9.

Articles on Sikhs. *Who's Who in the World Religions.* Ed. John R. Hinnells London: Macmillan (1991). Twenty-three articles.

The Sikh struggle in the eighteenth century and its relevance for today. *History of Religions* (University of Chicago) XXXI: 4 (May 1992), pp. 344–63. Reprinted in *Exploring Sikhism* (New Delhi: OUP, 2000), pp. 70–90.

The study of Sikh literature. *Studying the Sikhs: Issues for North America.* Ed. John Stratton Hawley and Gurinder Singh Mann. Albany: State University of New York Press (1993), pp. 47–68.

Articles in *The Encyclopaedia of Sikhism.* Editor-in-chief Harbans Singh. Patiala: Punjabi University. Volume 1 (1992) A–D: Adi Sakhian (9–10); Angad Dev, Guru (146–9); B40 Janam sakhi (232–3); Bala Janam sakhi (262–5). Volume 2 (1996) E–L: Haumai (265–7); Hukam (286–9); Janam-sakhi (337–40). Volume 3 (1997) M–R: Mani Singh Janam-sakhi (41–2); Miharban Janam-sakhi (85–6); Puratan Janam-sakhi (410–13). Volume 4 (1998) N–Z: Shabad (88–90).

Report entitled 'Sikhs and the Turban' prepared for the Justice Department, Government of Canada, for a court case John L. Grant et al. v. the Attorney General et al. (Federal Court file no. T-499-91) held in Calgary, Jan–Feb 1994. p. 22.

Where it all started. *The Sikh Review* 42: 1 (Jan. 1994) pp. 49–52.

Sikhism. *Collier's Encyclopedia.* New York: Collier (1994 edition), vol. 21, pp. 21–3.

Cries of outrage: history versus tradition in the study of the Sikh community. *South Asia Research* 14.2 (Autumn 1994), pp. 121–35. Reprinted in *Exploring Sikhism* (New Delhi: OUP, 2000), pp. 267–79.

The hagiography of the Sikhs. *According to Tradition: Hagiographical Writing in India.* Ed. Winand M. Callewaert and Rupert Snell. Wiesbaden: Harrassowitz Verlag (1994), pp. 15–41.

Three items in *Religions of India in Practice.* Ed. Donald S. Lopez, Jr. Princeton Readings in Religions. Princeton: Princeton University Press (1995). Translations with introductions and commentary. 'Sikh Hymns to the Divine Name', pp. 126–32. 'The Order for Khalsa Initiation', pp. 321–5. 'The Life of Guru Nanak', pp. 449–61.

Sikhism entries in *A New Dictionary of Religions.* Ed. John R. Hinnells. Oxford: Blackwell (1995). Revised and expanded version of *The Penguin Dictionary of Religions.* Sixty-three entries on Sikhism.

Sikhism. *Encyclopedia of Bioethics.* Rev. ed. Ed. in Chief Warren Thomas Reich. Vol. 5. New York: Simon & Schuster Macmillan, 1995. pp. 2397–9.

Phomen Singh. Entry in *The Dictionary of New Zealand Biography*, volume 3. Auckland: Auckland University Press/Department of Internal Affairs (1996).

Max Arthur Macauliffe. *British Association for the Study of Religions Bulletin*, no. 78 (June 1996), pp. 6–12. Reprinted in *Exploring Sikhism* (New Delhi: OUP, 2000), pp. 257–63.

Gender and the Sikh Panth. *The Transmission of the Sikh Heritage in the Diaspora*, ed. Pashaura Singh and N. Gerald Barrier. New Delhi: Manohar, 1996, pp. 37–43.

Articles on the Adi Granth; Authoritative texts and their interpretation, Sikh; Guru, in Sikhism; Guru Gobind Singh; Khalsa; Dasam Granth; Janamsakhis; Japji; Ks, the Five; Panjab; and Panth (related to Qaum). In *The Harper Collins Dictionary of Religion*, ed. Jonathan Z. Smith, in assoc. with the American Academy of Religion. London: HarperCollins, 1996.

Sikh Fundamentalism. *Journal of the American Oriental Society*, 118.1 (January–March 1998), pp. 15–27. Reprinted in *Exploring Sikhism* (New Delhi: OUP, 2000), pp. 162–86.

The turban: symbol of Sikh identity. *Sikh Identity: Continuity and Change.* Ed. Pashaura Singh and N. Gerald Barrier. New Delhi: Manohar, 1999, pp. 57–67.

What is History? *New Zealand Legacy,* Journal of the New Zealand Federation of Historical Societies, 11.2 (1999), pp. 16–22.

Discord in the Sikh Panth. *Journal of the American Oriental Society,* 119.3 (July–Sept 1999), pp. 381–9.

Sikhs and Muslims in the Punjab. *South Asia.* Special issue, Islam in History and Politics. Vol. XXII (1999), pp. 155–65.

Homeland, history, religion, and emigration. A Punjabi Community in Australia. Eds Rashmere Bhatti and Verne A. Dusenberry. Woolgoolga: Woolgoolga Neighbourhood Centre Inc, 2001, pp. 3–32.

The Sikhs today. A Punjabi Community in Australia. Eds Rashmere Bhatti and Verne A. Dusenberry. Woolgoolga: Woolgoolga Neighbourhood Centre Inc, 2001, pp. 266–7.

4.2 *Articles forthcoming*

Art. 'The Jap Sahib', for a book being edited by Professor Gurinder Singh Mann, University of California Santa Barbara.

Art. 'Sikhs in Australia and New Zealand', for a book on the Sikh diaspora being edited by Professor Gurinder Singh Mann, University of California Santa Barbara.

Art. 'Guru Nanak', for Encyclopedia of Religion in Canada.

Art. 'The Sikh Diaspora', for a book on the Sikhs to be edited by Mohinder Singh, New Delhi.

Notes

1. The excerpts of Dean Shirley Neuman's speech were taken from the video recording of the plenary session on Thursday, September 27, 2001.

2. Personal Letter, 28 February 1989.

Introduction-II
Sikhism in the Light of History

N. Gerald Barrier

The scholarly and public understanding of Sikhism has changed dramatically in the last three decades. A stream of publications reflecting a wide spectrum of ideological and historical perspectives now provide a base line for re-examining the nature of the Adi Granth and early Sikh tradition, changes and patterns culminating in the activist programmes of the Singh Sabhas and the Chief Khalsa Diwan, and contemporary issues. The intellectual climate for occasionally turbulent but always interesting debate has shifted. In the 1970s, books, articles, and conferences stirred debate but very little acrimony. Mounting tension arising from struggles among Sikhs and between them and others such as Nirankaris or Hindu activists, culminated ultimately in Operation Bluestar, the Delhi massacres, and a decade of turbulence in the Punjab and among Sikhs throughout the world. The emotions and sensitivity to any perceived attack from politicians or academics in turn led to a spiral of confrontations, conferences, and counter-conferences, and in general, made scholarly discourse very difficult. The fusion of politics and religion in the Punjab continues today, although with less violence and threats. Specific groups with agendas have used notable events such as the celebrations of the creation of the Khalsa and Ranjit Singh's reign as opportunities to attack opponents and to win legitimacy for their views on politics, religion, and tradition.

The leadership in addressing unexplored issues and traditions often has come from a growing group of Sikh and Western scholars trained and teaching in North American and European academic institutions. Earlier centres at Berkeley, Columbia, and Toronto have been joined by new programmes, often with Sikh chairs, at Santa Barbara, Michigan, and most recently, Hofstra and Milwaukee. These have begun to train scholars, to hold conferences, and to publish proceedings and articles. Similarly, in the UK, traditional centres of Indian studies at Cambridge, Oxford, and London have produced Sikh specialists, joined by a network of academic programmes associated with the University of Leicester and the Association of Punjab Studies. Numerous workshops and publications have resulted from such programmes, including the publication of the *International Journal of Punjab Studies*. As in the case of conferences in North America, most of the UK events have encouraged participation by local Sikhs and have attempted to initiate a variety of academic and public events connecting teaching, scholarship, and community concerns.

The earlier legacy of a period of distrust and acrimony still occasionally colours academic discourse and programmes, but the sincere efforts by scholars to address the questions raised by diaspora Sikhs have combined with a growing maturity of new generations of Sikh professionals to make possible an intellectual exchange that would have been unthinkable even ten years ago. For example, the Sikhs and scholars active on a leading list-serve, Sikh-Diaspora, daily engage in dialogue over interpretation of the Gurus, historical events, current problems facing Sikhs, and the implications of the new cultural contexts within which Sikhism now flourishes.

The Sikh Studies programme at the University of Michigan has been central to these positive developments. Three international conferences have brought together specialists and large numbers of participants from Michigan and nearby areas. The first dealt with the Sikh diaspora, local developments, communication, and the role of ideas and politics affecting Sikhs everywhere. The second, on the transmission of tradition, emphasized the interaction between heritage and culture, and history and politics. The third dealt with a range of certain contentious issues arising from an understanding of Sikh identity, especially in a diaspora context. All three have produced major volumes, and offered an opportunity for scholars and laypersons to meet together and address common concerns. Many specialists have attended some or all of the conferences, such as Arthur Helweg, Hew McLeod, Verne Dusenbery, Pashaura Singh, J.S. Grewal, and myself. Others from the Punjab or the UK have participated as time and funding permitted.

This fourth conference builds on past success and has once again offered older, as well as new specialists, an occasion to share ideas among themselves and with the Sikh community. Doris Jakobsh, a specialist on Sikh traditions and gender studies whose revised dissertation from British Columbia has been published recently by the Oxford University Press, attended her second Michigan session, as did Louis Fenech, whose revised Toronto dissertation on Sikh martyrdom has also been published by the Oxford University Press. The leading Western Sikh specialist whom the conference and this volume honours, Professor Hew McLeod, gave the keynote address and commented on virtually every paper. The leader of the Michigan programme, Pashaura Singh, has published two monographs with the Oxford University Press. I personally am delighted to have participated in and learned from a fourth conference, especially to have worked with noted scholars such as Arthur Helweg who also has attended each session. Pressing commitments forced J.S. Grewal to cancel his participation at the last moment, and two other veteran scholars from the Santa Barbara programme, Gurinder Singh Mann and Mark Juergensmeyer, gave short presentations but will not be contributing to this collection.

Four seasoned Sikh specialists joined the proceedings for the first time. Nikky-Guninder Kaur Singh, Professor and Chair of the Philosophy and the Religion Department at Colby College, has published major volumes and articles on Sikh women and theology. At the last minute, due to events relating to September 11, she could not attend in person but has contributed a revised paper. Robin Rinehart, whose earlier work on modern Hindu hagiography was published by the Oxford University Press, brought to the conference her insights on the Punjab and Sikh religious literature. Tony Ballantyne, whose revised Cambridge dissertation was published in 2001, shared his ideas on Maharaja Dalip Singh that will be part of a larger study on Sikhism, colonialism, and the diaspora. One of the most distinguished specialists on the Sikh diaspora, Darshan Singh Tatla, did not attend but submitted a paper growing out of his earlier monograph and current interest in the representation of Sikhism in public arenas.

The conference focused on important events, individuals, and institutions that have helped produce contemporary Sikhism. The research and ensuing discussion reflects the widely held assumption of participants that the Sikh religion and traditions can be fruitfully examined within a historical context. Other perspectives of course are useful and sometimes are offered as substitutes or correction of seeming over-emphasis on historiography and Sikhism as an evolving set of ideas and practices. For example, the recent workshop sponsored by the School of Oriental and African Studies, London, sought to bring together scholars primarily from within the Sikh community to advocate fresh approaches and understanding of Sikh religion, culture, and ethnicity.[1] Several of the London participants challenged some of the scholars involved in conferences at Ann Arbor and Toronto, especially Hew McLeod. In fact, McLeod, Jakobsh, and Pashaura Singh attended the workshop, but their papers were not included in the published proceedings.

The keynote address by Hew McLeod contributed to the tone and often congruent research findings emerging from the conference. McLeod and the many scholars influenced by his work believe that Sikhism must be evaluated in the light of documentary evidence and within a historical perspective. As McLeod notes: 'Apart from its historical context there can be no adequate understanding of Sikhism.' Traditions and approaches to both ideas and practice have undergone change over time, as in the case of any major world religion, a process particularly illustrated by McLeod's current study of the various *rahit-namas* or codes associated with the Khalsa tradition. His presentation, and the much longer analysis and collection of translated documents published by the Oxford University Press in 2003, emphasizes how the themes and specifics of the evolving *rahit* literature mirror the worldview of the authors and their historical milieu. Words and the meaning of words change over time, with some themes added or deleted. His paper and the book highlight a theme reflected in several papers, the marked degree that Singh Sabha publicists pursued agendas in light of perceived tradition and threats from within and outside the community. McLeod also notes major gaps in the historical record that must be addressed. At least a few of those missing links are beginning to be addressed by the papers and ongoing scholarship of specialists participating in the conference.

Two papers on Sikh tradition illustrate the role of methodology and individual training in influencing how events and major developments are framed. Nikky Singh uses anthropological and post-colonial literary analysis to re-examine the myths and common concerns linking Guru Nanak with Guru Gobind Singh and the creation of the Khalsa. Bringing to the discussion a personal understanding of Sikh faith, she poetically explores how ritual and myth influence individuals and community. Her paper also attempts to demonstrate that Guru Gobind Singh internalized key elements of the *Puratan Janamsakhi* tradition and distilled some of its internal codes and meaning. Emphasizing continuity, Nikky uses a model involving separation and death, transition and spiritual encounter with God, and honour and new status to denote both the comparative and unique features of Sikhism. Building on her earlier attention to feminist elements in Sikh tradition, she also discusses how male and female attributes combine in the Guru Granth Sahib and the regeneration of primal myths within Sikhism.

Pashaura Singh adopts a different approach to evolving Sikh tradition. He combines an intimate knowledge of Sikh scripture and history acquired during training and practice as a Granthi with excellent historical and exegetical training with McLeod at the University of Toronto. The resulting paper is a masterful review of how central Sikh concepts, symbols, and practice evolve over time, and yet maintain a core centrality based upon the teachings and experiences of the Gurus. Disagreeing at times with McLeod and also Harjot Singh Oberoi, whose work on the reconstruction of Sikhism in the Singh Sabha period remains central to any scholarly discourse, Pashaura Singh emphasizes continuity of practice rather than ideology, and suggests a model involving middle, centre and periphery to explain the complicated relationships emerging in the Singh Sabha world, c.1875–1920. He also stresses the transition toward emphasis on doctrine and legal definition as an underpinning of modern Sikhism. From his perspective, the new experiences of Sikhs in the diaspora will help redefine the Sikh faith as a modern world religion, and at the same time lead to a fresh rediscovery of Sikhism based on historical circumstance and cross-cultural encounters.

Lou Fenech also emphasizes historiography and the careful treatment of documents in his study of a Persian poet, Nand Lal Goya. Representing a new generation of scholars carefully trained in methodology, Punjab traditions, and necessary language skills, Fenech's earlier work on martyrdom focuses on the codification and often self-conscious framing of Sikh beliefs by Singh Sabha intellectuals. This paper, and the longer-term project it represents, builds on his careful attention to documents and the potential conflict between assumed tradition and actual historical event. He explores why Nand Lal's Persian works remain unreported in rahit literature, the value and limits of Persian in evolving Sikh tradition, sufi influence, and changing attitudes toward Islam and Muslims. The presentation ends with a series of questions and alternative suggestions about Singh Sabha influence, matters that he plans to develop within the structure of a lengthy monograph.

Attention to the Singh Sabha period, and broader efforts to review how traditions change and continue to influence contemporary Sikhism, also are central themes in four other papers. Robin Rinehart addresses the political and doctrinal issues surrounding the place of the Dasam Granth within Sikhism. Noting the problems of studying the text, including earlier oral and *Braj* renditions, she details some of the existing conflicts and their underlying assumptions. Part of the controversy arises from the perspectives and imagery within the Dasam Granth itself. Could Guru Gobind Singh in fact have written a work that reflects to some degree Hindu mythology and very negative views of women? During the Singh Sabha period, the tendency to accept the Dasam Granth as an authoritative scripture equal to the Adi Granth caused great division and launched innumerable tirades and tract wars. The continuing interaction of religious belief and politics in every current debate on the matter has led the SGPC (Shiromani Gurdwara Prabandhak Committee) and various religious leaders to try and dampen open discussion and research. Second, Professor Rinehart stresses the process of codification, the struggle over correct version, and printing. The problem, as she notes, is that firm evidence on authorship remains unclear. Either theological perspective informs approaches to the document or an alternative historical methodology influenced by literary criticism. Once again, the Singh Sabha advocates helped shape the debate and its outcome, just as today, various journals and research institutes/groups vie with each other in a renewed struggle that often tells us more about agendas and political motives rather than the legitimacy of particular arguments.

Moving from one controversy to another, Doris Jakobsh presents a historical and document-based analysis of 'Kaur' as nomenclature for Sikh women. At the same time, she uses the issues raised about names to explore a broader theme that influences her research, the role of women in Sikh society. Dr Jakobsh explores Rajput traditions and female names, suggesting how values about honour and male–female relations may have influenced Sikh usage. Linguistic discussion and definitions of 'Kaur' in nineteenth century reference works suggests a very undefined usage, with no accepted naming practice. In typical ambivalent fashion, the Singh Sabha discourse attempted to bridge disputing arguments and to minimize conflict on the subject despite the fact that stringent *Tat Khalsa* Sikhs such as Teja Singh Bhasaur and others insisted on distinct use of 'Kaur' for Sikh women and also other symbols of equality including carrying *kirpans* and wearing turbans. Over time, the apparent earlier tradition of using the term 'Devi' diminished, especially when particular values associated with the dramas of the Tat Khalsa publicist, Vir Singh, became popularized. Certainly until recent times, Kaur tended to be associated more directly with initiation of women and changing of name. In the last half-century, the Sikh *Rahit Maryada* promulgated by the SGPC in the early 1950s emphasized that girls should be named Kaur at birth and boys, Singh. Once again, as in the case of the Dasam Granth, assumed traditional views of symbols and literature have been questioned in light of historical evidence and also in terms of which groups and viewpoints will emerge as legitimate interpreters of Sikh identity.

In addition to heated debate over Sikh identity, much attention is being paid to the meaning and contributions of individuals associated with Sikh history. For example, seminars and books have focused recently on Bhai Ditt Singh of Lahore Singh Sabha fame, Bhagat Singh and his contribution to nationalism and the Sikh cause, and of course, Maharaja Ranjit Singh and Sikh rule just prior to British annexation of the Punjab. Similarly, the son of Ranjit Singh and the last Maharaja of the Punjab, Dalip Singh, has become an icon for nationalist historians as well as Sikh publicists who have tried to turn him into a 'true Sikh' freedom fighter, both in his lifetime and in current Sikh historical circles. Tony Ballantyne approaches Dalip Singh from another perspective, demonstrating the links between colonial policy and images and the ongoing interaction between Sikhs and English culture. The paper reflects themes that Ballantyne plans to develop in his forthcoming book on the Sikhs, colonialism, and the issues facing the community in a diaspora setting. He traces the increased prominence of Dalip Singh not only among Sikhs but also in the 'renegotiation of ethnicity and national identity' in England. His work further emphasizes the need to assess individuals in a historical context. Dalip Singh has been viewed from many angles, by colonial administrators and their allies or opponents within the Singh Sabha movement, as well as by Sikhs and the general public in the post-colonial period. A final point concerning how the historian's methodology and questions affect research is especially useful. Understanding the Sikh experience in the last two centuries involves combining an 'internalist' approach emphasizing texts, competing doctrines, and social change within Sikhism with the 'externals' model that highlights the role of colonial institutions and images.

Over the last three decades, my personal attempts to understand Sikh history and culture have reinforced my awareness of the links between Singh Sabha campaigns and the immediate concerns of Sikhs today. 'Authority, Politics and Contemporary Sikhism' traces the evolution of central institutions and ideas over the last century. Internal disputes among Sikhs and with outsiders took place in a colonial context that provided new intellectual and political challenges. As a minority community, Sikhs constantly struggled with balancing the need for consolidating traditions with the political task of expanding numbers and compromise. The 1925 Sikh Gurdwaras Act established the legal framework for controlling resources, political power, and legitimacy that have been a major part of Sikh public life ever afterward. At the same time, the Act and the Sikh Rahit Maryada that evolved in the first half of the twentieth century deliberately avoided controversial issues of identity or encouraged compromise positions that enabled Sikhs of many stripes to work together. The subsequent controversies over the SGPC and the Akal Takht involved both crises of identity as well as a fusion of religion and politics growing out of extreme competition among Sikh groups and personalities. The external constraints and the internal debates continue to interact with and influence Sikh public life in the Punjab. Similarly, the Indian Constitution and changing legal milieu in which Sikhs operate in India have affected politics and discussion of future legislation. Beyond the Punjab, the legal and cultural institutions of the countries where Sikhs reside across the world in turn contribute to ongoing discussion of political strategy and Sikh identity itself.

The last two essays in the volume focus on the Sikh diaspora in terms of anthropological paradigms, self-image, and representation. Arthur Helweg argues that the recent Sikh experience can be fruitfully understood from the comparative perspective of migration studies. Focusing on Sikhs in England, where he is a noted specialist, he applies a field theory framework that suggests three phases, decision-making, freedom and conflict, and nationalism, and illustrates how that helps explain initial Sikh reaction to life in England, changing norms and interaction with the homeland, and finally, the rise of new militancy and organizations.

The final essay by Darshan Singh Tatla explores how non-Sikhs view the community and portray Sikhs in fiction and history. He uses Bharati Mukherjee's journalistic account of the Canadian Air India tragedy attributed to Sikhs and her fictional writings as case studies for analysing themes and misconceptions. The essay places her work within the broader context of Hindus attempting to deal with the contradictions of India's cultural plurality. Tatla notes that Mukherjee attributes the blame for the bombing not only on Sikh extremists but also on Canadian policies (multiculturalism, reluctance to intervene more decisively in Sikh matters) that permitted the event to occur. He criticizes her focus on Hindu–Sikh conflict in Canada. Another questionable manipulation of image involves her contrasting educated and culturally sophisticated Hindus with coarse and often socially conservative and religiously fundamentalist Sikhs. Similar themes pervade Mukherjee's fiction. She discusses alienation of Sikhs, Sikh gangs, proclivity to violence, and the assumption that virtually all *amritdhari* Sikhs support Khalistan. Tatla challenges her portrayals and also some of the trends within post-colonial discourse.

Process, historical setting and change, identity, caricature, and symbols—these are common themes in the volume, and also within the broader, non-academic discourse found among Sikhs today. In gurdwara conflict, in the courts, and especially after September 11, 2001, in chat rooms and list-serves, Sikhs discuss virtually every issue explored by Sikh Studies scholars. Ritual, political history, the creation of the Khalsa, the meaning of rahit, the role of women, the importance of symbols and especially the *kirpan*, are persistent themes as Sikhs in the diaspora attempt to reassess who they are and how to mobilize the community in light of the threats and political challenges associated with recent events in North America and the UK.[2] Hopefully the essays arising from the Michigan conference will assist in that process. The possibilities for meaningful dialogue between academic specialists and the Sikh community certainly are greater now than ever before. As such an exchange continues, one thing is certain. Just as the Singh Sabhas and the Chief Khalsa Diwan helped create an institutional base and an ideological debate that has helped shape modern Sikhism, so now the programmes, spirit, and creativity current among Sikhs in the diaspora will contribute to the vitality of Sikhism as a major world religion in the twenty-first century.

Notes

1. Chrisopher Shackle, Gurharpal Singh and Arvindpal Singh Mandair, *Sikh Religion, Culture and Ethnicity* (London: Curzon Press, 2001).

2. Gurdwara issues and also the implications of the events of September 11, 2001 for Sikhs reviewed in *Understanding Sikhism* (January–June, 2002).

Keynote Speech
Researching the Rahit

W.H. McLeod

One statistic which I am fond of quoting is that there are evidently more Sikhs in the world than there are Jews. I say 'evidently' as the totals are very close (approximately seventeen or eighteen million in each case) and they are rather uncertain. Certainly though, the verdict would seem to favour the Sikhs. When one surveys the field of scholarship, however, the position is dramatically reversed. One need only consider the number of Sikh scholars or foreigners working on Sikh studies, and compare it with those in Jewish Studies, to become uncomfortably aware that the Sikhs receive nothing like the attention which they deserve.

There are, of course, reasons for this. The Jews are highly urbanized (at least outside Israel) and they have an extensive interest in things cultural. They have, moreover, a recent past which includes the Holocaust and the creation of the state of Israel. But then the Sikhs have a recent past which includes the Partition of India and the struggle for Khalistan, neither of which has aroused worldwide interest on anything like the scale of the Jewish events. The difference, I suggest, lies chiefly in who constitutes the Panth. The overwhelming majority of Sikhs live off the land in the Punjab, pursuing objectives which do not rate scholarly research very high.

This paucity of writers on Sikh Studies is reflected by its coverage in terms of thorough research and competent literature, by the treatment which it receives from institutions of higher learning, and by the interest which the outside world shows in it. Consider the first of these, the area which Sikh Studies covers in terms of competent research and literature. This, of course, raises that hoary question of just what the term 'competent' means.

Having discussed it in print on several occasions I am not going to launch again into a detailed analysis, merely saying that for me it means historical methodology of the critical variety.[1] For any research in Sikh Studies one requires both the study of History and that of Religion, the two being inextricably intertwined. It seems to me therefore that the historical approach is amply justified. This, indeed, is precisely the meaning which I attach to the theme of this conference, 'Sikhism in the light of history'. Apart from its historical context there can be no adequate understanding of Sikhism.

But even if this is disputed we can surely agree that there is plenty of territory which still remains to be covered in at least a tolerably adequate sense. Certainly there are distinguished contributions to be noted, some of them by individuals who are present here today. Elsewhere, however, there are glaring gaps, or at least gaps which are at best only partially filled. Some of these gaps I shall briefly notice.

The first is the Sant movement of northern India, the background out of which Guru Nanak and his message emerged. I have been strongly criticized for having suggested that this was the process whereby Guru Nanak acquired and preached his message, yet apart from asserting his uniqueness there has been little research in this area.[2] Let it not be supposed that I deny the uniqueness of Guru Nanak. Emphatically I uphold it, maintaining that no other representative equalled the fullness and the beauty of his expression. But there is more to be said about his message than that. The inescapable fact that Guru Nanak preached ideas that were common to other Sants must be faced if he is to be adequately understood.

The situation concerning the life of Guru Nanak is a little different. Biography after biography of him has appeared, yet few ever grapple with his life story. Most of them repeat the *janam-sakhi* tales of his having travelled to all manner of places such as Sri Lanka and Mecca, affirming as positively true that which is demonstrably false. Those that are aware of the case against these travels normally remain silent on the subject, preferring to avoid the censure which must inevitably await those who risk speaking out. There are a few good books which have been written concerning Guru Nanak (notably Jagtar Singh Grewal's *Guru Nanak in History*), but they are very few and the enthusiasm which marked the quincentenary of his birth seems to have faded.

But at least there was that period of brief enthusiasm in the case of Guru Nanak, and from it flowed an abundance of books and articles which signalled that here was a figure of very considerable importance. This situation has been very different with regard to his eight successors. We can accept that Nanak and Gobind Singh are clearly the two most popular of the Sikh Gurus and that they naturally attract the most attention. Even so, the general lack of scholarly interest in the other eight Gurus is regrettable, to say the least. It is true that there are the contributions of Harbans Singh, Fauja Singh, Gurbachan Singh Talib, and Gurudharm Singh Khalsa, yet these are only four names for a highly influential period of Sikh history spanning a century and a half.

To this judgment two qualifications should be added. The first is that one particular topic attracts periodic attention and is once again before us. This is the history and status of the Adi Granth, and the present interest is due to three works. One is Piar Singh's *Gatha Sri Adi Granth and the Controversy*; a second is Pashaura Singh's *The Guru Granth Sahib*; and the third is Gurinder Singh Mann's *The Making of Sikh Scripture*. From a different stance and dealing with the situation prior to the emergence of the Adi Granth there is Balwant Singh Dhillon's *Early Sikh Scriptural Tradition*. As a result of these and some earlier works we are now beginning to acquire a much clearer picture of the primary scripture of the Sikhs.

The second qualification is the obvious one, namely that we have hitherto confined our attention to works in English. What about all those books in Punjabi? It is true that there have been some notable contributions made in Punjabi, the works of Jodh Singh, Sahib Singh, and Taran Singh being obvious examples. There is, however, that same feature in the Punjabi works that we encounter in a majority of English contributions. This feature is that tradition serves as the dominant source in such cases. Appeals are certainly made to earlier works for support, but the source from which these narratives are drawn is normally Sikh tradition. We find ourselves again in the tumult of historical methodology and I can only assert once again that for the critical historian, tradition is at best a supplementary indicator.

And so we move onto Guru Gobind Singh and the foundation of the Khalsa order. This is an enormously influential period for Sikh history, but it is still served by only a limited number of books, monographs, and articles that we can accept as historically sound or adequate. The period of Guru Gobind Singh is followed by another of great importance, yet one of even less critical treatment. These are the years of Banda's uprising. The same applies to the period of the *misls*. Few works deserve serious notice, with the result that it would be idle to pretend that the middle decades of the eighteenth century have been adequately covered.

Fortunately we emerge into adequately covered territory with the reign of Ranjit Singh (thanks in particular to Jagtar Singh Grewal), but with the death of the Maharaja the limitations return. The period of the early Singh Sabha has been well covered by Harjot Oberoi's *The Construction of Religious Boundaries* and we await with much interest N.G. Barrier's forthcoming contribution. During the twentieth century the same pattern continues, with a small handful of works worthy of respect and the majority catering for a traditional or popular market. Studies which cry out for attention in the Singh Sabha years are the biographies of at least three of the prominent figures of this period. Most conspicuous is a critical life of Kahn Singh Nabha, a study which we badly need. There are, it is true, Punjabi biographies, but these contributions, though useful, fall well short of adequate analysis. The two remaining are Vir Singh and Principal Teja Singh. Others such as Ditt Singh could well be added. Fortunately we can expect thoroughly adequate coverage of Babu Teja Singh in Barrier's forthcoming work.

Spanning several such periods there are occasional works deserving notice. One which certainly deserves it is Louis Fenech's *Martyrdom in the Sikh Tradition*. Another subject, bridging at least three centuries, is the Sikh *Rahit* and it is on this subject that I intend to focus my attention. Actually it is incorrectly called the Sikh Rahit. It is of course the Khalsa Rahit, the means whereby Sikhs of the Khalsa were distinguished from other Sikhs. The word 'Rahit' is little known to speakers of English outside the narrow world of scholars interested in Sikh Studies, yet it designates the code of belief and conduct which all members of the Khalsa are required to obey and it is of absolutely fundamental importance for any understanding of Sikhism or of the Sikh Panth. Why is this so? There are, I suggest, two basic reasons for its importance.

The first reason has already been mentioned. Khalsa Sikhs are known by their obedience to the elements of the Rahit at least. This distinguishes the *amritdhari* (or at least the *kesdhari*) from the *sahajdhari Sikh*. The fact that the outside world blinks, believing as it does that all Sikhs are *kesdhari*, makes no difference to this statement. The opinion of the outside world is, of course, false, and it is particularly false with regard to the eighteenth century. At that time conditions were very different and Sikhs of the Khalsa were obviously only one part of the Sikh Panth. The Rahit was erected as a key marker. Sikhs of the Khalsa obeyed it, thus separating themselves from other Sikhs.

The second reason is the one that lends such intense interest to the study of the Rahit. It is that during the three centuries of its existence the Rahit has undergone extensive alterations, changing some central components of its structure in accordance with the prevailing concepts of the time. Others which may seem slightly incongruous to the outsider still persist, and one which once seemed rather absurd now earns for the Khalsa the admiration of all right-minded people. I refer of course to the ban on smoking. Not everyone will agree with this general claim concerning the Rahit, yet it seems to me to be proven beyond any shadow of doubt. We shall see some examples of it as we proceed with our description.

What are the sources available to the historian who seeks an understanding of the history of the Rahit? One of these has already been mentioned, though in some measure discounted. This is tradition. Sikh tradition does not deserve to be wholly discounted, serving as it does as an indicator of possible lines of enquiry and sometimes proving to be thoroughly reliable. It is, however, a source which should be used with much caution, and one which requires support from other sources before it can be accepted as authentic.

A second source is provided by the *rahit-namas*. The rahit-namas are manuals of Rahit principles, spelling out what a Khalsa Sikh may do and what he should avoid. They are, in other words, works which claim to record the Rahit as it was delivered by Guru Gobind Singh at the founding of the Khalsa order. These are much more promising, though their claims certainly cannot be accepted as they stand. There are several rahit-namas, of which six deserve close analysis. Two are attributed to Nand Lal, and one each to Prahilad Rai (or Prahilad Singh), Chaupa Singh, Desa Singh, and Daya Singh. In addition to these there are later rahit-namas such as the *Prem Sumarag* and two rahit-namas set in the *Sau Sakhian*. An additional work, also attributed to Nand Lal and commonly known as *Prashan-uttar*, contains very little material of the kind contained in a standard rahit-nama and may have been recorded before the actual founding of the Khalsa.

A third range of sources is provided by other eighteenth-century works which record features of the Khalsa discipline or which exercised a marked influence on the material recorded by rahit-nama authors. There are not many works which qualify in this respect, but two of these are of particular importance. One is *Gur Sobha*, a work by Sainapati which was almost certainly completed in 1711. The second is the miscellany known as the Dasam Granth, in particular the work known as *Var Sri Bhagauti ji ki*. One other that deserves analysis is *Guru kian Sakhian*, said to have been written by Svarup Singh Kaushish in 1790. This will receive a brief examination later.

We could begin with an analysis of the various authors to whom these various rahit-namas are attributed. The Nand Lal who has been popular as the putative author of two rahit-namas (plus the work known as *Prashan-uttar*) has traditionally been identified with the celebrated Nand Lal Goya, the Persian poet in the *darbar* of Guru Gobind Singh. As we shall be hearing later in the conference much mystery surrounds Nand Lal Goya, but there can be no doubt that the author of those Persian works could never have written the Punjabi (amounting to little more than doggerel) of the rahit-namas traditionally attributed to him. Nothing is known concerning Prahilad Rai (or Prahilad Singh). Chaupa Singh is traditionally understood to have been the *khidava* or adult play-mate and later the tutor of Guru Gobind Singh. Desa Singh is traditionally regarded as the tenth son of Mani Singh, who was executed by the Mughal governor of Lahore in 1738. And Daya Singh is traditionally believed to have been one of the *Panj Piare* first initiated into the Khalsa by Guru Gobind Singh.

Note how frequently the word 'traditionally' has been used. There is room for considerable analysis concerning the true identity of these various authors, and though this is one of the fascinations associated with this study of the Rahit, it is one that we shall have to leave aside. Instead I shall take up three of the many lines of research offered by this subject. I shall describe the experience of discovery which one encounters in the study of the rahit-namas; I shall examine some of the words which pose difficult problems, particularly when one seeks to present the rahit-namas in English translation; and I shall review the evidence presented by this late eighteenth century work, the *Guru kian Sakhian*.

First let us take up the question of discovery and of the manner in which a discovery enables us to place all the rahit-namas in an ordered sequence. The discovery to which I refer was not made by me. It was made by Dr Jeevan Deol in the research which he conducted in India, and to him we owe a considerable debt of gratitude. Dr Deol was going through some of the manuscripts held by the library of Guru Nanak Dev University in Amritsar, one of which proved to be a collection of various works and to bear in its colophon on folio 425a the date *S*. 1775 which corresponds to 1718–19 CE. One of the works recorded by this manuscript reproduces most of the text which later came to be known as the *Tanakhah-nama*, although that name is nowhere mentioned in this particular version. Nand Lal figures in the narrative, but the work as a whole is called the *Nasihat-nama*. (It should not be confused with the *Nasihat-na'ma'* which occurs in the hagiography concerning Guru Nanak.) The manuscript is numbered 770 in the library of the Guru Nanak Dev University.

S. 1775 (or 1718–19 CE) cannot be firmly and finally attached to *MS.* 770, but it certainly seems highly likely. Four conclusions follow from the discovery of this manuscript. The first is that it confirms that the text could not have been composed by the Nand Lal responsible for the Persian compositions attributed to Nand Lal Goya. As we have already observed they must have been by different hands. Second, the title *Tanakhah-nama* will have been attached to the work at some later date, displacing the original title of *Nasihat-nama*. Third, it provides us with the earliest extant rahit-nama. And fourth, it supplies crucial evidence which enables us to set the early rahit-namas in a general chronological order.

The last two conclusions require further examination. *MS.* 770 is certainly an early rahit-nama, but it is not the first. At least one manuscript lies behind it. This is made abundantly clear by the scribe's frequent errors, plainly indicating that he has copied his text from another. One of many examples is provided by a substantial portion which he has missed. On folio 415a he begins a *dohara* and continues on to the second line. Half way through that second line, however, the manuscript jumps ahead. Obviously a folio of the original manuscript had been detached or else (much more likely) the scribe has somehow missed it. Certainly the material must have been there originally because the scribe has failed to complete the *dohara* and is now in a *chaupai*.

The scribe's carelessness is important, for it means indisputably that he was copying an existing text. From this it follows that the version of the so-called *Tanakhah-nama* contained in *MS.* 770 cannot have been the original one. At least one other copy lies behind it. If the colophon is correct (and there seems to be no reason for questioning it) *MS.* 770 was copied only ten years after the death of Guru Gobind Singh, and there was at least one earlier copy of the rahit-nama now no longer extant. This conclusion explains why the discovery of this manuscript is dramatic. The *Tanakhah-nama* can be dated very close to *Gur Sobha*, and both can be dated within a few years of Guru Gobind Singh's death.

The fourth reason for the importance of Dr Deol's discovery is that it enables us to set the rahit-namas in an approximate order and to date the first of them at a very early date. This means abandoning the theory that the early rahit-namas belong to the latter part of the eighteenth century and to revert instead to the belief that the beginnings can be traced to early in that century. Dates have been approximately fixed for three rahit-namas. The earliest extant example of what comes to be called the *Tanakhah-nama* has been allocated to 1718–19. An even earlier manuscript may yet be found, but this seems unlikely. The earliest extant *Chaupa Singh Rahit-nama* has been placed in the period 1740 to 1765, with a strong probability that it was written during the 1740s. And the *Desa Singh Rahit-nama* was recorded at the very end of the eighteenth century or early in the nineteenth. *Sakhi Rahit ki* and the *Prahilad Rai Rahit-nama* are rather more doubtful, but seem to derive from the mid 1730s. That leaves only the *Daya Singh Rahit-nama*. Various factors have to be taken into account when reaching a decision and together these point to the late eighteenth century as the time when the rahit-nama was first recorded. Like the *Desa Singh Rahit-nama*, however, it too may date from the early nineteenth century.

Next we shall examine some of the words which pose difficult problems, particularly when one seeks to present the rahit-namas in English translation. Some of these are not really difficult if one retains the original form, taking care to explain its meaning. Two examples are the cognate terms *tanakhah* and *tanakhahia*. In Sikh usage tanakhah means a penance or fine imposed by a *sangat* on any member of the Khalsa who violates the Rahit. The person so convicted is called a *tanakhahia*.

The two words are said to have acquired their present meaning during the early eighteenth century. Tanakhah means 'salary'. In an attempt to protect their authority in the Punjab the Mughals evidently made grants of money to those who assisted them. Recipients included some Sikhs, and the Khalsa regarded such Sikhs as hirelings and traitors. From here the word evidently shifted to mean a Sikh guilty of an offence against the Rahit, and the offence came to be called a tanakhah. This may be the correct etymology of the two terms, but the process will have taken place later in the eighteenth century than is generally assumed. The process whereby the terms tanakhah and tanakhahia came into fashion appears to have taken place in the 1740s or even later. It is no accident that lists of tanakhahs are to be found in the later rahit-namas, not in the earliest ones.

A rather more tantalising example is the word *dharam*. In this case it is scarcely appropriate to leave the word in its original form, for it covers a variety of meanings. It is, of course, possible to consult Kahn Singh Nabha's *Gurushabad Ratanakar Mahan Kosh*, and after eliciting translations of all the various terms which he uses in defining the word dharam seek one word which comes closest to the meaning in English. This method is followed by Louis Fenech and produces for him the term 'righteousness'. For him this method works, for he is seeking the translation which best expresses the Singh Sabha understanding of the term *dharam yudh*. Kahn Singh writes from firmly within the Singh Sabha movement and 'righteousness' seems a justifiable equivalent for his understanding.

The rahit-nama situation, however, is different, though the difference is not great. Making righteous war against the enemy was, after all, a vital function of the true Khalsa, and in several instances 'righteousness' serves as an appropriate if approximate translation. In other instances, however, the meaning of dharam seems in varying circumstances to draw closer to one of the following: 'duty', 'religious duty', 'caste duty', 'religious obligation', 'faith', 'belief'. For the rahit-namas a better way seems to use the English word which comes closest, always adding dharam afterwards in brackets.

Perhaps the most interesting term, both for Punjabi as well as for English readers, is the word *turak*. The word carries the same meaning in both languages (as in many other languages besides) and means 'Turk'. In the languages of India, however, it carries a much greater weight than simply a member of the Turkish race or (to be more correct) the Turkish ethnic group. In Indian usage, including the rahit-namas, the word is normally translated as 'Muslim'. Is this a fair translation? We need to be clear about this. Understood and translated as 'Muslim' the term *turak* seems to offer definitive proof of the hostile eighteenth century relations between the Muslims and the Sikhs of the Punjab.

With regard to the rahit-namas the answer appears to be that sometimes *turak* does carry the meaning 'Muslim' exclusively; sometimes it does not carry it; sometimes it simultaneously means both Muslim and an associated religious or political term; and sometimes it extends over more than two or more of these meanings. It is in fact a very complex word, one which is not easy to translate into English.

During the first half of the eighteenth century the enemies of the Khalsa were the Mughals. The original Mughals were not ethnic Turks (Babur was a Mongol), but many of their servants in India were of Turkish descent, and the word 'Mughal' was applied indiscriminately to all these soldiers and administrators. These are the people who in certain contexts are unquestionably those whom the rahit-namas call Turks, and this in turn suggests that the meaning attached to turak in the rahit-namas should be 'Mughal'. For the early part of the growth of the rahit-namas they were the rulers of the Punjab and such instructions as refusing to bow to a turak seems certainly to indicate that the word must refer to a Mughal.

There are, however, objections to doing so. In the first place the word turak meaning 'Muslim' as a religious identity had already entered North Indian usage. 'Turk' was the chosen word because Islam had been carried into India by Turks who had come more than more than half a millennium before the arrival of the Mughals. The word does not appear frequently in the Adi Granth, but when it does, it clearly expresses this religious meaning. Obviously the word had entered everyday usage, at least as a term distinguishing Muslims from Hindus.

Second, the rahit-namas lay great stress on the iniquity of consuming meat killed in the Muslim manner. Sometimes this meat is called *kuttha*, a term which does not explicitly draw attention to its Muslim origins. At other times, however, it is labelled *turak ka mas* and of this designation there can be no doubt. The meat known as kuttha or turak ka mas is forbidden because it is meat from an animal killed by the *halal* method of the Muslims, not because it is associated with the Mughals. Other injunctions are likewise aimed at preserving Khalsa purity. Two which receive prominence are sexual relations with Muslim women and smoking the hookah.

Third, the works of the later eighteenth century show that the term was still used by rahit-nama authors after the Mughals had faded from the Punjab scene. The Mughals were succeeded by the Afghans who under Ahmad Shah Abdali mounted a series of invasions from 1747 to 1769, and in spite of the fact that only some of the Afghans could be strictly described as ethnic Turks it seems that the word turak was also applied indiscriminately to them. Obviously it was not applied exclusively to the Mughals. The word turak already designated Muslims generally as well as retaining its specific ethnic meaning or its wider political meaning which referred to the hostile rulers or would-be rulers of the Punjab.

With the rise of Ranjit Singh the threat from Muslim enemies receded, and by the beginning of the nineteenth century it was virtually over. The early rahit-namas had, however, been written during the preceding century, when deep suspicion alternated with open hostility and intense fighting.

Under such circumstances it was only natural that the rahit-namas should reflect the feelings of their people. These circumstances also explain why the rahit-namas lay such a strong emphasis on the need for every Khalsa to bear arms.

Under Ranjit Singh, feelings slowly became more subdued and by the time the Singh Sabha emerged there was some embarrassment at the unconcealed enmity of the inherited rahit-namas. Tat Khalsa scholars in particular viewed such anti-Muslim items as the kind of utterance that Guru Gobind Singh could never have made and quietly dropped them from their revised rahit-namas. Kahn Singh provides a clear example of this, and *Sikh Rahit Marayada* retains few examples of this anti-Muslim past. Feelings against Muslims have not entirely disappeared, but they are not emblazoned for all to see in the manner of the eighteenth century rahit-namas.

We are left with a word which can be very difficult to interpret in any given context. Does it require a narrow religious meaning? Does it possess a wider social meaning? Does it express an ethnic meaning? Does it suggest a political meaning? Or is it an amalgam of two or more of these meanings? It seems that the one-word translation must ultimately fail us. Although the word turak may be hesitatingly rendered 'Muslim' in many cases, we must always remember that frequently it means 'an enemy, commonly a ruler or an official, who is also a Muslim'.

Third, we shall examine, as an example of how other works can help or hinder our research, the case of the *Guru kian Sakhian*. This work is said to have been written in 1790 CE by Svarup Singh Kaushish. Svarup Singh Kaushish was one of two sons of Kesar Singh Bhatt of village Bhadason in Pargana Thanesar. *Guru kian Sakhian* therefore comes within the same area as the Bhatt *vahis* discovered by Giani Garja Singh. Like the Bhatt vahis it was originally written in a script called Bhattachchhari which (to quote Professor Grewal) was 'a kind of family code like *lande* and *mahajani*'. This was subsequently transliterated into Gurmukhi. The only manuscript copy of *Guru kian Sakhian* which has survived was transliterated by Bhatt Chhajju Singh Kaushish who performed the task in S. 1925 (1869 CE). A published version was produced by Piara Singh Padam in 1986 in which he provides an introduction explaining who the Bhatts were and what the term vahi means. The remainder of the volume then gives Garja Singh's version of the 112 sakhis attributed to Bhatts who were said to be companions of Guru Gobind Singh.

The portion of *Guru kian Sakhian* which deals directly with the Rahit indicates at least three points of interest. This portion concerns Guru Gobind Singh's inauguration of the Khalsa order which occurs in *sakhis* 58, 59, and 60. The first point of interest is the date of the inauguration which, according to *Guru kian Sakhian*, took place on Baisakhi Day, *S*. 1755. This is the equivalent of 1698 CE, not the 1699 which is the popular dating amongst the Khalsa of today. This dating actually enhances the claims of *Guru kian Sakhian* to have been written in 1790. During the eighteenth century there was no agreed dating, and if *Guru kian Sakhian* declares it to be *S*. 1755 that dating strengthens its claim to have been written in 1790 CE.

The second point of interest is that it specifies Five Ks and declares one of them to be the *kesaki* instead of the *kes*. This is not a disputable spelling, one which might separate *kes* from *ki* as two separate words. The item which is specified is *nili rang ki kesaki*, leaving no doubt at all that it is in fact the one-word *kesaki*. This news has been greeted with much jubilation by the Akhand Kiratani Jatha, and would also have been greeted with the same acclaim by the Panch Khalsa Divan were it still in existence. According to the Akhand Kiratani Jatha women must wear under-turbans or *kesaki* if they are to be true amritdhari Sikhs, and this particular reference points directly to the kesaki as mandatory for all Sikhs who receive initiation into the Khalsa.

The third point of interest is the fact that *Guru kian Sakhian* actually specifies the Five Ks. One of them is liable to cause controversy (that is the kesaki) and the *kara* may cause something of a dilemma because it has to be *sarab loh* (all iron), but the remaining three are precisely those that figure in the modern rahit-nama. Even though there may be disagreements concerning the precise constituency of those two items the fact that all five begin with *kakka*, and were declared mandatory as long ago as 1790, make this a reference of absolutely prime importance.

It is this third point which provides the real interest as far as a history of the Rahit is concerned. There appear to be three possible answers to the problem which it raises. The first is that these words must have been actually written in 1790. The second is that these words were a later insertion, perhaps introduced later during the nineteenth century. The third is that the whole of *Guru kian Sakhian* is a spurious work, dating from an appreciably later time.

Of these possibilities the third is perhaps the least likely. How otherwise would it contain Baisakhi Day, *S*. 1755, as the date of the founding of the Khalsa order? This alone does not rule out the possibility of the third explanation (particularly as one should evaluate all of the 112 sakhis with this possibility in mind), but it does serve to weaken it.[3]

That leaves a choice between the first and the second answers, and it seems to me that the second is by far the stronger. This answer is that the words represent a later insertion or modification, together with various other items which also seem to have been subsequently added. No other source provides the Five Ks at such an early date (almost a century before their first indisputable appearance), and all later works pre-dating the Singh Sabha provide a different set or ignore them altogether. It is difficult to see, for example, how they could have been overlooked by *Sarab Loh Granth* or Malcolm in his *Sketch of the Sikhs*, both of which date from the same period. As a foreigner this could perhaps be expected of Malcolm, but certainly not of Ratan Singh Bhangu or Santokh Singh had these symbols been current by the late eighteenth century. Serious offences against the Rahit (the *kurahit*) have also adopted a recent form and similarly the Five Reprobate Groups. In these respects it no longer seems possible to accept *Guru kian Sakhian*, or at least this portion of the work. It is too modern.

The element of doubt which clings to this view means, however, that it is high time *Guru kian Sakhian* and all the Bhatt vahis were subjected to critical scrutiny. This they have never received. Giani Garja Singh was the only person ever to work conscientiously on the vahis or *Guru kian Sakhian*. His contribution may well be entirely honourable and in the meantime we must accept that he genuinely believed that what he had found was the authentic truth. He was, however, no scholar. The manuscripts which he discovered have not been subjected to critical attention, and apart from *Guru kian Sakhian* and isolated fragments they have never been published. It is high time that these tasks were properly performed.

And so the task continues. I have outlined only three of the challenges or difficulties involved in the study of the Khalsa Rahit. There are many more. Like all such subjects it has its own fascination, though one must always remain aware that what I may regard from a strictly academic point of view many millions regard as sacred and wholly sacrosanct. In the preface to *Guru Nanak and the Sikh Religion*, published away back in 1968, I commented on the risks involved in such subjects and the need for caution at all times. The Rahit is just such a subject. In no way do I want to upset faith or give offence. I would be naïve, however, to imagine that such risks do not exist. The past thirty years should surely have convinced me otherwise.

Notes

1. The question is discussed in 'Cries of outrage: history versus tradition in the study of the Sikh community' in W.H. McLeod, *Exploring Sikhism: Aspects of the Sikh Identity, Culture, and Thought* (New Delhi, 2000), pp. 267–79.

2. Since this paper was written an exception to the rule has appeared in the *International Journal of Punjab Studies* 8: 1 (January–June 2001). This is Nirvikar Singh's 'Guru Nanak and the *Sants*: a reappraisal'. A reply was published in *IJPS* 9:1 (January–June 2002), together with Nirvikar Singh's reply to that response.

3. It should, however, be noted that in at least two places the text uses English words. This means that the third option is still a definite possibility.

Response to Keynote Speech

Pashaura Singh

A quarter of a century ago the first North American conference in the area of Sikh Studies was held in 1976 at the University of California, Berkeley. At that conference it was generally acknowledged that the Sikh tradition was indeed 'the forgotten tradition' in scholarly circles in North America. In particular, Mark Juergensmeyer argued that in the textbooks in world religions the study of Sikhism was either completely ignored or misrepresented. He examined the various reasons for this treatment, and suggested that there are two main prejudices in Indian Studies that function against the study of the Sikh tradition. The first prejudice is that against the modern ages. Many scholars, following the Orientalist perspective, have been more interested in the classical texts on Indian Philosophy rather than a medieval devotional tradition. Since the Sikh tradition is barely 500 years old and relatively modern, it has been completely ignored in Indian studies. The other prejudice that faces Sikh Studies in Indian literature is the prejudice against regionalism. Sikhism is not only relatively modern, but it is also almost exclusively Punjabi. In his arguments, Mark Juergensmeyer made the case for the utility of Sikhism for the studies of religion. Since then the study of the Sikh tradition has received some cautious scholarly attention.

Sikhism is the world's youngest major religion. It has had to address issues and divergent approaches in a more 'compact' time frame and within a context of persistent political turmoil than others. Often Christianity, Judaism, Islam and other major religions have spent literally centuries working through things. Sikhism has yet to make its impact in the scholarly world. Although we now have four Chairs of Sikh and Punjab Studies established in North America with the active financial support of the members of the Sikh community, a great deal of ignorance still exists in North America about the Sikhs and their religious traditions. Not surprisingly, the first victim of racial backlash during the recent crisis after the terrorist attacks of September 11 was a Sikh, Balbir Singh Sodhi of Arizona, who was shot dead by an angry gunman calling himself a patriot. Mr Sodhi became the target because of a mistaken identity. People simply do not know who Sikhs are. In his keynote speech Professor McLeod has rightly pointed out that Sikhs do not receive the scholarly attention which they deserve. He has underlined certain gaps in historical scholarship that need to be filled with competent research. He has raised some academic issues with sympathetic concern, ending his speech with the following words: 'In no way do I want to upset faith or give offence. I would be naïve, however, to imagine that such risks do not exist. The past thirty years should surely have convinced me otherwise.' Professor McLeod has always stressed that one must use extreme caution and circumspection while studying a living religious tradition. I will address this cautionary note at the end of my response. Let me first respond to the three main issues raised by Professor McLeod in his analysis of the available sources on the Khalsa Rahit or 'Code of Conduct'.

First of all, let us look at the issue of the Five Ks raised in the last point of the keynote speech because it must be fresh in the memory of this distinguished audience. It is commonly understood that all Sikhs initiated into the order of the Khalsa must observe the Rahit as enunciated by Guru Gobind Singh on Baisakhi Day 1699 and subsequently elaborated. The most significant part of the Rahit is the enjoinder to wear five items of external identity known from their Punjabi names as the Five Ks. These are unshorn hair (*kes*), a wooden comb (*kangha*), a miniature sword (*kirpan*), an iron wrist-ring (*kara*), and a pair of short breeches (*kachh*). Current scholarship has questioned the assertion made by orthodox Sikhs that the convention of the five Ks originated with Guru Gobind Singh's declaration at the Baisakhi of 1699. In his earlier work, for instance, Professor McLeod has argued: 'At the end of the [eighteenth] century the convention [of Five Ks] was still emergent rather than clearly defined.' In support of his thesis he offers two arguments. First, there is no clear eighteenth century Rahit-nama testimony. Second, no one drew the attention of the early Europeans to the actual convention as such. In his keynote speech, Professor McLeod examines *Guru Kian Sakhian* (written in 1790) that mentions the Five Ks in a slightly different form, replacing *kes* (hair) with *kesaki* (small turban).

This new source upsets his line of arguments and that is why he questions its authenticity by saying that 'the words represent a later insertion or modification, together with various other items which also seem to have been subsequently added.'

My response on the issue of the Five Ks is slightly different. From the authentic 'letters of command' (*hukam-namas*) of Guru Gobind Singh, it is quite evident that he gave the injunction to the Khalsa to wear five weapons: 'Appear before the Guru with five weapons on your person' (*hathiar panje bann ke darasan avana*). This injunction must be understood in the militaristic context of the contemporary situation. We have first-hand independent reports of early Europeans about the dress and weapons worn by Khalsa Sikhs. John Malcolm, for instance, mentions in his *Sketch of the Sikhs* (1812) that at the time of the Khalsa initiation 'five weapons'—a sword, a firelock, a bow and arrow, and a pike—were presented to the initiate. At the time of the annexation of the Punjab in 1849, however, the British put a legal ban on carrying weapons. In the light of this new historical situation Baba Ram Singh had to ask his followers to carry a simple staff. It is no wonder that in order to meet this new situation the organizers of the Singh Sabha movement replaced the tradition of 'five weapons' with that of 'five religious symbols', known as the Five Ks. They did not introduce these symbols for the first time. These five items were already there as part of the Khalsa discipline. They are mentioned in the scattered form in early rahit-namas, but they acquired new significance because of the Singh Sabha's new definition of orthodoxy. This is not surprising since every dynamic community is always involved in the process of re-definition and renewal in response to new historical situations.

Let me make a brief comment on the examination of original sources. The *Bhat Vahi* sources and the *Guru Kian Sakhian* were written down in *Bhatakashari* script, a kind of business shorthands written in *landel mahajani* forms without vowel signs. Bhai Svarup Singh Kaushish originally prepared *Guru Kian Sakhian* in 1790. Later on Bhai Chhajju Singh deciphered that material to put it in the transliterated Gurmukhi version in 1868. A century later Giani Garja Singh used that manuscript to publish *Guru Kian Sakhian* in 1961. He may well have read the word *kesaki* instead of *kes* to promote the agenda of Akhand Kirtani Jatha and the Panch Khalsa Divan. He was a contemporary of Bhai Randhir Singh, and his native village Rajpura in Patiala District was under the strong influence of Bhasaur Singh Sabha.

Unfortunately, we do not have the original *Bhat Vahi* sources to resolve this issue without the shadow of any doubt.

The second issue raised in the keynote speech examines certain key terms that pose difficult problems, particularly when one seeks to present the rahit-namas in English translations. For instance, the word *turk* is frequently translated as 'Muslim'. Let us look at the following translation of a passage from the rahit-namas: 'The true Khalsa is one who carries arms and slays Muslim.' Any Sikh who will read this translation will be stunned. This is certainly not the contextual meaning of the original passage. It is directly against the teachings of the Sikh Gurus to kill anyone because of one's religious affiliation. In fact, the word turk in the rahit-namas and early Sikh literature refers to an 'invader' or an 'oppressor'. In almost all cases, turk or *turkara* refers to Mughal rulers of the day or to Afghan invaders, although both of these groups did not belong to the Turkish ethnic group. In the early Sikh literature such expressions as *turk de mathe nahin lagana/ turk di mohar nahin manani/turkare di khushamad nahin karani* point towards those Mughal or Afghan officials who were perceived to be oppressors. Thus it was the fundamental duty of the Khalsa to 'slay oppressors'.

Finally, I would like to stress the point that Rahit is closely linked with the initiation ceremony that must be understood from the perspective of ritual studies. Rituals are generally passed orally from generation to generation. In the actual Khalsa initiation ceremony, the Cherished Five do not literally follow the written manuals that often provide sketchy details. The authors of these manuals wrote only those points that were significant to their contemporaries. They discarded other items that posed problems in their own historical situation. They also did not write certain items that were generally known to their contemporaries. Thus one must be extremely cautious in relying on the partial accounts available in the written sources. True, tradition must not be accepted uncritically, but it cannot be rejected outright either. What is 'believed to have happened' plays much more significant role in the life of a religious community than 'what actually happened'. Therefore, one must maintain a double focus on history and tradition in any analysis of the Rahit material. This is precisely what Professor McLeod has done in his study of the Khalsa Rahit. The modern version of the Khalsa Rahit available in the *Sikh Rahit Maryada* is certainly the evolved product of the last three centuries.

In conclusion, I come to the cautionary note about the risks involved in the area of Sikh studies. It is important to note that the kind of socio-religious controversy surrounding the works of the scholars of the Sikh tradition is not something new. It is surprisingly archaic and happens most of the time in homogenous old-world societies. There are certainly many conservative followers of Western traditions, too, who do not like much of the academic discourse about their traditions. They have, nevertheless, adapted to the existence of that discourse. Although they may ignore academic discourse as trivial in its disregard of real religious truth, they frequently glean insights from it despite perceived distortions. In the classroom, we frequently observe that analytic understandings help many contemporary students come to terms with their own traditions and appreciate them all the more. In the West, Sikh Studies is a new field, and much of the current reaction to scholars' work reflects the Sikh community's relative lack of experience with analytic understanding of their tradition. As that experience grows, Sikhs are likely to make adaptations and discoveries similar to those of their counterparts from other religious traditions—often ignoring analytic works as not serious, sometimes appreciating them in part.

Section Two

1

Mythic Inheritance and
the Historic Drink of the Khalsa

Nikky-Guninder Kaur Singh

> For there is no identity without memory—be it of a person, couple, family, neighborhood, community, tribe, people, nation, globe.
>
> Catharine Stimpson[1]

My chapter takes up the subject of Sikh identity, which has been deeply studied by Professor Hew McLeod from a historical perspective. With my focus on Guru Nanak's mythic initiation in the river Bein and Guru Gobind Singh's initiation of the Khalsa during Baisakhi 1699 in Anandpur, I want to examine Sikh identity from the perspective of feminist studies in religion. For millions of Sikhs the two events are an indelible part of their past, and their historical veracity is not questioned in Sikh practice. As irrefutable facts, they are remembered by generations of Sikhs and form the core of their belief and practice. The memory of these events is vital and carries a profound symbolic significance in the construction of their individual and that of their collective identity.

I want to return to those two moments which are an intrinsic part of the Sikh psyche and which lie mingled in some remote part of my own subconscious self. They have great personal value for me for these are the earliest narratives that I recall hearing from my parents and they constitute the most precious part of my past that I want to pass on to my daughter. We search the past to make use of it in the present. So with the help of phenomenological reflections of Mircea Eliade and Martin Heidegger, and the anthropological structures of Bronislaw Malinowski and Victor Turner,

I want to explore how the first Guru's mythic drink in the river Bein is recreated by his Tenth successor and feeds generations of Sikhs. My goal in remembering the past is to recover the possibilities and potentialities of the nutritious *amrit* so that we may create a more egalitarian and liberating future. The cultural stereotypes and inscriptions of female otherness and subjugation that should have been severed through the *amrit* drink have ended up being reinforced and internalized over the centuries. The emancipatory value of the amrit received by Nanak and prepared by the Tenth is submerged in an androcentric memory, which reproduces structures of domination and authority. From a feminist perspective, selfhood and autonomy are the crucial ingredients in amrit. It is my hope that my feminist commemoration of these will retrieve the full force of Sikh identity envisioned by the Gurus—for both men and women.

The amrit rite of passage practiced by Sikhs all over the globe evokes the primal moment of Sikhism—Guru Nanak's sipping of amrit recorded in the *Puratan Janamsakhi*. The myth narrates how Nanak, a simple worker at a grocery store, was initiated by the Divine in the River Bein, and became the founder Guru of the Sikh religion. The diaphanous and flowing waters of the north Indian river form the placenta in which the Sikh religion was initially lodged. The Janamsakhi relates the Sikh *gesta*, the primal sacred act, and fulfills Mircea Eliade's definition that myth is 'always an account of a "creation"; it relates how something was produced, began to *be*.'[2]

In a very meaningful way, the Tenth Sikh Guru returns to this primal moment of Sikhism and opens it up into the future through his inauguration of the amrit initiation at Anandpur on Baisakhi 1699. Although there may not be sufficient historical documents to provide the perfect testimony to exactly what happened on that particular day, the event is deeply etched in the collective memory of Sikhs. Professor McLeod's approach is most appropriate: 'It matters little whether five volunteers were actually summoned or whether five goats were actually slain. The overriding fact is that in its essential outline the story is firmly believed and that this belief has unquestionably contributed to the subsequent shaping of conventional Sikh attitudes.'[3] Rather than empirical evidence or historical explorations, I am drawn to the imprint that Baisakhi 1699 has left on the Sikh popular imagination, and the responses, attitudes, and emotions that it continues to elicit. Across the continents and through the generations, the initiation of Sikhs into the community has been modelled on the ritual performed by Guru Gobind Singh on that day. As Pashaura Singh observes, there may be variations in the actual practice amongst Sikhs, 'Nevertheless, each group claims to follow the "correct" procedure laid down by Guru Gobind Singh at the Baisakhi of 1699 and transmitted orally through successive generations.'[4]

What I find most intriguing is that the 'beginning' of Sikhism embodied in the private, individual, and mystical experience of the First Guru, culminates in a public, social, and institutional ritual by the Tenth. Through Guru Gobind Singh's unique performance on Baisakhi 1699, Guru Nanak's experience is organized and systematized into an essential rite. The Tenth Guru unleashes the force from Guru Nanak's mythic narrative and brilliantly choreographs it into a *fixed* and *enduring* ritual for the present and future of his community. In Eliade's words,

By virtue of the continual repetition of a paradigmatic act, something shows itself to be *fixed* and *enduring* in the universal flux .... ritual abolishes profane, chronological Time and recovers the sacred Time of myth.[5]

By grounding the Khalsa initiation in the primal moment, the apodictic value of the Janamsakhi is reconfirmed, and in turn, Guru Gobind Singh's ritual is endowed with significance and authenticity. The vigour of Nanak's amrit is thrust into perpetuity—the metahistoric account becomes an essential part of the psyche and practice of the Sikh community—Sikh sacred history as enduring and integral part of daily life. We will analyse how Guru Gobind Singh transcreates the Janamsakhi narrative into a vital ritual act and accomplishes Malinowski's goal of lifting myth from its 'existence on paper', and placing it 'in the three-dimensional reality of full life.'[6]

Specialists on the study of myth and ritual have shown the two to be parallel phenomena. With its preterpunctual and eternal happenings, myth is distinguished from ritual, which consists of punctual and immediate events. Whereas myth expresses a situation in its ideal, transcendent aspect, the ritual is an actual event taking place in historic time and involving everyday people. Although myth and ritual are two distinct processes, anthropologists, sociologists, and psychologists have claimed the powerful connection between them. Mythos leads to ethos; stories control moral and social behavior. Malinowski, the pioneer in functional anthropology, inspired the study of the practical result of myth in a living society. His research of Melanesian culture and his voluminous contributions elaborate his thesis that 'an intimate connection exists between the word, the mythos, the sacred tales of a tribe, on the one hand, and their ritual acts, their moral deeds, their social organization, and even their practical activities, on the other.'[7] Malinowski's theoretical formulations are valuable to us, for they enable us to understand the cultural force of Guru Gobind Singh's undertaking. As the 1699 initiation rite moves into the past, it gains great force and momentum, building a sense of continuity, stability, and direction for future generations. Time and timeless, history and myth are blended together in the potent amrit.

I disagree therefore with usual perceptions that Guru Gobind Singh forms a contrast to and deviation from Guru Nanak. A recent study on the institution of the Khalsa enumerates how modern historians continue to reiterate Toynbee's view that the Tenth Guru wrought 'a process of transformation for the Sikhs from a pacifist fraternity into a militant political community.'[8] As the crusader against tyranny and oppression, the Tenth Guru is opposed to the peace-loving Guru Nanak.

Even in popular imagination, the two are presented quite differently. In most Sikh paintings, Guru Nanak is portrayed in the dress combining Hindu and Muslim elements. He wears a patched cloak with arabesque designs, and his spherical turban has a rosary on it. While he is rapt in contemplation, with his right palm imprinted with 'Ikk Oan Kar', we find Guru Gobind Singh richly dressed and ready for action. Instead of a rosary placed on a hat-like turban, he is decked with a jeweled crest upon a lofty, cone-shaped turban. He is either standing erect, or seated on his horse, armed with various weapons, including a bow and a quiver of arrows, a sword, a discuss, a shield, and a spear. He is shown with a handsome bluish-gray horse, and often, a white hawk is perched on his left hand. G.S. Talib, sums up Guru Gobind Singh's portrait: 'In contradiction to the other preceptors of the Sikh faith he is thought of as the warrior, the hero with a resplendent, knightly figure fighting against tyrants and evil-doers, somewhat like Saint George of the Christians.'[9]

When we get stuck on such contrasts and contradictions, we overlook the powerful message of continuity and tradition at the heart of the Sikh religion. Such preoccupations lead to historical aberrations, and they deflect us from understanding the liberating process inherent in the Amrit initiation. An exclusive reliance on the 'warrior', and the 'knightly' figure of the Tenth Guru distracts us from the maternal and feminine dimension of his personality and undertakings. Consequently, amrit initiation is primarily understood as a male rite performed by men, for men, and through men, which was not Guru Gobind Singh's intention. It seems to me that the interrelationship between the First and the Tenth illuminates the full meaning of the Sikh rite, and gives us a taste of the peace and the freedom and the newness each sip carries for all members, high and low, both male and female. It is my contention that the motherly waters of the river Bein function as the primordial womb from which the Khalsa Amrit is made: the waters in which Guru Nanak had his divine encounter constitute the material substance of Guru Gobind Singh's Amrit.

The continuity between them is expressed in the *Bachittar Natak*. Most Sikhs believe that the *Bachittar Natak* is composed by Guru Gobind Singh himself though some modern scholars in the West argue that it may be written by one of his associates. In either case, it accurately represents Guru Gobind Singh's outlook. The author unequivocally acknowledges that it is the same light passing through the Ten Gurus.

bhin bhin sabh hun kar jana
ek rup kinhun pahicana
jin jana tin hi sidhi pai
binu samajhe sidhi hathi na ai [10]

All know them distinct and apart
Only the rare recognize their single form;
Those who know are successful
Without understanding, spiritual powers cannot be grasped.

Guru Gobind Singh is conscious of his heritage, and confidently accepts that his own ideology, poetics, and practices are rooted within an existing structure. In an essay on the theory of influence, contemporary critic Harold Bloom explores the anxiety that writers and poets feel about their literary heritage. Bloom comments, 'Every major aesthetic consciousness seems peculiarly more gifted at denying obligation as the hungry generations go on treading one another down.' [11] The Sikh Guru is no way reticent about acknowledging his indebtedness to his precursors, and in fact, he even celebrates his rich legacy.

Although Guru Nanak's initiation in the River Bein is not specifically mentioned by Guru Gobind Singh, he was deeply aware of it at some unconscious level. He was the tenth Guru to succeed Nanak, and as he inherited his precursor's history, he inherited his metahistory as well. According to Anil Chander Banerjee, the tradition of Puratan Janamsakhi was quite well known in Guru Gobind Singh's time. [12] The reference to Guru Nanak's revelation in the Bein is even found in the work of Nand Lal

Goya, a leading poet in Guru Gobind Singh's literary entourage.[13] Apparently janam-sakhis had become popular by then. Whether they were factually true does not matter. What is important is that the stories of the birth and life of the founder of the Sikh religion became an essential part of his successor's memory and imagination, and came to play in his own life. As Victor Turner says, 'It is only when we bring into relation with the preoccupying present experience the cumulative result of similar or at least relevant, if not dissimilar, past experiences of similar potency, that the kind of relational structure we call "meaning" emerges.'[14]

As Guru Gobind Singh intentionally and/or unintentionally reaches back to his predecessors, there is a constant interrelation between Guru Nanak and Gobind Singh, in Gadamer's sense, that is, a 'fusion of horizons'. Certainly, Guru Gobind Singh does not simply repeat and reproduce the mythical account for his is not a mechanical output. Guru Gobind Singh is creative and innovative, and his is an authentic development and formation of his predecessors' voice and action. His tendency towards the dramatic gives a new fervour to the ritual format. Guru Gobind Singh was a superb poet himself, and his artistic sensibilities would have absorbed the paradigmatic myth and developed it into a new creation of his own. Martin Heidegger reminds us,

All creation, because it is such a drawing-up, is a drawing, as of water from a spring. Modern subjectivism, to be sure immediately misinterprets creation, taking it as the self-sovereign subject's performance of genius. The founding of truth is a founding not only in the sense of free bestowal, but at the same time foundation in the sense of this ground-laying grounding.[15]

By returning to the earliest moments of Sikhism, Guru Gobind Singh draws out layers of meaning, sustenance, and experience from his past and mingles it with the Amrit. When we recognize their philosophical, social, and aesthetic horizons fusing together, we experience the full power and dynamism of the amrit drink. Many symmetrical relationships and fascinating parallels emerge in our analysis. The Khalsa initiation becomes an exciting hermeneutic opening for Guru Nanak's vision, revealing Guru Gobind Singh as a perfect fulfillment and certainly not a 'contradiction to the other preceptors of the Sikh faith'.

Amrit initiation is a uniquely Sikh phenomenon which debunks centuries-old rites and customs. A radical departure from traditional rites of passage such as the *upanyana* or circumcision prevalent in Guru Gobind Singh's society, it is grounded in Nanak's experience. The paramount significance of initiation rites has been discussed by Eliade in his comparative work *Rites and Symbols of Initiation*. He begins by delineating three categories: puberty initiations which establish sexual identity and adult status, secret fraternities which establish membership in a secret society, and voluntary or involuntary initiations which establish higher religious status.[16] Eliade focuses upon the first type of initiation, which is an essential part of all communities and elaborates its extraordinary patterns and variety. His extensive study unfolds the construction of male superiority and dominance as the standard outcome of such rites.

Instead of a puberty rite, the janam-sakhi literature presents Nanak as going through another type of initiation that would correspond to the third category enumerated by Eliade—the transition into a higher religious status. The passage does not establish his sexual identity or adult status; it is simply a transition into a liberated and liberating mode of existence. We learn that Nanak in his early years was a contemplative person who spent most of his time outside, tending the family herd of cattle, conversing with wayfaring sadhus and sufis, and devoting his time to solitude and inward communion. Later, at the invitation of his sister Nanaki, and her husband Jai Ram, he moved to Sultanpur where he worked in the Muslim Nawab's *modikhana* (grain stores). It was at Sultanpur that Nanak went through a critical transition. This was his rite of passage, a symbolic birth which redefined Nanak's personal and social identity, and becomes the starting point of the Sikh religion. As the Tenth successor to Guru Nanak deconstructs established social borders and reconstructs new formations, he models his momentous Khalsa initiation on Nanak's rite of passage. Both discourses conform to the archetypal tripartite pattern: (a) separation; (b) liminality; and (c) reincorporation.

Separation

The first stage of initiation in both cases is marked by death. Nanak goes for a bath in the river. He leaves behind his clothes—indicative of his set of codes and insignias; he leaves behind his attendant—indicative of his home, family, and society at large. He possesses nothing. His concomitant identity is left behind. Nanak has stripped off his cultural conditions and divested himself of social structures. He disappears in the Bein for three days. His Muslim employer summons the fishermen, has nets thrown into the river, and has his men search everywhere in vain. Nanak is nowhere to be found, and Nanak's employer leaves dejected thinking how good a minister Nanak was.

Just as Guru Nanak was considered dead in the river Bein, Guru Gobind Singh's Five devotees are also assumed dead by the Baisakhi gathering in Anandpur. Across cultures, the theme of death has been posited as a resource for dynamic new beginnings. In the *Katha Upanishad*, Nachiketa discovers true living after his encounter with Yama, the God of Death. Closer to our own times, Malinowski writes, 'And he who is faced by death turns to the promise of life.'[17] Nanak's true vocation began after his 'death' in the River Bein. The realistic perspective of death in the janam-sakhi narrative becomes the template for Guru Gobind Singh's recreation of the initial stage of separation. Turner observes that the transition of the initiates in different cultures is similar to death and compares it to the womb, darkness, bisexuality, and to a lunar or solar eclipse.

But rather than being 'likened to death', the initiates in both of the Sikh instances as are depicted being dead in a very realistic manner. Guru Nanak is searched for and ultimately declared dead by his contemporaries. Guru Gobind Singh emulates Nanak's crisis by 'making up'—in the sense of Aristotle's *poiesis* (crafting)—the death of his Five Beloved. In order for the Khalsa to enter a new womb, death was necessary. How else could the Khalsa be born into a new family? How could the Khalsa have new parents? A new name? A new personality? A new residence? Nanak's 'accident' in the river Bein is metamorphosed into a deliberate act. The natural and silent hazard recounted in the *Puratan Janamsakhi* changes into a willful and audible requirement during Guru Gobind Singh's ritual recreation. Whereas Nanak 'disappears' in the Janamsakhi account, death during Baisakhi 1699 blatantly appears and reappears through Guru Gobind Singh's crimson sword dripping with warm blood. The Guru asks for the lives of five of his devotees; five times the audience hears a thud and sees a flow of blood. No darkness or colour or paint represents death.

Blood and water are cast as its agents: the river Bein for Nanak, the flowing blood for the Khalsa. In both discourses, the fluids are not represented through pigments or any images; they exist in actuality and create real dramatic scenarios. Both retain an element of mystery for the transparent waters reveal nothing about Nanak, nor the blood anything about the five devotees who offered themselves to the Guru's sword. Their spectators remain equally bewildered. The vital fluids lead us to the concealment of the mother's womb where the menstrual blood and the placental waters fuse together to feed and sustain the embryo. The light, white, and life-giving water of the Janamsakhi account does not form a contrast with the dark, red, and life-taking blood of the Baisakhi celebration. The Tenth Guru rents the goats during the Sikh *akedah* in such a fashion that the blood flows like a river. Perhaps the Sikh Guru shared Empedocles's view of blood as 'the perfect substance, containing all elements united in equal measure' for him to display it so openly![18] Through the Guru's performance, the frightening and dangerous fluid acquires the primacy and sustaining power of the waters of the River Bein. Rather than an end to life, the red elixir becomes the embryonic fluid that nurtures and sustains the germination of the Khalsa. It becomes both life and life-giving, and as Trumbull described over a century ago, an 'analogon of life', a 'means of inspiration'.[19]

Death is definitely a major plot in both Guru Nanak's mythic account and in the ritual enactment of the Khalsa initiation, but their emphasis is on the acceptance of the finitude of life. If anything, death is made light of. That death is a natural phenomenon, something common to both men and women, issues forth in each case. Men and women realize that Nanak is dead. It is noteworthy, that women stayed in the Baisakhi congregation and witnessed the Sikh *akedah*. Feminist scholars remind us that Socrates' wife, Xanthippe, was banished from his presence during his last hours: 'reminder of gender, birth, and embodied life. ... her presence cannot be tolerated while Socrates practices the philosophical life ...'[20] Even in the Jewish *akedah*, Sarah is left at home while Abraham goes by himself to sacrifice their son Isaac. During Baisakhi 1699, women with their male counterparts receive the Guru's call, and with them, witness the graphic scenes of death. They are not excluded.

The acceptance of death has been a central concern for feminist scholars. According to Grace Jantzen, western philosophy is obsessed with death, and this obsession she detects is 'connected with the obsession with female bodies, and the denial of death and efforts to master it are connected with a deep-seated misogyny.'[21] From the sensitive global lenses she wears, Rita Gross envisions that for the post-patriarchal transformation of religion, affirmation of death and our embodied condition is essential. In *Feminism and Religion*, Gross discusses the different ways in which Rosemary Ruether, Carol Christ, Sally McFague, Naomi Goldenberg, and even herself from her Buddhist perspective, condemn the dualism of death and life, finitude and transcendence. Feminist thinkers universally argue that such a dualism carries dangerous consequences for humanity and the earth: 'Women are identified with the despised body that constantly changes and finally gives evidence of its finitude by dying, and the entire natural world of change and decay is also rejected in favour of the spiritual, other worldly ideal.'[22]

Instead of idealizing release from bondage to the mortal body, a natural cycle of birth, growth, and death emerges in our accounts. Just as the feminist scholars claim, death is not a punishment, and guilt is not attached with being human. In either case, eschatological joys are not offered as an antithesis to life, for there are no scenes celebrating any paradisal existence of beauty or bliss in contrast with life here on earth. The Janamsakhi does not extol Nanak's end of suffering and entry into a beatific world; in fact, the Khan returns dejected for having lost a good worker in Nanak. In the same vein, Guru Gobind Singh does not promise a life of joy after death: he demands but the supreme *gift of life* from his devotees. That death is not to be feared, that death is not to be mastered over by miraculous deeds, that death does not lead to some wonderful world beyond, but rather death simply is and that it be accepted, and even embraced, so that we can have a just and egalitarian society here and now, is played out in the Baisakhi of 1699. Guru Gobind Singh did not put his beloved Sikhs through the tortuous ordeal to prepare them for some other distant world but rather to usher in an authentic mode of existence for them *here and now*. In both our mythic and ritual discourses death is a part of life, not opposite of life, and in both instances, it leads to new life in this world, with the full experience of being human in and through the body.

Betwixt and Between

The ambiguous and paradoxical stage in both of the Sikh discourses conforms to an archetypal pattern. Features from Turner's study of the 'Betwixt and Between: the Liminal Period' apply to our myth and ritual. In their 'interstructural situation', Guru Nanak and the Five Beloved are 'at once no longer classified and not yet classified'.[23] As Guru Nanak is ushered into the realm of the Divine, he is no longer the store employee, nor is he yet the Guru who would attract millions to a new world religion. Similarly, when Guru Gobind Singh ushered his Five devotees out of the congregation, they no longer had their social cultural identity, nor were they yet the Khalsa. Each of them is at a dynamic threshold where the past borders are gone and future possibilities are yet to come.

During the three days that he is deemed drowned, Guru Nanak has a numinous experience. The reader is drawn into the depths of the river where Nanak has a vision of the Transcendent—to an opening of infinite possibilities. The waters are the womb in which Nanak gestates. With the fecund and fertile waters of the river as the backdrop, the *Puratan Janamsakhi* narrates a sequence of events leading up to Nanak receiving the religious status of Guru:

1. In the multi-layered mythic account, Nanak is ushered into the divine presence and receives a cup full of amrit: '*ehu amritu mere nam ka piala hai*— this amrit is the cup of my Name.'[24] Enclosed in the waters of Bein, Nanak receives the drink of immortality—*amrita* (literally, *a*=not+*mrita*=death). The voice he hears does not come from some high mountaintop, but from the inside of the river. Drink is our most basic and primal function and need: upon entry into the world we first drink our mother's milk. The account validates a basic human process. The Divine command '*pio*' (drink) substantiates the human body with its capacity to drink and taste and grow and nourish, and its capacity to produce the elixir as well.

What Nanak received was *nam ka piala*—the cup of Name. *Nam*, the cognate of Name, is the identity of the Transcendent One. The immortal drink that Nanak receives and drinks is the sapiential experience of the transcendent One. Amrita as immortality is not a renunciation or end of life, rather, it is the full intensity of the human experience. By drinking, Nanak cognizes the Divine Reality. In this encounter in the River Bein, Nam and Amrita are declared as synonymous. The drink enables Nanak to enter into the depths of his own being and recognize the utterly transcendent within. Nanak's vision is a vision of his own Self—the infinite and transcendent experienced by his finite body.

Nanak is then asked to go and instruct others. But there is also the implication in the Janamsakhi narrative that he is put through a test. Before he departs—he has made his salutations and stood up—Guru Nanak is ordered to illustrate his method and technique. 'How does one praise my name? Recite!' Guru Nanak responds with a hymn that was his song—and proof—of praise. We find here a striking affinity between '*kahu*' (recite in Punjabi) the command that Nanak receives, and '*kun*' (recite in Arabic), the order given by God to the Prophet Muhammad through the Archangel Gabriel. While the Prophet Muhammad hears the Word in the caves of Mount Hira, Guru Nanak, in the river Bein. Neither was previously known for his poetic genius, but after passing through the feminine spaces, both of them become the matrix for a voluminous, momentous, and most artistic text—the Qur'an and the Guru Granth, respectively.

2. Guru Nanak passes the test through the poetic syntax and is accepted by the Divine. The hymn he recites is an excellent testimony of his psychic and spiritual power (its melody is unstruck—'dhuni anhadu udthi'), and of his artistic sensibility. To cite just its final verse:

> If I had a supply of bottomless ink, and could write with the speed of the wind;
> I would still not be able to measure your greatness,
> Nor signify the glory of Your Name![25]

Nanak becomes the poet. He explodes human language. He uses poignant similes and analogies and metaphors to describe That which is utterly ineffable. Feminist philosophers have shown the contrast between the abstract, intellectual, and patriarchal theology and the feminist theology that is 'the reawakening of sensitivity to the forgotten dimensions, to the spheres of the senses, the psyche, the body, the imagination.'[26] Through his poetic outpour Guru Nanak incorporates the feminist reawakening of sensitivity into the very foundations of the Sikh faith. Hearing Guru Nanak's poetic outpour, the Voice spoke: 'Nanak, you discern My will.' The Janamsakhi thus attests to Nanak's success. He has passed his divine examination; in fact, he has triumphed in his praise of the Formless One. Nanak then recites the *Japu*. Although the Janamsakhi does not cite the entire text of Guru Nanak's hymn, it specifies that Nanak 'concluded the Japu—*japu sampuran kita*'. The *Japu* would be Guru Nanak's acknowledgement of his acceptance. Recited at this particular juncture of his spiritual encounter, the *Japu* becomes an expression of Nanak's gratitude. The *Japu* constitutes the core of Guru Nanak's metaphysics, and forms the opening text of Sikh scripture, the Guru Granth.

3. In the third phase of his sacred liminality, Guru Nanak is given the robe of honour (*sirpao* or commonly known as *saropa*). As the Janamsakhi narrative continues,

The Voice was heard again: 'Who is just in your eyes, Nanak, shall be so in Mine. Whoever receives your grace shall abide in Mine. My name is the Supreme One; your name is the divine Guru.' Guru Nanak then bowed in gratitude and was given the robe of honour from the divine court. A sonorous melody in the Raga Dhanasari rang forth ... Arati ....

Nanak is initiated as the Guru. He is conferred a new status and identity. The sacra or the physical object that marks his special dispensation is the *sirpao*—the robe of honour. Nanak receives it from the divine court. Literally, it is a piece of material that goes from head (*sir*) to foot (*pao*). But the dress does not carry any male or female codifications. It is not tailored for either– or, and could be worn by both men and women. Immediately following his conferral, the Guru rapturously recites *Arati*, in which he celebrates the transcendent light permeating every being. *Joti*, the insubstantial light, is the feminine dimension of the Ultimate One.[27] Contained by the fecund waters of the River Bein, Nanak recognizes the ontological basis of the universe and is called upon to disseminate what has been vouchsafed to him.

Nanak's initiation does not establish his sexual status, and if at all, his rite of passage shatters the construction of a male identity. Although he is a son, brother, husband, and father who entered the river, the mythic initiation endows him with his essential humanity. Located in the placental waters, he goes through the process of physical drinking which gives him the metaphysical insight into the feminine *joti*. He responds in a sensuous, poetic outpour, and receives gender-inclusive clothing from the divine court. The space, the process, the revelation, the result, the gift, all pulsate with female imagery and activity. Through them, Nanak recovers the fullness and intensity of the human experience, and is called upon to enlighten others.

The symbolic form of the Janamsakhis is inherited by the Tenth Guru and is realized and materialized in his ritual event. Guru Nanak's initiation in the river Bein serves simultaneously as a 'model of' and 'model for' Guru Gobind Singh's Khalsa initiation. According to Clifford Geertz, this double aspect is important because only through the two senses—an 'of' and a 'for' sense—do cultural patterns give meaning to 'social and psychological reality both by shaping themselves to it and by shaping it to themselves.'[28] The leitmotif of death, and the liminal experience of drinking amrit, reciting sacred poetry, and robing recounted in the *Puratan Janamsakhi* are historically transmitted to the Tenth Guru; it is his 'system of inherited conceptions'. And in a most subtle and artistic way, the First Guru's mythic experience becomes a 'model of' and 'model for' Guru Gobind Singh's enactment of the Khalsa initiation.

The sequence, however, differs. The Guru first gives an extremely difficult test, and only after that does he offer the drink of amrit. As the poetic sources tell us, Sikhs had gathered in Anandpur from far and wide for the annual Baisakhi celebrations in 1699. According to Sainapati who writes some twelve years after the event

gobind singh kari khushi sangati kari nihal
kio pragat tab khalsa cukio sakal janjal
sab smuh sangati mili subh satiludr ke tir
ketak sun bhae khalsa ketak bhae adhir[29]

Gobind Singh ushered joy, made the community happy,
He then created the Khalsa, and so removed all traps.
The entire community gathered on the banks of the auspicious Sutlej
Hearing him, many became his Khalsa, and many discontent.

Brief though it may be, Sainapati unequivocally points to a specific historical event: '*kio pragat tab khalsa*—he then manifested the Khalsa', '*tab*' (meaning 'then'). The passage also indicates that Guru Gobind Singh said something awesome which inspired many to adopt Khalsahood but many others were left discontent and doubtful (*adhir*). Sainapati is alluding to the intensity and suspense of Guru Gobind Singh's examination that elicited different kinds of responses from the congregation, making Sainapati a rather realistic resource.

We can well imagine what the audience must have felt when their revered Guru addressed them with sword in hand, asking for a head! In the words recorded by another poet:

'*sanmukh pura sikh hai koi,*
sis bhet gur deve joi'[30]

'Is there a complete Sikh present here,
who would offer his/her head to the Guru?'

Indeed, it is a most painful demand, especially made on such a festive occasion. The Guru provides no rationale whatsover. Although the poet recording the event years later keeps repeating that the motivation behind the Guru's Word was the refinement of his community, the Baisakhi congregation at that point could have found no discursive meaning behind the Guru's tortuous request. The ultimate faith and commitment of his devotees is put on trial. When he repeats his demand three times, a volunteer comes up. We are not told where the Guru goes with his volunteer. Or for how long. But we do know he 'returns outside again'. But this time it is only the Guru. The devotee enters a womb-like dark and mysterious world, utterly unknown to the audience outside, and so Guru Gobind Singh recreates Guru Nanak's disappearance in the River. Separated from his Baisakhi congregation, separated from his social role and rank, he is left in an ill-defined marginal space. The volunteer has made his passage into a liminal sphere, which Turner shows is full of positive and active qualities. Meanwhile, the Guru becomes the recipient of the ultimate gift of his devotee's life.

The Guru returns triumphantly carrying the sword bathed in the essential substance of his 'volunteer'; the sight of the crimson fluid dripping around its sharp and strong and sparkling body would have been deeply unsettling. The blood here is not dark or congealed or dead in any sense, its life-force is palpably visible which creates an awesome tension, heightened even further by Guru Gobind Singh's demand for yet another head. The tough test is repeated five times. Each time the Guru puts his Sikhs on trial—examining their courage, endurance, love, and devotion. All together, five men end up being taken away from the congregation into a sacred liminality. But the Five—like Guru Nanak—succeed splendidly. The Guru had not killed the Five Beloved; he had killed five male goats. Just as men and women witness Guru Nanak stepping out of the Bein, the Baisakhi congregation witnesses the Five returning with the Guru.

The Five Beloved then receive sacra, which for Turner is the crux of liminality. Guru Nanak and the Five Beloved are communicated the typical three sacra: exhibitions (what is shown), actions (what is done), and instructions (what is said). However, Turner's overall premise that the liminal sacra are imbued with secrecy does not quite fit in the Khalsa initiation, for Guru Gobind Singh brings out Guru Nanak's encounter in the depths of the River Bein on to the lofty stage at Anandpur. The cup of Divine Name that Guru Nanak drank in seclusion is drunk by the Five Beloved in front of the huge gathering on a bright Baisakhi day. In contrast with Turner's observation, 'great importance is' *not* 'attached to keeping secret the nature of the sacra',[31] and a description like that of the Swazi liminality wherein people become one only in darkness, silence, celibacy, and in the absence of merriments and movement,[32] does not hold true for the Khalsa initiation.

Actually, we find the Heideggerian strife between the earth and the world at the heart of the Khalsa liminality. According to Heidegger, art is created from the conflict between the grounding, founding and sheltering 'earth' and the open, flamboyant, and the soaring 'world'. In his unforgettable essay on 'The Origin of the Work of Art' Heidegger explains that the relationship between earth and world is not an insipid and vacant coming together of opposites, nor is it a destructive relation of any sort. Rather, there is an intimacy with which the two belong to each other: 'The world grounds itself on the earth, and earth juts through world.'[33]

Genuinely poetic projection is the opening up or disclosure of that into which human being as historical is already cast. This is the earth and, for an historical people, its earth, the self-closing ground on which it rests together with everything that it already is, though still hidden from itself. It is, however, its world, which prevails in virtue of the relation of human being to the unconcealedness of Being. For this reason, everything with which man is endowed must, in the projection, be drawn up from the closed ground and expressly set upon this ground. In this way the ground is first grounded as the bearing ground.[34]

In his creation of the Khalsa, the Tenth Guru discloses and preserves the historical grounding and founding of the First Sikh Guru. In his artistic projection, Guru Gobind Singh draws upon the liminality of Guru Nanak from under the waters and sets it openly and firmly upon the ground. As such, 'Art is history in the essential sense that it grounds history.'[35]

When Guru Gobind Singh ushered his Beloved Five back into the Basiakhi congregation, the first object he asked for was 'sarita jal'—water from the river flowing by. Water thus forms the starting point of the Khalsa initiation. We are struck by the formal simplicity of Guru Gobind Singh's sacra. His simple request takes us through the waters of memory to Nanak's experience two hundred years earlier. The sacra become an expression of the Tenth Guru's desire to capture the fluidity of time for his community. What had been creatively flowing needed to be held together and formulated into an everlasting ritual. The water put in an iron bowl (patr loh in Koer Singh's rendition) and placed near the Guru revokes chronological time and recovers the mythic time. Its placental nutrients form the intrinsic self, the very ground of the Khalsa's being.

The quintessential sacred action of the liminal stage is the drinking of Amrit. Guru Nanak received the bowl full of nectar and heard the command: 'Nanak! This Amrit is the cup of Name-adoration. You drink it.' Then Guru Nanak paid his respects, drank the cup .... During Baisakhi 1699, Guru Gobind Singh actively prepares the amrit that Guru Nanak directly received from the Divine: after getting the water from the river, he stirred it with his double-edged sword while reciting sacred poetry. Mata Jitoji added sugarpuffs to the mixture.

The recipe for Guru Gobind Singh's Amrit is in fact provided by Guru Nanak. In our mythic account Guru Nanak does not witness the preparation of Amrit, but is aware of its contents. The final stanza of the *Japu*—which the Puratan Janamsakhi explicitly states he recited in full (*japu sampuran kita*) in the Bein—specifies the ingredients and the procedure for the ambrosial compound. During Baisakhi 1699, Guru Gobind Singh reconstitutes the very fusion of physio-chemical and spirito-psychological elements that are proposed by the first Guru:

jatu pahara dhiraju suniaru
ahrani mati vedu hathiaru
bhau khala agani tap tau
bhandha bhau amritu titu dhali
ghariai sabadu saci taksal[36]

Let smithy be the continence, patience the goldsmith;
Let anvil be wisdom, knowledge the hammer;
Let bellows be divine fear and fire be inner control and heat;
On the crucible of divine love, let the ambrosial gold flow,
In this True mint forge the transcendent word.

The Tenth Guru does not make strict use of the smithy scenario that the First used to underscore the importance of Divine love. Perhaps by restricting himself to the fires of a smithy, Guru Gobind Singh would have only confused his people with the ascetic heat and reinforced current rituals and practices which restrained the natural flow of senses, emotions, and thoughts. Eliade discusses how in both Hinduism and Buddhism, and especially in their schools of Tantrism, heat and fire represent magico-religious power. He provides several important examples: Prajapati generates the world by heating himself up to an extreme degree of asceticism, Buddha burns with heat because he practices asceticism, Kundalini arouses an intense heat in the Yogi, Tantric texts transmute sexual energy into magical heat, and as he says, 'all over the world shamans and sorcerers are reputedly masters of fire, and swallow burning embers, handle red-hot iron and walk over fire.'[37] Rather than ascetic heat, or fiery magic, or a transmutation of the sexual energies, the cool waters of the River, essential to life and living, dominate Guru Gobind Singh's configuration.

And yet, by his innovation, Guru Nanak's metaphor of the goldsmith seated in his smithy with its anvil and bellows and hammers forging Amrita, the immortal gold, is made into a reality by Guru Gobind Singh. In front of the Baisakhi gathering he performs a metallurgical and chemical operation: he stirs the iron bowl of water with his double-edged sword and recites sacred verse while Mata Jitoji adds sugarpuffs to his mixture. Just as the ambrosial gold in the goldsmith's crucible, the ambrosial Nam flows into the Guru's iron bowl. The receptacle in both instances is made of *bhau*, divine love, but the metaphorical container of the goldsmith (*bhanda*) is concretely held in Guru Gobind Singh's hands (*patr loh*). The motion (*phora*) across (*meta*) the metallic and the spiritual which Guru Nanak introduced in his *Japu* is practically followed through by his Tenth successor. The First Guru's words contained in the myth are transformed into deed.

The Guru then offers amrit to his five initiates. Anthropologists and sociologists have repeatedly remarked that commensality leads to the formation of *societas*: 'Of all human behaviors, there is none more conducive to the integration of society than the ritual sharing of food.'[38] Guru Gobind Singh extended Guru Nanak's individual drinking of Amrit to his five initiates. The Tenth Guru's act signifies that Nanak's initiation was not just reserved for a chosen one but was meant to be a wide opening for his entire society. The spirit of unity and mutual belonging underlies the communal drinking. The Five initiates came from different castes and professions, but by drinking the Amrit together all societal conditionings and divisions were eradicated; together, they were bound to the new family of the Khalsa. While the elixir tied them together through bonds of sentiment and obligation, it also gave the members a new life, a new birth into freedom and immortality.

The initiates respond to the drink with the exclamation: '*Waheguru*'. (*wahe*=wonderful+*guru*=enlightener), expressing their appreciation for the divine wonder and beauty they feel. The initiates' response evokes the exultation that Nanak experienced when he drank the *nam piala*. Nanak burst into song of praise for the greatness and infinity of the Divine. He did not see any being at all and yet acquired insight into the very ground of Being. The hearing of the command, the holding of the cup, the savouring of the nectar of Its Name—these together constituted the fullness of his enlightened vista. In that transcendent state, Guru Nanak began to recite hymns including the *Japu* and *Arati*. Guru Nanak's overwhelming sentiments expressed in those hymns are recapitulated in the singular exclamation, *Waheguru*. Like Guru Nanak, the imagination of the Sikh initiates is startled to awarenes and a sense of wonder.

What Guru Nanak experienced by drinking the ambrosial cup transformed him forever. This sacred historical account was exemplary for the Tenth Guru, who wanted a radical transformation for his community. Eliade's theory about mythology that 'not only does it relate how things came to be; it also lays the foundations for all human behavior and all social and cultural institutions' comes true.[39] His aim for his Khalsa was to taste what the First Sikh Guru had tasted. In the river Bein, Nanak did not see the Divine in any form, male or female, god or goddess: the cup of amrita constituted the medium of his revelation. The Janamsakhi describes him drink the ambrosial cup and rejoice. How could Guru Gobind Singh's initiates re-see Guru Nanak's revelation? How could they re-experience the joy of Nanak's vision? Like Guru Nanak's own experience in the River Bein, which I termed 'aestheticontological' in an earlier work, the Khalsa initiation is intrinsically a rejoicing in Divine beauty and wonder. Drinking the ambrosia signifies the sapiential quality of Divine. By drinking the Amrit, the senses are heightened, and the infinity of the Being is recognized. The utterly simple yet most viable and highly penetrating portrayal of Guru Nanak's encounter with the Transcendent is reaffirmed in the Khalsa rite.

Guru Gobind Singh's amrit initiation reinforces the feminist emphasis on the union of mind and body. The connectedness seriously endangered by patriarchal dualism is recovered: by drinking the Amrit, Guru Gobind Singh's Khalsa can renew Guru Nanak's unified experience that bypasses all divisions and hierarchies. Feminist scholars have studied the terrible consequence of such polarizations for women. By associating *her* with the body, women are given a negative identity and are kept subordinate to the mind/spirit–male supremacy. The Sikh initiation rite, restores the co-existence of sensuous knowledge—hearing the word, holding the amrit, drinking it, and absolute Truth—insight into the Infinite One.

Reincorporation

After their radically new liminal experience, the protagonists in both our mythic and ritual discourse, return to society: the former as the Guru; the latter as the Khalsa. In their new status and role, they had gained a new awareness of their self, and were constructed in a profound way. Unlike other initiation rites there are no additions to or subtractions from the body: tattoos, circumcision or scarring did not mark the transition of either Guru Nanak or the Khalsa. In each case, their new identity was marked by the unity of *bana* (dress) and *bani* (divine Word), body and mind, exterior and interior, *sirpao* and *nam*.

As they reincorporate into society, 'antistructure' becomes the mode of existence for both Guru Nanak and the Khalsa. The first Sikh community that developed with Guru Nanak at Kartarpur fits in with Turner's description of 'antistructure' because the neat horizontal divisions and vertical hierarchies of society were broken down. Three important institutions of Sikhism: *seva* (voluntary labour), *langar* (community meal), and *sangat* (congregation) evolved in which men and women from different castes and religions took equal part. Together they listened to, and recited, the sacred hymns, together they cooked and ate *langar*, together they formed a democratic congregation without priests or ordained ministers. The Amrit initiation underscored the antistructure of Guru Nanak's worldview. The new rite of passage shattered traditional social and religious structures where people were divided and stratified, and entered the family of the Khalsa in which all of them are to have the same name—Singh for men, and Kaur for women, the same parents—Guru Gobind Singh and Mata Jitoji, the same birth place—Anandpur, and even the same physical format—*kesh, kangha, kirpan, kara,* and *kacch.*

Guru Gobind Singh marked the internal transformation of his newly constructed subject with the five Ks which are patterned on the Sirpao that the First Guru received in the River Bein. For me it is absolutely essential to realize that Guru Nanak's Sirpao is the paradigm for the code of dress that the Khalsa wears. The Sirpao was the symbol of honour bestowed on Guru Nanak from the divine court—'*sirpao baba dargaho milia*', and the five Ks are also a symbol of honour and respect for both men and women. Guru Nanak received the Sirpao after he passed his test; the Five Beloved received the five Ks after they successfully passed their severe examination. Corresponding to the open and expansive Sirpao that Nanak received from the transcendent One, the five Ks are to be worn by people from all classes, castes, and ages. Indeed, they are external signs that the Khalsa wears as a mark of self-respect and respect for one another. They immediately identify the wearer as a Sikh, but they also enable the person to participate in a deeper universal reality. Thus they serve as both signs and symbols.

The five Ks become public symbols with a variety of socially significant meanings. They give rise to relationships between and among individuals, and thereby promote the crystallization of the Sikh community. While they shape personal identity, they help integrate the person with society. Thus they have the force to carry on and illuminate the legacy of the divine gift that the first Sikh Guru received in the River Bein. Unfortunately, they have been interpreted from men's experiences, for history has emphasized the masculine and militaristic definition of these five emblems. Guru Nanak's

Sirpao is an inclusive material permeated with the potential to be stitched and tailored into many creative patterns and forms: the only exception, it cannot be designed into any exclusionary or ostracizing shape (like that of the *janeu* exlcusively for upper class males which Guru Nanak loudly denounced). Sikh community has yet to recognize the primal pattern of Guru Nanak's Sirpao in the five Ks. How do they endorse self-respect and dignity for *both* men and women? How do they impart value to the individual? How do they articulate the body as resource for and object of significance and power? How can they be worn other than as patriarchal symbols?

The outer mode is linked with the interior. In his new role Guru Nanak was commanded 'to go and recite the Divine Name and teach others to recite as well—*tun jai kari mera namu japi, aur loka thin be japae.*' Sacred poetry was the medium and object of Guru Nanak's mission that the Tenth inherited and fully absorbed. His Khalsa is required to recite and live in accordance with the verses of the Sikh Gurus. In fact, the amrit is prepared and drunk in the sight and sound of the sacred poetry. Through the divine name the Khalsa is born, through the divine name the Khalsa is nurtured. It is not merely that the body be dressed in the five Ks (*bana*), and the mind think about the hymns (*bani*), but a real fusion of the self was wrought by the Tenth Sikh Guru.

V—— ——ch like the Sirpao, the divine name is open and inclusive. It is
directs the individual to the
ges and multivalent symbols.
id mother. In the five hymns
d as the emotions that expand
nite One. Sikh Gurus do not
does not choose love and the
love and heroism are essential
transcendence in and through

irus, meant for both men and
and they have been taken over
iman and universal meaning of
d interpreted from a male point
that to be universal is to be not
ominated by men. Since men
ces and hands have seized the

practical modality of bani. Instead of the union of male and female, only male procedures are applied for the procreation of the Khalsa. Sikh women are tacitly barred from fusing the semiotic verses with the placental waters; their voices from welding with the momentum of the double-edged sword, their hands from caressing and sprinkling the verbally energized waters. The feminine dimension that gave birth to the First Sikh Guru and the Khalsa is forgotten; the initiation into a liberated mode of existence is often aborted and instead a patriarchal structure is reproduced in the Sikh world. The significant opening for women ushered in by the Janamsakhi narrative and Baisakhi 1699 have pretty much remained forgotten.

Fused with his own socio-historical horizon, Guru Gobind Singh's interpretation and transcreation of the Puratan Janamsakhi discourse has the energy to produce more new and powerful phenomena. Eliade's theoretical views make a lot of sense: 'Though the myths, by presenting themselves as sacrosanct models, would seem to paralyze human initiative, actually they stimulate man to create, they are constantly opening new perspectives to his inventiveness.'[40] The primal myth so inspired Guru Gobind Singh that he created his own 'dramatic breakthrough'; in turn, it can stimulate and empower generations of Sikhs into entering exciting new horizons. The origins of their faith and the energetic actions of their heroic past are crystallized in the alchemical amrit. Whatever part of the world the Sikhs may be in, amrit initiation brings meaning to their lives, linking their personal experience to that of their Ten Gurus. 'Meaning arises when we try to put what culture and language have crystallized from the past together with what we feel, wish, and think about our present point in life.'[41] Most of the time, rites of passage underscore the biological and physical make-up of the person and demarcate gender roles that the initiates are to follow for the rest of their lives. Guru Nanak's aspiration to deconstruct such exclusionary rites, and to reconstruct an emotional and spiritual rite of passage, is accomplished in Guru Gobind Singh's Amrit initiation.

But the real transformative power of his rite of passage has yet to be fully reclaimed. As June O'Connor says, 'oversight as well as insight marks human knowing', and in our instance, the horizon that the historic Baisakhi could have opened for women remains unseen.[42] It is frequently recalled that the Five Beloved who were initiated into the Khalsa were men and that women did not actually stand up to offer their head during Baisakhi 1699. Feminist scholarship has cautioned us about the ways in which the powerful erase those out of power from public consciousness and forge the collective memory that they select. 'Hegemony means the ability to control the formal machinery of representation; to design the past that a specific culture will then naturalize and teach', writes Catherine Stimpson.[43] Concentrating on the malehood of the protagonists, Sikh collective memory has ignored the liberating implications for women in that historic drink.

Our memory of the Amrit entails that we recognize the Tenth Guru's intention and his moral vision. It requires that we squarely face the fact that even after centuries, Guru Gobind Singh's radical vision of equality is far from being practiced. Sexism prevails in Sikh families, and attitudes towards boys and girls contrast from the very conception of a child. Modern technology is abused to promote the abortion of foetuses that are determined to be female. No sweets are distributed at *her* birth. They may be born into the same family, but the son and daughter are chartered out different roles and given a whole different set of obligations. To come to think of it, how can Sikh society claim that a woman is reborn equally into the Khalsa family when she is even denied the position her male counterpart is entitled from the moment of his birth? The liberty granted by the *Rahit Maryada*, the Sikh Ethical Code, that, 'Any man or woman of whatever nationality, race, or social standing, who is prepared to accept the rules governing the Sikh community, has the right to receive amrit initiation' serves more as a licence rather than a true fulfillment anticipated by Guru Gobind Singh.

For the 300th anniversary of the Khalsa there were conferences and celebrations all around the world, but the Guru's fundamental principle of equality is far from being commemorated. Sikh patriarchs proudly expound the radical processes of liberation championed by the Sikh Gurus, but without praxis what good are mere recitations? For how long can we continue to hide our gross misconduct behind the revolutionary actions of our Gurus? A true commemoration of Guru Gobind Singh's creative event charges us with the obligation that we break all the inequities and hegemonies that confound us today. In fact, the more clearly we remember the egalitarian birth of the Khalsa in Anandpur, the more intensely we feel the tragic inequities prevailing in our homes and in our communities, and the more urgently we react to eradicate them.

We must go back to Anandpur and sit in the congregation; we must recognize *her* presence in the public consciousness of the Sikhs. What was the cultural conditioning of the women in the Baisakhi gathering of 1699? If a woman had actually stood up in public, how would her husband, father, brother, uncle, or son have reacted? Would it have been her act of honour or shame? If women did not stand up then, does it mean they never can or never should? And if a woman had stood up, Guru Gobind Singh would not have barred *her* from being one the Five Beloved. The Guru had made his tortuous request to the entire Baisakhi gathering including Shudras and Brahmins, Hindus and Muslims, men *and* women too. Memories of course are selective. And they have a future. When we remember Guru Gobind Singh's action we must remember that he himself remembers the First Guru, and we too must keep alive their shared experience of transformation and liberation.

Notes

1. Catharine Stimpson, 'The Future of Memory: A Summary' in *Michigan Quarterly Review* (Winter 1987), p. 262.

2. Mircea Eliade, *Myth and Reality* (NY: Harper and Row, 1963), p. 6.

3. W.H. McLeod, *Who is a Sikh: The Problem of Sikh Identity* (Oxford, 1989), p. 29.

4. Pashaura Singh and N. Gerald Barrier, eds, *The Transmission of Sikh Heritage in the Diaspora* (Delhi: Manohar, 1996), p. 169.

5. *Myth and Reality*, p. 140.

6. Bronislaw Malinowski, *Magic, Science and Religion and Other Essays* (NY: Doubleday Anchor Books, 1948), p. 146.

7. Ibid., p. 96.

8. Prithipal Singh Kapur and Dharam Singh, *The Khalsa* (Patiala: Punjabi University, 1999), p. 51.

9. G.S. Talib, *The Impact of Guru Gobind Singh on Indian Society: A Socio-Ethical Interpretation of the Sikh Religion* (Chandigarh: Guru Gobind Singh Foundation, 1966), p. 12.

10. *Bachitar Natak*, 5:10 in Bhai Randhir Singh (editor), *Shabdarath Dasam Granth Sahib* (Patiala: Punjabi University, 1985), p. 70.

11. Harold Bloom, *The Anxiety of Influence* (NY: Oxford University Press, 1973), p. 6.

12. Anil Chandra Banerjee, *Guru Nanak to Guru Gobind Singh* (New Delhi: Rajesh Publications, 1978), p. 218.

13. Ibid., p. 218.

14. Victor Turner in 'Dewey, Dilthey, and Drama: an Essay in the Anthropology of Experience' in *The Anthropology of Experience* edited by V.W. Turner and E.M. Bruner (Chicago: University of Illinois Press, 1986), p. 36.

15. Martin Heidegger, *Poetry, Language, Thought* (translated by Albert Hofstadter) (NY: Harper and Row, 1975), p. 76.

16. Mircea Eliade, *Rites and Symbols of Initation: The Mysteries of Birth and Rebirth* (Dallas: Spring Publiications, republished 1994), pp. 2–3.

17. Malinowski, *Magic, Science, and Religion*, p. 47

18. Bruce Lincoln, *Myth, Cosmos, and Society: Indo-European Themes of Creation and Destruction* (Cambridge: Harvard University Press, 1986), p. 38.

19. H. Clay Trumbull, *The Blood Covenant: A Primitive Rite and Its Bearings on Scripture* (NY: Charles Scribners, 1885), p. 100.

20. Grace M. Jantzen, *Becoming Divine: Towards a Feminist Philosophy of Religion* (Indiana University Press, 1999), p. 138.

21. Ibid., p. 132.

22. Rita Gross, *Feminism and Religion: An Introduction* (Boston: Beacon, 1996) p. 237.

23. V.M. Turner, *The Forest of Symbols: Aspects of Ndembu Ritual* (Cornell University Press, 1967), p. 96.

24. *Puratan Janamsakhi Guru Nanak Devji*. Published in Amritsar by Khalsa Samachar, 1946. 'Bein Parvesh', pp. 16–19.

25. Ibid.

26. Elizabeth Moltmann-Wendel, *A Land Flowing with Milk and Honey: Perspectives on Feminist Theology* (NY: Crossroad, 1986), pp. 74–5.

27. Discussed in my earlier work, *The Feminine Principle in the Sikh Vision of the Transcendent* (Cambridge University Press, 1993), pp. 33–47.

28. Clifford Geertz, *The Interpretation of Cultures: Selected Essays* (HarperCollins, Basic Books, 1973), p. 93.

29. Sainapati, *Sri Gur Sobha* edited by Ganda Singh (Patiala: Punjabi Universiy, 1967), chapter 5, verse 5, p. 20.

30. Koer Singh, *Gurbilas Patshahi 10* edited by Shamsher Singh Ashok. (Patiala: Punjabi University, 1968) Chapter 9, verse 10; p. 127.

31. Ibid., p. 103

32. Ibid., p. 110.

33. Hiedegger, *Poetry, Language, Thought*, p. 49.

34. Ibid., pp. 75–6.

35. Ibid., p. 77.

36. Final stanza of the Japu (#38)

37. Mircea Eliade, *Myths, Rites, Symbols* (edited by Wendell C. Beane and William G. Doty), volume 1, (Harper Colophon books, 1976), pp. 192–3.

38. Bruce Lincoln, *Discourse and the Construction of Society* (NY: Oxford University Press, 1989), p. 88.

39. Eliade, *Rites and Symbols of Initiation*, p. ix.

40. Mircea Eliade, *Myth and Reality* (NY: Harper and Row, 1963), p. 141.

41. Turner in *The Anthropology of Experience*, p. 33.

42. See June O'Connor, 'The Epistemological Significance of Feminist Research in Religion' in Ursula King (editor) *Religion and Gender* (Blackwell, 1995).

43. In 'The Future of Memory: A Summary', p. 260.

2

Sikh Identity in the Light of History
A Dynamic Perspective

Pashaura Singh

I

The question of identity is an important subject for academic discussion. It covers a wide range of important issues pertaining to the complex process of 'coming to be', frequently referred to as a classic notion of identity-formation. The complexity of this process of 'coming to be' is confounded and compounded by the inter-connections between the formal, conscious and organized processes of institutional development, and the informal, unconscious and spiritual ways in which people come to know themselves. Outward religious practices and inward beliefs are, therefore, always the important factors that define human beings. All these identity markers in turn fashion responses to how others understand and accept identity. A comparison with the other prevailing traditions sharpens the process of self-definition. In fact, every encounter with a new society or a new culture brings with it new self-discovery. As such, the crystallization of a religious community is an ever-evolving process, a process which continues as a creative response to the changing historical situation. There is always a need to meet the challenge of changing times and answering the new questions each age presents. Thus the process of self-definition is an ongoing phenomenon of a dynamic nature.

The first in-depth analysis of the problem of Sikh identity from an historical perspective was produced by W.H. McLeod in his perceptive work *Who is a Sikh?* (Oxford: Clarendon Press, 1989). It is thus quite appropriate to engage with his arguments in this volume to be published in his honour.

McLeod offers a range of answers to the question 'Who is a Sikh?' along the line of history and across the arc of traditional Sikh understanding. As a modern historian, he frequently addresses the issues of history versus tradition, the nature of authority in the Sikh *Panth* (community), and the ever-evolving nature of Sikh identity. Throughout his analysis McLeod assumes 'uniformity' to be the standard criterion which he applies to understand the various issues related to Sikh identity. In doing so he is looking for certain 'fixed' categories to make sense of the diverse nature of the Sikh Panth. This assumption, however, becomes the key problematic in our understanding of the dynamic nature of Sikh identity. Not surprisingly, McLeod admits at the end of his discussion that 'complex communities can never be summarized in neat, concise, unqualified terms.'[1] We will return to his arguments from time to time in our analysis.

This chapter examines some of the central issues in the process of identity-formation in the Sikh tradition in different historical periods. The first section focuses on the early Sikh Panth. It addresses the questions: What did it mean to be a Sikh in the early phase of the community? How did the Sikh Panth evolve during the period of Guru Nanak's early successors? The second section addresses the question of Sikh identity from the institution of the Khalsa in 1699 to the fall of sovereign Sikh rule in 1849. It focuses on the pre-modern understandings of Sikh identity. The third section deals with the issues of religious and cultural transformation that took place under the British Raj. It examines the issue of how Sikh identity was constructed from a modern perspective influenced by the ideology of the Enlightenment. We will examine the impact of the Singh Sabha and Akali movements on the emerging Sikh community self-consciousness. The final section addresses the issues of Sikh identity from the post-colonial and post-modern perspectives. Throughout our arguments we will address the fundamental question: Who is a Sikh?

II

Any discussion of Sikh identity must begin with the understanding of the question of how the early Gurus became the spearhead of a process of demarcation which clearly defined the distinctiveness of the Sikh tradition. Notably, Sikhism is rooted in a particular religious experience, piety, and culture and informed by a unique inner revelation of its founder, Guru Nanak (1469–1539), who declared his independence from the other thought forms of his day. He tried to kindle the fire of autonomy and courage in those who claimed to be his disciples (*sikhs*, learners). Notwithstanding the influences that he absorbed from his contemporary religious environment, that is, the devotional tradition of the medieval *Sants* (Poet-saints)[2] of North India with which he shared certain similarities and differences, Guru Nanak laid down the foundation of 'true teaching, practice and community' from the standpoint of his own religious ideals. Of the religious figures of North India, he had a strong sense of mission which compelled him to proclaim his message for the ultimate benefit of his audience and to promote socially responsible living. At the end of his missionary travels, in the 1520s, therefore, Guru Nanak purchased a piece of land on the right bank of the Ravi River in West Punjab and founded the village of Kartarpur (Creator's Abode). There he lived for the rest of his life as the 'spiritual guide' of a newly emerging religious community. His attractive personality and teaching won him many disciples who received the message of liberation through religious hymns of unique genius and notable beauty. They began to use these hymns in devotional singing (*kirtan*) as a part of congregational worship. Indeed, the first Sikh families who gathered around Guru Nanak in the early decades of the sixteenth century at Kartarpur formed the nucleus of a rudimentary organization of the Nanak-*panth*, the 'Path of Nanak', referring to the community constituted by the Sikhs who followed Guru Nanak's path of liberation.

Guru Nanak prescribed the daily routine, along with agricultural activity for sustenance, for the Kartarpur community.[3] He defined the ideal person as a Gurmukh (one oriented towards the Guru) who practiced the threefold discipline of 'the divine Name, charity and purity' (*nam dan ishnan*).[4] Indeed, these three features, *nam* (relation with the Divine), *dan* (relation with the society), and *ishnan* (relation with the self) provided a balanced approach for the development of the individual and the society. They corresponded to the cognitive, the communal, and the personal aspects of the evolving Sikh identity. For Guru Nanak, the true spiritual life required that 'one should live on what one has earned through hard work and that one should share with others the fruit of one's exertion.'[5] In addition, service (*seva*), self-respect (*pati*), truthful living (*sach achar*), humility, sweetness of the tongue, and taking only one's rightful share (*haq halal*) were regarded as highly prized ethical virtues in pursuit of liberation. At Kartarpur, Guru Nanak gave practical expression to the ideals which matured during the period of his travels and combined 'a life of disciplined devotion with worldly activities, set in the context of normal family life and a regular *satsang* [or true fellowship].'[6] As part of the Sikh liturgy, Guru Nanak's Japji (Meditation) was recited in the early hours of the morning, and So Dar (That Door) and Arti (Adoration) were sung in the evening.[7]

Guru Nanak's spiritual message found expression at Kartarpur through key institutions: the *sangat* (holy fellowship) where all felt that they belonged to one large spiritual fraternity; the *dharamshala*, the original form of the Sikh place of worship; and the establishment of the *langar*, the inter-dining convention which required people of all castes to sit in status-free lines (*pangat*) to share a common meal. The institution of langar promoted the spirit of unity and mutual belonging, and struck at a major aspect of caste, thereby advancing the process of defining a distinctive Sikh identity. Finally, Guru Nanak created the institution of the Guru, who became the central authority in community life. Before he passed away in 1539, Guru Nanak designated one of his disciples, Lehna, as his successor by renaming him Angad, meaning 'my own limb'. Thus, a lineage was established, and a legitimate succession was maintained intact from the appointment of Guru Angad (1504–52) to the death of Guru Gobind Singh (1666–1708), the tenth and the last human Guru of the Sikhs. Indeed, a theory of spiritual succession was advanced in the form of 'the unity of Guruship' in which there was no difference between the founder and the successors. They all represented one and the same light (*jot*) as a single flame ignites a series of torches.

The analysis of the works of the first five Gurus reveals that they followed a policy of both innovation and preservation. Although they never departed radically from the legacy of Guru Nanak, they met the challenge of the religious pluralism of the sixteenth century by establishing a clear basis for a distinct Sikh identity. This sense of distinct identity was marked by distinctive belief system, modes of worship, socio-religious institutions and an over-arching organization with the Guru as its pivot. Indeed, the institution of the Guru carried an aura of divinity for the Sikhs. In this context, McLeod rightly maintains that veneration of Guru Nanak and his line of successors qualified a person as a Nanak-panthi or Sikh.[8] This early Sikh identity, he argues, was defined by 'a common loyalty, by common association, and by common practice'.[9] For the Nanak-panth the principal mode of worship was devotional singing (*kirtan*), a corporate practice that served to weld a group of disparate followers into a society with a common sense of identity. This sense of identity was further strengthened by the poetic beauty and durable nature of *gurbani* (utterances of the Gurus) used in such kirtan sessions.[10]

The second Guru, Angad, consolidated the nascent Sikh Panth in the face of the challenge presented by Guru Nanak's eldest son, Baba Sri Chand, the founder of the ascetic Udasi sect. His sixty-two *saloks* (couplets or stanzas) in the Sikh scripture throw considerable light on the historical situation of the Panth during his period and mark the doctrinal boundaries of the Sikh faith in strict conformity with Guru Nanak's message. In the first place, Guru Angad mentioned his predecessor as 'Guru Nanak' for the first time, thereby stressing the necessity of the institutional Guru in the spiritual growth of his audience.[11] Second, he established a new Sikh centre at Khadur where the community kitchen (*langar*) was run by his wife Khivi, who used to serve a pudding of rice boiled in milk to the congregation.[12] It confirmed an organizational principle that the communal establishment at Kartarpur could not be considered a unique institution, but rather a model which could be cloned and imitated elsewhere. Third, Guru Angad made the early-morning bath obligatory for the practice of meditation on the divine Name.[13] Fourth, in contrast to the worldview of the Hindu religious texts he claimed the exclusive status of the *bani* (divine Word), delivering all people from the shackles of *karma* and from discriminatory aspects of the caste system through divine grace.[14] Thus by stressing the inspired nature of the bani Guru Angad laid down doctrinally the requirement of the compilation of Sikh scripture parallel to the Vedas. The idea that the revealed Word was to be assumed as an objective abstract—in no way a personal affect—had far-reaching implications in the development of Sikhism, both in terms of consolidation of authority and in terms of the evolving scriptural tradition.

Finally, Guru Angad further refined the Gurmukhi script for recording the compilation of the Guru's hymns. The original Gurmukhi script was a systematization of *lande/mahajani* business shorthands, of the kind Guru Nanak doubtless used professionally as a young man. This was the script which was certainly familiar to the Khatri merchants of the Punjab. Its use in early Sikh literary tradition was an emphatic rejection of the superiority of Devanagri and Arabic scripts (along with Sanskrit and the Arabic and Persian languages) and of the hegemonic authority they represented in the scholarly and religious circles of the time. The use of the Gurmukhi script added an element of demarcation and self-identity to the Sikh tradition. In fact, language became the single most important factor in the preservation of Sikh culture and identity and became the cornerstone of the religious distinctiveness that is part and parcel of the Sikh cultural heritage.

A major institutional development took place during the time of the third Guru, Amar Das (1479–1574), who introduced a variety of innovations to provide greater cohesion and unity to the ever-growing Sikh Panth. These included the establishment of the city of Goindval, the biannual festivals of Divali and Baisakhi that provided an opportunity for the growing community to get togtether and meet the Guru, a missionary system (*manjis*) for attracting new converts, and the preparation of the Goindval *pothis*, collections of the compositions of the Gurus and some of the medieval poet-saints. This early move toward the establishment of a more comprehensive administrative system speaks both of the rapidity with which the spiritual appeal of Guru Nanak's message was gaining ground, and also of the practicality of those to whom the tradition had been entrusted in dealing with this broadening appeal. The location of Goindval on the right bank of the Beas River was close to the point where the Majha, Malwa, and Doaba areas converge. This may help account for the spread of the Panth's influence in all three regions of the Punjab. Further, Guru Amar Das provided the distinctive ceremonies for birth and death and added his hymn of 'divine bliss' (*Anand*) to Sikh liturgy which was meant to be recited on happy occasions. All these innovations reflect the geographical and institutional expansion of the Sikh Panth during the period of the third Guru. One could also read in them a response of a second-generation Panth passing through a predictable process of self-definition and crystallization.[15]

The fourth Guru, Ram Das (1534–81) founded the city of Ramdaspur, where he constructed a large pool for the purpose of bathing. It was named Amritsar, meaning 'the nectar of immortality'. To build an independent economic base, the Guru appointed deputies (*masands*) to collect tithes and other contributions from loyal Sikhs. He contributed a large body of sacred verse by expanding the range of available musical modes (*ragas*) and composed the wedding hymn (*lavan*) for the solemnization of Sikh marriage.[16] Indeed, it was Guru Ram Das who for the first time explicitly responded to the question 'Who is a Sikh?' with the following definition: 'He who calls himself Sikh, a follower of the true Guru, should meditate on the divine Name after rising and bathing and recite *Japji* from memory, thus driving away all evil deeds and vices. As day unfolds he sings *gurbani*; sitting or rising he meditates on the divine Name. He who repeats the divine Name with every breath and bite is indeed a true Sikh (*gursikh*) who gives pleasure to the Guru.'[17] Thus, the liturgical requirements of reciting and singing of the sacred Word became part of the very definition of being a Sikh. The most significant development was related to the self-image of the Sikhs who perceived themselves as unique and distinct from other religious communities of North India. In this context, Guru Ram Das proclaimed that 'loyal Sikhs of the Guru' (*gursikhs*) were spiritually greater than the *Bhagats*, *Sants*, and *Sadhs*.[18] The new status of the word 'Gursikh' points to the greater cohesiveness of the Sikh community. Indeed, the distinction between 'us' and 'them' was complete during the period of the fourth Guru.

The period of the fifth Guru, Arjan (1563–1606), was marked by a number of far-reaching institutional developments. First, at Amritsar he built the Harimandir, later known as the Golden Temple, which acquired prominence as the central place of Sikh worship. It became *the* integral identity marker for the Sikhs parallel to the famous Hindu *tiraths* and Muslim Mecca. Second, he compiled the first canonical scripture, the Adi Granth (Original Book), in 1604, which advocated the doctrine of the unity of *Akal Purakh* (Timeless One), stressing an uncompromising monotheism in which there was no place for incarnation or idol-worship. It provided a framework for the shaping of a text-centred community and hence it was a decisive factor for Sikh self-definition. McLeod rightly maintains that the Adi Granth served to enhance the clarity of definition which distinguished the Sikhs from people of other faiths.[19] Third, Guru Arjan established the rule of justice and humility (*halemi raj*) in the town of Ramdaspur, where everyone lived in comfort.[20] He proclaimed: 'There is no other place like the beautiful and thickly populated Ramdaspur. The divine rule prevails in Ramdaspur due to the grace of the Guru. No religious tax (*jizya*) is levied, nor any fine; there is no collector of taxes.'[21] The administration of the town was evidently in the hands of Guru Arjan, although in a certain sense Ramdaspur was an autonomous town in the context and the framework of the Mughal rule of Emperor Akbar. Finally, by the end of the sixteenth century the Sikh Panth had developed a strong sense of independent identity, which is quite evident from Guru Arjan's assertion 'We are neither Hindu nor Musalaman.'[22] In this context, McLeod aptly remarks: 'The Panth now possessed a line of Gurus, a growing number of holy places, distinctive rituals, and its own sacred scripture. There could no longer be any question of vague definition nor of uncertain identity.'[23]

The emphasis on a strong sense of Panthic identity may also be seen in the works of Bhai Gurdas. In contrast to the two prevailing dominant traditions of Hindus and Muslims, Bhai Gurdas made an exclusive claim for the 'third distinctive path' (*tisar panth*) of Sikhs who followed the teachings of the Sikh Gurus.[24] McLeod makes the point that the Adi Granth and the works of Bhai Gurdas provide a 'normative response' to the issue of Sikh identity. He further argues that an analysis of the hagiographical literature known as the *janam-sakhis* (birth narratives) offers a popular view. As refracted through the janam-sakhis the Nanak-Panth was still 'in the process of self-definition' but had 'not yet achieved a clear awareness of separate identity.'[25] It was in the process of 'becoming' without a sure awareness of 'having arrived'. McLeod draws this conclusion from the janam-sakhis in which Guru Nanak says that he is a 'Hindu'. The actual context, however, makes it abundantly clear that he was not a 'Muslim'. The Sikhs could be regarded as Hindu in the sense of non-Muslim Indians. As such, they stood bracketed with millions of other Indians.[26] Nevertheless, the *B-40 Janam-sakhi* portrays the Sikhs of Guru Nanak as distinct from adherents of other faiths in the sense that they had their own distinctive place of worship: Vaishnavas have their temple, Yogis have their *asan*, Muslims have their mosque, and Nanak-panthis have their *dharamsala*. The same text further claims that Nanak-panthis had their own unique mode of salutation (*pairi pavana satiguru hoia*).[27] McLeod concludes that the intellectual elite within the Sikh Panth moved more rapidly towards a sense of distinctive identity than the general body of the Panth. The 'boundaries' might be indistinct but not the 'centre'. McLeod thus makes a good case for distinct identity in the pre-Khalsa Sikh tradition, but he qualifies it by bringing in the notion of the elite and the masses.

Here, it is equally important to note the perception of the outsiders about the Sikh Panth in the process of identity-formation. With the increasing socio-cultural articulation of the Sikhs, their consciousness of self-identity was strengthened. The outsiders were quick to perceive the distinction. It is no wonder that the distinctive identity of the Sikhs was duly recognized by other people who were around them during the early period. For instance, the author of *Dabistan-i-Mazahib* ('The School of Religions'), a mid-seventeenth century work in Persian, provides us with the earliest account of Sikh beliefs and practices under the title of *Nanak-panthis*. He knew two of the Sikh Gurus, Guru Hargobind (1595–1644) and Guru Har Rai (1630–61), and met them at Kiratpur. He maintains that 'loyal Sikhs of the Guru' (gursikhan) were a distinct community. He writes: 'The disciples of Guru Nanak condemn idol worship. Their belief is that all their Gurus are Nanaks. They do not read the mantras of the Hindus. They do not venerate their temples or idols, nor do they esteem their avatars. They have no regard for the Sanskrit language which, according to the Hindus, is the speech of the angels.'[28] The author further elaborates the Sikh concept of the 'unity of Guruship' as follows: 'They [the Sikhs] say that he who does not know Guru Arjan Mall as Baba Nanak is a manmukh, i.e. non-believer.'[29] The distinctive identity of early Sikhs was, therefore, based on their peculiar doctrines, their institutions and their social attitudes—including their sense of commitment to both temporal and spiritual concerns.

The question of 'normative self-definition', however, encompasses far more than doctrinal and institutional developments. The traditional history-of-ideas approach which focuses purely on philosophical or theological topics cannot do justice to understand the complex phenomenon of identity-formation. We need to examine the social setting as well as the driving forces which pushed the Sikh Panth more and more to insist not only that it was important to be Sikh, but also to be so in a certain way. Moreover, self-definition cannot arise apart from conflict. But which conflicts were decisive and with whom? These are certain features of the evolving Sikh Panth that deserve to be noted.

First, we need to examine the social constituency of the early Panth. Guru Nanak and the succeeding Gurus emphatically proclaimed that the divine Name is the only sure means of liberation for all the four varnas: the Khatri, the Brahmin, the Shudra, and the Vaish.[30] Doctrinally, caste was not one of the defining criteria of Sikh identity. In the sangat, there was no place for any kind of 'injustice or hurtful discrimination based on caste status.' Sikhs were, however, free to observe it as 'a marriage convention'.[31] Identifying the caste identities, a general profile of Panth's leadership may be reconstructed with the help of the eleventh var (ballad) of Bhai Gurdas which provides the lists of the names of prominent followers of the early Gurus. There were certainly some Brahmins among the Sikhs and some outcastes. For instance, the name of Paira Chandal appears in the list of prominent Sikhs. The Khatri caste was particularly prominent among the trading communities, and this was the caste to which all the Gurus belonged. There was a clear preponderance of Jats among the cultivators, who were followed by members of artisan castes, notably Tarkhans or carpenters. It should be emphasized that Bhai Gurdas deals only with the more notable members of the Panth.[32] On the whole, identities based on caste were not obliterated completely but caste had nothing to do with access to liberation.

Second, the issue of dissensions within the ranks of the Panth deserves our careful attention. A great number of Guru Arjan's compositions are focused on the issue of dealing with the problems created by 'slanderers' (nindak) who were rival claimants to the office of Guruship. The Udasis and Bhallas (descendants of Guru Amar Das's eldest son, Baba Mohan) had already established parallel seats of authority and paved the way for competing views of Sikh identity. The rivalry of the 'dissenters' was heightened when Guru Arjan was designated for the throne of Guru Nanak in preference to his eldest brother, Prithi Chand, who even approached the local Mughal administrators probably to claim the position of his father. At some point Prithi Chand and his followers were branded Minas (dissembling rogues). Indeed, the successful resisting of the challenges posed by Minas involved a heightened loyalty on the part of those who adhered to the orthodox line.[33] Thus, the conflict created within the Sikh community by dissidents originally worked to counter and then, paradoxically, to enhance the process of crystallization of the Sikh tradition.

Finally, there is clear evidence in the compositions of Guru Arjan that a series of complaints were made against him to the functionaries of the Mughal state, giving them an excuse to watch the activities of the Sikhs. In response to such complaints, for instance, Sulhi Khan came to attack the Guru's establishment, but he was killed by his own 'bolting horse' before his evil intentions materialized.[34] The Mughal authorities, it seems, were seriously concerned about the extensive Jat allegiance to the Panth. It is quite possible that the militant traditions of the Jats may have brought the Panth into increasing conflict with the Mughal authorities. The liberal policy of Emperor Akbar may have sheltered the Guru and his followers for a time, but it could not remove the nefarious designs of the Guru's enemies for good. Thus, the external and internal pressures on the Sikh Panth were largely responsible for the crystallization of the Sikh tradition.

In sum, the quest for normative self-definition was linked with the emergence of a new kind of doctrinal self-identification among Sikhs in this early phase of history. Based initially on religious ideology, however, the distinctive Sikh identity was reinforced with the introduction of distinctly Sikh liturgical practices, including ceremonies on the occasions of birth, marriage and death. Indeed, the Sikh community self-consciousness was further heightened by the in-group conflict created by dissenters and slanderers. The conflict with the local Mughal authorities provided another challenge to the Sikh Panth. To a large extent, the liberal policy of Emperor Akbar's reign provided the overall context for the peaceful evolution of the Sikh Panth. However, within eight months of Akbar's death in October 1605, Guru Arjan, under torture by the orders of the new emperor, Jahangir, was executed in May 1606. The Sikh community perceived Guru Arjan's death as the so-called 'first martyrdom'.[35] In this context, Wilfred Cantwell Smith aptly points out that Guru Arjan's martyrdom is of crucial significance in Sikh history, contributing very basically to the growth of Sikh community self-consciousness, separatism, and militancy.[36] In other words, it became the most decisive factor for the crystallization of the Sikh Panth.

III

A radical reshaping of the Sikh Panth took place after Guru Arjan's martyrdom. The sixth Guru, Hargobind (1595–1644), signalled the formal process when he traditionally donned two swords symbolizing the spiritual (*piri*) as well as the temporal (*miri*) investiture. He also built the *Akal Takht* (Throne of the Immortal Lord) facing the Harimandir, which represented the newly-assumed role of temporal authority. Under his direct leadership the Sikh Panth took up arms in order to protect itself from Mughal hostility. From the Sikh perspective this new development was not taken at the cost of abandoning the original spiritual base. Rather, it was meant to achieve a balance between temporal and spiritual concerns. A Sikh theologian of the period, Bhai Gurdas, defended this new martial response as 'hedging the orchard of the Sikh faith with the hardy and thorny *kikar* tree.'[37] After four skirmishes with Mughal troops, Guru Hargobind withdrew to the Shivalik hills, and Kiratpur became the new centre of the mainline Sikh tradition. Amritsar fell into the hands of Minas, who established a parallel line of Guruship with the support of the Mughal authorites.

During the time of the seventh and eighth Gurus, Har Rai (1630–61) and Harkrishan (1656–64), the emphasis on armed conflict with the Mughal authorities receded, but the Gurus held court and kept a regular force of Sikh horsemen. During the period of the ninth Guru, Tegh Bahadur (1621–75), however, the increasing strength of the Sikh movement in the rural areas again attracted the Mughal attention. Guru Tegh Bahadur's ideas of a just society inspired a spirit of fearlessness among his followers: 'He who holds none in fear, nor is afraid of anyone, Nanak, acknowledges him alone as a man of true wisdom.'[38] Such ideas posed a direct challenge to the increasingly restrictive policies of the Mughal Emperor, Aurangzeb (r.1658–1707), protecting the interests of Sunni orthodoxy. The emperor had imposed Islamic laws and taxes, and ordered the replacement of Hindu temples by mosques. Not surprisingly, Guru Tegh Bahadur was summoned to Delhi by the orders of the emperor, and on his refusal to embrace Islam he was publicly executed in Chandni Chowk on 11 Novemeber 1675. The Sikhs perceived his death as the 'second martyrdom', which involved the 'larger issues of human rights and freedom of conscience'.[39]

Tradition holds that the Sikhs who were present at the scene of Guru Tegh Bahadur's execution shrank from recognition, concealing their identity for fear they might suffer a similar fate. In order to respond to this new situation, the tenth Guru, Gobind Singh, resolved to impose on his followers an outward form that would make them instantly recognizable. He restructured the Sikh Panth and instituted the *Khalsa* (pure), an order of loyal Sikhs bound by common identity and discipline. On Baisakhi Day 1699 at Anandpur, Guru Gobind Singh initiated the first so-called 'Cherished Five' (*panj piare*), who formed the nucleus of the new order of the Khalsa. These five volunteers who responded to the Guru's call for loyalty, and who came from different castes and regions of India, received the initiation through a ceremony that involved sweetened water (*amrit*) stirred with a two-edged sword and sanctified by the recitation of five liturgical prayers.

From the perspective of ritual studies, three significant issues were linked with the first amrit ceremony. First, all who chose to join the order of the Khalsa through the ceremony were understood to have been 'reborn' in the house of the Guru and thus to have assumed a new identity. The male members were given the surname *Singh* (lion) and female members were given the surname *Kaur* (princess)[40], with the intention of creating a parallel system of aristocratic titles in relation to the Rajput hill chiefs of the surrounding areas of Anandpur. From that day onwards, Guru Gobind Singh was their spiritual father and his wife, Sahib Kaur, their spiritual mother. Their birthplace was Kesgarh Sahib (the gurdwara that commemorates the founding of the Khalsa) and their home was Anandpur, Punjab. This new sense of belonging conferred on the Khalsa a new collective identity.

Second, the Guru symbolically transferred his spiritual authority to the Cherished Five when he himself received the nectar of the double-edged sword from their hands and thus became a part of the Khalsa Panth and subject to its collective will. In this way he not only paved the way for the termination of a personal Guruship but also abolished the institution of *masands*, which was becoming increasingly disruptive. Several of the masands had refused to forward collections to the Guru, creating factionalism in the Sikh Panth. In addition, Guru Gobind Singh removed the threat posed by the competing seats of authority when he declared that the Khalsa should have no dealings with the followers of Prithi Chand (Minas), Dhir Mal (Guru Har Rai's elder brother, who established his seat at Kartarpur, Jalandhar) and Ram Rai (Guru Harkrishan's elder brother, who established his seat at Dehra Dun). Indeed, abandoning these five reprobate groups (*panj mel*) led to the 'greater awareness of boundaries and a heightened consciousness of identity'.[41]

Finally, Guru Gobind Singh delivered the nucleus of the *Rahit* (Code of Conduct) at the inauguration of the Khalsa. By sanctifying the hair with amrit, he made them 'the official seal of the Guru', and the cutting of 'bodily hair' was thus strictly prohibited. The Guru further imposed a rigorous ban on smoking. In addition, he made the wearing of 'five weapons' (*panj hathiar*) such as sword, disc, arrow, noose, and gun obligatory for the Khalsa Sikhs: 'Appear before the Guru with five weapons on your person' (*hathiar panje bann ke darsan avana*).[42] This injunction must be understood in the militaristic context of the contemporary situation.

The inauguration of the Khalsa was the culmination of the canonical period in the development of Sikhism. Guru Gobind Singh also closed the Sikh canon by adding a collection of the works of his father, Guru Tegh Bahadur, to the original compilation of the Adi Granth. Before he passed away in 1708, he terminated the line of personal Gurus, and installed the Adi Granth as the eternal Guru for the Sikhs. Thereafter, the authority of the Guru was invested together in the scripture (Guru Granth) and the corporate community (Guru Panth). The twin doctrine of Guru-Granth and Guru-Panth successfully played a cohesive role within the Sikh tradition during the eighteenth century. The *gurmata* (intention of the Guru) system provided an effective means of passing resolutions in the presence of the Guru Granth Sahib.

J.S. Grewal compellingly argues that Sikh identity was visibly sharpened by the institution of the Khalsa.[43] Indeed, the Khalsa Sikhs were distinct from 'Hindus' and other religious communities of India. However, all Sikhs did not embrace the Khalsa discipline, and the Sikh Panth was larger than the Khalsa. A considerable number of urban Khatris continued to live as

Nanak-panthis who were scattered in large cities throughout India.[44] Udasi Sadhus catered to the religious needs of these people. Moreover, the continuing presence of non-Khalsa Sikhs is attested by the literature of the eighteenth century. For instance, the *Chaupa Singh Rahit-nama*, compiled in the middle of the eighteenth century, provides us with references to *sehajdhari* Sikhs who continued to live as Nanak-panthi Sikhs. They maintained an identity which was less precise than that of an initiated member of the Khalsa. It is, however, instructive to note that *sehajdhari* Sikhs too were expected to keep their facial hair and whiskers uncut.[45] Like the initiated members of the Khalsa they were also expected to wear only turbans on their heads.[46] Finally, there were those Sikhs who followed the rival lineages of Prithi Chand (Minas), Dhirmal and Ram Rai. In the beginning of the eighteenth century, however, the Minas lost control of Amritsar to the Khalsa. Although Jiwan Mal (sixth in line from Prithi Chand) re-established the lineage at the village of Guru Har Sahai (named after his son) in 1752, his grandson, Ajit Singh (d. 1813) worked out a close relationship with the Khalsa.[47] Similarly, the exclusion of the Sodhi family of Kartarpur (*Dhirmalias*) from the Panth was lifted in the second half of the eighteenth century. It was Vadbhag Singh who was able to win this reprieve with the help of Jassa Singh Ahluwalia.

Interestingly, the observations made by early Europeans provide us with some helpful commentaries on Sikh identity late in the eighteenth century. Almost all the foreign observers are unanimous that following an initiation ceremony the Sikhs refrained from cutting their hair, wore an iron 'wrist-ring', and strictly avoided the use of tobacco. For instance, George Forster writes: 'They permit the growth of hair of the head and beard, they generally wear an Iron Bracelet on the left hand and the use of Tobacco is proscribed among them.'[48] The Swiss observer Colonel A.L.H. Polier noticed 'a pair of blue drawers' as part of the few garments typically worn by the Sikhs whom he observed.[49] William Francklin's following remark may draw our attention to the use of comb: '[A]fter performing the requisite duties of their religion by ablution and prayer, they comb their hair and beards with peculiar care.'[50] One can assume that the sword (*kirpan*) must have been part of the weaponry worn by the Khalsa Sikhs of the eighteenth century, and the comb (*kangha*) would be concealed in their conspicuous turbans. Thus the five items, now known as five Ks, were already there in the eighteenth century, though they were not defined as such.

In a letter written in 1783, George Forster mentioned that all Sikhs did not belong to the military order of the Khalsa. He described the two main categories of Sikhs late in the eighteenth century. On the one hand, there were 'Khualasah Sikhs' who did not observe the outward forms of the Khalsa and lacked visible identity. In fact, the Persian word 'Khualasah' means 'to be free', signifying those Sikhs who were free from external observances of the Khalsa.[51] Forster further mentioned that the boundaries between the 'Khualasah Sikhs' and 'the ordinary class of Hindoos' were quite blurred. The Khalsa Sikhs, on the other hand, were known for their rustic coarseness which clearly distinguished them from everybody else.[52] In a similar vein, John Malcolm distnguished the 'followers of Guru Gobind' or Khalsa Sikhs from those whom he variously called 'followers of Guru Nanak' or 'Khalasa Sikhs'.[53] The 'Khalasa Sikhs' (Forster's 'Khualasah Sikhs') were of course, the sehajdhari Sikhs.

The coexistence of Khalsa and sehajdhari identities has been variously explained by scholars. For instance, Harjot Oberoi considers it as a 'part of the complex process of state formation'. His argument goes like this: The Khalsa Sikhs, in their drive to carve out an empire for themselves, realized that for their project to succeed they required allies both within and outside the Sikh Panth. Therefore, an internal alliance was quickly forged with the sehajdharis, and their religious culture was conceded to be legitimate.[54] For McLeod, however, the situation of Khalsa/sehajdhari divide presents the 'problem of defining the Panth'. Thus a single definition did not cover all the Sikhs. Indeed, McLeod assumes uniformity to be relevant for identity. Addressing the question of uniformity Grewal maintains that there can be no objective 'homogeneity' among all the members of a community identified as distinct from others. If we are expecting that everyone in a community should be exactly the same, then we are looking for the impossible. This never happens. Neither fluidity nor diversity can invalidate distinct identity. Thus we need to think of the centre, middle, and periphery in terms of the distance or nearness of what is regarded as the central part of the tradition which makes for the normative identity. Grewal offers a new definition of 'identity' that rules out homogeneity.[55]

The issue of multiple Sikh identities aside the Khalsa identity had become predominant during the Sikh rule. In the 1840s Joseph D. Cunningham refers to the merging of castes, the Khalsa rite of initiation, 'devotion to steel', uncut hair, blue clothing, use of the name 'Singh', and a strict ban on smoking. The presence of the Guru was recognized in the Adi

Granth, and in any gathering of five Sikhs. Further, Cunningham made an important observation as follows: 'Thus the prominent division into "Khulasah", meaning "of Nanak", and "Khalsa", meaning "of Gobind" ... is no longer in force. The former term, Khulasah, is almost indeed unknown in the present day, while all claim membership with the Khalsa.'[56] This perception is strongly supported by the contemporary Sikh literature such as Rattan Singh Bhangu's *Prachin Panth Prakash* (1841).

In sum, Sikh identity evolved in pre-modern period in response to four main elements. First of these was the ideology based on religious and cultural innovations of Guru Nanak and his nine successors. This was the principal motivating factor in the evolution of the Sikh Panth. The second was the rural base of the Punjabi society. During the period of Guru Arjan the founding of the villages of Taran Taran, Sri Hargobindpur and Kartarpur in the rural areas saw large number of converts from local Jat peasantry. Further, Guru Tegh Bahadur's influence in the rural areas attracted more Jats from the Malwa region, and most of them became Khalsa during Guru Gobind Singh's period. It may have been the militant traditions of the Jats that brought the Sikh Panth into increasing conflict with the Mughals and Afghans, a conflict that shaped the future direction of the Sikh movement. The third factor was the conflict created within the Sikh community by dissidents, which originally worked to counter and then, paradoxically, to enhance the process of the crystallization of the Sikh tradition. The fourth element was the period of Punjab history from seventeenth to eighteenth centuries in which the Sikh Panth evolved in tension with Mughals and Afghans. All four elements combined to produce the mutual interaction between ideology and environment that came to characterize the historical development of Sikhism. On the whole, the pre-modern understandings of Sikh identity were primarily based upon orthopraxy rather than orthodoxy. Although the earlier Nanak-panth had permeable boundaries with the Hindu society at the popular level, the institution of the Khalsa sharpened the process of the emergence of a separate Sikh identity.

IV

The introduction of the British administration into Punjab at the time of annexation in 1849 brought profound changes in Punjabi society. First, the colonial rulers introduced a large measure of bureaucracy and the rule of law, which established a new kind of relationship between the individual and the state. It is no wonder that the 'paternal' rule of the early decades was eventually replaced by the 'machine rule' of laws, codes and procedures.[57] Second, the British introduced a worldview grounded in the secular, modernizing ideology of the Enlightenment. Third, the British sought to cosset and to control the Sikhs through the management of the Golden Temple and its functionaries.[58] In this context, the British even sidestepped the dictates of statutory law which required them to maintain 'the separation of secular and religious matters, neutrality in the treatment of religious communities and the withdrawal from involvement in religious institutions.'[59] Indeed, for the alien British, the need to control the Golden Temple was the greater. Finally, they put a legal ban on carrying of weapons. In fact, this decision was meant to disarm the Khalsa who had fought valiantly against the British in two Anglo-Sikh wars in 1845 and 1849.

In the light of this altered historical situation Baba Ram Singh had to ask his Namdhari followers to carry a simple staff if the colonial rulers do not allow the wearing of a *kirpan* (sword).[60] One can assume that in order to reach an understanding with the British authorities organizers of the Singh Sabha movement replaced the tradition of 'five weapons' with that of 'five religious symbols', known as Five Ks. It is not surprising that M.A. Macauliffe, who faithfully offered a Singh Sabha mode of interpretation of Sikh history and tradition throughout his writings, wrote in 1881 that

all orthodox Sikhs must have five appurtenances whose names begin with the letter K. They are spoken of by the Sikhs as five K's, and are—the Kes or long hair, the Kirpan, a small knife with an iron handle round which the Kes, thus rolled, is fastened on the head, the Kachh or drawers, and the Kara, an iron bangle for the wrist.[61]

Here, the 'Kirpan' no longer remains a 'weapon' worn diagonally across the right shoulder in a sash-like *gatara* (or belt). Rather it is worn as a matter of religious conviction along with the long hair (*kes*) and concealed under the turban. Macauliffe's understanding of the ceremonial sword (*kirpan*), therefore, reflects the contemporary Sikh response to the British policy of banning weapons. Similarly, at the close of the nineteenth century Captain R.W. Falcon explicitly mentions the tradition of five Ks in his handbook for the use of regimental officers.[62] The British reinforced the legitimacy of the five Ks through its recruitment policy. In this context, N.G. Barrier writes: 'Only Sikhs with the five Ks could join the army and part of their initiation was baptism and a pledge to maintain "orthodox" practices.'[63] Thus the five items which were already there as a part of the Khalsa discipline, acquired new significance because of the Singh Sabha's new definition of orthodoxy. This is not surprising since every dynamic community is always involved in the process of re-definition and renewal. In this context, Grewal skillfully argues that it is necessary to make a distinction between the formulation of the five Ks and its substantive prototypes. The formulation came later but the substantive symbols were there from the time of instituting the Khalsa.[64]

It is instructive to examine the impact of the nineteenth century Singh Sabha movement on Sikh identity. Here, it will be useful to take a note of Harjot Oberoi's major work on this socio-religious movement. For him, the Singh Sabha consisted of two components: the *Sanatan* and the *Tat Khalsa*. Sanatan Sikhs accepted the authority of the Vedas and Puranas in addition to the Sikh scriptures, thereby believing in incarnations and the ideas of pollution and purity based upon the caste system. Tat Khalsa, on the other hand, rejected all Hindu accretions prevalent in the Sikh society in the nineteenth century. Applying a social scientific method of analysis, Oberoi argues how the Tat Khalsa, the dominant wing of the Singh Sabha movement, succeeded in eradicating all forms of religious diversity at the turn of the century and in establishing uniform norms of religious orthodoxy and orthopraxy.[65] As a consequence of the success of the Tat Khalsa reformers, Sikhs in the early twentieth century came 'to think, imagine and speak in terms of a universal community of believers united by uniform rites, symbols and scripture.'[66]

In his analysis, however, Oberoi tilts the balance of evidence artificially in favour of Sanatan Sikhism. There is no doubt that some Sikhs did embrace Hindu practices in the nineteenth century. By projecting this backward, Oberoi seems to imply that Sikh identity was always predominantly fluid, with free mixing of Sikh and Hindu practices. This is questionable. From as early as the period of Guru Arjan, Sikhs clearly were encouraged to think of themselves as a distinct community. Not surprisingly, Grewal criticizes Oberoi's view of the Singh Sabha 'as a new episteme arising out of praxis' since it precludes the 'possibility of any meaningful linkages with the past'.[67] Nevertheless, Oberoi's work offers a valuable contribution in the ongoing debate on the process of identity-formation in the Sikh tradition.

McLeod recognizes continuity in the Sikh tradition from the time of Guru Nanak but he also notices changes coming in from time to time. He emphatically states that the Khalsa tradition was 'systematized and clarified' by the Singh Sabha reformers to make Sikh tradition consistent and effective for propagation. The Tat Khalsa conception of Sikh identity was both old and new, a point which McLeod forcefully makes in his analysis. In a similar vein, Ian Kerr maintains that the emerging Tat Khalsa identity espoused by the dominant wing of the Singh Sabha 'had been forged, admittedly from the pre-existing ores, in the crucible of colonial encounter'.[68] In addition to the economic and military policy of the British, there were other elements which meshed together to produce a great impact on the emerging Sikh identity. These additional elements in the larger colonial context were: new patterns of administration, a new technology, a fresh approach to education, the entry of Christian missionaries, and the modernist perspective based on the scientific paradigm of the Enlightenment. All these factors produced a kind of neo-Sikhism, characterized by a largely successful set of re-definitions in the context of the notions of modernity and religious identity imposed by the dominant ideology of the colonial power closely associated with Victorian Christianity.[69] As such, modern Sikhism became a well-defined 'system' based on a unified tradition and the Tat Khalsa understanding of Sikh identity became the norm of orthodoxy.

Also, Sikh identity was the key issue in the religious debate between the Tat Khalsa reformers and the Arya Samaj leaders, representing the voice of neo-Hinduism formulated by the Gujarati brahmin Dayanand Saraswati in the Punjab. This debate was greatly intensified when the widow of Dyal Singh Majithia went to the Punjab High Court after his death in 1898 to contest his will on the plea that he was not a Hindu. The court, however, ruled that he was. In the meantime, two pamphlets entitled *Sikh Hindu Hain* (Sikhs are Hindus) appeared under the name of Sikh authors. In this context, Kahn Singh Nabha's *Ham Hindu Nahin* (We are not Hindus) may be seen as a classic statement of independent Sikh identity as well as a declaration of Sikh ethnicity. Two major claims of the Tat Khalsa reformers gained general acceptance: one, that Sikhs are not Hindu and the other, that a true Sikh will normally be a Khalsa. A new definition of sehajdharis as 'slow adopters' was advanced with the intention of including them in the larger Sikh Panth.

In 1891, census enumerators were instructed to return as Sikhs all those who kept their hair and abstained from smoking. Thus, the kesdharis alone were to be treated as Sikhs. The sehajdharis could, of course, return themselves as Nanak-Panthis. In 1901, sects were not included. But in 1911 it was decided to enter as a Sikh any person who claimed to be one. The category of 'Sikh-Hindu' was also permitted. No change was, however, made in 1921 and 1931. Interestingly, the results of these census reports point to a well-defined pattern. Given the changing approaches to Sikhs from 1901 onward, the procedures and classifications may be involved in framing these statistics. The number and proportion of kesdhari Sikhs showed a remarkable increase, rising from about 840,000 in 1891 to nearly 3,600,000 in 1931. The number of sehajdhari Sikhs fell from nearly 580,000 in 1891 to less than 300,000 in 1931. Thus, the percentage of kesdhari Sikhs rose from less than seventy per cent to more than ninety per cent in less than half a century.[70]

The Akali movement began in 1920 as a non-violent agitation. This is sometimes described as the 'Third Sikh War' of 1920–5, although it is better known as the Gurdwara Reform Movement. The Tat Khalsa reformers demanded control of Sikh shrines in opposition to the British supported *Mahants* and *Pujaris*. The last gasp effort of the British to manipulate the Sikhs via management of the Golden Temple and its priests proved an ignoble failure in 1919 when General Dyer's invited visit to the Temple failed to pacify the Sikhs. The Akali answer was given in the agitations over the Keys Affair, at Guru-ka-Bagh, at Jaito, and elsewhere. The Akali campaign was finally terminated by the drafting and passing of the Sikh Gurdwaras Act of 1925. Chapter 1 of the Act defined a Sikh as 'a person who professes the Sikh religion', adding that the following declaration should be required if any doubt should arise: 'I solemnly affirm that I am a Sikh, that I believe in the Guru Granth Sahib, that I believe in the Ten Gurus, and that I have no other religion.'[71] The point to be noted in this definition is that it was based upon modernist assumption that doctrine dominates practice. This was the beginning of the definition of a 'Sikh' by legislation. The definition was deliberately broad because legislators did not want to be specific in terms of either detailed beliefs or practices and boundaries. This approach indeed set the precedent later continued by the *Sikh Rahit Maryada* (1950) and all the way upto 1971 Delhi Gurdwara Act.

In sum, the dominant Sikh response to modernity was conditioned by the need to to enforce clear definitions of authority and community in the face of the double challenge of colonialism and of neo-Hinduism.[72] The main impetus behind this response was to secure permanent control of Sikh institutions in the Punjab. The effect of the Sikh Gurdwaras Act was to make available to the Shiromani Gurdwara Prabandhak Committee (SGPC, Chief Management Committee of Sikh Shrines) and thus to Akali Dal the enormous political and economic benefits that came from control of the gurdwaras. A government within a government was created as the price of a restored acceptance of the British among Sikhs.[73] In the course of time the SGPC became the 'authoritative voice' of the Sikhs. As a democratic institution it has always represented the majority opinion. As such, it has laid the claim to represent the authority of the 'Guru-Panth', although it has been frequently challenged by Sikhs living outside the Punjab.

V

The Constitution of independent India came into force on January 26, 1950, which is treated as the date of the commencement of the Constitution. Its amended form defines India as a secular state. Western notions of this designation aside, for India this has always involved the state in religious matters. According to Article 25 [1], all persons are guaranteed the right 'freely to profess, practise, and propagate religion', although this freedom is subject to 'public order, morality and health'. Further, it is to be clearly distinguished from 'economic, social, political or other secular' activities which might be found in close proximity with religious practices. These 'secular' matters can be directly regulated by the state. Furthermore, the state is obliged to engage in social welfare and reform, and legislation to that end cannot be set aside on the grounds that it interfers with religious freedom. Nor can temple entry laws be set aside because they restrict practices that are admittedly religious (Article 25 [2][b]). Indeed, Hindu religious institutions of a public nature can legitimately be opened to all classes of Hindus, even to those who were previously excluded because of untouchabiltiy.[74]

Explanation II of Article 25 [2][b] states that 'the reference to Hindus shall be construed as including a reference to persons professing the Sikh, Jaina, or Buddhist religion, and the reference to Hindu religious institutions shall be construed accordingly.' Robert Baird compellingly argues that this explanation is a constitutional admission of two things. First, it admits that there is a difference between the 'Hindu religion' and 'Hindu' as a legal category. For, the stipulation that 'Hindus' in Article 25 [2][b] is to be taken to include persons professing the Sikh, Buddhist or Jaina *religion* suggests that *as religion* these are distinguishable from 'Hinduism' *as a religion*, but *before the law* they *are* to be included within the category of 'Hindu' (emphasis in the original). While Article 25 [2][b] deals with the temple entry, it also includes welfare and reform more broadly conceived.[75] Indeed, the legal net of 'Hinduism' is cast very widely in the Constitution of India in such a way that it raises the fundamental problem of defining 'Hinduism'.

It is instructive to note that the Sikh members of the Constituent Assembly refused to sign the draft constitution to be adopted by the people of India on 26 January 1950. They resented the fact that the Constitution of India did not recognize the independent identity of the Sikhs and failed to establish a separate personal law for them. This resentment surfaced again during the 1980s when Akali leader Parkash Singh Badal publicly burned a copy of Article 25 in New Delhi. In contrast to this popular interpretation, however, a leading Sikh legal specialist, Kashmir Singh, has emphasized that 'the separate identity of Sikhism and that of Jainism & Buddhism is specifically conceded' in Explanation II to Article 25 [2][b].[76] He further argues that Explanation I to Article 25 [2][b] (that is, 'The wearing and carrying of Kirpans shall be deemed to be included in the profession of Sikh religion.') refers to the autonomous character of Sikh religion. Thus the separate Sikh identity 'is not annihilated by Explanation II because it itself admits the same.'[77] Nevertheless, both Sikh and Hindu politicians have used the popular interpretation of constitutional wording for their own purpose in ensuing confrontation.[78] Therefore, to remove this misunderstanding the National Commission to Review the Constitution headed by the former Chief Justice of India, Justice M.N. Venkatachaliah, has made the following recommendation: 'The commission, without going into the larger issue on which the contention is based, is of the opinion that the purpose of the representations would be served if Explanation II to Article 25 is omitted and subclause (b) of clause (2) of that article is re-worded as follows—(b) "providing for social welfare and reform or throwing open of Hindu, Sikh, Jain or Buddhist religious institutions of a public character to all classes and sections of these religions".'[79] When this amendment to Article 25 takes place, the Indian Constitution will duly recognize the distinct and independent identity of Sikhism.

It is equally important to underline the historical coincidence that the SGPC published the standard manual of the 'Sikh Code of Conduct' known as *Sikh Rahit Maryada* in 1950. This manual begins by defining a Sikh in the following terms: 'Any person, female or male, who believes in One God (Akal Purakh); in the Ten Gurus (Guru Nanak to Guru Gobind Singh); in Sri Guru Granth Sahib and the *bani* and teachings of the ten Gurus; in the Khalsa initiation ceremony (*amrit*) instituted by the tenth Guru; and who does not believe in any other religion, is a Sikh.' This defintion implies preference for the amritdhari, includes the kesdhari, and does not exclude the sehajdhari. It is certainly based upon modernist assumptions. Its wording is carefully chosen so that one is required to 'believe in' or 'have faith in' (*jo…nisacha rakhada hai*) the need to take amrit. That is, one will certainly be expected to take amrit at some time in life when one is ready for the full range of Khalsa discipline (*rahit*), but it is not an immediate step. The essential requirement, as McLeod argues, is that one should affirm the value of so doing.[80]

The gurdwaras of Delhi and New Delhi were beyond the jurisdiction of the SGPC, and hence, there was a need for fresh legislation to regularize their administration. The parliament of India, therefore, passed two such Acts in 1971. First of these was the the Delhi Gurdwara (Management) Act 24 of 1971, in which the word 'Sikh' was defined in terms closely following those of the 1925 Act. The latter Act, however, amended this definition. The definition of a 'Sikh' in the Delhi Gurdwara Act 82 of 1971 is given as follows:

'Sikh' means a person who professes the Sikh religion, believes and follows the teachings of Sri Guru Granth Sahib and the ten Gurus only *and keeps unshorn hair*. For the purpose of this Act, if any question arises as to whether any living person is or is not a Sikh, he shall be deemed respectively to be or not to be a Sikh according as he makes or refuses to make in the manner prescribed by rules rules the following declaration:

'I solemnly affirm that I am a *Keshadhari* Sikh, that I believe in and follow the teachings of Sri Guru Granth Sahib and, the ten Gurus only, and that I have no other religion.'[81]

This defintion has indeed become more exclusive than the one given in the Gurdwara Act of 1925. It includes the kesdhari, but does not include the sehajdhari. It may well reflect the influence of a particular pressure group among the Sikhs of Delhi at that time.

Much has happened within the Panth since the tragic events of 1984, including the Operation Blue Star of June and the killings of the Sikhs nationwide in November after Indira Gandhi's assassination. Consequently, 'Sikh identity became sharper, less incoherent, consciously integrated, and one in which the martial tradition was particularly enlivened.'[82] The year 1984 itself became the turning point in the history of the Sikhs in post-colonial and post-modern world. It created the identity crisis among the Sikhs throughout India and abroad. As a diaspora Sikh writes: 'Who am I was a question that never crossed my mind until the cataclysmic events of

1984—caused by the Hindus declaring an open season on Sikhs—were to jolt me from my long, self-induced amnesia.'[83] Many Sikhs who had abandoned their turbans and beards returned to their traditional ways. One estimate records that during the decade of militancy (1981–1990) as many as 79,100 persons took 'amrit' in various districts of Punjab.[84] In particular, the frequency of arranging the amrit ceremony increased among the diaspora Sikhs, which was once a rare occurrence. As a result the significance and need for full commitment to the Khalsa discipline has received new recognition by the diaspora Sikhs (especially by young adults).[85] More recently, the Delhi Sikh Gurdwara Management Committee organized an amrit ceremony on 1 October 2002 in which 15,000 persons were initiated into the Khalsa order 'under one roof on a single day'.[86] In my personal observations of North American Sikhs during the last two decades, I have witnessed a dramatic change in their attitudes and life styles. In my recent visits to California and Calgary, for instance, I met certain full-fledged Khalsa Sikhs who were earlier clean-shaven (*mona*) Sikhs.[87] These examples point towards the dynamic nature of Sikh identity. No single category is a 'fixed' category. A Mona Sikh of yesterday, could be a kesdhari today, and who might be an amritdhari tomorrow. Similarly, the process in the reverse direction is also possible when an amritdhari becomes an apostate by cutting his/her hair. In this context, Deepankar Gupta rightly maintains that 'identities are not permanently inscribed on our psyches but undergo context-related changes.'[88]

At the beginning of twenty-first century, there are more than twenty-two million Sikhs in the world. Among them approximately fifteen to twenty per cent are the amritdharis (those who have taken amrit or nectar, that is, 'Initiated') who represent the orthodox form of the Khalsa. There is, however, a large majority of those Sikhs who 'retain their hair' (kesdhari, 'Unshorn') and maintain a visible identity. In particular, male Sikhs are easily recognized by their beards and turbans. They follow most of the Khalsa Rahit without having gone through the initiation ceremony. Further, there are others who have shorn their hair and are less conspicuous, but their number is quite large in North America and the United Kingdom. They are popularly known as 'clean-shaven' Sikhs, although they do not like the term 'Mona' (Shorn) as the designation of their status within the Panth. In order to overcome this difficulty, I propose to use the term *ichhadhari* (lit. *ichha* means 'desire' or free choice) for them. I have avoided the use of its equivalent *manmukh* (self-willed) for being loaded with pejorative connotation. I am using the term ichhadhari with two meanings in mind. In the first place, most of the icchadharis 'desire' to keep their hair intact, but cut them under the pressure of circumstances at a particular moment (which may be a temporary phase in their life). The moment they feel secure in their life they start keeping the hair again. This may be illustrated with the recent example of a young Sikh from New York, who cut his hair after he was attacked after the terrorist attacks on the Twin Towers of New York and the Pentagon Building of the Department of Defense of the United States of America on September 11 2001. It was an act brought not so much by individual considerations but by social terror. He explained his mental anguish as follows: 'I am not happy that I cut my hair. I went against my religion and I disrespected my parents … I am growing my beard and may be by next week, I will start wearing turban again.'[89] Secondly, there are those ichhadharis who cut their hair because of reasons of their own choosing, but retain their affiliation with the Khalsa families. They use the Khalsa names 'Singh' and 'Kaur' without inhibition. Neither do they consider themselves as 'lesser Sikhs' in any way, nor do they identify themselves with the 'Hindus'. In fact, there has emerged a new sense of identity among them in recent times. Being majority in the diaspora, they participate with equal zeal in all Sikh rituals and in the management of the gurdwaras.

The Icchadharis are frequently confused with the so-called Sehajdhari ('Gradualist') Sikhs who have never accepted the Khalsa discipline. Although the Sehajdhari Sikhs practice *nam simaran* and follow the teachings of the Adi Granth, they do not observe the Rahit and, in particular, cut their hair. The recent debate within the Sikh community is again focused on the issue of the inclusion of Sehajdharis in the voters' list in the SGPC elections.[90] The number of Sehajdharis has continued to decline in the last few decades, although they certainly have not disappeared completely from the Panth. This impression, however, concerns only true Sehajdharis. It does not apply to those who violate the Khalsa Rahit and cut their hair after initiation. They are lapsed Amritdharis who are known as '*Patit* Sikhs' ('Apostates'). Being directly opposite to the category of Amritdhari, I propose to use the term *Bikh-dhari* ('one who has taken "poison", leaving the life of amrit or "nectar" behind') for this category of Sikhs who become apostates after committing any one of the following four prohibitions (*char kurahit*): 'cutting the hair, using tobacco, committing adultery, and eating meat that has not come from an animal killed with a single blow.' This condition has occured largely in the Sikh diaspora.

Let us now represent these various categories of Sikhs in the following figure 1 of a 'soccer-ball', and try to understand the dynamic nature of each category within the large body of the Sikh Panth. At the centre stand the amritdharis (15–20 per cent) who represent the orthodox form of the Khalsa. The bulk of the middle of the 'ball' consists of the kesdharis (70 per cent) who belong to the Khalsa tradition, and who could either become amritdhari when they are ready to take amrit or become icchadhari when they cut their hair. The next category represent the ichhadharis who are affiliated to the Khalsa tradition. Their number is less than 10 per cent in the worldwide Sikh population, although they are in majority in the Sikh diaspora. They are followed by sehajdharis who do not belong to the Khalsa tradition. However, as 'slow-adopters' they could also join the Khalsa ranks at any time. For instance, a sehajdhari Ragi (Sikh musician), Bhai Chaman Lal, who used to perform kirtan in major cities beyond Punjab, has become an amritdhari in the recent past to win the confidence of large Sikh congregations.[91] On the fringe of the 'ball' come the bikhdharis who have become apostates (*Patit*). They can become amritdhari once again when they confess their guilt and accept 'penance' (*tanakhah*) from the Cherished Five at the time of re-initiation with amrit. In this context, the personal narrative of a North American Sikh jouranlist offers an interesting reading:

I was 13 years old when my mother enthused me to partake of Amrit at the school ceremony. I vividly remember the day of ceremony at Khalsa High School Gujarkhan (Rawalpindi). My mother had bought two Kirpans at Amritsar a couple of years prior to the occasion. Next day she took away the big Kirpan (about a feet or so long) and put a small one, about three or four inches long around my neck, which stayed with me till my high school days. That ceremony had in-buil[t] Sikhee in my thought. In spite of the fact that I went under the influence of Marxists, accepted apostasy, abandoned attending religious rituals, the spirit of Sikhee remained in some corners of my mind. As the time passed it sprung out. Had I not partaken the Amrit, perhaps I would still be an atheist.[92]

This personal narritive underlines the changing perceptions of the self through different phases of one's life. The author may have become an apostate 'under the influence of Marxists,' but the 'spirit of Sikhee' remained with him. It is no wonder that he regained his original 'status' and became a full-fledged Khalsa Sikh once again. Thus any one individual might go through different stages in one's life, each referring to a different status within the Panth. Therefore, to think of the five categories of Sikhs as 'predetermined' or 'fixed' permanently (as in the case of the caste system of the Hindus) would be misleading.

In addition to Fig. 2.1 which represents the global Sikh population, we need to look at Fig. 2.2 carefully from the perspective of diaspora Sikhs. Both figures highlight the dynamic nature of Sikh identity:

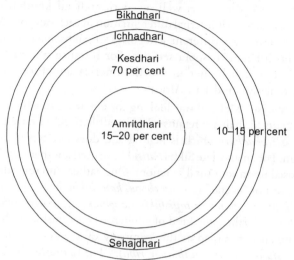

FIG. 2.1   Worldwide Sikh Population (22 million)

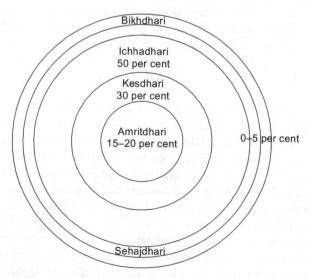

FIG. 2.2   Diaspora Sikh Population (1.5 million)

It should be emphasized here that all these five categories of Sikhs are not fixed permanently. The movement from one category to another takes place frequently and therefore, it refers to their dynamic nature. For instance, all amritdharis are kesdharis as well, even though all kesdharis are not amritdharis. Also, there is internal differentiation in each category. Moreover, the actual numbers of different categories of Sikhs may show marked variations in different diaspora settings. For instance, the percentage of ichhadharis is much higher in North America and England than in Singapore, Malasiya, and East Africa.

In his analysis, McLeod was looking for a new term 'which designates a Sikh who cuts his hair yet retains a Khalsa affiliation.'[93] I have coined this new term as *ichhadhari* which is neutral and does not carry any negative connotation. For an apostate Sikh (*Patit*) I have used another term *bikhdhari* which is based upon scriptural sanction: 'One gathers "poison" after leaving the life of amrit or "nectar" (*amritu chhodi kahe bikhu khai ...; amritu chhodi maha bikhu pivai ...; amritu tajji bikhu sangarahi ...; amritu chhadi bikhai bikhu khahi*).'[94] Further, any kind of adulterous relationship with any other man or woman is regarded as the 'company of a poisonous snake' (*jaisa sangu bisiar siu hai re taiso hi ihu pargrihu*).[95] Furthermore, the Desa Singh Rahit-nama employs the term *bikhia* (poisonous substance) for smoking tobacco in a hookah-bowl.[96] All these considerations justify the use of the term bikhdhari for an apostate, although it may appear highly loaded with strong condemnation. Indeed, the process of formalization becomes complete with these 'five' categories of Sikh identity.

VI

In sum, the discussion of this paper has addressed the question 'Who is a Sikh?'. It has offered different perspectives on the ever-changing historical context in which a distinct Sikh identity finds expression in different ways. Although the objective realities of the Sikh Panth and the self-image of the Sikhs from the days of Guru Nanak to the present day have changed dramatically, the consciousness of distinction from the 'others' has remained constant throughout history. What it meant—and means—to be a Sikh has also been shaped in part by the policies and actions of governing authorities, whether they be the Mughals, or the British, or the Government of India. Recently, Sikh scholars have, however, vehemently argued that the State has no right to define who is a Sikh.[97] It is no wonder that the protagonists of nationalist discourse have often invoked Sikh identity as the basis of their politics. Indeed, we have witnessed the increasing estrangement of Sikhs from the Republic of India before and after the assault on the Golden Temple in 1984 which has been labelled 'the nation-state phase of Sikh identity-formation.'[98] More recently, Sikhs are seeking fresh inspiration from the Guru Granth Sahib for the reconstruction of self and gender within the Sikh tradition from the post-modern and post-colonial perspectives.

The Sikh community has always been involved in the process of 'renewal and re-definition' throughout the world. In fact, the question 'Who is a Sikh?' occupies much of the attention in the online discussions among the various Sikh networks, although the debate frequently becomes acrimonious. Each generation of Sikhs has to respond to this question in the light of new historical situation and to address the larger issues of orthodoxy and orthopraxy. Not surprisingly, the diaspora Sikhs have to respond to these issues from their own particular situation in different cultural and political contexts. In fact, they rediscover their identity in cross-cultural encounters as well as through their interaction with other religious and ethnic communities. They have to face new challenges which require new responses. It is no wonder that they are starting to provoke fresh responses to the notions of self, gender, and authority in the postmodern world. On the whole the process of Sikh identity-formation is an ongoing phenomenon of a dynamic nature.

Notes

1. W.H. McLeod, *Who is a Sikh?: The Problem of Sikh Identity* (Oxford: Clarendon Press, 1989), p. 121.

2. For details, see W.H. McLeod, *The Sikhs: History, Religion, and Society* (New York: Columbia University, 1989), pp. 16–31.

3. During my visit to Darbar Sahib, Kartarpur (Pakistan), on May 30, 1999, I found out that about one thousand acres of land was still recorded in the name of 'Baba Nanak'.

4. M1, *Ramakali Siddh Gost 36*, AG, p. 942.

5. M1, *Var Sarang*, 1 (22), AG, p. 1245.

6. W.H. McLeod, *Guru Nanak and the Sikh Religion* (Oxford: Clarendon Press, 1968), p. 228.

7. Bhai Gurdas, *Var 1, pauri 38*.

8. McLeod, *Who is a Sikh?*, p. 21.

9. Ibid., p. 19.

10. W.H. McLeod, *Exploring Sikhism: Aspects of Sikh Identity, Culture, and Thought* (New Delhi: Oxford University Press, 2000), pp. 51–2.

11. M2, *Var Majh*, 1 (27), AG, p. 150.

12. Satta and Balvand, *Ramakali Ki Var 3*, AG, p. 967.

13. M2, *Var Majh*, 1 (18), AG, p. 146.

14. M2, *Var Sarang*, 1 (16), AG, p. 1243.

15. McLeod, *Who is a Sikh?*, p. 12.

16. M4, *Suhi Chhant 2*, AG, pp. 773–4.

17. M4, *Var Gauri*, 2 (11), AG, pp. 305–6.

18. M4, *Var Sorathi*, 18, AG, p. 649.

19. McLeod, *Exploring Sikhism*, p. 55.

20. M5, *Siri Ragu 2*, AG, p. 74.

21. M5, *Bilavalu 3*, AG, p. 817 and *Asa Astapadian 1*, AG, p. 430. For details, see Grewal, *The Sikhs of the Punjab*, p. 56.

22. M5, *Bhairau 3*, AG, p. 1136.

23. McLeod, *Exploring Sikhism*, p. 55.

24. See Susan Elizabeth Prill, 'Bhai Gurdas' *Vars* and the Formation of Sikh Identity' (MA diss., Centre for South Asian Studies, University of Michigan, 2000).

25. McLeod, *Who is a Sikh?*, p. 18.

26. J.S. Grewal, 'Sikh Identity, the Akalis and Khalistan', in J.S. Grewal and Indu Banga, eds, *Punjab in Prosperity and Violence* (Chandigarh: K.K. Publishers for Institute of Punjab Studies, 1998), p. 92.

27. McLeod, *Who is a Sikh?*, p. 17.

28. Harbans Singh, ed., 'Dabistan-i-Mazahib', *The Encyclopaedia of Sikhism*, Vol. I (Patiala:: Punjabi University, 1992), pp. 484–5.

29. Ibid.

30. M5, *Maru 1*, AG, p. 1001.

31. McLeod, *Who is a Sikh?*, pp. 21–2.

32. Bhai Gurdas, *Var 11, pauris* 22–31.

33. McLeod, *Exploring Sikhism*, p. 55.

34. M5, *Bilaval 18*, AG, p. 825. The expression 'axed to death by the Lord' in this hymn refers to the actual incident in which Sulhi Khan's horse bolted and fell in the brick-kiln, killing the rider instantaneously.

35. For different perspectives on Guru Arjan's martyrdom, see Louis E. Fenech, 'Martyrdom and the Execution of Guru Arjan in Early Sikh Sources', *Journal of the American Oriental Society*, Vol. 121, No. 1 (January–March 2001): pp. 20–31.

36. Wilfred Cantwell Smith, 'The Crystallization of Religious Communities in Mughal India', *On Understanding Islam: Selected Studies* (The Hague, The Netherlands: Mouton Publishers, 1981), p. 191.

37. *Varan Bhai Gurdas*, 26: 25.

38. M9, Salok 16, AG, p. 1427.

39. Harbans Singh, *Guru Tegh Bahadur* (New Delhi: Sterling Publishers Private Limited, 1982), p. 104.

40. Doris Jakobsh's article in this volume presents the argument that 'Kaur' as nomenclature for Sikh women was part of the Singh Sabha project in the twentieth century. However, we have evidence that 'Kaur' was used by Sikh women in the pre-modern times (Guru Har Rai's daughter's name was Bibi Rup Kaur and then there were Sada Kaur, Raj Kaur, Mehtab Kaur, Rup Kaur, and so on). The actual practice was already there, though the formulation of the convention may have come as the result of Singh Sabha reforms.

41. J.S. Grewal, *Historical Perspectives on Sikh Identity* (Patiala: Punjabi University, 1997), p. 30.

42. Ganda Singh, ed., *Hukam-name* (Patiala: Punjab University, 1967), pp. 179, 194.

43. Grewal, *Historical Perspectives on Sikh Identity*, p. 31.

44. See Jeevan Deol, 'Eighteenth Century Khalsa Identity: Discourse, Praxis and Narrative', in Christopher Shackle et al, eds, *Sikh Religion, Culture and Ethnicity* (UK: Curzon Press, 2001), pp. 26–9.

45. W.H. McLeod, *The Chaupa Singh Rahit-nama* (Dunedin: University of Otago Press, 1987), pp. 64 and 100 (nos. 53, 54 and 287).

46. Ibid., p. 234, no. 303.

47. See Gurinder Singh Mann, *The Making of Sikh Scripture* (New York: Oxford University Press, 2001), p. 34.

48. See Ganda Singh, ed., *Early European Accounts of the Sikhs* (Calcutta: Indian Studies Past & Present, 1962), p. 79. Also see pp. 18, 63, 65, 79, 92, and 103–4.

49. Ibid., p. 63.

50. Ibid., p. 103.

51. Ghulam Ali Khan Sayyid mentions in his *Imad-us-saadat*, written in 1808 as follows: 'The disciples of Baba Ji (Guru Nanak) with hair are known as "Khalsa" and without hair are called "Khulasa".' See Gurbax Singh, *Masti Da Namazi Guru Baba Nanak* (Patiala: Punjabi University, 1970), p. 41.

52. George Forster, *A Journey from Bengal to England*, Vol. I (London: R Foulder, 1798), pp. 268–9. Ganda Singh's text omits this reference.

53. Lt. Col. Malcolm, *Sketch of the Sikhs: Their Origin, Customs & Manners*, with notes by Subhash C. Aggarwal (Chandigarh: Vinay Publications, reprint 1981; Original London 1812), pp. 105–6.

54. Harjot Oberoi, *The Construction of Religious Boundaries: Culture, Identity and Diversity in the Sikh Tradition* (Delhi: Oxford University Press, 1994), pp. 87 and 90.

55. Grewal, *Historical Perspectives*, p. 29.

56. Joseph Davey Cunningham, *A History of the Sikhs*, ed. H.L.O. Garrett (New Delhi: S. Chand & Co., reprint 1966; original Oxford University Press, 1849), p. 81.

57. J.S. Grewal, *The New Cambridge History of India: The Sikhs of the Punjab* (Cambridge: Cambridge University Press, 1990), p. 128.

58. Ian J. Kerr, 'Sikhs and State', in Pashaura Singh and N.G. Barrier, eds, *Sikh Identity: Continuity and Change* (New Delhi: Manohar Publications, 1999), p. 153.

59. Ibid., p. 164.

60. Grewal, *The Sikhs of the Punjab*, p. 142.

61. Max Macauliffe, 'The Sikh Religion Under Banda, and its Present Condition', *The Calcutta Review*, Vol. 66 (1881), p. 162.

62. Captain R.W. Falcon, *Handbook on Sikhs: For the Use of Regimental Officers* (Allahabad: Pioneer Press, 1896), p. 9.

63. N. Gerald Barrier, 'The Singh Sabhas and the Evolution of Modern Sikhism, 1875–1925', in Robert D. Baird, ed., *Religion in Modern India* (New Delhi: Manohar, 2nd edn, 1989), p. 204.

64. J.S. Grewal, *Contesting Interpretations of the Sikh Tradition* (New Delhi: Manohar, 1998), p. 303.

65. Oberoi, *Construction of Religious Boundaries*, p. 25.

66. Harjot Oberoi, 'From Ritual to Counter-Ritual: Rethinking the Hindu-Sikh Question, 1884–1915', in Joseph T. O'Connell et al, eds, *Sikh History and Religion in the Twentieth Century* (Toronto: Centre of South Asian Studies, 1988), p. 154.

67. Grewal, *Historical Perspectives*, p. 73.

68. Kerr, 'Sikhs and State', p. 161.

69. Christopher Shackle, 'Sikhism' in Linda Woodhead et al, eds, *Religions in the Modern World: Traditions and Trasformations* (London and New York: Routledge, 2002), p. 70.

70. Grewal, *The Sikhs of the Punjab*, pp. 137–8. For details, see Rajiv A. Kapur, *Sikh Separatism: The Politics of Faith* (London: Allen & Unwin, 1986), pp. 9–32.

71. McLeod, *Who is a Sikh?*, 93.

72. Shackle, 'Sikhism', p. 83.

73. Kerr, 'Sikhs and State', p. 166.

74. Robert D. Baird, 'On Defining "Hinduism" as a Religious and Legal Category', in Robert D. Baird, ed., *Religion and Law in Independent India* (New Delhi: Manohar Publications, 1993), p. 41.

75. Ibid., pp. 41–2.

76. Kashmir Singh, 'Article 25 of the Indian Constitution', in Madanjit Kaur, ed., *Co-Existence in Pluralistic Society: Punjab Issues and Prospects* (Amritsar: Guru Nanak Dev University, 1991), p. 95.

77. Ibid.

78. I am grateful to Professor N.G. Barrier for showing me the manuscript of his insightful paper, 'Sikhs and the Law: A Century of Conflict over Identity and Authority'.

79. T.R. Ramachandran, 'Sikhism favoured as Separate Religion', *The Tribune* (Wednesday, April 3, 2002).

80. McLeod, *Who is a Sikh?*, p. 96.

81. Cited in ibid., p. 98.

82. Dipankar Gupta, *The Context of Ethnicity: Sikh Identity in a Comparative Perspective* (Delhi: Oxford University Press, 1996), p. 125.

83. Bhupinder Singh Mahal, *Punjab: The Nomads and The Mavericks* (New Delhi: Sanbun Publishers, 2000), p. 2.

84. Pramod Kumar, 'Violence in Retrospect', in *Punjab in Prosperity and Violence*, p. 137.

85. See my 'Observing the Khalsa Rahit in North America: Some Issues and Trends', in Pashaura Singh and N. Gerald Barrier, eds, *The Transmission of Sikh Heritage in the Diaspora* (New Delhi: Manohar Publication, 1996), pp. 168–9.

86. See '15,000 baptisms', *The Tribune* (Saturday, October 5, 2002).

87. Some prominent Sikh leaders of North America like Hardev Singh Shergill of Sikh Centre, Roseville (CA), Paul Singh Purewal of Edmonton, author of *Sikh Jantari* (Calendar), and Avtar Singh Sekhon of Edmonton were all 'clean-shaven' Sikhs when I met them in the past. Now they are Khalsa Sikhs. Similarly, Didar Singh Bains and Gian Singh Sandhu, the past Presidents of World Sikh Organization were also clean-shaven Sikhs in the past.

88. Gupta, *The Context of Ethnicity*, p. 1.

89. See the report by Leela Jacinto, 'Bias Fallout: How One Sikh-American Learned a Hard Lesson in Identity Politics', in *abc.NEWS.com* (October 30, 2001): <wysiwyg://5/http://abcnews.go.com/.../us/DailyNews/sikh011030_hair.html>.

90. See H.S. Mattewal, 'Should Sehajdharis have a right to vote in SGPC elections?', *The Tribune* (May 01, 2003), editorial page. This question has assumed particular importance in view of the resolutions passed by the SGPC proposing amendments to the Sikh Gurdwara Act, 1925, for limiting the right to vote only to the Kesdhari Sikhs as in the case of the Delhi Sikh Gurdwara Act, 1971. By an

amendment in 1959, a new Section (10A) was added to the Sikh Gurdwara Act, 1925, offering the definition of a Sehajdhari Sikh as a 'person (1) who performs ceremonies according to Sikh rites; (2) who does not use tobacco or *kutha* (*halal* meat) in any form; (3) who is not a 'patit'; and (4) who can recite Mul Mantar.' Since then Sehajdharis have been participating in the general elections to the SGPC. For instance, during the SGPC elections in 1996 the number of 'Sehajdhari' voters was 6,33,495 out of the total 36,23,974. Leaders of various Akali factions apprehend that 'non-Sikhs' posing as 'Sehajdharis' will get themselves registered as voters and thereby, usurp the SGPC. Currently, 8 lakh 'Sehajdhari' Sikhs figure on the draft of the revised electoral rolls of 62 lakh voters prepared by the Gurdwara Election Commission, a Union Government organization, to conduct the forthcoming SGPC general elections. See Sarbjit Singh Dhaliwal, '8 lakh sehajdharis on the draft of SGPC poll rolls,' *The Tribune* (August 7, 2003). Clearly, the percentage of Sehajdhari voters has gone down from 17.5% in 1996 in 12.9% in the forthcoming elections.

91. I met the family of Inder Singh Gulati of Ambala who were earlier sehajdhari Sikhs. The whole family took amrit and joined the Akhand Kirtani Jatha. Inder Singh Gulati founded the Guru Granth Sahib Mission Trust.

92. Pritpal Singh Bindra's missive of February 19, 2002 on Sikh-Diaspora online discussion. I had seen Mr Bindra in the clean-shaven form in an international Sikh Studies conference, organized by the University of Toronto in February 1994.

93. McLeod, *Who is a Sikh*, p. 114.

94. M1, *Suhi 2*, AG, p. 728; M1, *Maru 7*, AG, p. 1013; M3, *Var Sorathi*, 2(4), AG, p. 644; and Kirat, *Savayyie Mahale Chauthe Ke*, AG, p. 1406.

95. M5, *Asa 127*, AG, p. 403.

96. See W.H. McLeod, *The Sikhs of the Khalsa* (Oxford University Press, 2003).

97. See Jasbir Singh Ahluwalia, 'Should the right to define a Sikh be surrendered to the State?', *Hindustan Times* (January 22–3, 2001).

98. See Harjot Oberoi, 'From Punjab to "Khalistan": Territoriality and Metacommentary', *Pacific Affairs*, 60: 1 (Spring, 1987): 38–40.

3

Bhai Nand Lal 'Goya' and the Sikh Tradition

Louis E. Fenech

Far off Ghazni ... is known to the people of India as the home-town of two gigantic figures. One belonged to the field of battle and the sword, and the other to thought and the pen. One was Mahmud of Ghazni and the other was Bhai Nand Lal ... Bhai Nand Lal[was drawn to India] by the soundless call of the spirit.[1]

I

Introduction

So begins B.P.L. Bedi's enthusiastic introduction to his English translation of the Persian Divan of Bhai Nand Lal 'Goya', who was according to Sikh tradition the premiere Persian poet and litterateur in the *majlis* or 'literary assembly' of Guru Gobind Singh (1666–1708), the tenth Guru of the Sikhs.[2] This assembly, tradition continues, was composed principally of poets who wrote in the Punjabi *lingua franca* of the period, a form of *Braj Bhasha* which we will refer to as Punjabi in this paper. It was mainly through this form of Braj, a language intimately related to the *Sant Bhasha* language of the Adi Granth that Sikh thought and theology was conveyed in the early eighteenth century.

The use of Persian words and idioms in Sikh literature is not unique to Nand Lal. The Sikh Gurus themselves conversed with Muslim audiences and in so doing utilized the language, especially Persian terms of royalty, with which their educated Muslim listeners in northern India would have been familiar.[3] Nand Lal's usage of Persian goes well beyond the mere appropriation of terms, however, but rather to the deployment of an entire genre, that of the mystical Persian ghazal a form which in the late seventeenth and early eighteenth centuries was considered quintessentially Islamic.[4] What we must therefore ask is why Nand Lal wrote in this specifically Islamic language, clearly and consistently employing the language of Islamic mysticism in his *Divan* to describe concepts which were to be understood as Sikh rather than as Muslim.[5] That he did so at a time when Sikh hostility towards Islam and the Mughals was coming into fruition is particularly surprising and may tell us something about the development of this well-known antagonism.

Let us be wary of such conclusions, however, for the evidence on which Nand Lal's authorship of the *Divan* is claimed, is tenuous indeed. Ultimately, if one excludes Sikh tradition, the only reasonable claim on which his authorship of the *Divan* is founded is that the pen-name Goya which appears in every ghazal is the same as Nand Lal's.[6] To be sure there are Persian works attributed to Nand Lal that can only be the work of a Sikh poet. While the *Zindagi-namah* sometimes includes terminology which may be considered Sikh, the Persian *Joti Bigas* and the *Ganj-namah* incessantly praise the Sikh Gurus by name. Such praise is also recognized in the lengthiest of the Persian works ascribed to Nand Lal, the *'Arz-ul Alfaz*, though less frequently.[7] None of these works, however, are in the ghazal format but appear to be, rather, a type of *masnavi* (*mathnavi*).[8]

However 'Sikh' some of these other Persian works may appear, their general nature and even more so that of Persian ghazal poetry, with its strict rules of prosody, its set conventions, and its emphasis on mystical themes, is nevertheless understood as inclusive, as a poetry with which the people of any number of religious traditions in eighteenth century northern India could identify. This was perhaps one of the reasons why Persian was self-consciously chosen, initially, as the language of the Mughal empire and promoted under the emperor Akbar. According to Muzaffar Alam,

> Persian poetry, which had integrated many things from pre-Islamic Persia and had been an important vehicle of liberalism in the medieval Muslim world, helped in no insignificant way in creating and supporting the Mughal attempt to accommodate diverse religious traditions.[9]

There are thus no grounds within the *Divan-i Goya* itself to see it as the product of a pious Sikh rather than that of a Muslim or Hindu for that matter.[10] There is, we will see, no contemporary late seventeenth- or early eighteenth-century evidence to attribute the poems of the *Divan* to Nand

Lal. In the eighteenth- and nineteenth-century Sikh *rahit-nama* literature, for example, a literature which makes a habit of buttressing its claims with passages from the Adi Granth, Dasam Granth, and the works of Bhai Gurdas, there is to the best of my knowledge never a reference to the Persian poetry of Nand Lal nor does the name Nand Lal (who also authored three Punjabi rahit-namas according to tradition) ever appear with his famous sobriquet Goya.[11] Nor do we find references to the Persian poetry of Nand Lal in Sainapati's *Sri Gur-Sobha*, one of the earliest examples of the literature of the *gur-bilas* genre or in the mid eighteenth century *Bansavali-nama* of Kesar Singh Chhibbar.[12] What are we to make of this state of affairs, of these profound silences in Sikh history and literature as opposed to tradition in regard to Nand Lal Goya? The following paper is thus an attempt to come to terms with the historical Nand Lal and the Persian poetry which is attributed to his hand, especially the *Divan-i Goya*, and offer some tentative answers to (as well as some more questions accentuating) this dilemma. Let us start off with the standard Sikh narrative of Bhai Nand Lal Goya.

General Sikh tradition begins its account of Nand Lal with his birth in 1633 to Chhajju Mall, a Hindu Khatri well learned in Persian and stationed in Ghazna in the employ of the Mughal state. Although tradition is confused about the place of Nand Lal's birth[13] it is sure that it was here in Ghazna that Goya was raised and educated by his father according to the exacting Islamic standards of his day.[14] With the death of Chhajju Mall in 1652 Nand Lal made his way south into India, eventually occupying the post of scribe or *munshi* under one Nawab Wassaf Khan in the Court of Multan. Through diligence and hard work, tradition maintains, Nand Lal was elevated to the position of chief scribe or *mir* munshi. This would not be the last of his promotions. Recognized for both his literary talent and military acumen the Bhai ji secured a station in Delhi on the staff of the future Mughal emperor Bahadur Shah, Prince Mu'azzam.[15]

Sometime in the 1680s Nand Lal left the service of the prince for reasons as yet unknown. Various Sikh traditions maintain that Nand Lal's extraordinary skill at Quranic exegesis had reached the very ears of the emperor Aurangzeb who claimed that anyone who could so accurately convey the meaning of the scripture's *ayats* must certainly become a Muslim.[16] Nand Lal thus left the Mughal court and journeyed to Anandpur to escape conversion to Islam.[17] In Anandpur he became a beloved disciple and leading poet in the court of Guru Gobind Singh here preparing the Punjabi and Persian literary works for which he is known.[18]

Composing prose and poetry was not the sole reason for which Nand Lal was famed, however, for while with the Guru he served the Panth faithfully in the *langar* (communal kitchen) under his charge. Tradition claims that one day when Guru Gobind Singh had toured the various langars throughout Anandpur incognito he had found only Nand Lal's to be in perfect order and to give food to all regardless of their caste or the time they arrived at the kitchen.[19] After the evacuation of the city and fort of Anandpur in 1705 Nand Lal retired to Multan where he established a school of Arabic and Persian.[20] It is possible, however, that Nand Lal may have rejoined the court of Prince Mu'azzam sometime after the evacuation (perhaps after the death of Aurangzeb on 3 March 1707/1118) as he is claimed to have been present at the then emperor Bahadur Shah's court in southern India in 1708 just before the death of the tenth Guru.[21] Apparently, claims Ganda Singh, Nand Lal may have then returned from the Deccan with the emperor in 1710 in the latter's attempt to deal with Banda Bahadar. Tradition continues that sometime after or before the death of Bahadur Shah in 1712 Nand Lal left once again for Multan where he 'became a heaven-dweller' (*surgavas hoe*) soon after his arrival.[22]

II

Questions: *Prashan*

General Sikh knowledge regarding Nand Lal and his poetry is at best rudimentary. This may be because the best of the poetry attributed to Nand Lal Goya is in Persian, a language with which very few Sikhs of the eighteenth and nineteenth centuries were familiar. This ignorance continues today as an acquaintance with the Persian language remains the sole prerogative of a very small group of educated (and Iranian) Sikhs.

It is true, however, that since the 1950s knowledge of our poet has been enhanced by the brief references to Nand Lal and his poetry in the *Sikh Rahit Maryada*, the normative Khalsa Sikh code of conduct. The first of two allusions appears under the section headed *kirtan*, the congregational singing of hymns:

Within the community of the faithful only the utterances of the Gurus(*gur-bani*) or the commentaries(*viakhia-sarup*) upon those utterances, [that is] the *bani* of[both] Bhai Gurdas ji and Bhai Nand Lal ji, may be sung as kirtan.[23]

This enrichment though is exceedingly minor and tells us nothing of Nand Lal's life, apart from the belief that he composed commentaries on the Adi Granth, the sacred Sikh scripture which contains Gur-bani. Whether such poetry was written purposefully as commentary and *bani* or if it was understood as such in the time of Nand Lal or immediately afterwards is not mentioned, however.

The reference to Nand Lal's commentaries in the *Sikh Rahit Maryada*, moreover, is unclear since it does not actually specify which of Nand Lal's poetry is considered bani. As the Punjabi works for which Nand Lal is known such as the *Tanakhah-nama* (Manual of Penances), the *Prashan-uttar* (Question and Answer), and the *Sakhi rahit ki* are written in a language that can be best described as pedestrian, it is probably more to the Persian compositions that the *Sikh Rahit Maryada* alludes.[24] This should be the case since these works, especially the *Divan-i Goya*, easily the best of the lot in terms of poetic artistry, are certainly the products of a highly skilled Persian poet and rank well with the output of other traditional Indo-Persian poets of Nand Lal's time. Most scholars of Sikhism tend to agree as to which texts deserve this status. W.H. McLeod ultimately withholds judgement but seems to acknowledge the Persian texts as bani. Piara Singh Padam is convinced that only the Persian poetry merits the status.[25] Kahn Singh Nabha is less clear. Section 7 of his *Gurmat Sudhakar* for example is titled '*Bhai Nand Lal ji di bani*' and includes only Persian compositions while section 8 has no title and includes the Punjabi writings often attributed to Nand Lal.[26] In his posthumous *Gurumat Maratand*, moreover, Kahn Singh claims that one of the works which enunciates the Rahit of the tenth Guru is *Bhai Nand Lal ji di bani*.[27] *Gurmat Sudhakar* thus implies that the Punjabi rahit-namas attributed to Nand Lal are not bani while *Gurumat Maratand* suggest that they are so considered. Such conclusions are quite helpful in that they lead us into a fresh direction in terms of Nand Lal and his poetry: that is, understanding Nand Lal's Persian works as bani ultimately tells us much more about the attitudes of men such as Kahn Singh of Nabha and his contemporaries, Vir Singh, and Teja Singh, all of whom were major Sikh ideologues of the Singh Sabha project fundamental in authoring today's *Sikh Rahit Maryada* and earlier rahit texts, than it does about Nand Lal. This is a point to which we shall eventually return.

For now, however, it will be principally upon these Persian texts, especially the *Divan*, that I shall focus. The reasons for this are not at all difficult to fathom. For one, while the authorship of the Punjabi/Braj texts attributed to Nand Lal is clearly in dispute the authorship of the Persian texts has never been seriously questioned (at least in print). The inquiry into the Punjabi texts, moreover, is based on the assumption that the Nand Lal Goya of Sikh tradition authored the Persian texts attributed to him. As W.H. McLeod has often noted it seems unlikely that the doggerel Punjabi in which the *Tanakhah-nama* and the other rahit-namas attributed to Goya are written could be the product of a Persian poet as highly skilled as Nand Lal is said to have been.[28]

This conclusion is debatable but may nevertheless be buttressed from another angle as there is to my mind a major concern with the claims in the Nand Lal rahit-namas. The exceedingly hostile attitude towards Muslims we discover in both the earliest extant manuscript of the *Tanakhah-nama* (MS 770 at GNDU dated *S.* 1775 or 1718–19 CE), and its later recensions is well understood in the light of the early eighteenth century history of the Khalsa.[29] According to this manuscript:

A Khalsa [is a Sikh] who smites [all] Muslims (*khanu*).[30]

and

A Khalsa [is a Sikh] who slays Turks.[31]

But it seems highly implausible that this hostility could belong to the author of the *Divan* with his clear affection, at times reverence, for Sufi ideas and attitudes.[32] This marked difference of opinion could simply not be the product of a single author. Recent Sikh scholarship suggests that there were actually two men named Nand Lal, one the author of the Punjabi texts, the other the author of the Persian ones.[33] This is certainly a possibility in light of the fact that in seventeenth- and eighteenth-century northern India the name Nand Lal was most likely a common one and may have led to some confusion among Sikh interpreters of the late nineteenth and early twentieth centuries.

But possibilities are not certainties. Until we have a less opaque historical picture of our poet, the only conclusion we can come to in the light of the above questioning is that there are few personalities in the late seventeenth- and early eighteenth-century history of the Sikhs who are as inscrutable as Nand Lal Goya.

III

Nand Lal in Sikh Tradition and Literature

Let us begin by stating categorically that there was indeed a Nand Lal in the court of Guru Gobind Singh. The evidence for this is clear. In MS 770 of 1718–19 the name appears six times.[34] Since for reasons noted above Nand Lal Goya cannot be the author of the copy of the *Tanakhah-nama* on which the scribe of MS 770 based his text we must conclude that the name Nand Lal is mentioned to impart authenticity to this work by associating it with a well-known disciple of the tenth Guru. Which Nand Lal this was, however, is a question that merits some consideration. Indeed, MS 770 seems to refer to a Nand Lal who composes only in Punjabi. It is later tradition which makes us equate this Nand Lal with the Goya of our Persian texts. Let us thus pause for a moment and search out other Nand Lals noted in Sikh tradition one of whom may be responsible for the Punjabi rahit-namas credited to Nand Lal Goya.

Tradition presents us with a number of seventeenth century Nand Lals. Most of these men were somehow associated with the courts of either the ninth or the tenth Guru and thus deserve some scrutiny. In Kahn Singh Nabha's extraordinary *Gurshabad Ratanakar Mahan Kosh* for example we are introduced to at least four Sikh Nand Lals: Nand Lal Goya; Nand Lal 'Sohana', who was initially a *chela* of two of Guru Hargobind's Muslim disciples, Khwaja and Jani;[35] Mihan, or Mihansahib the famous Udasi Sikh who was nicknamed 'Mihan' or 'Rain-bringer' by the ninth Guru after his habit of sprinkling water on the ground on which the *sangat* (congregation) would sit (Bhai Mihan was the son of Nand Lal Sohana); and, finally, a brahman, the brother of Pandit Pindi Lal, who became a Sikh in the time of Guru Gobind Singh.[36]

As Nand Lal Sohana died, according to tradition, in S. 1732 or 1675 CE and is first mentioned almost 175 years after his death in Santokh Singh's *Gur-pratap Suraj Granth* (1843), he can be excluded. It is plausible though highly unlikely that a rahit-nama of the sort attributed to Nand Lal Goya could have been written before the guruship of Guru Gobind Singh. So too may we excuse Mihansahib who, it appears, was included in Kahn Singh's list solely because of his father (Kahn Singh's entry suggests that the name Nand Lal would have been appended to his name by virtue of his descent).

The brahman Nand Lal may probably be excused as well but not as hastily for it is possible that he could have prepared the Punjabi texts attributed to Nand Lal. According to Piara Singh Padam this Nand Lal, along with his elder brother Pindi Lal, was a member of the tenth Guru's literary court. And although Padam is quite clear that this Nand Lal should be distinguished from the famous Persian poet who shares his name,[37] he only provides a very short specimen of the brahman's poetry without mentioning just which works the brahman Nand Lal is alleged to have produced.[38] Until clear evidence comes to light therefore we must suspend our judgement about the latter's authorship of the Nand-Lal Punjabi rahit-namas.[39] One feature of the Nand Lal rahit-namas which may work against brahman authorship, it should be noted, is that the rahit-namas of Nand Lal have no injunctions privileging brahman Sikhs such as those we find in the rahit-nama of Chaupa Singh Chhibbar.[40] What we discover in MS 770, in fact, are statements disparaging both brahmans and their rituals.[41]

There is one Nand Lal, however, who cannot be so readily dismissed. This Nand Lal appears in two of the *hukam-namas* which were sent to the sangat of Patna by Guru Tegh Bahadar in, we may only assume, the late 1660s or early 1670s after he had passed through this area.[42] Here we have perhaps the most intriguing of our Nand Lals as we can tentatively place him in Patna during the childhood years of the tenth Guru who was born in Patna in 1666 and remained there until early 1672 when he and his mother moved to Lakhnaur near Ambala.[43] It may well be that the young, future Guru was perhaps acquainted with this Nand Lal. Although his name is not listed amongst the more prominent Sikhs of this sangat such as Bhai Dayal Das and Bhai Ram Rai it is nevertheless mentioned. That he was thus included by the ninth Guru with other important members of the Patna sangat may well indicate the esteem in which he was held. There is a possibility that he could have become the 'other' Nand Lal to which recent Sikh scholarship points.

Why so much time has been spent narrowing the field of Nand Lals down is because outside of Sikh tradition mention of Nand Lal is exceptionally rare. Even in Multan where Nand Lal is claimed to have worked, reference to him is virtually non-existent. According to tradition Nand Lal left Ghazna and attached himself to a caravan bound for Multan. Multan was an obvious destination for a career-minded scholar as it had already become a very important commercial and cultural hub between the Mughal empire and the Uzbek and Safavid empires, an importance that is clearly implied in the number of princes who had been bestowed with the governorship of the province.[44] The need for scribes would have thus been paramount and this would undoubtedly have made Multan especially enticing. As well, Sikh tradition claims Multan as the ancestral home of the family of Chhajju Mall. But by coincidence Dara Shikoh had replaced his younger brother Aurangzeb as the governor of Multan in the same year as Chhajju Mall's death in 1652. And although Dara was an absentee governor during his tenure in Multan, his influence in securing a position for the son of one of his scribes is certainly plausible and, also, would add weight to Nand Lal's choice of Multan as an area for potential employment.[45] Sikh tradition names one Wassaf Khan as the governor of Multan during Nand Lal's stay there but my efforts to unearth this figure (or any of his aliases) have thus far proved unsuccessful.[46]

In Multan, Nand Lal compiled an *insha*. In Arabic *insha* literally means 'construction' or 'creation'. The term is used for a collection or compilation of stylised form-letters and correspondence which was, according to Jan Rypka, 'grist to the Indian mill ... for it offered opportunity for extravagance of expression in the most brilliant form, both in word and thought.'[47] As is well known, in India these *insha* were often the prerogative of those Hindu castes which, in Mughal times, had extensively mastered Persian and Arabic such as the Kayasthas and the Khatris.[48] It is to the latter that Nand Lal belonged according to tradition. Nand Lal's insha was titled the *Dastur-ul Insha* or 'Guide to letter-writing'. Although Lala Parmanand Arora claims that this text is 'a valuable treasury of the history of Multan and the Punjab' a glance at its contents should certainly qualify such a conclusion.[49]

What Arora fails to note is that the choice of letters to be included within an *insha* was based far more on style, expression, and even penmanship than on the particular events narrated within. These letters, in other words, are not without importance in terms of biographical or historical data, but 'their factual contents stand in inverse ratio to their verbosity.'[50] The advice to read these texts guardedly is further emphasized in recent studies on *insha* literature in India. These have made clear that scribes and clerks sometimes fabricated letters to dignitaries and members of the Mughal royal family and others to serve as stylistic examples. In fact, Zahur-ud Din Ahmad has determined that such was done by the great Abu'l-Fazl himself.[51] The amount of information we can extract is therefore limited.

Fortunately, limited data is far better than none at all. If the *Dastur-ul Insha* is indeed authentic, a question which has yet to be answered satisfactorily,[52] then some interesting information about Nand Lal may be extracted from its signature line, portions of which may be used to both corroborate and contest the claims of Sikh tradition:

The book *Dastur-ul Insha* is here completed. The compilation was done by me, Munshi Nand Lal Goya Multani.[53]

This passage, like the other final signature lines of the various Persian texts attributed to Nand Lal,[54] corroborates claims since it proves that there was certainly a munshi in Multan named Nand Lal. Internal evidence also supports this contention. This may seem a moot point from the perspective of Sikh tradition. But by no means should this be the case. A careful scrutiny of Multani records during the period of Nand Lal's supposed employment (*circa* 1650s to 1680s or 1690s in some accounts) fails to reveal the name of our poet. We certainly hear of other non-Muslim munshis, the most prominent of whom was Munshi Lal Chand Multani (also known as Malik Zadah) author of the *Nigar-namah*.[55] It was Malik Zadah, according to imperial records, who was the munshi of Prince Mu'azzam.[56] But the search for a Munshi Nand Lal in the accounts of Multan has been thus far a fruitless endeavour and so the significance of the closing statement of the *Dastur-ul Insha* and those of the other Persian Nand Lal texts which definitely place Nand Lal in Multan at one point in his career.

These lines also contest claims since it seems clear that Nand Lal had taken the pen-name Goya before he had allegedly met with the tenth Guru in the 1680s. These suggest that at least some of the poetry which, tradition claims, Nand Lal wrote under the name Goya, principally the ghazals we find in the *Divan-i Goya*,[57] was written before he met Guru Gobind Singh and perhaps before Nand Lal's intimate acquaintance with the Sikh religion.[58] This in turn suggests that the 'Sikh meaning' which is often extracted from at least some of the ghazals by Sikh interpreters may be a strained one as many of these odes were probably written before Nand Lal had taken *charan-amrit* (foot-wash) from the tenth Sikh Master as the tradition claims he did.[59]

Yet the importance of the final passages in the majority of the Persian Nand Lal texts has not yet been exhausted. It is certainly worth noting that in regard to the historical Nand Lal these are the only passages in both the Persian and Punjabi literature attributed to the tenth Guru's poet which make it beyond doubt that the name Nand Lal is appended with the *takhallus* Goya. As we know, the very nature of the *Divan* as Persian mystical poetry makes extracting historical and biographical data a very dubious enterprise.[60] Leaving a historical record for the benefit of posterity was usually not what these poets had in mind. Their concerns were far more often spiritual or poetical not historical.[61] In regard to the name Nand Lal Goya, for example, we note that although the pen-name Goya appears in the final line of almost every single ghazal of the *Divan*, the word *nand* (a diminutive of the Sanskrit *ananda* or 'bliss') is never seen. This is just as well since it is extremely rare to find ghazal poets placing their entire name so transparently within their poetry. After all where is the poetic skill in such a blatant inclusion? Inserting one's name in a more subtle and rhetorically playful way demonstrated a greater command of the Persian language and its theory of tropes and figures. For this reason perhaps, Persian terms equivalent to *anand* such as *khush* or *shadi* which do appear throughout the *Divan* may be allusions to the name Nand Lal.[62]

The term *la'l* does appear, however, and whenever it does so interpreters of the *Divan* take it for granted that this is an allusion to the poet's name, Nand Lal. This last word play is by all means possible but it is worth noting that the term *la'l* is a very common word in Persian ghazal poetry generally, used as a trope for the 'ruby-red lips of the Beloved' (*mashauq*, i.e. the Divine). There is a case to be made for this nevertheless as in the *Joti Bigas*, the *Arz-ul Alfaz*, and the final portion of the *Tausif o Sana'* titled the *Khatimah* (epilogue), it is this word, *la'l*, which appears as the poet's sobriquet a fact which may add weight to the claim that the appearance of the term *la'l* in the *Divan* and elsewhere is indeed an allusion to the name Nand Lal (assuming that one author penned both works):

Let it be that the head of La'l becomes a sacrifice [placed] at the feet [of the Beloved]. Ensure [that both] the life and heart [of La'l become] secret wealth (*nawa*) on account of [the Beloved].[63]

Poets did sometimes change their pen-names but such alteration was very uncommon. It may also be, however, that the appropriation of a different pen-name suggests that there was more than one Indo-Persian Sikh poet in the eighteenth century.[64] It can also suggest that the 'Goya' works were written before the 'La'l' works since the latter are clearly Sikh whereas the former are more open to interpretation. This seems unlikely though, as there are ghazals in the *Divan* which indicate that Nand Lal used the pen-name Goya at an advanced age.

What Sikh tradition takes for granted then we as historians cannot. Connecting the name Goya to Nand Lal makes the possibility of Nand Lal's authorship of the ghazals that much stronger especially when we consider the existence of another Indo-Persian poet who chose this very same pen-name, the Kashmiri poet Kamran 'Goya'.[65] It is very tempting to see this Goya as the author of the *Divan-i Goya* since his pen-name and dates coincide remarkably with those of Nand Lal.[66] One can speculate that since the kingdom of Kashmir, the court to which Kamran Goya and his brother Juya were attached, had been absorbed by Maharaja Ranjit Singh in 1819 (one year after his annexation of Multan) it would have been a rather simple matter for pious Sikhs to mistake the poetry of Kamran Goya for that of Nand Lal, especially since Persian ghazal poetry is not particularly exclusivist and can be thus interpreted by the followers of any number of religio-cultural traditions as their own. There is, let us emphasize, less internal evidence in the *Divan* itself suggesting that Kamran Goya is the poet than there is evidence to propose Nand Lal Goya's authorship.[67]

We have, it seems, gone as far as we can in placing Nand Lal in Multan after the demise of his father. To recount, it seems highly likely based on the evidence of the *Dastur-ul Insha* and the other Persian poetry attributed to Nand Lal that our esteemed poet was a munshi in Multan and that he had appropriated the pen-name Goya while there. Evidence for Sikh tradition's account of Nand Lal's life after Multan, however, is on less stable ground. As we noted earlier, tradition maintains that while in Multan, Nand Lal eventually came into the employ of the crown prince, Mu'azzam, and in due course secured the post of mir munshi. It has already been implied that this appointment is unlikely since imperial records claim that Malik Zadah of Multan was the Prince's chief scribe.[68] Unfortunately, moreover, as in every case we have examined thus far, Nand Lal's name also fails to appear in the various chronicles recounting both the activities of Prince Mu'azzam and his later incarnation as Bahadur Shah (of which there are many).[69] It seems, therefore, that the reference to Nand Lal in the Persian *Amar-namah* of Dhadhi Nath Mall,[70] the only source, Sikh or otherwise, implying that Nand Lal had rejoined the Prince's retinue after the tenth Guru's evacuation of Anandpur in 1705 cannot be substantitated by the many Mughal records of the period and immediately afterward which we have at our disposal.

IV

Answers: *Uttar*

While placing Nand Lal in the court of the emperor Bahadur Shah has been unsuccessful we do know that there was certainly one Nand Lal and perhaps more at the court of Guru Gobind Singh in Anandpur sometime in the late eighteenth century. It seems that early to late eighteenth century Sikh sources probably refer to the celebrated Nand Lal in an attempt to ensure that their own works would be understood as authentic. These very same sources, however, make no references to Nand Lal's Persian works. This failure is particularly noticeable in eighteenth century Sikh rahit literature such as the rahit-nama of Chaupa Singh Chhibbar, a text which like all rahit-namas often supported its injunctions with various quotations from the Adi Granth and other Sikh literature considered sacred in that period to impart to these enjoinders a scriptural legitimacy.[71]

There may be a reason for this deficiency, however, which goes beyond the fact that the authors of the rahit-namas simply did not know Persian. This was that Persian was specifically considered a language of Islam. Given the context of Khalsa–Muslim relations in the eighteenth century, such Persian Sikh texts would have become something of an embarrassment after both the declaration to have Sikhs executed in 1710 and the execution of Banda Bahadur in 1716.[72] Though we cannot make this claim with absolute certainty we do know that by the later eighteenth century and well into the nineteenth, Khalsa Sikh literature contains an overtly hostile attitude towards both Islam and the languages in which its tenets were traditionally conveyed, most notably Persian. Within the confusing late eighteenth- or early nineteenth-century rahit-nama attributed to Daya Singh, for example, the following statement appears:

If a Sikh reads Persian I am not his [Master] and he is no [Sikh] of mine. Do not drink water from this Sikh's hand. Do not trust anyone who reads Persian.[73]

A near-contemporary text, the *Sau Sakhian* of 1834, contains similar disdain for those Sikhs and others who know Persian.

I will give nothing to the Sikh who commits adultery or learns Persian. I will take nothing from this person. Never drink water [from the hands of this Sikh]. Never accept anything from the house of the person who reads Persian. Trust him at no time. Do not touch his food [as it is polluted] since he has strayed from the path of *dharam*.[74]

This attitude towards Persian was one which probably developed much earlier than the late eighteenth and early nineteenth centuries. This can be based on the enmity between Khalsa Sikhs and Muslims after 1710, and also on the fact that these statements were penned during the reign of Maharaja Ranjit Singh whose empire conducted a good deal of its official business in Persian.[75]

We may now turn to the question asked at the beginning of this paper: why would a Sikh poet like Nand Lal write in Persian, a language which not only had no prior importance in the communication of Sikh thought and theology but which was recognized as the language of Islam? Perhaps the most straightforward answer lies within the realm of tradition. The appropriation of a language understood as Islamic to convey Sikh thought would be another attempt to underscore the universal nature of the Sikh tradition, a tradition which could be conveyed in any language and encompass any people, even those later considered the oppressors of the Khalsa. Is this 'universalist' explanation not the reason for the inclusion in the Adi Granth of the *bhagat bani*, the hymns and sayings attributed to non-Sikh saints such as Shaikh Farid Shakar-ganj and Bhagat Kabir? This is certainly a possibility though, I believe, an unlikely one as the 'universalist' explanation is one more situated in modern Orientalist understandings of the Sikh tradition. There are other such possibilities, however, and these like the answer above are tentative, verging more on the side of speculation. Since the testimony of the putative Sikh author of the *Divan-i Goya* does not exist, speculation it seems, is our best option.

It is well known that before the second decade of the eighteenth century had come to a close, Sikh enmity towards Islam was acute. This was especially so in the light of the execution of the tenth Guru's younger sons and the incursions and eventual 'martyrdom' in 1716 of Banda Bahadur. One answer we may thus provide is that Nand Lal, cognizant of the Muslim hostility towards Sikhs, was perhaps attempting to soften the Muslim attitude towards his co-religionists. If the *Divan* and *Zindagi-namah* are Sikh works they present a Sikhism very much commensurate with the values and ideals of mystical Islam. Could Nand Lal then have been attempting to legitimate Sikh theology in the eyes of an Islamic audience, adopting a language and style with which every educated Muslim gentleman and mystic of his period would be familiar?[76] Nand Lal's life as a munshi in the court of Multan and later as perhaps a minor secretary to Prince Mu'azzam ensured that he came into contact with numerous Islamic legal and religious personnel, with pious

Muslims, in other words, some of whom with, we may assume, he would have engaged in discussion and debate and perhaps formed lasting friendships. This line of speculation could possibly explain why Nand Lal's poetry is so conspicuously non-martial in the period of the Khalsa's gradual ascendancy.

This last feature of the poetry may have to do with the Muslim attitude towards the Sikhs and their understanding of what constituted the Sikh community. In the early eighteenth century the Mughal administration took a relatively hard stand towards what they perceived as martial Khalsa Sikhs. With this in mind it may be that few of the educated Muslims of the period with whom Nand Lal was familiar would have wished to understand their spiritual tradition. Relationships with those who espoused the tenets of Guru Nanak, however, would have probably been a different matter altogether. It seems that Muslims generally and the Mughals specifically had little trouble accepting Nanak-panthis despite the wording of the imperial decrees of 1710 and 1712 to slaughter the *nanak-parastan*, the disciples of Guru Nanak. Indeed, educated Muslims seem to have thought highly of Guru Nanak and his followers as evidenced by the *Ibrat Maqal* of Sayyid Muhammad Qasim of Lahore.[77] It could thus be for this reason that Nand Lal's poetry emphasizes those features of Sikhism which correspond to the values found in the Adi Granth rather than those of the more martial portions of the Dasam Granth.

Yet the other possibility which an 'Islamic introduction' to Sikhism supports is the offer of an alternative religious tradition to his Persian-knowing audience, most of whom would have been Muslim. In other words the idea that Nand Lal was, in effect, attempting to convert Muslims to Sikhism.[78] Tradition supports such contentions maintaining that Nand Lal persuaded a number of Muslims to become Sikhs in the early eighteenth century. Nand Lal's poetry, moreover, can also be interpreted in this light. The following ghazal for example appears as number 27 in various editions of the *Divan-i Goya*:

Along the [true] path thousands of jewel-encrusted thrones have fallen by the wayside. Your wandering mystics (*qalandaran*) do not desire crowns (*taj*) or signet rings.

Everything in this world is transitory (*fana*) except for lovers who are aware of the secrets of love.

Everything is capable of becoming a [pure-seeing] eye which constantly looks for Him. Thousands of bosoms wither in the passion of separation.

[True seekers] give all the world's wealth in exchange for a glimpse [of the Beloved]. Know for certain that these people, his beggars, are the kings of kings.

O Goya! Always seek the company of men who know the truth (*mardan-i haqq*) because the seekers of <u>khuda</u> are united to Allah.[79]

The first bait here seems straightforward in its claim that true mystics (*qalandaran*) have no need for the trappings of worldly power. Yet when we consider that the crown or *taj* is also a term for a Sufi's cap we receive the distinct impression that Nand Lal is deriding the common Sufi garb and thus by extension Sufism and Islam generally. The third couplet too can be read in this way by employing the common poetic device of *iham* or ambiguity. This reading scorns far more than headgear:

In the world everything is capable of *fana'* except for [true] lovers who are aware of the secrets of love.

Here the Sufi idea of *fana'*, annihilation in the divine, the final stage along the mystical path seems to be decried. This particular ghazal may be thus understood as contesting Sufi claims that mystical insight is the sole prerogative of Islamic mystics, a claim we do sometimes recognize in Persian mystical poetry.[80]

Yet although the general tone of Nand Lal's work may possibly be understood as a cumulative criticism of both Islamic and Sufi ideas, conventions, and symbols, this is still a far cry from a desire to convert Muslims to Sikhism.[81] Nand Lal is here most probably following the time-honoured conventions of Islamic mystical poetry as even Sufi poets themselves, thoroughly grounded in the tenets of Islam and understanding themselves as intimately pious Muslims, often disparaged features of Islamic orthodoxy such as the Hajj and the prayer carpet, and the mullah and the qazi in their quest for the Beloved, privileging in their place the wine-tavern and the idol (features considered *haram* or forbidden in legalist Islam).[82] The problem of assigning a conversion mandate to Nand Lal (and to all the Sikh Gurus for that matter), moreover, is certainly compounded by the fact that religious boundaries were particularly flexible and fluid in the early eighteenth century and that religious conversion as a category has its origins not in late seventeenth century northern India but rather in the epistemologies generated by the European Enlightenment.[83]

The final explanation we can offer for our poet's use of Persian is perhaps the most mercenary: Nand Lal wrote a Persian *Divan* and various Persian masnavis in a Sikh court to demonstrate his versatility with the two traditionally Islamic genres. Such literary displays were quite common. Since at least the time of Amir Khusrau in the thirteenth century, Indo-Muslim poets in northern India wrote ghazals and masnavis in Persian, and later Urdu, to make evident their skill at manipulating the poetic principles of these genres.[84] Sikh tradition certainly implies as much for Nand Lal who is said to have excelled in his conventionally Islamic education in mid seventeenth century Ghazna (a point to which, as we have seen over and over again, Nand Lal's *Divan* as well as his other Persian works readily testify). Recent examinations make it seem very likely that the Persian *Zafar-namah* attributed to Guru Gobind Singh, despite its rather controversial position in modern-day Sikh discourse and tradition's tenuous claim that it had actually reached the emperor Aurangzeb, was composed as just such an exercise.[85]

V

Concluding Remarks

We are, I am afraid, not much better off than we were at the beginning of this paper. All we have offered throughout is speculation in the attempt to come to terms, both historically and literally, with this most enigmatic poet. It is comforting in a way that the history of Nand Lal Goya is as veiled as the deeper meanings of his ghazals, as it forces us to dig to ever deeper depths to uncover what on the surface are his long-departed traces. In other words, this paper is certainly not the last word on the historical Bhai Nand Lal Goya and his Persian poetry.

We may fortunately pick up the debate two centuries after our poet's demise. We mentioned some time ago that the inclusion of Nand Lal's Persian poetry in the Sikh canon would ultimately tell us more about the scholars of the Singh Sabha who likely saw something of their own understandings of Sikhism in the words of Persian mystical poetry. Let us now make good on that claim. These men to be sure were highly educated and it seems very likely that Persian couplets would have formed a part of their upbringing as well-rounded late nineteenth- and early twentieth-century gentlemen and scholars.[86] The privileging of Nand Lal's poetry may have thus been an attempt to further secure for the Sikh literary tradition and thus for Sikhism, generally a footing clearly equal to that of mystical Islam, a tradition which was somewhat admired in Europe thanks to the early nineteenth century European fascination with the Persian masnavis and ghazals of Hafez and Rumi.[87] This would in a way complement the work of M.A. Macauliffe whose six-volume *The Sikh Religion: Its Gurus, Sacred Writings, and Authors* of 1909 was indeed designed to introduce Sikhism to the West, presenting it as a tradition as worthy of study and respect as mystical Islam.[88] We may also note, however, that the inclusion of Nand Lal's Persian poetry in the canon may have also been an attempt to demonstrate the universality of the Sikh tradition as these men saw it.

Yet the opposite may also be true: that the inclusion of Nand Lal's poetry was actually an exercise in further distancing. Let us recognize this development in the light of the fierce politicization of language in the Punjab of the early twentieth century that saw all three Punjabi communities attempt to safeguard and promote what they understood as their language and thus their own unique contributions to Punjabi identity and culture.[89] Certainly the language which educated Sikhs promoted was Punjabi in the Gurmukhi script. Not only was this the language and script of the Adi Granth but the script was formulated, according to tradition, by the second Sikh Guru, Guru Angad. As such its sanctity and its identification as the premiere Sikh language was assured. The Persian language, however, was also a part of the Sikh history and literary heritage these men were attempting to reconstruct.

Ironically Persian was the language associated with the oppressors of the Khalsa in the early- to mid-eighteenth century. This much we have made clear. Since the rise of Sikh power in the later eighteenth, however, this attitude began to soften. The adoption of this language by the court of Maharaja Ranjit Singh and the devaluation of Persian as the language of politics and bureaucracy after the annexation of the Punjab in 1849 probably relegated Persian to the status of the language of the learned.[90]

On the one hand, therefore, the existence of Sikh Persian texts would have ensured that Sikhs and Sikh identity were kept separate from what the Singh Sabha considered to be the overwhelming tide of Hinduism. Educated Hindus of the period, especially those of the Arya Samaj, championed Hindi in the Devanagiri script as the official language of the Punjab and ultimately of Indian nationality. On the other hand Persian, though considered a language of Islam, was not the Islamic *lingua franca* of contemporary Punjabi Muslims. This position had been eclipsed a century earlier by Urdu the language which educated Muslims privileged in early twentieth century Punjab. Persian would have thus been an odd non-Sikh vehicle to promote Sikh interests given that it shared its script with Urdu, but in the changed political circumstances of the early to mid 1900s in which Khalsa Sikhs of the Singh Sabha painted the Hindu tradition as its principal foe, it may have been able to simultaneously demonstrate Sikh difference from the Hindus of their day and as well the more obvious separation of Sikhs from Punjabi Muslims.[91] The appropriation of Persian Sikh materials such as the *Divan-i Goya* and the *Zafar-namah* attributed to Guru Gobind Singh, we must note, may have also been a way to underscore the royal heritage of the Sikhs as Persian still possessed an aura of prestige as the language of the court of Akbar and the language of high culture. In a way therefore, Sikhs of the Singh Sabha may have unintentionally demonstrated a closer affinity with Islam by the inclusion into the sacred canon of Nand Lal's Persian poetry in order to more loudly declare *ham hindu nahin*, 'We are not Hindus'.[92]

Notes

Acknowledgements: I would like to express my gratitude to Christine Fenech, Hew McLeod, Pashaura Singh, and Maria Subtelny who offered help and encouragement on various parts of this paper.

1. B.P.L. Bedi (trans.), The Pilgrim's Way: Diwan of Bhai Nand Lal Goya Poet Laureate at the August Court of Guru Gobind Singh Maharaj (2nd edn, Patiala: Publication Bureau Punjabi Univ., 1999), p. xi.

2. Gurbachan Singh Talib, 'Nand Lal Bhai' in Harbans Singh (ed.), *Encyclopaedia of Sikhism* II (Patiala: Punjabi Univ. Press, 1997), pp. 195–6.

3. The *janam-sakhis* often insert hymns with Persian content in stories dealing with Baba Nanak's discussions with Muslims. Piar Singh, *B40 Janam-sakhi Sri Guru Nanak Dev ji* (Amritsar: Guru Nanak Dev Univ., 1989), pp. 48–9. An analysis of Persian terms in the Adi Granth appears as Christopher Shackle, 'Approaches to the Persian loans in the Adi Granth', in the *Bulletin of the School of Oriental and African Studies* 4:1 (1978), pp. 73–96.

4. There is also the Persian *Zafar-namah* attributed to Guru Gobind Singh.

5. This is an argument I put forth in my 'Persian Sikh Scripture: The Ghazals of Bhai Nand Lal Goya' in the *International Journal of Panjab Studies* I:1 (1994), pp. 49–70. Since its publication I have modified my views.

6. Sikh tradition sometimes claims that individual couplets were produced in response to actual situations.

7. *Arz-ul Alfaz baits* 127 and 132, Ganda Singh (ed.), *Kulliyat-i Bhai Nand Lal Goya* (Malaka, Malaya: Sikh Sangat, 1963), p. 213 (hereafter *Kulliyat*).

8. Masnavis are composed of more than eight couplets and follow a AA BB CC ... etc. rhyming convention while ghazals are usually under eight couplets following

a AA BA CA ... etc. scheme. The *Joti Bigas* and the *Ganj-namah* appear in *Kulliyat*, pp. 109–25; 159–69.

9. Muzaffar Alam, 'The Pursuit of Persian: Language in Mughal Politics,' in *Modern Asian Studies* 32, 2 (1998), pp. 317–49.

10. There may be one exception to this rule in what I term the 'Holi ghazal', the 33rd in the *Divan-i Goya*. *Kulliyat*, p. 62.

11. Even in the Punjabi rahit-namas attributed to Nand Lal we do not find the pen-name.

12. Ganda Singh (ed.), *Kavi Sainapati Rachit Sri Gur-sobha* (Patiala: Punjabi Univ. Press, 1988) and R.S. Jaggi (ed.), *Kesar Siôgh Chhibbar da Bansavali-nama Dasan Patshahian ka* (Chandigarh: Panjab University, 1972).

13. Ganda Singh speculates that Nand Lal was probably born somewhere near Agra if not in the city itself. Ganda Singh (ed.), *Bhai Nand Lal Granthavali* (Patiala: Punjabi Univ. Press, 1989), p. 2. (Here after *BNLG*).

14. These standards are outlined in Mohiuddin, *The Chancellery and Persian Epistolography*, pp. 40–4.

15. Details in *BNLG*, p. 5.

16. Virtually every account of Nand Lal mentions this incident.

17. This much is claimed in the controversial *Guru kian Sakhian* of Bhatt Svarup Singh Kaushish. Piara Singh Padam (ed.), *Guru k-an Sakhian krit Bhai Svarup Singh Kaushish* (2nd edn, Amritsar: Singh Bros., 1991), p. 91.

18. The apocryphal *Sau Sakhian* (c. 1830s) notes the importance of Nand Lal to Guru Gobind Singh. See sakhi 62 in Gurbachan Singh Naiar (ed.), *Guru Ratan Mal: Sau Sakhi* (3rd ed., Patiala: Punjabi Univ. Publication Bureau, 1995), p. 71.

19. Haribhajan Singh (trans.), *Sachi Priti: Ghazalan Bhai Nand Lal ji 'Goya' ate 'Ganj-nama' chon 'Salatanat-i Dahamm' Satik* (Amritsar: Singh Bros., 1989), p. 21. There is also a passage in Santokh Singh's *Gur-pratap Suraj Granth* (*ritu* 3, *ansu* 26) on which this tradition may be based as noted in Kahn Singh's *Gurmat Maratand* (4th ed., Amritsar: SGPC, 1992), p. 24, n. '+'. There may be some merit to this tradition as within the rahit-nama credited to Desa Singh there are lengthy descriptions of the langar and the method of conducting one attributed to Bhai Nand Lal. The tradition of Nand Lal's langar, however, may have arisen from just such claims. Piara Singh Padam, *Rahit-name* (5th ed., Amritsar: Bhai Chatar Singh Bhai Jivan Singh, 1991), pp. 153–5.

20. Kahn Singh claims that on his return to Multan (after the tenth Guru had gone to the Deccan) he spent all of his time preaching Sikh doctrine. Kahn Singh, *Gurmat Sudhakar* (5th ed., Patiala: Bhasha Vibhag Panjab, 1988), p. 238.

21. This information comes from the controversial *Amar-namah* attributed to Dhadhi Nath Mall. See *Kulliyat*, p. 25.

22. *BNLG*, pp. 12–13. In Kahn Singh's Nand Lal narrative, our poet leaves Anandpur in 1703 for Multan where he dies in 1705. Kahn Singh, *Gurumat Maratand*, pp. 23–4, n. '+'.

23. *Sikh Rahit Maryada* (16th ed., Amritsar: SGPC, 1983), p. 13. Also, p. 16.

24. The works attributed to Nand Lal Goya are the *Divan-i Goya* (Persian), *Zindagi-namah* (Persian), *Ganj-namah* (Persian with some Punjabi), *Joti Bigas* (Punjabi), *Joti Bigas* (Persian with Punjabi), *Tanakhah-nama* (Punjabi), the *Sakhi rahit ki* usually appended to the text of the Chaupa Singh rahit-nama (Punjabi), *Prashan-uttar* (Punjabi), *Dastur-ul Insha* (Persian), *Arz-ul Alfaz* (Persian with some Punjabi), and the *Tausif o Sana'* (Persian).

25. W.H. McLeod (ed. and trans.), *Textual Sources for the Study of Sikhism* (Manchester, UK: Manchester Univ. Press, 1984), pp. 69–70; Padam, *Darbari Ratan*, p. 70.

26. Kahn Singh, *Gurmat Sudhakar*, pp. 237–76.

27. Kahn Singh, *Gurumat Maratand* (3rd ed., Amritsar: SGPC, 1993), p. 796.

28. W.H. McLeod (ed. and trans.), *The Chaupa Singh Rahit-nama* (Dunedin: Univ. of Otago Press, 1987), p. 11. (Hereafter *CSRn*).

29. I would like to thank Hew McLeod for sharing his images of and thoughts on MS 770.

30. MS 770, f. 416b.

31. MS 770, f. 417a.

32. The Perso-Arabic edition of the *Divan* I have generally followed is in *Kulliyat*, pp. 49–73.

33. This is probably claimed in order to demonstrate that the Nand Lal of the rahit-namas did in fact take Khalsa initiation. See Haribhajan Singh, *Sachi Priti*, pp. 22–3. Other scholars do not readily accede to this point.

34. MS 770, ff. 415a, 415b (twice on each though only *lalji* appears as the second reference on 415b); 416a, 417a, 417b. There is one earlier reference we will note later.

35. *MK*, pp. 230–1; 723.

36. 'Nandlal' and 'Nandlal Bhai', in *MK*, p. 723. For Mian or Miansahib see 'Miansahib Mianshahi' in *MK*, p. 973.

37. Padam, *Darbari Ratan*, p. 217.

38. This short specimen incidentally does not compare with any of the poetry attributed to Nand Lal Goya.

39. Like Nand Lal Sohana the brahman Nand Lal is also first mentioned in Santokh Singh's *Suraj Prakash*. Padam, *Darbari Ratan*, pp. 217–18.

40. *CSRn*, pp. 36–7.

41. MS 770, f. 416b.

42. Ganda Singh (ed.), *Hukam-name: Guru Sahiban, Mata Sahiban, Banda Singh ate Khalsa ji de* (Patiala: Publication Bureau Punjabi Univ., 1985), pp. 105, 106.

43. J.S. Grewal and S.S. Bal, *Guru Gobind Singh* (Chandigarh: Dept. of History, Panjab Univ., 1967), pp. 30–7.

44. *BNLG*, p. 4. Background on Multan appears in Chetan Singh, *Region and Empire: Panjab in the Seventeenth Century* (New Delhi: Oxford Univ. Press, 1991), pp. 205–55.

45. Humaira Faiz Dasti, *Multan: A Province of the Mughal Empire (1525–1751)* (Karachi: Royal Book Company, 1998), pp. 148–156. Dara Shikoh was the governor of Multan from 1652–58 while Aurangzeb governed the province from 1648–1652.

46. For a history of viceroys and governors of Multan after Dara Shikoh see Humaira Faiz Dasti, *Multan*, pp. 148–177.

47. Rypka, *Iranian Literature*, p. 315. The best analysis of *insha* materials in India remains Momin Mohiuddin, *The Chancellery and Persian Epistolography*.

48. Aziz Ahmad, *Studies in Islamic Culture in the Indian Environment*, p. 106.

49. *BNLG*, p. 4 paraphrases: '... *multan te panjab di tarikh da ik kimati khazana hai*'.

50. Rypka, *Iranian Literature*, p. 316.

51. Zahur-ud Din Ahmad, *Abul Fazl—Ahwal o Asar* (Lahore: Punjab Univ. Press, 1975), pp. 185–97 as noted in Ishtiyaq Ahmad Zilli, 'Development of *Insha* Literature to the End of Akbar's Reign', in Muzaffar Alam et al. (ed.), *The Making of Indo-Persian Culture: Indian and French Studies* (New Delhi: Manohar, 2000), pp. 309–49.

52. *BNLG*, pp. 15–16.

53. *Kulliyat*, p. 205.

54. The majority of closing lines in the Persian texts follow the same format as the final passage of the *Dastoor-ul Insh*.

55. Malik Zadah, *Nigar-Namah-'i Munshi* (Lucknow: Newal Kishore Press, 1882). Also Muzaffar Alam, *Crisis of Empire*, p. 323.

56. Humaira Faiz Dasti, *Multan*, p. 289.

57. The pen-name Goya also appears in the *Zindagi-namah*, baits 84 and 507 for certain and perhaps in bait 401. *Kulliyat*, pp. 82, 102, 108. Also see *Ganj-namah* bait 26, *Kulliyat*, p. 111.

58. Ganda Singh claims, on the contrary, that all of Goya's writings appear to have been written 'under the influence of the teachings of the Sikh religion'. *BNLG*, p. 13. It is unclear just when Nand Lal did become acquainted with Sikhism.

59. Kahn Singh, *Gurumat Maratand*, pp. xviii, 280, 572, 594, 723, 847.

60. Sometimes a poet may reflect upon his advanced age. The 37th ghazal of the *Divan* may certainly be read in this light (*Kulliyat*, p. 64).

61. Jan Rypka, *Iranian Literature*, p. 85.

62. See ghazals 3: 2; 20: 3; 37: 1. Also 44: 1, 3. *Kulliyat*, pp. 50, 57, 64, 66.

63. *Joti Bigas* 175, *Kulliyat*, p. 169. Also *Arz-ul Alfaz*, 136, *Kulliyat*, p. 214.

64. The *Arz-ul Alfaz* and the *Joti Bigas* in which this other pen-name appears are probably Sikh works.

65. Wladamir Ivanow, *A Concise Descriptive Catalogue of the Persian Manuscripts in the Collection of the Asiatic Society of Bengal* (Calcutta: Asiatic Society of Bengal, 1924).

66. Since Kamran Goya's brother, Mirza Darab Beg 'Juya', died in 1707 it seems likely that Kamran Goya died within a decade or so of this year. Tikku, *Persian Poetry in Kashmir*, pp. 117–24.

67. There seems to be no allusion to the name Kamran (*kam-ran*, 'fortunate') in the *Divan-i Goya* while as we have seen terms such as *la'l* (ruby) which may allude to our poet do appear.

68. William Irvine in his *Later Mughals* (p. 140), however, does not speak about Malik Zadah.

69. My sources for this period are all noted in Irvine, *Later Mughals*; Muzaffar Alam, *Crisis of Empire*; and Ganda Singh, *Life of Banda Singh Bahadur* (Patiala: Punjabi Univ. Publication Bureau, 1990).

70. The 'history' of this text ensures that its evidence must be met with skepticism. See Bhagat Singh, 'Amarnama', in *The Encyclopaedia of Sikhism* I, pp. 90–1.

71. In the addendum of the rahit-nama of Chaupa Singh Chhibbar we have a reference to *kabitt* 503 of Bhai Gurdas. See *CSRn* 646, p. 131.

72. Ganda Singh, *Life of Banda Singh Bahadur*, pp. 103–24.

73. P.S. Padam (ed.), *Rahit-name*, p. 77.

74. Gurbachan Singh Naiar (ed.), *Gur Ratan Mall: Sau Sakhi*, p. 79. See also line 10, p. 76.

75. Charles Joseph Hall, 'The Maharaja's Account Books: State and Society Under the Sikhs'. PhD dissertation, University of Illinois at Urbana Champaign, 1981.

76. Some scholars speculate that in the later eighteenth and early nineteenth centuries Udasi and Nirmala Sikhs expounded Sikh principles in Sanskrit in order to foster this very same legitimacy amongst brahmanical orthodoxy. Ratan Singh Jaggi, *Gur-bani Tike: Anandaghan* (Patiala, 1970); also Nripinder Singh, *The Sikh Moral Tradition* (Delhi: Manohar, 1991), pp. 245–7.

77. S.H. Askari, 'Baba Nanak in Persian Sources', in the *Journal of Sikh Studies* II:2 (Aug., 1975), pp. 112–16.

78. I offered this explanation in my 'Persian Sikh Scripture'.

79. *Kulliyat*, p. 43.

80. Perhaps Nand Lal is following a Sikh precedent set in the hymns of Guru Nanak, who also scorned Sufi claims and practices. J.S. Grewal, *Guru Nanak in History* (Chandigarh: Panjab University Publication Bureau, 1969), pp. 62–103.

81. Fenech, 'Persian Sikh Scripture'.

82. For example Ghulam Abbas Dalal, *Ethics in Persian Poetry* (New Delhi: Abhinav, 1995).

83. I discuss these points in my 'Conversion and Sikh Tradition', in Rowena Robinson (ed.), *Conversion and Indian Religious Traditions* (New Delhi: Oxford Univ. Press, forthcoming).

84. And so the title of Carla Petievich's wonderful book *An Assembly of Rivals: Delhi, Lucknow and the Urdu Ghazal* (Delhi: Manohar, 1992).

85. Suggested in Christopher Shackle's 'The *Zafar-namah* of Guru Gobind Singh'.

86. The *baits* of famous masters were known to educated Sikhs, Muslims, and Hindus.

87. Annemarie Schimmel, *As Through a Veil*, pp. 1–10.

88. M.A. Macauliffe, *The Sikh Religion: Its Gurus, Sacred Writings, and Authors* I (Oxford: Clarendon Press, 1909), pp. v–lxxxviii.

89. Background in Paul Brass, *Language, Religion, and Politics in North India* (Cambridge: Cambridge Univ. Press, 1974).

90. V.S. Suri, 'The Importance of Persian', in J.S. Grewal and Indu Banga (ed.), *Maharaja Ranjit Singh and His Times* (Amritsar: Guru Nanak Dev Univ. Press, 1980), pp. 243–4. In the rest of India Persian was replaced by Urdu in 1837.

91. I am of course speculating here as I have yet to discover any Sikh defense of the Persian language.

92. This phrase belongs to Kahn Singh Nabha.

4

Strategies for Interpreting
the *Dasam Granth*

Robin Rinehart

The *Dasam Granth*, a lengthy and diverse collection of compositions attributed to the tenth and final human guru of Sikhism, Guru Gobind Singh (1666–1708), has a complex and controversial history. There are many disagreements about how the text may be understood, and its contents have generated a wide range of fascinating interpretations and impassioned arguments. Pronouncements about the *Dasam Granth* are found not only within the province of academia in India and the West, but in newspapers, journals, and most notably of late, internet discussion groups. The issues raised by the *Dasam Granth* are not merely arcane pedantry; they go straight to the heart of matters relating to theology, liturgy, and the life of one of Sikhism's most revered figures, Guru Gobind Singh. Controversies have swirled round the literary and religious implications of the *Dasam Granth*, and its connection to matters relating to religious identity and communal relations have made it the focus of political controversy as well. Indeed the debate about this text became so fierce in the year 2000 that the *jathedar* of the Akal Takhat, Joginder Singh Vedanti, issued a directive that Sikh scholars should not comment on the text publicly lest they be excommunicated from the faith.[1] There is some irony in the fact that Guru Gobind Singh, remembered for his role in establishing a firm boundary between Sikhism and other religious traditions through the creation of the Khalsa, should also be associated with a text held up as evidence for the lack of such boundaries in actual religious practice. Given its association with so many potentially inflammatory issues, it should come as no surprise that the range of scholarly commentary surrounding the *Dasam Granth* includes widely disparate opinions. Examination of this range of opinions itself can tell us much about the history of Sikhism, but the intense nature of the debates regarding the *Dasam Granth* may also have obscured some of the potentially more fruitful avenues of research it presents to scholars.

The controversies surrounding the *Dasam Granth* revolve primarily around two key issues: the inclusion of lengthy tales from the Hindu mythological tradition[2], and the *Charitropakhian* and the *Hikayat*, which consider, among other things, the 'wiles of women' (these two categories of compositions comprise the majority of the *Dasam Granth*). The Hindu mythological material (including accounts of the lives of Krishna, Rama, Chandi, and others) has been the source of some political controversy as groups such as the Rashtriya Swayamsevak Sangh (RSS) have sought to claim this as evidence that Sikhism is not a distinct religious tradition, but rather a part of the larger Hindu tradition. But why should there be apparently 'Hindu' material in a Sikh text, and why should a text ostensibly concerned with spiritual matters devote such detailed examination to deceit, treachery, and the seamier side of male/female relations? The primary approach that commentators on the *Dasam Granth* both from inside and outside the faith have taken is to make arguments about the authorship of the text, either by asserting that Guru Gobind Singh did indeed compose the entire *Dasam Granth* and that we must therefore understand *why* it contains the material it does, or by asserting that certain portions clearly could *not* have been the work of Guru Gobind Singh and are therefore not authentic.

Although there have been countless publications and pronouncements on the authorship of the *Dasam Granth*, there has been little consensus; rather, the same arguments are presented over and over, often without full consideration of the available evidence. In published studies of the *Dasam Granth*, the focus on authorship typically remains the defining feature of the discussion; each person who weighs in seems to do so with the hope that his or her argument will settle the matter once and for all. The assumption seems to be that if someone could establish beyond a shadow of a doubt which portions of the *Dasam Granth* are indeed Guru Gobind Singh's, the debate would cease. Indeed in the wake of the most recent debates over the *Dasam Granth*, the Shiromani Gurdwara Prabandhak Committee (SGPC) in 2000 announced plans to convene a committee which would further investigate the controversy and issue a definitive statement on the official status of the text as Sikh scripture. Yet earlier pronouncements of this kind have not resolved the controversies by any means.[3]

The problem with making an ostensibly definitive statement about the status of the *Dasam Granth* is that the existing evidence may not be sufficient to reach a conclusion on authorship which will satisfy everyone. And even if such evidence were to be found, it is quite likely that it would not necessarily follow that everyone would accept the validity of such evidence and come to an agreement. Verifiable philological and historical evidence alone will not be enough to defuse the debate, in part because the vast majority of assertions about the *Dasam Granth*, though typically couched in the rhetoric of critical textual scholarship, are at least partly theological in nature. Where verifiable philological and historical evidence is either unavailable, inconclusive, or disputed, theological assertions have been brought in to fill in the gaps, resulting in a complex range of assertions whose presuppositions are not always immediately apparent. There is not always a clear demarcation between studies informed primarily by a theological perspective and studies guided by some sort of historical and/or literary critical approach. (I am of course not arguing that it is wrong to make theological claims about the *Dasam Granth*; the problem is that assumptions which are at heart theological in nature [e.g. about the nature of Guru Gobind Singh's thinking] have been used as the basis for what are historical, not theological claims.)

The *Oxford English Dictionary* defines theology as 'the study or science which treats of God, His nature and attributes, and His relations with man and the universe.'[4] If we expand this definition somewhat, keeping in mind the limitations of the gender-specific nature of this definition, and assuming that 'god' may be conceived in different ways, we may use this term broadly as a means of identifying certain kinds of arguments about the *Dasam Granth*. That is, first of all many compositions within the *Dasam Granth* are quite clearly concerned with theological matters: the nature of God (and goddesses), the attributes of gods and goddesses, and their relations with humans and the universe, for example through the agency of *avatars*. As a result, interpreters of the text may themselves read it with particular theological principles in mind—certain parts of the text may or may not accord with their own theological perspective. For example, someone might read the text with the position that Sikhism does not endorse the notion that God manifests in the form of an avatar and as such become directly involved in human affairs, and such a reader would be likely either to reject or to make some sort of qualifying argument about compositions such as the *Chaubis Avatar*. This would in part be a *theological* argument (though of course such an argument might include historical information as well). The point is that there are certain kinds of claims about the *Dasam Granth* which are either wholly or partially theological, informed to some extent by one's faith in a particular understanding of Sikhism.

Many claims about the *Dasam Granth,* whether for or against its composition by Guru Gobind Singh, are ultimately resolved by recourse to what is essentially a theological position about what Guru Gobind Singh could or could not have composed[5] (again using a broad conception of the term 'theological' which includes an understanding of the nature of the guru and the guru's relationship to God within Sikhism). Thus the focus on determining the authorship of the text is at least partially driven by an underlying theological agenda. Explicit acknowledgement of the theological component of some positions on the *Dasam Granth*, as contrasted with those governed more by historical and/or literary critical methods might help to clarify the different aims of analyses of the *Dasam Granth* and perhaps allow the debate on the text to move forward. The distinction here between theological versus historical/literary critical approaches is intended primarily as a heuristic device; we may not always be able to draw a clear line between the two kinds of approaches, and we may be able to identify theoretical presuppositions within some historical/literary critical approaches which in effect function in the same way as theological claims; nonetheless, a greater distinction between the two types of arguments and the different forms of evidence which support them would be beneficial.

Virtually all the studies of the *Dasam Granth*, whether informed by theological concerns or not, seem to operate with the same set of assumptions. The thought process behind analyses of the *Dasam Granth* seems to be something like this: the *Dasam Granth* is in some way associated with Guru Gobind Singh. If it is indeed the composition of Guru Gobind Singh, it is therefore a text of paramount importance for the Sikh faith. The *Guru Granth Sahib* preserves the compositions of the other Sikh gurus and the *bhagats*, and it, along with the *panth*, holds the status of guru. Thus if we have a collection of the compositions of the tenth guru, then these too should be worthy of deep study and reverence. Further, since relatively uncontroversial portions of the text (e.g. the opening stanza of *Var Sri Bhagauti Ji ki*, used in the *ardas* prayer[6]) are already a central and beloved feature of daily liturgy, it is therefore important to understand the text as a whole.[7] But here problems arise for commentators, for the text as a whole is potentially problematic. While normative Sikh theology views god as *nirguna* [without qualities], vast portions of the *Dasam Granth* seem to describe god as *saguna* [with qualities], indeed as an embodied avatar. While many people are inclined to draw distinctions between matters considered appropriate in a spiritual context and matters secular, even profane, the *Dasam Granth* includes rather graphic discussions of sexuality. And so the *Dasam Granth* in its entirety presents a challenge: if some of it is indisputably in line with normative Sikh thought, then what is one to do with those portions of it which may not be? At this point the lines of thinking among commentators diverge: some look for reasons to conclude that Guru Gobind Singh could not have composed anything which does not fit in with one's own thinking about the appropriate content of a Sikh religious text, and others look for reasons that explain the presence of the controversial content.[8]

Such explanations, whether they assert Guru Gobind Singh as the author of the entire *Dasam Granth* or not, are typically based on a particular reading of Guru Gobind Singh's life and personality. For example, the extensive mythological material in the *Dasam Granth* may be explained either as the work of poets in Guru Gobind Singh's court who translated Sanskrit materials, or as the work of Guru Gobind Singh himself, who is said to have translated this material not in order to advocate worship of Hindu gods, goddesses, and avatars, but in order to inspire his followers to greater heroism in battle through the examples of gods, goddesses, and avatars slaying demons.[9] One side may argue that the stories of deceitful women and such in the *Charitropakhian* may under no circumstances be the work of Guru Gobind Singh, because to tell such tales would have been wholly out of character for him. The other side asserts that Guru Gobind Singh felt it important to consider all sides of human nature, even the less savoury, and hence related these stories for moral edification; or, it may be suggested that the reasons for the inclusion of such material may be beyond the understanding of the ordinary person.

What is interesting about these arguments—whether for or against Guru Gobind Singh as the author of the entire *Dasam Granth*—is that both sides can be bolstered by known details from Guru Gobind Singh's life. There are numerous historical references to the poets in Guru Gobind Singh's court,[10] which lend credence to the notion that these poets could have composed or translated the mythological material and the *Charitropakhian*. But there are also many references to Guru Gobind Singh's own interest in composing poetry—thereby supporting the idea that he might indeed have composed all that is found in the *Dasam Granth*. Guru Gobind Singh is of course remembered as a deeply intelligent and spiritual man, and therefore one could plausibly argue that he would not have been interested in the sort of ribald anecdotes in the *Charitropakhian*. But it is also indisputable that Guru Gobind Singh fought a number of battles against neighbouring rulers as well as the Mughals. His army drew members from diverse backgrounds, and they often lived under very difficult circumstances, far from their families and loved ones. In such a situation, perhaps the tales from the *Charitropakhian* would have been useful both for entertainment and didactic purposes.[11] On the surface, it may appear that a historical fact has confirmed a particular position, but given that historical details may be used to establish conflicting positions, there must be some other set of criteria in operation, whether acknowledged or not. Thus the biographical information available about Guru Gobind Singh alone may not be adequate to reach a definitive conclusion about the *Dasam Granth's* authorship.

In addition to assumptions about the life of Guru Gobind Singh, arguments about the *Dasam Granth* typically presuppose particular conceptions of Hinduism and Sikhism and their relation to one another. If Hinduism and Sikhism are separate, distinct religious traditions, and the mythology of the *Puranas* is considered to be definitively Hindu, then the inclusion of such mythology in a Sikh text raises difficult questions. The particular conceptions of Hinduism and Sikhism in operation in the Punjab of Guru Gobind Singh's time, however, need to be further explored and elucidated. Earlier Sikh literature (such as the compositions of Guru Nanak) makes distinctions among a number of different Hindu groups (e.g. the Naths, worshippers of the goddess, etc.), and there were various divisions within Sikhism itself based upon disputes about the succession of gurus as well as particular interpretations of Sikh teachings and practices. And of course Guru Gobind Singh's establishment of the Khalsa brought about changes in the conception of what it meant to be a Sikh (and was not by any means the only conception available of what it meant to follow the teachings of the Sikh gurus). If we are to conceive of matters relating to the *Dasam Granth* in terms of the relationship between Hinduism and Sikhism, it is essential that we clarify how those terms might actually have been used when the different parts of the *Dasam Granth* were composed, and how their use may have changed subsequently. Neither 'Hinduism' nor 'Sikhism' was a monolithic, unified tradition, and relations among different groups were likely much more complex than the conception of two separate, distinct religious traditions would imply. We must also keep in mind that there were likely people who would not necessarily have identified themselves as exclusive followers of either tradition, but may instead have participated in both 'Hindu' and 'Sikh' practices (as is still the case). There also clearly existed within Sikh tradition itself the notion that some forms of religious expression from outside the tradition were meaningful enough that they should be preserved along with the compositions of the gurus themselves (as evidenced by the inclusion of the works of the *bhagats* in the Adi Granth), a fact which in and of itself raises interesting questions about the rigidity of boundaries among seemingly distinct religious traditions.

It is equally important to recognize that conceptions of Hinduism and Sikhism are not fixed either synchronically or diachronically. It is well-established that conceptions of religious identity underwent radical changes during the colonial period in India, which brought about a sense of distinct boundaries among religious traditions where those boundaries had previously been more fluid. There nonetheless remain competing conceptions of the level of distinctness between Sikhism and Hinduism in the present day, as evidenced by the recent RSS agitation in the Punjab which sought, among other things, to publicize the so-called 'Hindu' portions of the *Dasam Granth* as evidence for Sikhism as a sub-sect of Hinduism and not a distinct religion.[12] In understanding pre-colonial texts such as the *Dasam Granth*, it is essential that we do not use post-colonial definitions of religious identity as our sole framework of interpretation. Just as details from Guru Gobind Singh's biography may be used to support a range of different opinions about the *Dasam Granth*'s authorship, so too may different aspects of the text itself be used to promote different conceptions of the relationship between Hinduism and Sikhism.

As is the case with so many studies of pre-colonial Indian literature, the questions asked about the *Dasam Granth* are grounded in assumptions about the nature of authorship, about biography and its relation to oral and literary production, and about the categories into which religious experience and expression are placed. And so despite research into the earliest manuscripts of the *Dasam Granth*, close examination of its use of language and metre, the relationship of certain compositions to Sanskrit myths, and so forth, the debate about who actually composed this material continues unresolved, and this is likely due to the fact that the unspoken terms of the debate restrict it from progressing beyond what are thus far unanswerable questions. Questions informed by such assumptions may themselves lead us away from what the text and its history might teach us about the development of Sikhism and its relationship with other religious traditions in the Punjab. Suppose, then, we were to approach the *Dasam Granth* by first assuming that given the nature of the extant manuscripts and other sources of information, there is unlikely to be a wholly satisfying answer to the authorship question.[13] Acknowledging the difficulties in making a definitive conclusion regarding the authorship of the *Dasam Granth* allows us to evaluate the text and its ongoing reception in different ways.

What other presuppositions might help us to frame a different set of questions about the *Dasam Granth*? One is to posit that the text itself has varied in content in different times and places both in terms of the specific compositions included or left out as well as variation within particular compositions, as suggested by the earliest manuscripts of the text itself.[14] Thus when we think of the *Dasam Granth*, we must keep in mind that the title itself has designated different texts at different times (and indeed the title itself has evolved, from *Bachitar Natak* to *Dasven Patshah ka Granth* to the later *Dasam Granth*). Notions about its authorship have varied throughout its history, as evidenced, for example, by the variations in use of the phrase *Sri mukhvak patshahi dasvin* (or variations thereof) which is found at the beginning of some versions of some compositions within the *Dasam Granth*, indicating that someone had concluded that the composition was the work of Guru Gobind Singh himself. Similarly, different Sikh texts offer different explanations for the origins of the different portions of the text; some, for example, state that certain portions of the *Dasam Granth* are translations of Sanskrit texts completed by poets in Guru Gobind Singh's court.[15] More recently, printed editions of the text may include only selected portions, indicating a variety of editorial decisions about which compositions are the most significant. (For example, the 1995 edition issued by the Publications Bureau of Punjabi University, Patiala omits the *Charitropakhian*. A text called the *Das Granthi*, printed regularly by the Shiromani Gurdwara Prabandhak Committee, includes *Japu*, *Sabad Patshahi Das*, *Akal Ustati*, *Bachitar Natak*, *Chandi Charitar I* and *II*, *Chandi di Var*, and *Gian Prabodh*.)

Just as particular notions of authorship have shaped the analysis of the *Dasam Granth*, unexamined notions of 'text' have also influenced interpreters' approaches. A 'text' is literally 'that which is woven' (etymologically related to 'textile'), semantically quite similar to *granth* (from the Sanskrit root *grath*), something 'bound' or 'strung together'. Both words connote a unified whole, something put together with a purpose. This notion has been cemented by the shift from transmission via handwritten manuscript to transmission via print. The greater longevity and widespread dissemination of printed texts have contributed to an understanding of a text as something which exhibits fixity and consistency. Within the Sikh tradition in particular, the careful preservation and transmission of the Adi Granth may have led to certain assumptions about any other composition deemed a *granth*. If the *Dasam Granth* (despite the changes in its title, the word granth seems always to have been attached to it) is truly a granth, something tied or woven together, this suggests that it ought to have some coherence. That this assumption is behind interpretations of the text is proven by precisely the kinds of assessments people have made—either it is a single text, the product of a single author (indeed notions of text and author are inextricably linked) and therefore its purpose can be determined, or it is not a coherent text, not the work of a single author, and only those portions which conform to a particular principle of coherence may be deemed authentic and constitutive of a true granth.[16]

Whatever conclusions on philological grounds one may reach about the *Dasam Granth*, we may also posit that there is substantive evidence to suggest that this text, including those portions of it which are problematic with respect to normative Sikhism (e.g. the Hindu mythological material) has nonetheless been important to some Sikhs in some times and places. Whatever one may conclude about the actual role of goddes or *devi* worship in the founding of the Khalsa, for example, there is a strand of Sikh historiography which presents this as part of Guru Gobind Singh's activities, and thereby places those portions of the *Dasam Granth* which mention goddesses in a different light. A number of interpreters have suggested that Anandpur's location within a region in which goddess-worship is prevalent might also have had some bearing on the nature of the text.[17] In his 1966 study of the *Dasam Granth*, Dr Rattan Singh Jaggi noted that in some parts of the former Punjab and East Patiala States Union, the *Dasam Granth* and the Adi Granth were held in equal esteem, and that at gurdwaras particularly associated with Guru Gobind Singh, *path* or recitation of portions of the *Dasam Granth* was a regular occurrence.[18]

In addition to a more nuanced understanding of the diverse religious milieu in which the compositions of the *Dasam Granth* presumably arose, it would be useful to develop further, our understanding of the political and historical context so that analyses of the text are not grounded solely in particular readings of Guru Gobind Singh's life, but also take into account the possible wider implications of his leadership. Guru Gobind Singh maintained a court at Anandpur and displayed symbols of sovereignty such as a large drum and other accoutrements of kingship. He was also the patron of a number of poets, the traditional number being fifty-two. How might Guru Gobind Singh's use of royal symbolism, including the patronage of poets, illuminate larger issues regarding the ongoing development of Sikhism's role as both a spiritual and military/political force? If indeed, most of the text was composed at Anandpur and Paonta, and if the composition of some forms of poetry was in part a symbol of one's status and power as a ruler, to what extent might have Guru Gobind Singh's complex relationships with neighbouring rulers influenced the choice of subject matter? It is also useful to consider that if indeed some of the material in the *Dasam Granth* was composed by court poets, Guru Gobind Singh's having sponsored its composition does not necessarily imply that he would have endorsed or agreed with its contents. It is possible, after all, to study other points of view without adopting them.

Perhaps the *Dasam Granth* could be read not only within the context of Sikh theology, but also within the larger framework of *Braj* literature and court poetry of the period. It is significant, after all, that the vast majority of the text is in Braj, and not the Punjabi of earlier Sikh scripture. Placing various portions of the *Dasam Granth* in the larger context of Braj poetry, and court poetry in particular, might be particularly helpful in understanding the purpose of the anecdotes told in the *Charitropakhian* and the *Hikayat*. There seems to have been a great deal of poetry composed in Braj in the Punjab region, but it has not been well-preserved and that which has survived has received little scholarly attention.[19]

Placing the *Dasam Granth* within the wider context of the literature of the period might allow us to generate new hypotheses about the reasons for the text's contents which have as yet been unanswered by studies of the earliest manuscripts and references to the writings of Guru Gobind Singh in various sources. Indeed there remain significant uncertainties about the compilation of the text (claims about which range from the text as accident to anti-Sikh conspiracy). While the traditional view had long been that Bhai Mani Singh had compiled the writings of Guru Gobind Singh sometime after the Guru's death, the evidence for this is inconclusive. Although there have been some recent arguments that the *Dasam Granth* may not actually have been compiled until the nineteenth century, there does seem to be good evidence that some texts attributed to Guru Gobind Singh (even if not exactly in the current form of the *Dasam Granth*) were in circulation by the late eighteenth century. As with the authorship problem, the extant evidence may not be sufficient to establish conclusively the circumstances of the *Dasam Granth*'s compilation. Even so, substantial numbers of people have understood some or all of the text to be the authentic work of Guru Gobind Singh, and that fact alone makes the ongoing interpretation and use of the text significant for Sikh history. J.S. Grewal, for example, (who does not believe that Guru Gobind Singh was the author of the entire text), has noted that 'the question of [the *Dasam Granth*'s] influence among the Sikhs during the eighteenth century does remain to be answered.'[20]

While closer analysis of the importance of the *Dasam Granth* in earlier periods of Sikh history may present a challenge to certain normative paradigms of Sikh historiography, such as those which view Sikh history from the perspective of the Singh Sabha reform movement of the late nineteenth and early twentieth centuries, analysis of the text's importance need not follow the outlines of the argument advanced by those who suggest that it evidences a close relationship or even a complete lack of distinction between Sikhism and Hinduism[21] (which has led some to opine that the compilation of the *Dasam Granth* was the result of a conspiracy to discredit Sikhism, as suggested for example in a resolution passed by the Institute of Sikh Studies in Chandigarh in April, 2000). As noted earlier, conceptualizing the issue purely in terms of 'Hinduism' and 'Sikhism' is not necessarily the most effective strategy. One possibility to explore is that some parts of the text were a means of communication between Sikhs and members of various Hindu groups, particularly during the tumultuous situation during and after Guru Gobind Singh's lifetime. While we tend to think of the *Dasam Granth* as primarily a written text, it is quite plausible that, like much poetic composition of the time, it was initially presented (and later circulated) orally, whether by Guru Gobind Singh himself or by poets in his court. Perhaps there was accompanying commentary or even criticism of the material that has not survived; the rich and creative commentarial tradition which later developed certainly suggests that the contents of the text would have provoked discussion from the very beginning.

A further possibility which some commentators have pursued is to treat the issues raised by the *Dasam Granth* as primarily a matter of literary genre by proposing to distinguish between 'Sikh scripture' and 'Sikh literature'. Those parts of the *Dasam Granth* not in accord with normative Sikh theology could be deemed 'literature' and thereby become subject to a different sort of use and interpretation. While some have explicitly made such a distinction, it is implicit in many analyses of the text, such as those which argue that the tales of avatars slaying demons in battle are presented as a means of inspiring warriors to greater bravery in battle through the example of the avatars' persistence against all odds. Such arguments imply that the tales of the avatars are not strictly for so-called religious purposes such as belief in and worship of particular avatars, but instead may also function as a sort of shared cultural idiom. Jaggi has argued that during Guru Gobind Singh's era there was little distinction between Hindu and Sikh, and that it was not a time of debating principles, but of defending all Indian tradition. The diverse compositions of the *Dasam Granth* for him thus reflect the needs of a *dharma-yuddh*, or battle in defense of religious tradition.[22]

The inclination towards making a genre distinction with respect to the contents of the *Dasam Granth* is also evidenced in Kesar Singh Chibbar's 1769 accounts of the lives of the gurus, the *Bansavalinama Dasan Patshahian ka*, which relates that when the suggestion was put to Guru Gobind Singh that he combine his own compositions with those of the previous gurus and the bhagats, he declined, saying that while the other works were spiritual in nature, his own works were more for entertainment [*granth hai oh, ih asadi hai khel*].[23] Similarly, the account of the *Dasam Granth* given in sources such as Bhai Kahn Singh Nabha's *Gurshabad Ratnakar Mahan Kosh* indicates that some Sikh scholars thought that not all the compositions in the *Dasam Granth* fit together logically in a single compilation. According to this account, the *Dasam Granth* was sent to Damdama Sahib after Bhai Mani Singh's martyrdom in 1737, provoking lengthy deliberation among Sikh leaders about what to do with the material it contained. While some argued that it should remain as is, others suggested that it be separated into two parts, one with those compositions of the tenth guru which seemed in keeping with the sentiments of the previous gurus, and another containing the rest of the text. Yet no agreement could be reached until one Bhai Mahitab Singh proposed a novel solution. He had stopped at Damdama Sahib en route to Amritsar, where he had heard that Massa Ranghar was defiling the Golden Temple with illicit activities. Mahitab Singh planned to kill Massa Ranghar, and he suggested that if he succeeded in his mission, the *Dasam Granth* should be kept as it was, and that it should be divided if he were to be killed.[24] Since he was indeed successful, the *Dasam Granth* remained as a single text.

This story shows that there has long been debate about the *Dasam Granth* (whatever the origin of this tale, which seems to be relatively late), with particular unease about whether all the material was worthy of being considered religious literature of some kind. And although the story does not go into detail about the specific nature of the discussions that took place, it highlights the fact that learned Sikh authorities, even after lengthy deliberations, could not reach a consensus on the text's status. Resolution of a sort came only when the text's fate rested upon the demise of Massa Ranghar, which had no direct bearing on the contents of the *Dasam Granth*. We might infer that the agreement to let the text's status rest upon Bhai Mahitab Singh's actions reflects a tacit acknowledgement that resolution was unlikely, and that perhaps maintaining unity among the leaders at Damdama Sahib was important enough that the theological issues raised by the *Dasam Granth* could be deflected.

Such strategies have prevailed throughout the controversial history of the text which has come to be known as the *Dasam Granth*. Analyses of the text necessarily delve into topics which can be quite delicate in the recent climate surrounding the study of Sikh history, such as the dating and interpretation of early manuscripts, the interpretation of the biographical evidence for the Sikh gurus, the relationship between Sikhism and other religious traditions, and the issue of diversity within Sikh theology and practice. The composition, compilation, dissemination, use, and ongoing interpretation of the *Dasam Granth* are clearly matters deserving greater attention, and one way to advance our knowledge is to rethink the strategies we use in considering the text.

Notes

1. 'Jathedar warns Sikh scholars'. Aug. 8, 2000. http://news.indiaabroad.com/2000/08/08/jathedar.html. The initial directive was issued on May, 14, 2000.

2. The portions of the *Dasam Granth* which are generally understood to include Hindu mythological material (primarily from the *Puranas* and the *Mahabharata*) include sections of the *Bachitar Natak, Chandi Charitar, Chandi Charitar Ukti Vilas,* parts of *Var Sri Bhagauti Ji Ki*, parts of *Gian Prabodh, Chaubis Avatar, Brahma Avatar, Rudra Avatar,* and *Shastra-nam-mala.*

3. See, for example, http://www.rolmnet.com/potnet/religion/linkrel.html. In a brief personal interview on February 27, 2001, Joginder Singh Vedanti and an

assistant reiterated to me their wish that public comment on the *Dasam Granth* be suspended pending the findings of the committee. An earlier but similar effort sponsored by the Amritsar Gurmat Panth Pracarak Sabha resulted in an 1897 report which asserted that the entire *Dasam Granth* was the work of Guru Gobind Singh, but the goal of the committee issuing the report was not so much to solve the authorship problem as to standardize recitation of the text. See Rattan Singh Jaggi, *Dasam Granth dù Kartritav* (New Delhi: Punjabi Sahit Sabha, 1966), pp. 35–7 for further discussion of this report.

4. Some critics of recent scholarship on Sikhism have argued that it is wrong to apply 'western' methods of study to Sikh tradition, and might suggest that this definition of theology, derived as it is from its initial application in Christian theology, is misplaced. However, I would argue that it is appropriate here and need not be seen as imputing some sort of 'western' bias into the study of the *Dasam Granth* so long as it is clear that terms such as 'God' are representing Sikh conceptions of divinity.

5. An example is Pritpal Singh Bindra and S.S. Sodhi's 'Could Guru Gobind Singh Have Written Such Things?' in *Sikh Studies Quarterly*, 2, 4 (2000), pp. 53–8. This journal is published by the Institute of Sikh Studies.

6. Among those who argue that Guru Gobind Singh composed only portions of the *Dasam Granth*, there are varying opinions as to which those texts are. However, there seems to be general agreement that it is safe to attribute authorship of the *Jap*, *Akal Ustati*, *33 Savaiye*, and the *Zafarnama* to Guru Gobind Singh. Some also accept all or part of the *Bachitar Natak*, all or part of *Gian Prabodh*, and all or part of *Var Sri Bhagauti Ji Ki*.

7. An example is the argument made by Baba Virsa Singh in his introduction to the five-volume edition of the *Dasam Granth*, that because the *Dasam Granth* contains the *Japu*, which is clearly *bani*, the text as a whole must be accepted as bani, just as one cannot accept someone's arms but not their head since they are all part of the same body. See '*Baba Virsa Singh Ji Maharaj Valon Asis*' in Rattan Singh Jaggi and Gursharan Kaur Jaggi, eds, *Sri Dasam-Granth Sahib: Path-sampadan ate Viakhia*. 5 vols. (New Delhi: Gobind Sadan, 1999).

8. See, e.g., Jodh Singh's '*Anuvadakiya*' in his '*Sri Dasam Granth Sahib (Hindi Anuvad Sahit Nagari Lipyantaran), Pahli Sainci*,' 2nd ed. (Lucknow: Bhuvan Vani Trust, 1990).

9. For an argument against Guru Gobind Singh as author of the *Dasam Granth*, see 'Appendix 4' in Khushwant Singh, *A History of the Sikhs, vol. 1: 1469–1839* (Delhi: Oxford University Press, 1977). For an argument for Guru Gobind Singh as author of the entire text, see Dharam Pal Ashta, *The Poetry of the Dasam Granth* (New Delhi: Arun Prakashan, 1959).

10. For a useful general discussion of court poetry as well as consideration of the evidence regarding Guru Gobind Singh's court poets in the work of Santokh

Singh, Giani Gian Singh, Bhai Vir Singh, and others, see Harmendra Singh Bedi, *Gurmukhi Lipi Men Upalabdh Hindi Bhaktisahitya ka Alocnatmak Adhyayan* (Amritsar: Guru Nanak Dev University, 1993), pp. 203–48.

11. This type of argumentation is found throughout studies of Indian religious literature. For a more detailed exposition of this argument with respect to critical studies of the poetry attributed to Bullhe Shah, see Rinehart, 'The Portable Bullhe Shah: Biography, Authorship and Categorization in the Study of Punjabi Sufi Poetry', *Numen* 46, 1, (1999), pp. 53–87.

12. See Praveen Swami, 'RSS Forays into Punjab'. *Frontline* 17, 11 (May/June 2000), http://indiaserver.com/frontline/2000/05/27/17110410.htm. See also 'Sangh Settles its Confusion over Sikhs', (2001) http://www.indian-express.com/ie/daily/20010117/ina17048.html.

13. The most thorough examination of the manuscript tradition thus far is Rattan Singh Jaggi's *Dasam Granth da Kartritav* (New Delhi: Punjabi Sahit Sabha, 1966), which also includes a detailed examination of studies of the text up to the time Jaggi published his own work. Jaggi's research shows that there is extensive variation in the earliest available manuscripts and that the manuscripts cannot be dated as early as some have claimed. While many sources attest to Bhai Mani Singh's compilation of Guru Gobind Singh's works, Jaggi has argued convincingly that the manuscript identified as the 'Bhai Mani Singh Vali Bir' is likely not an original compilation of Bhai Mani Singh, and that the letter to Mata Sundari attributed to Bhai Mani Singh is almost certainly a later forgery. More recently, Daljeet Singh has argued that the text presently known as the *Dasam Granth* is most likely an early nineteenth century compilation based on earlier *pothis* in circulation. See his article 'Dasam Granth–Its History' in Daljeet Singh and Kharak Singh, eds, *Sikhism: Its Philosophy and History* (Chandigarh: Institute of Sikh Studies, 1997), pp. 710–22. Daljeet Singh surveys references to Guru Gobind Singh's writings in eighteenth- and nineteenth-century Sikh sources and uses Jaggi's work, but his assessment suffers from flawed argumentation. See also J.S. Grewal, *Contesting Interpretations of the Sikh Tradition* (New Delhi: Manohar, 1998), pp. 262–4.

14. See, for example, the chart on pp. 100–1 of Rattan Singh Jaggi's *Dasam Granth da Kartritav*. Jaggi shows that there is considerable variation within even the earliest identifiable manuscripts of the *Dasam Granth*.

15. This is the position stated in Sarup Das Bhalla's *Mahima Prakash* (1776) as well as Santokh Singh's *Sri Gur Pratap Suraj* (completed 1843).

16. In this regard the references to the *Dasam Granth* in Sikh tradition bolster the position that it was not the work of a single author, but rather a somewhat haphazard assortment of manuscripts, some of which may have been intentionally discarded only to be subsequently recovered. If indeed the material was not originally intended to be saved, it is possible that some of the material that was ultimately recovered may not have been in its final form; there may well have been unedited 'drafts' that inadvertently survived the chaotic situation in Guru Gobind Singh's era.

17. See, e.g., W.H. McLeod, *The Evolution of the Sikh Community* (Oxford: Clarendon Press, 1976), p. 81. See also Jaggi, *Dasam Granth da Kartritav*, pp. 176–94.

18. See Jaggi, *Dasam Granth da Kartritav*, p. 10, and also his *Dasam Granth Paricay* (New Delhi: Gobind Sadan, 1990), p. 1. In addition, particular groups such as the *namdharis* and the Nihangs have held the *Dasam Granth* in especially high esteem.

19. See, for example, Manmohan Sahgal, *Panjab Men and Sudama-carit Kavya* (Delhi: Vani Prakashan, 1978).

20. Grewal, *Conflicting Interpretations of Sikh Tradition*, p. 265.

21. The classic example is Dharam Pal Ashta's *The Poetry of the Dasam Granth*.

22. Jaggi, *Dasam Granth da Kartritav*, p. 194. As an analogy, one might consider the Christian appropriation of the Hebrew Bible as the 'Old Testament', that is, using the same text but within a different context and with a completely different interpretive framework.

23. Kesar Singh Chibbar, *Bansavalinama Dasan Pathshahian ka*. Gurtej Singh makes the interesting observation that none of the scholars writing on the *Dasam Granth* has noted that there is no use of the name 'Nanak' in the compositions of the text, whereas all the earlier gurus used this name in their poetry. His implication, of course, is that if Guru Gobind Singh were composing poetry which he intended to be worthy of inclusion with the compositions of the earlier gurus preserved in the Adi Granth, he would have used the name 'Nanak'. See his 'Two Views on Dasam Granth', in Daljeet Singh and Kharak Singh, eds, *Sikhism: Its Philosophy and History* (Chandigarh: Institute of Sikh Studies, 1997), p. 706.

24. Kahn Singh Nabha, *Gurshabad Ratnakar Mahan Kosh* (Delhi: National Book Shop, 1990), p. 616.

5

Maharaja Dalip Singh, History, and the Negotiation of Sikh Identity

Tony Ballantyne

I have to say the Sikhs are a bit of a nightmare ... sometimes they look, well, er, rather strange. I suppose we're not used to people like that round here.[1]

A villager from Elveden, 1993

Although it is some 7,000 miles from Punjab, the village of Elveden in rural Suffolk has been a crucial site for the construction of Sikh history and identity over the last one hundred and fifty years. Formerly home to Maharaja Dalip Singh, the last sovereign ruler of the independent Punjab, the village has become an important pilgrimage site for British Sikhs. But the village's centrality in the cultural life of the *Panth* (community, lit. way) has opened up acrimonious debates over the position of the British Sikh community and the very definition of Britishness itself. This halting, yet thoroughgoing, assertion of difference by an inhabitant of Elveden encapsulates the 'systematic racial and religious codes' identified by the recent *Parekh Report* as occupying a central position in British cultural life.[2] In insisting on the fundamental otherness of Sikhs, this quotation not only articulates a deep-seated fear of the Sikhs who visit Elveden from London, Coventry, or Bradford, but also in emphasizing the 'strangeness' of Sikhs implicitly equates Britishness with both Christianity and whiteness. Over the last decade Elveden has intermittently entered the public eye, as metropolitan newspapers have highlighted the village's prominent role in the life of the British Sikh community and exposed the racial and religious tensions that have erupted over efforts to commemorate Dalip Singh. The stakes in these 'memory battles' are high, as rural Britons and supporters of the 'countryside movement' proclaim that the countryside embodies the nation's heritage, a past grounded in tightly-knit communities structured around the country-house (the source of employment and the site of key rural rituals such as the hunt) and the Church. The efforts of British Sikhs to celebrate Dalip Singh, contest and disrupt such narratives, as they emphasize not only the long history of the British Sikh community but also the Maharaja's key role as a patron and benefactor in the supposedly homogenous rural world evoked by the villagers of Elveden.

This paper, part of a larger project that reassesses the entangled pasts of the British empire and Sikhism, examines these conflicting understandings of Dalip Singh's life and legacy. While the first section briefly sketches Dalip Singh's career and discusses his place within discourses on Sikh identity within India, my primary focus is on a series of British debates surrounding Dalip Singh in the 1990s. Dalip Singh returned to prominence in the British public sphere in a major 1990 exhibition that re-examined the Raj at the National Portrait Gallery and subsequent debates triggered by the foundation of the Maharaja Duleep Singh Centenary Trust have ensured that the last Maharaja of the Punjab occupied an important position in end-of-the-millennium reappraisals of British history and identity.[3] The paper concludes by suggesting that careful analysis of the shifting representations of Dalip Singh subverts both the dominant 'internalist' approach to Sikh history (an analytical tradition that focuses narrowly on developments within the Panth) and exposes the limitations of the existing work on the encounter between Sikhs and Britons. The interweaving of Punjabi and British culture necessitates a new approach to modern Sikh history, one that is grounded in a recognition of the mutually constitutive nature of colonial encounters and that is dedicated to delineating the multiple forces and contexts that frame the construction and performance of various Sikh identities, both 'at home' in Punjab and 'away' in North America, Australasia and especially the United Kingdom.

Dalip Singh: In Life and in Memory

The details of Dalip Singh's life are well-known, thanks to the pioneering work of Ganda Singh, a detailed biography produced by Michael Alexander and Sushil Anand, and a recent short reappraisal by David Jones.[4] Here, I will not review the details of his short life at length, rather I will offer a thumbnail sketch before proceeding to discussion competing interpretations of his life and significance. Born in September 1838, the young Dalip Singh succeeded Maharaja Sher Singh to the Lahore throne in September 1843, but was stripped of his kingdom with the annexation of the Punjab by the East India Company in March 1849. After his arrival in England in 1854 Maharaja Dalip Singh became a well-known public figure both in London and in Suffolk where he acquired a large estate at Elveden: his fame was such that he led the 'foreign princes' at the wedding of Prince Edward and became a favourite of Queen Victoria herself. His time in Britain was marred by recurring financial worries that were exacerbated by his increasingly fraught relationship with the India Office. As a result of his commitment to reclaiming his sovereign powers and a resurgent interest in Sikhism (he had 'quietly' converted to Christianity before travelling to England), Dalip Singh was effectively exiled in Paris from 1886 until his death in 1893. He was buried alongside his wife and youngest child at Elveden and his grave has subsequently become a popular pilgrimage site for the British Sikh community.

Of course, the meaning of individual lives are not fixed, rather they are shaped, contested, and re-formed through stories, graphic images, biographies, works of fiction, and various forms of private and public performance.[5] By recounting exemplary lives, acts of heroic martyrdom, or villainous treachery, these representations mould both individual and collective memory. In this sense, memory works both constructively and unevenly: it orders and shapes the complexities of the past, highlighting key points while simultaneously omitting or effacing other qualities, practices or events, shaping fragments of the past into coherent, if partial, images and narratives. Thus memory plays a central role in the 'invention of tradition', the fashioning of narratives that enable the definition of community and the construction of beliefs and practices that tie individuals together into larger collectives defined by ethnicity, faith, or nationality. As the rest of this paper demonstrates, these processes have played a central role in the constitution of Sikh traditions and are an important, if under-explored, problematic in Sikh studies: indeed, questions of community memory run through Hew McLeod's work on the *janam-sakhis* and his pioneering volume on bazaar prints.[6]

Dalip Singh is a rich case for a study of the constructive and uneven work of memory, especially given his mobility and shifting fortunes. The complex tangle of his life and the religious and political ambiguities that surround him inhibit the search for an authoritative vision of Dalip Singh. The multi-faceted nature of his character has meant that he has been an extremely useful figure for many—often competing—visions of Sikh history and identity: in fact, there seems to be as many Dalip Singhs as there have been tellers of his tale.

In mapping these divergent visions of Dalip Singh's life and meaning, we must begin by noting that he occupies significantly different positions in texts produced by Sikh authors based at home in India and those in Britain and, in turn, both of these bodies of literature contrast with the seemingly limited significance of Dalip Singh for North American Punjabis. Indeed, one of my Sikh students in Illinois, who had just returned from visiting cousins in Bradford, seemed perplexed by Dalip Singh's popularity in Britain, reflecting that: 'He is no Dip Singh'.

If this young Chicago-domiciled Sikh feels that Dalip Singh falls short of legendary heroes like Baba Dip Singh, there is no doubt of Dalip Singh's continued importance within the Indian context. Despite his effective exile in Britain, he occupied an important position in community memory, remaining a potent figure for Punjabis. McLeod, for example, notes that the Maharaja was amongst one of the twelve Sikh heroes reproduced in nineteenth century woodcuts.[7] The tumultuous reception he received from Sikh soldiers while in Calcutta in 1861 alarmed the British to such an extent that his planned up-country tour was cancelled and he was ordered to return to Britain by the Governor-General himself.[8] In 1883, when news reached India that Dalip Singh was planning to return to his homeland, the fledgling nationalist movement seized upon Dalip Singh as an icon, circulating pamphlets entitled *Maharaja Dalip Singh ki jai*.[9] Much of this impetus came from Bengal rather than Punjab: Bengalis played a central role in this campaign and Sardar Dayal Singh Majithia—who had strong ties with the Brahmo Samaj and an abiding interest in Bengali culture—used his *Tribune* to rally support for Dalip Singh.[10] In its obituary for the Maharaja, *The Tribune* affirmed Dalip Singh's abiding love of his homeland: 'He had forgotten nothing of his life at Lahore. He loved to talk of his old days, and his eyes were filled with tears, as he spoke of his old playmates, his *tahlias* [attendants], his favourite horse and the gorgeously uniformed regiment of infants consisting of the cadets coming of the noblest houses in the Punjab.'[11]

For many Sikhs in the 1880s, however, Dalip Singh was a contentious figure. Baba Nihal Singh's *Kurshid-i-Khalsa* (1885) not only undercut traditional understandings of the Adi Granth as embodying the Guruship after the passing of the tenth Guru by celebrating Ram Singh, the leader of the Kuka movement, as a new Guru, but also anticipated the imminent restoration of the Lahore throne to Dalip Singh. In response to these claims Gurmukh Singh, the Chief Secretary of the Khalsa Diwan (which in 1885 was attempting to foster Sikh interest in the Punjab while negotiating a difficult path through the growing rift between the Lahore and Amritsar Singh Sabhas), declared that *Kurshid-i-Khalsa* was 'unauthorized' and excluded Baba Nihal Singh from all Singh Sabhas.[12] British officials were pleased with this swift response: one noted that 'it is a gratifying testimony to the loyalty of the leaders of the Sikh community.'[13]

Not all Sikh leaders, however, were antithetical to the possibility of Dalip Singh's return. While the members of the Lahore Singh Sabha rejected Dalip Singh's grand schemes for the reconstruction of his authority, he found active support in Amritsar, particularly from Sardar Thakur Singh Sandhanwalia. A moving spirit behind the foundation of the Singh Sabha, Thakur Singh Sandhanwalia played a central role as Dalip Singh's 'local informant' in the Punjab, remitting a detailed sketch of the property and *jagirs* that Dalip Singh had claim to in Punjab in November 1883.[14] While this correspondence was crucial in the initial formation of Dalip Singh's plans to return to India, Thakur Singh Sandhanwalia was also instrumental in coordinating operations in 1886–7 intended to facilitate Dalip Singh's political resurgence. He dispatched Thakur Singh of Wagha to Aden to perform the *pahul* rite, formalizing Dalip Singh's re-admittance into the Khalsa. In light of these activities both Thakur Singh Sandhanwalia and Thakur Singh of Wagha were under close British surveillance: in November 1886 Thakur Singh Sandhanwalia arrived in French-controlled Pondicherry, in the hope that this new base would allow him to function as an effective agent for the Maharaja's interests in India, while avoiding the very real possibility of arrest within British India.[15] Thakur Singh Sandhanwalia's deep commitment to Dalip Singh, however, effectively marginalized him within contemporary Sikh politics: this once influential figure died in Pondicherry in August 1887, far from home, championing an unlikely political cause at a moment when Singh Sabha reformers were locked in crucial exchanges over the very nature of Sikhism and the future of their community.

A more detailed assessment of responses to Dalip Singh's life and death could be assembled from Ganda Singh's important collection of documents published in 1977 as the third volume in the *History of the Freedom Movement in the Punjab*, a work that rehabilitated Dalip Singh as a key Punjabi figure within the mainstream of Indian nationalism. Ganda Singh's volume was the first in a line of publications produced by South Asians that celebrated Dalip Singh's nationalist credentials.[16] Baldev Singh Baddan's 1998 edited collection embodied this explicitly nationalist approach to the Maharaja's life. Frustrated at histories that have emphasized Dalip Singh's acculturation, depicting him as 'a thorough English country gentleman of his times' or, even worse, 'a pathetic, helpless figure, an object of pity and in British eyes an object of ridicule', Baddan cast Dalip Singh as a precocious nationalist leader.[17] Baddan's volume was an act of nationalist recuperation, as he set about recovering the 'rebellious facet' of Dalip Singh's life, especially in the anti-British *avatar* of his later years.[18] In short, Baddan celebrated Dalip Singh as 'one of the early and most important freedom fighters of India.'[19]

Nishaan: Dalip Singh in the Age of a Global Khalsa

Baddan's conventionally nationalist approach, which shows no interest in Dalip Singh's significance for British Punjabis or in Britain more generally, has been challenged by the emergence of explicitly transnational visions of Sikhism, such as those documented in Brian Axel's recent *The Nation's Tortured Body*.[20] India-based community organizations have constructed increasingly dense and elaborate networks that reach out to North America and Great Britain in the hope of knitting diasporic and India-based communities together. Within this context, Baddan's nationalist vision of Dalip Singh has been revised in light of an increased awareness of the authority of Dalip Singh for the British diasporic community and his value as an icon for Sikhs in a 'global age'. One such organization, the Nagaara Trust, an 'apolitical organization' whose mission is to propagate 'the wonderful message of the Sikh tradition for all mankind', has committed itself to strengthening Sikhism's international profile and cementing the transnational status of the Khalsa.[21] The Nagaara Trust's preferred media indicate its commitment to the globalization of Sikhism: alongside its *Khalsa 300: A Vision Re-visited*, a video targeted at an international audience (available 'on both VHS-PAL and NTSC systems'), the Trust runs a web page and publishes a journal *Nishaan*, available both in print and online. That the journal was launched by Dr Manmohan Singh, the architect of the reforms that liberalized India's economy in the 1990s, (as *Nishaan* reminds us, Manmohan Singh 'transformed the country's insular economy into a global one') and who is closely associated with the World Bank, confirms the Trust's dedication to an explicitly global agenda.

In the premier issue of *Nishaan*, alongside articles on 'Gurmat Sangeet', 'The Mystic Year 1999' and 'Anandpur Sahib: Vaisakhi 300', two articles explored Dalip Singh's life and legacy. The first, a brief biographical sketch, emphasized Dalip Singh's role as a modern, highlighting his transformation of Elveden from a 'run-down estate into an efficient, modern game preserve' and noting his commitment to the organization of Sikh political activity and anti-colonial struggles late in his life. Despite echoing Baddan's insistence on Dalip Singh's role as a pioneering architect of pan-communal nationalism, the overwhelming emphasis of *Nishaan* is on Dalip Singh's commitment to the Sikh kingdom of Lahore. The Elveden estate—even while Dalip Singh remained a nominal Christian (the article avoids any direct discussion of his Christianity)—is cast as a material expression of Sikh power and an extension of the glorious court of Ranjit Singh. From its 'halls decorated with glass mosaic in the fashion of the *shish mahal* and dominated by the huge oil paintings of Ranjit Singh in darbar or at the Golden Temple and of his brother Sher Singh in regal splendour' to 'sculptures of past glories and cases of jewels', Elveden embodies the lost glories of Sikh kingdom of the Punjab.

This vision was extended in a second article entitled 'A defining moment of posthumous glory' which described the efforts of the British Sikh community to commemorate the memory of Dalip Singh. Again the emphasis here was on Dalip Singh as an icon of Sikh faith and political commitment. Dalip Singh's rekindled devotion to Sikhism is highlighted, as are the efforts of the British government to stifle his desire to 'return to his beloved Punjab'. The concluding sentence—'Even today The Sikh Nation aspires to regain its Sovereignty'—effectively casts an unbroken chain of Sikh activism that reaches across time and space, from Punjab to Britain and from the Nagaara Trust through Dalip Singh back to the very foundation of the Khalsa itself.

Dalip Singh as a Post-colonial Icon

Nishaan's attempts to stress Dalip Singh's emblematic status for a global Sikh community must be read at least in part as being of the product of the efforts by British Sikhs to elevate Dalip Singh as an icon of the community. In contrast to Dalip Singh's marginal position within the cultural memory of North American Punjabis, his image has been increasingly prominent amongst the British Punjabi community and, more generally, within a British public sphere that has increasingly grappled with questions of religious difference, race, and Britain's place in Europe and the world beyond. These debates over ethnicity and national identity have operated at a variety of levels: from an avalanche of academic and popular works on Britishness to numerous documentaries that have re-evaluated British history and the contribution of migrant groups to British culture, from debates in the House of Commons to violent clashes in the streets of northern cities, from sermons in village churches to football stadium chants. The work of community activists or think-tanks like the Runnymede Trust—which has examined the power of Islamophobia in addition to identifying pernicious 'racial and religious codes' (the equation of Englishness and Britishness with whiteness) at the heart of contemporary discussions of British identity in its *Report on the Future of Multi-Ethnic Britain*—have invested political reform and cultural change with new urgency, as well as making persuasive cases for the active reimagining of Britishness.[22] Although these processes predated Labour's landslide victory in 1997, they have proceeded at pace under the Labour government (particularly in contrast to the Thatcherite regime that was wedded to a narrow, exclusivist interpretation of British history and identity) which has struggled to redefine Britain's relationship with Ireland, to revisit its relations with both the United States and Europe, and to confront the racial violence and institutional racism embedded in the police and justice system revealed by the murders of Stephen Lawrence and Lakhvinder 'Ricky' Reel.

The effects and legacies of colonialism were a prominent thread in these discussions of Britishness in the 1990s. As the decade dawned, a landmark exhibition 'The Raj: India and the British, 1600–1947', held at the National Portrait Gallery, undertook a major re-assessment of British colonialism under the lingering shadow of the 'Raj nostalgia' that was so prominent in British culture in the 1980s.[23] It was within this context that Dalip Singh re-entered the British public sphere in a dramatic way as C.A. Bayly—a leading British historian of South Asia and the organizer of the exhibition—selected a portrait of Dalip Singh as its 'central image'.[24] Bayly argued that the painting by Francis Xavier Winterhalter, a renowned Continental portraitist, captured the central tensions and ambivalences that characterized the Raj as a whole. While the image depicted Dalip Singh as confident (in contrast to Francis Hayman's famous image of Mir Jafar's submission to Clive) and exotic (bedecked with jewels, with minarets in the distant mist), Bayly notes that in reality Dalip Singh had been reduced to a 'mere pensioner' after his 'kingdom, his religion, and even the famous Koh-i-Noor diamond had been snatched away from him'. In short: 'The image suggests the vigourously exotic; the reality was defeat and dispossession.'[25]

The ambivalence of Dalip Singh's experience was also highlighted in reviews of the exhibition. Michael Ratcliffe, writing in *The Guardian*, observed: 'Winterhalter had painted his glittering portrait of Dalip Singh at Buck House, under the enthralled eye of the Queen herself. This is one of the most glamorous images, and most deceiving, of the Raj. During the sittings the converted young Christian Maharaja of the Punjab was actually shown the Koh-i-noor diamond, nicked from him on Victoria's behalf five years before.'[26] Nina Poovaya-Smith echoed this analysis, suggesting that:

Winterhalter's portrait of the young Maharaja Dalip Singh (1838–93) is a studied exercise in presenting or mimicking the veneer of power and authority, a gloss as superficial as the varnish that overlays the painting .... For by the time this work was produced in 1854, Dalip Singh had already been dispossessed of his kingdom, his wealth and, for a time, even of his Sikh religion. He lived in England as something of a pet of Queen Victoria, and it is her portrait he wears round his neck. His later sad attempts at a new selfhood, when he reverts to Sikhism and dreams of a Sikh state, confer on him a tragic dignity.[27]

Although Bayly, Ratcliffe, and Poovaya-Smith all alluded to Dalip Singh's later anti-colonial career, they emphasized his dispossession and dependency: in short, the Winterhalter portrait was a potent reminder of the disempowerment and dislocation enacted by colonialism, a verdict supported in a recent article by Simeran Mann Singh Gell.[28] In the wake of the exhibition British Punjabis, however, would fashion a very different reading of Dalip Singh, one that shifted weight from his subject status and the power of colonialism to a celebration of Dalip Singh as the founder of a diasporic community. If, for Bayly, Dalip Singh's significance lay in his position as 'the heir to the last, great free Indian state', for British Punjabis Dalip Singh's iconic status is not because his image marks the culmination of Company colonialism but rather because his travels and his life in Britain laid the very foundations of their community.

These divergent readings reflect the different temporal logics and analytical aims of these historical narratives. Bayly was organizing an exhibition that examined British colonialism in South Asia and as such he located Dalip Singh within a political narrative that traced the rise of the Company as a territorial power, the consolidation of its influence, the shift to Crown Raj after 1857, and the gathering strength of nationalism, culminating in independence and Partition in 1947, the terminal point of the exhibition.[29] British Sikh narratives, however, were organized by a different temporal logic and to meet a particular cultural need: the desire to fashion a long and celebratory history that might cement the community's distinctiveness and its contribution to British life. Living within a nation deeply concerned with 'heritage' and where history is a highly marketable commodity, the construction and dissemination of a 'long history' is crucial to claiming legitimacy within the public sphere: indeed David Lowenthal has suggested that this pressure to claim distant origins or originary status is an overwhelming feature of the British 'heritage industry.'[30] Recently the role of 'heritage' (and other forms of cultural memory) in the constitution of the nation have been explored by Raphael Samuel and Patrick Wright, but while both these authors interrogate notions of Englishness, they pay limited attention to the role of the empire in constituting metropolitan culture.[31] Scholars working on the South Asian diaspora have drawn our attention to the powerful metropolitan influence of empire, but the significance and contribution of the British Sikh community to national life has received surprisingly little attention from historians. While Rozina Visram's *Ayahs, Lascars and Princes* celebrated the long history of South Asians in the United Kingdom (and was warmly received by notable figures such as Salman Rushdie), its focus on the *collective community* of South Asians did not provide the kind of specific and serviceable history that British Punjabis might have looked for.

Nor did leading scholars on the British Sikh community provide this. Where Visram devoted four pages to a discussion of Dalip Singh in a chapter on 'Indian pioneers in Britain', Roger Ballard entirely effaced the Maharaja in his essay on the Sikh community in his influential collection *Desh Pardesh*. Under the heading 'Sikhs in Britain—the early pioneers', Ballard excised Dalip Singh from the community's history as he located the origins of the British Sikh community in the early twentieth century, observing: 'Although mass migration did not begin until the 1950s, the pioneer founders of Britain's Sikh settlement had arrived much earlier. Details are scanty, but it seems probable that the earliest settlers were Sikh soldiers who had fought in France during the First World War, and stayed on in Britain'.[32]

Dalip Singh as British Settler

The arguments, narratives and images produced by the Maharajah Duleep Singh Centenary Trust (hereafter MDSCT) countered the identification of Dalip Singh as the embodiment of colonialism's contradictions and extended the truncated vision of British Sikh history elaborated by Ballard. The MDSCT was established in 1992 by a group of British Sikhs to raise public awareness of Sikhism and to underline the long history of the British Sikh community. The Trust's web page explains the particular importance of Dalip Singh:

As the last Maharajah of the Punjab he remains an important symbol of Sikh sovereignty. The 1993 centenary represented an ideal opportunity to mark a period of great significance in Anglo/Sikh history. The annexation of the Maharajah's Sikh empire marked the commencement of an association between the nations which would eventually see Sikh troops serving with unparalleled gallantry in the World Wars. As we enter a new millennium, this association is today represented by a Sikh diaspora which plays an active and responsible part in British society. Through its work, the Trust seeks to remove the veil of anonymity that has hitherto shrouded the life of its last sovereign and by implication the enormously rich heritage of the Sikh nation.[33]

This statement encapsulates the complex cultural and intellectual moves made by the Trust to fashion a very precise understanding of Dalip Singh (and, by extension British–Sikh relations). While the Trust does emphasize the Maharaja's function as an 'important symbol of Sikh sovereignty', it downplayed the role of colonialism in extinguishing that sovereignty. The significance of British colonialism was gestured towards, but 'annexation' is an impoverished term that fails to encapsulate the profound transformations enacted by British colonialism. In effect, the Trust reconfigured the highly unequal power relations of the colonial past into a potentially positive development: colonialism initiated the 'commencement of an association between the nations' forging not only a unique partnership between Britons and Sikhs, but also, as Brian Axel has pointed out, provided the 'historical condition' for the constitution of Sikh nation within a colonial (and post-colonial) framework.[34]

The MDSCT emphasized the centrality of military service in cementing this cultural and political relationship, highlighting the 'unparalleled gallantry' of Sikh soldiers under imperial service.[35] Most importantly, however, the Trust insisted on Dalip Singh's significance within the local British context of a global Sikh diaspora. His life, it suggested, belonged not simply to a purely Sikh past, but rather to a long and continuing 'Anglo/Sikh history'. The role of Dalip Singh (and his descendants) as grandees of the Suffolk countryside—as patrons of hunting and as generous benefactors to local charities and institutions—foreshadowed the important public role of the contemporary British Sikh community, 'which plays an active and responsible part in British society'. The Trust's insistence on the positive contribution of Sikhs not only served to remind fellow Britons of the willingness of Sikhs to engage with British culture, but (in the wake of Operation Blue Star and the growing strength of the Khalistani movement) also counteracted any fears that Dalip Singh might function as a potentially symbol for 'radical' political action *within Britain*, an important move given the efforts of the Khalistan Commando Force to celebrate Dalip Singh as the last raja of the Khalsa Raj.[36]

This emphasis on Dalip Singh as a symbol of cultural interdependence and cooperation culminated in the unveiling of a statute of Dalip Singh on horseback by Prince Charles in the centre of Thetford in July 1999. This image, the product of six years of concerted fundraising and organization by the MDSCT, is an important site in the cultural and religious landscape for British Sikhs. There is no doubt that the MDSCT hoped that the statue would be a unifying force for a British Sikh community that has marked generational divisions and is strongly differentiated along caste lines. The image of the Maharaja proclaimed a potent past to British Sikhs who were used to the urban labour and landscapes of city life: it evoked the power of the Sikh kingdom of the Punjab, and celebrated the martial values central within Sikh iconography, and popular tradition. As a memorial, the statue also attempted to provide what we might term a 'memory anchor', a fixed vision of a key element of the collective past, a constant referent within a community that is constantly reshaped by migration, class mobility, intermarriage, doctrinal reformulations, and schisms.[37]

At its most basic level, however, the statue is a strong proclamation of an important cultural presence within Britain that could be traced back to almost 150 years. The Trust emphasized that '[t]he intention of the memorial itself is to provide a memorial to the Maharaja Dalip Singh, and to illustrate the links symbolized between Indian and English history, and between Sikh and western cultures.' This agenda was made explicit in the statute's inscription, which under the heading 'Bringing History and Cultures Together', underscored the interweaving of the British and Sikh Crowns, noting that Dalip Singh was a 'close favourite of Queen Victoria' and that his Koh-i-noor 'passed to the British authorities' and was eventually incorporated into the Crown jewels. While the inscription reaffirmed that: 'To this day the Sikh nation aspires to regain its sovereignty', the Statue cannot be read as a repudiation of Britishness or as a claim against the Crown: in fact, in this formulation at least, Britishness and a desire for a Sikh homeland are not incompatible in the least.

Race, Religion and Britishness in Elveden

As the quotation that opened that this paper suggests, the Trust's identification of Dalip Singh as a symbol of 'Anglo-Sikh' relations and its insistence on the 'constructive' role played by the Sikh community within Britain have been contested in Suffolk. Since the 1960s inhabitants of Thetford and more especially Elveden have expressed discomfort, resentment, and open hostility towards Sikhs who have made the pilgrimage to Elveden from the Midlands and cities of the north. In 1961, the discovery of a Sikh at worship in the church adjoining the cemetery where Dalip Singh was buried, outraged villagers, and some demanded the immediate re-consecration of the church.[38] The graveyard resurfaced as a flashpoint in the 1990s, when increasing numbers of Sikhs journeyed to Elveden and the MDSCT mooted plans for its statue and formulated a proposal to formally commemorate Dalip Singh's memory with a cultural festival. In response, locals attempted to limit access to the graveyard and rejected the existence of any abiding bonds between the Sikh community and Elveden. Mabel Schofield, a villager whose close family is interred at Elveden, complained that visiting Sikhs 'walk over other graves and leave plastic swords about. They don't think of others. They take too much on themselves, but they probably think I'm prejudiced. It's not worth bothering putting up a plaque [to Dalip Singh], but it's their prerogative ... If they have celebrations here, I won't go.'[39]

Access to the Elveden estate also became a contentious issue in the early 1990s as the Guinness family, which has owned the Elveden estate since the early twentieth century, attempted to limit access to the estate and gave 'the cold shoulder' to proposals for celebrations 'involving city dwellers in turbans'. *The Guardian* reported that: 'Callers at the estate office are told that the only public place is the churchyard, and once they've had a look at the grave the best thing is to continue along the A11 [motorway].'[40] In response to these developments, Harbinder Singh, a member of the MDSCT, argued that racism underpinned the hostility of both the locals and the Guinness family and suggested that this development was a special concern for Sikhs 'because they are such a visible minority with the turban they wear.' Again he insisted that the aim of the Trust was to celebrate the interweaving of British and Sikh culture:

We want to take away this veil of anonymity about our history and get people to realise that the link between the British and Sikhs is not just as immigrants but as equal partners. We've now found an historical link—all commonwealth immigrants have the link of empire—but we have found a special link. We're trying to strengthen Anglo-Sikhism.[41]

Memory Battles: History and Identity

Harbinder Singh's arguments, however, were not acceptable to vocal opponents of the MDSCT in Suffolk. Where Winterhalter's romanticized portrait of Dalip Singh as an exotic prince, which graced billboards and posters in London's Underground (in addition to the cover of the Exhibition catalogue), might function as a suggestive signifier of Britain's imperial entanglements to a metropolitan audience, the image of Dalip Singh had a very different cadence in the Suffolk countryside. Villagers rejected the Maharaja as an alien, an irrelevant intrusion upon accepted understandings of the region's past and dismissed contemporary Sikhs as 'foreign' interlopers and 'nightmarish' intruders.[42]

These clashes over the rights of Sikhs to gain access to the cemetery and plans to formally recognize Dalip Singh's contribution to the region can be seen as battles over memory, disputes over the history of various communities of identification (whether British Sikh, Elveden or Suffolk, or, at the broadest level, Britain itself). If we can understand the project of the MDSCT as fashioning and publicizing a particular form of community memory that would simultaneously unite British Sikhs while drawing the attention of non-Sikhs to the iconic status of Dalip Singh, the local population attempted to excise Dalip Singh from their community memory and protect their vision of Elveden and its surrounds as a rural English idyll.

The insistence that the villagers were 'not used to people like that round here' invoked racial and religious homogeneity as the foundation of local life. Implicitly, 'the people round here' were white and Christian, not South Asian Sikhs. The willingness of Sikhs to travel to Elveden and the MDSCT plans to formally celebrate his memory punctured the 'peace', the predictability, and Protestantism that villagers treasured. Not only were Sikhs visiting Elveden, but they were laying claim to its Britishness, as *The Guardian* observed: 'The coach-loads of Sikh children from Wolverhampton who went to Elveden last summer were thrilled. It's the very Englishness of Elveden which makes the story so potent. The wrought iron gates, the empty mansion and the romantic sweep of parklands exert a snobbish fascination. All this once belonged to their co-religionist.' *The Guardian* suggested that it was in cultural encounters such as these in Elveden—'this chocolate-box remnant of 19th century England'—that the future shape of national identity was being defined:

It's a tale for our times—two bits of England representing two nations as disparate as anything Benjamin Disraeli ever considered. Only this time, it's not wealth that divides. A multicultural urban Britain schooled in racial tolerance meets the quintessential rural England—an area on the Norfolk–Suffolk border where landed gentry still hold sway over their estates.[43]

These oppositions between the city and country, between tradition and the future, between diversity and homogeneity are striking and run through the debates surrounding the activities of the MDSCT. As we have already seen, the managers of the Elveden estate made it clear in 1993 that they did not welcome 'city dwellers in turbans' in the Suffolk countryside.[44] Yet this insistence that Sikhs had no part to play in rural Britain, that the people of Suffolk were 'not used to people like that', was only possible because of the disavowal of Dalip Singh's important contributions to the region's cultural life in the late nineteenth century.

Oral histories produced by the inhabitants of Elveden celebrate rural pastimes and values, identifying them as providing the bonds of community and the basis of daily life. The reminiscences of Reg Trett, for example, are full of accounts of farming, the fruits of the harvest, sports, and hunting.[45] Although the very existence of an Elveden village web page, a project initiated by the Forest Heath District Council and funded by the National Lottery Board, chafes against the insistence of the village as an embodiment of the old rural order, the site nevertheless celebrates the two bastions of rural community, the estate or country house—the 'Hall'—and the Church.

Although passing references are made to Dalip Singh (noting for example that his generosity enabled the repair of the church in 1869), his connection with the estate is almost entirely effaced, which in effect denies his crucial role in the development of the Estate as one of the premier sites for hunting in Britain and its popularity with the Victorian elite. In short, the village's web page excises Dalip Singh from community memory and this works to de-legitimize the claims of British Sikhs about the significance of the Hall or cemetery.[46]

It seems that the people of Suffolk, like Punjabi nationalists, are at great pains to expunge Dalip Singh's brief but prominent role as a bastion of the British rural elite. Although villagers respond to the presence of Sikhs in Elveden by insisting that they are not used to 'people like that', a wealth of material establishes Dalip Singh's rapid adoption of the life of a country squire. In many ways, his early childhood at the Lahore court, where the young Dalip Singh was schooled in falconry and the use of weapons from a very early age, and subsequent exile in Fatehgarh, where he kept elephants and hawks, prepared the Maharaja well for elite life in rural Britain where bloodsports were a highly valued cultural tradition.[47] Dalip Singh's initial renown as enthusiast for British rural life and as a skilled hunter was based on his leasing of Castle Menzies in Perthshire. Dalip Singh gained national renown as a sportsman after setting a new shooting record at Grandtully in Perthshire (some 440 grouse in a day).[48] It was at Elveden, however, that he became a bulwark of the rural establishment, a reputation he cemented by shooting some 780 partridges with 1000 cartridges. At the Elveden Estate, Dalip Singh hosted famous shooting parties that included the Prince of Wales as an invited guest. As Alexander and Anand note, Dalip Singh welcomed 'all the great shots' at Elveden and he hosted 'half the grandees in the land.'[49] There is also evidence to suggest that for his contemporaries in Suffolk, Dalip Singh embodied the ideals of rural masculinity: T.W. Turner, who eventually became head game keeper at the Elveden estate, noted that it was after watching the Maharaja partridge-shooting that he decided: 'When I get to be a man I will be a gamekeeper if I can.'[50]

Thus, Dalip Singh's love of horses, hunting, and firearms—passions central to the courtly culture of the Punjab of Ranjit Singh—provided an important entrée into elite British society and formed a common idiom that temporally transcended, or at least mitigated, differences of race and religion.[51] Such skills were crucial markers of masculinity and gentility for the British aristocracy and *The Times of India* celebrated the Maharaja's ability to 'play the role' of a 'a fine gentleman'. Despite the implication that this was in some sense a performance, *The Times of India* recognized Dalip Singh's abilities as 'landlord, a patron or a host'.[52] The statue of Dalip Singh in Thetford suggests these 'rural values': the regal Maharaja on horseback not only evokes images of great British heroes—such as the famous statue of Richard the Lionheart outside the Houses of Parliament—but also embodies the rural, masculine ideals so prominent in Sikh iconography and the popular prints produced for the bazaars of Punjab and Southall.

Here we can extend Brian Axel's insights into the iconic status of Dalip Singh and identify another important layer of meaning that attached to what Axel terms 'the Maharaja's glorious body'.[53] Unlike other South Asian male travellers (but especially Bengalis such as Rammohan Roy and Keshub Chandra Sen) who were, as Antoinette Burton has demonstrated, represented within feminized idioms that stressed their 'sweetness' and 'gentleness', Dalip Singh's masculinity was consistently emphasized within metropolitan discourses.[54] Embodying a military and religious heritage that was juxtaposed against the effeminacy of popular Hinduism, vegetarianism, and the supposed innate femininity of Bengali culture, Victorian reportage hailed Dalip Singh as the antithesis of the effete *babu*. Of course, these heavily gendered understandings of race and religion had powerful material and cultural effects: the equation of Sikhism with a masculine warrior tradition underpinned the 'Punjabization' of the Indian army, while simultaneously rendering Sikh women silent and invisible.[55]

Gender continues to be a crucial element within the performance of Sikh identities within contemporary Britain. The statue at Thetford allows the contemporary British Sikh community to maintain this insistence on the distinctive masculinity of the Sikh tradition, a masculinity that is used to mark the Panth off from other South Asian communities and to forge a common bond between Britons and Punjabis out of a hyper-masculinist discourse. A cultural commensurability between Britons and Sikhs grounded in a shared masculinity—or, at least, perceived commensurability—remained important even in the late twentieth century, as the feminizing discourse of the *babu* was reworked within the British public sphere to insist on the fundamental otherness of Britons of Bengali/Bangladeshi descent, most notably in the controversial Morrissey song 'Bengali in Platforms'.[56]

Conclusion: Dalip Singh and the Project of Sikh Studies

As Brian Caton has recently demonstrated, the 'British rural ideal' has functioned as a crucial influence on the construction of Sikhism from the mid-nineteenth century. British accounts of the court of Ranjit Singh emphasized his attachment to all things military, his love of hunting, and his attachment to horses. Colonial ethnographers and military recruiters celebrated the 'stout' Jat who was close to the land and deeply attached to traditions of military service.[57] But Dalip Singh's enthusiastic embrace of such values within a metropolitan context disrupts many of the key fictions about heritage, history, and Britishness. Dalip Singh's prominence as an 'English squire' and the Sikh community's celebration of his memory punctured the oppositions drawn by the Guinness family and *The Guardian* between city and country, urban multiculturalism, and rural homogeneity. As the squire of Elveden, Dalip Singh destabilizes any attempts to cast the countryside, rural life, or hunting as refuges for an unreconstructed Englishness that is grounded in the traditions of the past: in essence, Dalip Singh subverts the oppositions between the country and the city that have structured British life from the early modern period and dichotomies that continue to resonate in debates over the role of farming and hunting in the British economy and identity.[58]

Dalip Singh's life and his contested afterlife in community memory remind us of the interweaving of British and Punjabi cultures since the nineteenth century, a theme that has received surprisingly limited treatment in the historiography of Sikhism. The dominant tradition within Sikh studies is what we might term an 'internalist' approach. In this view, Sikh history should be mainly understood in light of the internal dynamics of the Panth: the elaboration of Sikh tradition through a genealogy of texts, competing visions of doctrine and community, and the shifting social composition of the Panth are the key analytical problematics.

Despite the profound epistemological break marked by Harjot Oberoi's *The Construction of Religious Boundaries*—a work that embraced the ethnographical sensibility of anthropology and a Foucauldian vision of the new episteme fashioned by the Singh Sabha—Sikh history continues be cast as largely independent, a story best understood from within the community. Although Oberoi's radical re-reading of the Singh Sabha movement has driven intense and often inaccurate criticism, his *The*

Construction of Religious Boundaries does not seriously challenge this inherited analytical tradition and can be read as the most theoretically sophisticated statement of the internalist model. While Oberoi noted that colonialism was an important cultural backdrop, he stressed the role of indigenous elites and propagandists in the reordering of indigenous identity along communal lines. Oberoi detailed the clash between the Sanatan tradition and the systematized religious vision of the Tat Khalsa that inscribed clear lines between *kesdharis* (unshaven Sikhs who maintain their *kes* (hair) as a symbol of their religious identity) and other Sikhs by insisting on the maintenance of a cluster of new rituals and social practices as markers of community. Thus *The Construction of Religious Boundaries* detailed the erosion of an 'enchanted universe' of popular faith in rural Punjab by a highly ordered pattern of practice and a clearly delineated Tat Khalsa identity elaborated by urban reformers.[59] As such, Oberoi's work is best read in conjunction with the work of K.W. Jones on religious debate within the Punjab, Anil Sethi's recent thesis on late nineteenth century Punjabi culture, and N.G. Barrier's work on Sikh institutions and the colonial state. Nevertheless, we await a work that moves beyond the internalist and externalist approaches: Barrier's forthcoming study, anticipated in part in his essay in this volume, is our best hope in the near future.[60]

The debates surrounding Dalip Singh that this paper has examined have the limitations of the dominant internalist interpretative tradition. While his elite status and wealth mean that we must guard against reading Dalip Singh's life as an 'exemplar' of Sikh experience,[61] many of his Punjabi contemporaries—especially those in the military—travelled widely, encountered Britons on a regular basis, and practiced their faith and articulated their identity within the hybridized cultural formations borne out of colonialism. But, if we must move beyond an 'internalist' approach to recognize the transformative power of colonialism, we must also guard against the excesses of the 'externalist' model developed by Richard Fox in his *Lions of the Punjab*. Fox argued that the colonial administration were pivotal in the constitution of the orthodox 'Singh' [i.e. Khalsa] identity as the British hoped a distinctive and loyal Sikh soldiery would form a bulwark to imperial authority. Unfortunately, Fox entirely effaced the importance of the previous four centuries of Sikh history, neglecting the importance of military values and symbols in pre-colonial Sikh tradition and erasing Sikh agency in the reformulation of cultural practice and political idioms.[62]

Here I have attempted to balance a sensitivity to the importance of Sikh agency and the power of community organizations with an emphasis on the crucial cultural and political contexts that shape post-colonial Sikh identity, particularly within the British context. In locating the increased prominence of Dalip Singh in the British public sphere within the broader context of the re-negotiation of ethnicity and national identity in post-Thatcher Britain, this paper has not attempted to disavow the claims of British South Asians (particularly those of Punjabi descent) about the significance of Dalip Singh, rather it has emphasized that community identity is never simply the product of the dynamics internal to that community. Sikh identity is constantly remade through encounters with other communities (whether of faith, ethnicity, or allegiance) and access to public institutions and the machinery of government. In other words, Sikh identities are constantly formed and reformed through an uneven dialogic, or more correctly polylogic process, whereby understandings of community are constantly formulated, performed, and re-formed in response to other groups, whether Punjabi Hindus, Muslims, or *patit/mona* Sikhs who are seen to be occupying the margins of the community and, within the British context, South Asians of Gujarati or Bangladeshi origin, or Britons of Afro-Caribbean or Anglo-Celtic descent.[63] It is important to emphasize that such processes are not confined to the last few decades: indeed, the mutually constitutive nature of such cross-cultural encounters have been stressed in recent historical work by Rozina Visram, Antoinette Burton, and Michael Fisher on South Asians in Britain from the eighteenth century on.[64] As yet, however, such work on the articulation of Punjabi and more specifically Sikh identities within Britain is fragmentary: in addition to Axel's work on transnational representations of the male Sikh body, Saloni Mathur's recent essay on the beleaguered Tulsi Ram and Susan VanKoski's study of Punjabi soldiers in Britain and France during World War I hint at important avenues for future enquiry and reflection.[65]

For over a century and a half, the Sikh community, whether at home or abroad, has lived within a world fundamentally reshaped by British colonialism. As we are increasingly aware, the transformative power of colonialism not only engendered new social structures and cultural formations in the periphery, but also played a central role in the constitution of metropolitan cultures, including understandings of gender, religion, race, and national identity. If this essay has warned that internalist approaches to the Sikh past erase important connections with other religions, regions, and nations, it has also demonstrated that the British past can no longer be imagined as 'island story', a tale of 'splendid isolation'. This paper has insisted on the interweaving of the Punjab and Britain, the colonial past and the post-colonial present: from understandings of Sikhism as an 'Indian Reformation' to the popularity of contemporary forms of *bhangra* on British dance floors, from the 'Punjabization' of the Indian army in the late nineteenth century to the Gurudwaras of Southall, Bradford, and Coventry, from the impact of Aitchison college to Dalip Singh's Elveden Hall, the enmeshment of Sikh and British cultures is clear. One of the most important projects for Sikh studies in the future is to map the power relations that underpin these cultural formations and to trace their development over the broad sweep of the last 150 years of Sikh history.

Notes

1. *The Guardian*, March 3, 1993. I would like to thank Hew McLeod for initially directing me to this reference.

2. The Runnymede Trust, *The Future of Multi-Ethnic Britain: The Parekh Report* (London: Profile, 2000).

3. Brian Keith Axel, *The Nation's Tortured Body: Violence, Representation, and the Formation of a Sikh 'Diaspora'* (Durham, NC: Duke University Press, 2001).

4. Ganda Singh, ed., *Maharaja Duleep Singh correspondence* (Patiala: Punjabi University, 1977); Michael Alexander and Sushila Anand, *Queen Victoria's Maharajah: Duleep Singh 1838–93* (London: Weidenfeld and Nicolson, 1980); David Jones, 'Maharaja Dalip Singh', *Arts of the Sikh Kingdom* (London: V&A, 1999).

5. Deborah E. McDowell, 'In the First Place: Making Frederick Douglass and the Afro-American Narrative Tradition', *Critical Essays on Frederick Douglass*, ed. William L. Andrews (Boston: G.K. Hall, 1991, 1991), pp. 192–214; Gary Daynes, *Making Villains, Making Heroes: Joseph R. McCarthy, Martin Luther King Jr., and the Politics of American Memory* (New York: Garland, 1997).

6. W.H. McLeod, *Early Sikh Tradition: A Study of the Janam-sakhis* (Oxford: Clarendon, 1980); *The B40 Janam-sakhi* (Amritsar: Guru Nanak Dev University, 1980) and *Popular Sikh Art* (Delhi: Oxford University Press, 1991).

7. McLeod, *Popular Sikh Art*, 19 and figs. 2, 4, and 5.

8. M.L. Ahluwalia, 'Duleep Singh—the crusader', *Fighter for Freedom: Maharaja Duleep Singh* Baldev Singh Baddan, ed., (Delhi: National Book Shop, 1998), p. 92.

9. ibid., p. 95

10. *The Tribune*, August 1883. On Sardar Dayal Singh Majithia and *The Tribune* see: Prakash Ananda, *A History of the Tribune* (Chandigarh: The Tribune Trust, 1986).

11. *The Tribune*, October 25, 1893.

12. *Kurshid-i-Khalsa* (Jalandar, 1885). Baba Nihal Singh's invocation of Bhai Ram Singh and Dalip Singh was somewhat ironic given that Ram Singh denounced Dalip Singh as a beef-eating foreigner to his followers: *Kookian di Vithia*, 234. For British views of these debates see Secy of Punjab Govt to Foreign, *Summary of Correspondence in the Case of Maharaja Dalip Singh* (Shimla, 1887).

13. See W.M. Young to H.M. Durand May 24, 1886, Enclosure C, Ganda Singh, ed., *Maharaja Duleep Singh correspondence*, p. 321.

14. Sardar Thakur Singh Sandhanwalia to Maharaja Dalip Singh, November 9, 1883, Ibid., pp. 117–18.

15. British surveillance of Thakur Singh Sandhanwalia and Thakur Singh of Wagha is recorded in Ibid., pp. 321–2, 346, 467–72.

16. E.g. Rishi Ranjan Chakrabarty, *Duleep Singh: The Maharaja of Punjab and the Raj* (Oldbury: D.S. Samra, 1988); S.P. Gulati, ed., *The Tragic Tale of Maharaja Duleep Singh* (Delhi: National Bookshop, 1998); Prithipal Singh Kapur. ed., *Maharaja Duleep Singh: The Last Sovereign Ruler of the Punjab* (Amritsar, 1995).

17. Baddan, 'Introduction', *Fighter for Freedom*, p. 7.

18. Ibid., p. 11.

19. Ibid., p. 12.

20. A telling indicator of Baddan's narrowly nationalist vision is the complete omission of any reference to the work of Alexander and Anand. Compare this approach with Brian Axel's important study of the transnational articulation of Sikh identities.

21. < http://www.nishaan.com/nagaara.htm>.

22. Runnymede Trust, *Islamophobia* (London: Runnymede Trust, 1997) and *The Future of Multi-Ethnic Britain: The Parekh Report*.

23. C.A. Bayly, 'Exhibiting the Imperial Image', *History Today*, 40 (October 1990), p. 13.

24. Ibid.

25. Ibid., p. 14.

26. *The Observer*, December 9, 1990.

27. *The Guardian*, November 12, 1990.

28. Simeran Mann Singh Gell, 'The Origins of the "Sikh Look": from Guru Gobind Singh to Dalip Singh', *History and Anthropology* 10:1 (1996), pp. 37–83.

29. While the exhibition catalogue puts great emphasis on social and cultural history, the primacy of political events is not only suggested by the chronological sweep of the exhibition (from the foundation of the East India Company through to independence), but also in Bayly's comment directed towards British South Asians that the exhibition tried 'to represent Indian nationalism and Muslim movements as fully as it does British conquests, bugles and tiger-shots'. p. 13.

30. Teri Brewer. ed., *The Marketing of Tradition: Perspectives on Folklore, Tourism and the Heritage Industry* (Enfield Lock: Hisarlik, 1994); J.M. Fladmark. ed., *Heritage and Museums: Shaping National Identity* (Shaftesbury: Donhead, 1999).

31. Raphael Samuel, *Theatres of Memory* (London: Verso, 1994); Patrick Wright, *On Living in an Old Country: The National Past in Contemporary Britain* (London: Verso, 1985).

32. Ballard, 'Differentiation and disjunction among the Sikhs', *Desh Pardesh: the South Asian Presence in Britain* (London: Hurst, 1994), p. 93.

33. <http://www.mdsct.org.uk/mdsctwebpage/background_trust_was_originally_established.htm>

34. Axel, *Nation's Tortured Body*, p. 60.

35. This interpretation is also borne out in the Trust's selection of speakers: in 1997 its annual lecture was delivered by Major Robert Henderson a former officer in a Sikh Regiment, ibid.

36. Axel, *Nation's Tortured Body*, p. 73.

37. This notion of a 'memory anchor' elaborates upon Sybil Milton's observation that: 'Memorials provide fixed places in a chaotic and shifting landscape, where groups can project shared symbols to consolidate notions of pride, heritage, power, and self.' Sybil Milton, 'Memorials', *The Holocaust Encyclopedia* Walter Laqueur, ed., (New Haven: Yale University Press, 2001), p. 414.

38. *The Guardian*, March 3, 1993

39. Ibid.

40. *The Guardian*, January 20, 1993.

41. *The Guardian*, March 3, 1993.

42. Ibid.

43. Ibid.

44. *The Guardian*, March 20, 1993.

45. Gillian Turner interview with Reginald Allen Trett http://www.elveden22.freeserve.co.uk/spoken.htm. All of the interviews on this site discuss the arrival of American servicemen in Elveden during World War II, it seems that it is only at this point the 'outside world' intruded on life in Suffolk.

46. The history presented of the Estate is, 'A brief outline of the development of Elveden Estate during the ownership of the Guinness family 1894–to the present day', eliding Dalip Singh's ownership of the estate from 1869. <http://www.elveden22.freeserve.co.uk/elveden_estate.htm>.

47. The early cultivation of these skills is suggested by a portrait produced in the early 1840s, probably by Imam Bakhsh, that depicts a bewelled infant grasping a rifle. 'Maharaja Dhelip Singh', Musée national des Arts asiatiques-Guimet, (39750).

48. Alexander & Anand, *Queen Victoria's Maharajah*, p. 112.

49. Ibid. p. 111.

50. T.W. Turner, *Memoirs of a Gamekeeper* (London, 1954), cited in *Ibid.*, p. 113.

51. On the importance of these in the moulding of British self-perceptions and in imperial culture see John MacKenzie, *Empire of nature: hunting, conservation and British imperialism* (Manchester: Manchester University Press, 1997).

52. *The Times of India*, May 6, 1873.

53. Axel, *The Nation's Tortured Body*, chapter 1.

54. Antoinette Burton, *Indians and the Colonial Encounter in Late-Victorian Britain* (Berkeley: University of California Press, 1998), p. 36.

55. Elements of the *babu* stereotype and the very different representation of Punjabis, and Sikhs in particular are explored in Tony Ballantyne, 'Resisting the "Boa Constrictor" of Hinduism: the Khalsa and the Raj', *IJPS*, 6:2 (1999), 195–216; Burton, *Heart of empire* 35–7; Mrinalini Sinha, *Colonial Masculinity: The 'Manly Englishman' and the 'Effeminate Bengali' in the Late Nineteenth Century* (Manchester: Manchester University Press, 1995).

56. This song, from Morrissey's 1988 *Viva Hate* album, proved a contentious statement of Englishness with its warning addressed to a young 'Bengali in platforms' who 'only wants to embrace your culture/And to be your friend forever'. The Bengali is told 'Shelve your Western plans/'Cause life is hard enough when you belong/Life is hard enough when you belong here'. For conflicting visions of the significance of these lines, see *Melody Maker*, March 19 and December 3, 1988 and *Sounds*, June 18, 1988.

57. Brian P. Caton, 'Sikh Identity Formation and the British Rural Ideal, 1880–1930', *Sikh Identity: Continuity and Change* Pashaura Singh and N. Gerald Barrier, eds, (Delhi: Manohar, 1999), pp. 175–94.

58. Raymond Williams, *The Country and the City* (London: Chatto and Windus, 1973).

59. Harjot Oberoi, *The Construction of Religious Boundaries: Culture, Identity and Diversity in the Sikh Tradition* (Delhi: Oxford University Press, 1994).

60. Kenneth W. Jones, *Arya Dharm: Hindu Consciousness in 19th-century Punjab* (Berkeley: University of California Press, 1976); 'Ham Hindu Nahin: Arya-Sikh Relations 1877–1905', *Journal of Asian Studies*, 32 (1973), 457–75; Anil Sethi, 'The creation of religious identities in the Punjab, c.1850–1920', (University of Cambridge, PhD 1998); see N.G. Barrier's essay in this volume.

61. C.f. Simeran Man Singh Gell, 'The Origins of the Sikh "Look": from Guru Gobind to Dalip Singh', *History and Anthropology* 10,1 (1996), pp. 37–83.

62. Richard G. Fox, *Lions of the Punjab: Culture in the Making* (Berkeley: University of California Press, 1985).

63. On 'dialogics' see Eugene Irschick, *Dialogue and History: Constructing South India, 1795–1895* (Berkeley: University of California Press, 1994). Of course, it is crucial to underline the deep-seated inequalities that structured such processes, both under colonialism and in this postcolonial age: my use of the phrase 'uneven dialogics' is an attempt to draw greater attention to this disparities, which Irschick acknowledges, but doesn't emphasize. An important essay on inter-regional contexts of identity construction is Himadri Banerjee, 'Sikh Identity Question: A View from Eastern India', *Sikh Identity*, Singh and Barrier, eds, 195–216. Also see Steven Vertovec, 'Caught in an Ethnic Quandary: Indo-Caribbean Hindus in London', *Desh Pardesh*, pp. 272–90.

64. Burton, *At the Heart of the Empire*; Michael Fisher, *The First Indian Author in English: Dean Mahomed (1759–1851) in India, Ireland and England* (Delhi: Oxford University Press, 1996); Rozina Visram, *Ayahs, Lascars and Princes: Indians in Britain 1700–1947* (London, 1986).

65. Susan Van Koski, 'Letters Home, 1915–16: Punjabi Soldiers Reflect on War and Life in Europe and their Meanings for Home and Self', *IJPS*, 2:1 (1995), pp. 43–63.

6

What's in a Name?
Circumscribing Sikh Female Nomenclature

Doris Jakobsh

Early sources delineating the injunctions of Guru Gobind Singh for his newly founded order asserted that not only were members of the Khalsa brotherhood to be recognized as such by outward symbolism and garb, they also placed considerable emphasis on the naming practices to be followed within the Khalsa. Those installed into the brotherhood were required to take on the surname 'Singh' and strictly prohibited from omitting the appellation in addressing another member of the brotherhood.[1] Needless to say, while a distinct naming practice for Sikh males was a prescribed and central aspect of Sikh identity, things were not nearly as clear for Sikh women. Injunctions regarding Khalsa naming conventions focused exclusively on males; ordinances wholly neglected naming specifications for Sikh women folk.

Nonetheless, a tradition whose origin is highly obscure existed among a significant proportion of the Sikh populace, namely, the usage of the appellation 'Kaur'. As the term 'Singh' meaning 'lion' was adopted from the Rajputs, so too was the name 'Kaur', a derivative of the Rajput term 'kanwar' customarily defined as 'prince' or 'bachelor'.[2] Early sources indicate that the name 'Kaur' was given to both males and females in Punjab. The appellation appears in both the Adi Granth and the *Dasam Granth*, the former utilizing the term in its traditional delineation of 'prince',[3] the latter referring to a woman's name during the time of Guru Gobind Singh.[4]

Given the paucity of sources that address Punjabi patterns of nomenclature during the early and late Guru periods it is difficult to move beyond a mere verification of its usage for both males and females. It must also be noted that individuals, apart from those playing a central role in the formation of the Sikh panth or those of the upper echelons of society were seldom named in Sikh historical sources, especially the *women* of Sikh history. As a result, the early *janam-sakhi* literature, while claiming to be authoritative on the life of Guru Nanak is at considerable variance with regard to both his mother's and his wife's names. Questions regarding the application and incentive for the naming practices among the early Sikhs can thus at best be speculative. It does appear however that some variances in the usage of the name 'Kaur' emerged during the seventeenth and nineteenth centuries between the Jats and Khatris of Punjab. 'Kaur' continued to be utilized by both males and females of the Khatri caste, but by the eighteenth century exclusively referred to females among the Jats.[5]

Appropriation of highly specific Rajput distinctions such as 'Kanwar/ Kaur' and 'Singh' can most likely be attributed to active attempts by specific segments of the Sikh population during the mid-to-late Guru period to *rajputize* their identity.[6] Early European accounts certainly make the connection between Guru Gobind Singh's adoption of the title 'Singh' for his warrior-brotherhood, and the heretofore exclusively assumed name of the Rajputs, the foremost warrior-class among the Hindus. According to Syad Muhammad Latif, by taking on this Rajput signifier 'the Sikhs felt themselves at once elevated to rank with the highest, and their leader opened to them the dazzling prospect of earthly glory, rousing their military valour and inciting them to deeds of courage.'[7] This process of 'rajputization' becomes intelligible particularly in light of the elevation of the lowly Jat to a hegemonic position within the social hierarchy of the Sikh Panth, but the continued stigma attached to the Jat within the wider social arena.[8] Jats, far more than the highly established and traditionally respected Khatris were in need of signifiers that connoted their rise in the social hierarchical patterns of the day. While Khatris were content to stay with the established customs of nomenclature, traditional biases against the inferior societal position of the Jats were compelling incentives to consolidate their hegemonic position within Punjab society by taking on distinctive Rajput and thus highly esteemed names.[9] By the nineteenth and twentieth centuries British assumptions pertaining to the 'manliness' of both the Rajputs and the Jats had accomplished a great deal in upgrading the status of the Jat; at least for the colonial masters the heritage of the Jats and the Rajputs were inextricably intertwined. Thus, according to Denzil Ibbetson in the early twentieth century, whatever the original lineage of both groups 'the two *now* form a common stock, the distinction between the Jat and the Rajput being social rather than ethnic' [italics mine].[10] The similar naming practices of the Jats and Rajputs presumably benefited colonial claims regarding this kinship.

It would be entirely plausible that with the consolidation of Rajput martial identity through the inauguration of the Khalsa, particularly with the adoption of 'Singh' nomenclature for Jat males, the Rajput name 'Kanwar' and its Punjabi equivalent 'Kaur' was embraced as its natural ancillary for females. By the eighteenth century women of the newly established aristocracy, the leadership of the misldoms that were largely dominated by Jat leadership, were invariably given two names, the latter as 'Kaur'.[11] The usage of 'Kaur' for Sikh princesses, given the term's implications of royalty is highly understandable among the newly established Sikh nobility of the Punjab. The naming practices of the elite however offer little insight into the patterns of nomenclature among the masses. While the signifier 'Kaur' eventually came to be embraced by the wider populace as well, single names were more common for women, before and after the eighteenth century, than dual names.[12]

Unfortunately the earliest attempt made to elucidate the linguistic conventions of the Punjab offers little guidance or insight in this regard. The first dictionary of the Punjabi language published in 1854 by the Ludhiana Mission retained the princely definition of 'Kaur' and its alternate reference to a *male* child.[13] Although evidence points to the signifier being utilized by both Sikh males and females throughout the eighteenth and early nineteenth centuries, this inaugural *Dictionary of the Punjabi Language* makes no reference to its usage by Sikhs in particular. Nor does it refer to specific cultural conventions of the term as an addendum for females. The dictionary of Bhai Maya Singh of 1895 also refers exclusively to its masculine and princely delineation.[14] The latter definition is indeed surprising for by the late nineteenth century British accounts indicate that the customary usage of the appellation 'Kaur' for males had apparently ceased and it was henceforth consigned to an exclusively feminine signifier.[15]

Needless to say, the scant sources available with regard to the appellation 'Kaur' as well as its wide though inconsistent application throughout Sikh history make a definitive explication of the normative naming practices among Sikh females impossible. Even the increasingly authoritative *Prem Sumarg* offers little insight in this regard; it does however point to the variability of female patterns of nomenclature among the Sikhs. Completely omitting mention of the appellation 'Kaur' in its injunctions, females after being initiated into the Khalsa order were instructed to add the epithet '*Devi*' alongside their given name.[16] Given the paucity and divergence of source material with regard to Sikh female naming practices, certitude can only be replaced by speculation. At *best* until the beginning of the twentieth century, 'Kaur' as a feminine epithet can only be delineated as indicative of a diffuse *cultural* identity but as having no definitive *religious* and *ritual* signification. On the other hand, by the mid-nineteenth century the epithet '*Singhni*' had become the *linguistic* complement to 'Singh'.[17] Its linguistic correspondence must be stressed given the appellation's lack of ritual signification.

The parameters of that which constitutes 'ritual' has been aptly delineated by the anthropologist Gilbert Lewis, based on his extensive fieldwork among the Gnau in Papua New Guinea.[18] According to Lewis, ritual is exceedingly difficult to define in that its identification is inextricably bound not only to specific expressions and codes, but also to the ability to interpret what is being communicated. Ritual in essence can be likened to a form of language, art, performance, or a specific code of conduct. Yet not just any formula of communication, action, or behaviour can be construed as ritual; Lewis delineates what *is* essential to ritual:

> To say the action is prescribed, that there is some ruling about the circumstances for its performance, moves closer to an answer ... What is always explicit about ritual, and recognized by those who perform it, is that aspect of it which states who should do what and when. It is practical. It guides action. And phrases like 'prescribed routine', 'standardized behaviour', 'behaviour with incongruous rigidity', which appear in most of the definitions given ... refer to this ... The explanations for what is done may be clear, or complicated or uncertain, or multiple, or forgotten: but what to do is clear.[19]

Further Lewis notes, to conform to a particularized ritual is to acknowledge that one is part of the specific group for whom the ritual has meaning.[20] By implication then, the *lack* of conformance to a particularized ritual would by the same token attest to restrictions placed upon comprehensive membership within the specific group. The argument can easily be extended to explicate the status of a *segment* of the group within that of the larger body. For the purposes at hand it is useful in coming to a gendered understanding of the mechanisms of inclusion and exclusion in the context of group formation and identity. The appellation 'Singh' *was* a specifically prescribed injunction and consequential to the rite of initiation; it was also central to the identity formation of Khalsa Sikhs at large. Clearly, in comparison to the highly standardized naming routine for males within the Khalsa, female naming patterns among the Sikhs were *not* uniform, *not* precise, and *not* explicit.

Gilbert Lewis' clarification of the explicit separation between men and women in terms of ritual identity among the Gnau is particularly helpful in also understanding this divergence in ritual behaviour among the Sikhs. For example, among the Gnau, children and women were not granted the equality or the responsibility that was accorded to men. While Lewis maintains that there are a variety of influences shaping these gender differences, 'rites have a special place in creating it and providing impressive direction to male aspiration. By excluding others, making some knowledge and experience esoteric, they find a justification for their capacity to act in these matters and enhance the value of what they do.'[21] In essence, *control* of ritual knowledge and behaviour allowed for the creation of a tightly bonded brotherhood equipped to face the traditionally 'masculine' realities of war, disputes, and defence. Similarly, the continued divergence between male and female naming practices in the discourse of Sikh reform stemmed from a perceived need to control access to full-fledged and equal membership within the Khalsa order. Thus, the propensity to demarcate women as 'different' and ultimately to exclude them from the consummate 'brotherhood' continued well into the twentieth century. Indeed, the very obscurity and lack of standardization among women's naming practices can be viewed as an apt indicator of their status within the 'reformed' Sikh panth under the Singh Sabha reformers, and their continued negligible role within the Khalsa brotherhood on the whole.

The Re-writing of Ritual: Singh Sabha Formulations of Women's Identity

The diversity of women's naming patterns continued well beyond the nineteenth century.[22] There were however distinct rumblings of a shift in the significance of female naming patterns among the Tat Khalsa reformers. The impetus for this change is not difficult to appreciate or to understand. While Hindu and Muslim women of Punjab were securely distinguished by appellations distinct to their communities such as 'Devi' or '*Begum*' respectively, Sikh female identity remained indistinct and multifarious.

Lakshman Singh tells of an encounter that brings the distinctions between women of the Hindu and Muslim community based on the naming conventions of each community to light. The incident revolved around the 'language issue' in Punjabi schools, in this case, whether Sanskrit or Persian was to be taught. Bhagat Lakshman Singh was an avid promoter of Sanskrit and took it upon himself to convert students to the cause. Addressing a Hindu boy, Lakshman Singh queried of him:

'[w]ill you give up Persian and take up Sanskrit instead?' 'Why should I? I am not going to turn into a Brahman priest', was the reply. I then turned to a Musalman child, 'Kaka', repeated I, 'Will you take up Sanskrit in place of Persian?' 'Am I a Hindu?' was this child's reply. I again turned to the previous Hindu child and said, 'Are you a Musalman, my boy? Yes you are. You see you are learning a language of the Musalmans'. And, added I, *Is your mother's name Bibi Jamalo or Begam Bano?'* *'No, my mother's name is Bishen Devi' was the angry reply* ... [italics mine].[23]

Albeit barely discernible, opposition to the ambiguous nature of Sikh female nomenclature was beginning to make an impression on the Sikh literary horizon. Bhai Vir Singh's novel *Sundri* published just before the dawn of the twentieth century brings what would appear to be an inconsequential censure to the fore. For Surastri's (Sundri's earlier name) initiation into the Khalsa fold by the *amrit* ceremony was accompanied by a change of name; henceforth she was to be known as Sunder *Kaur* and popularly as Sundri.[24]

Another seemingly innocuous though important indicator of this shift can be traced to Bhai Kahn Singh Nabha's celebrated tract, *Ham Hindu Nahin* [We Are Not Hindus]. According to Kahn Singh, Guru Gobind Singh pronounced himself as the father, and Sahib *Kaur* not *Devan* as the mother of the Khalsa.[25]

The context of this change in nomenclature, from Sahib Devan to Sahib Kaur is highly significant. For according to the worldview of Kahn Singh of Nabha, Sikhs were not Hindus; 'Hindu' names, particularly those associated with the inauguration of the Khalsa necessitated transformation into a form acceptable to the increasingly defined ideology of the Tat Khalsa. This purging of 'hinduized' names can best be understood within the context of the *larger* issue of Singh Sabha reformers' attempts to distance themselves from the ever menacing Hindu aspects from *within* their own history. For, within the *gur-bilas* genre of literature from the eighteenth and nineteenth centuries, the Goddess Devi continues to play a significant role; these early Sikh accounts consistently maintained that Guru Gobind Singh not only paid homage to the Goddess Devi, but that she also associated with the Khalsa. The *Gurbilas Patshahi 10* attributed to Koer Singh of the mid-eighteenth century insists that the Devi is responsible for its very creation.[26]

More specifically, Kalika or Devi is the 'mother' of the new order.[27] Another important account is Sainapat's *Sri Gur Sobha*, the earliest example of the *gur-bilas* literature; while Sahib Devan receives no mention, the author does present the earliest perspective on the parentage of the Khalsa. For Sainapat, Guru Gobind Singh is *both* the father and the mother of the Khalsa.[28] Clearly, the authors of the later *gur-bilas* writings needed to make sense of this anomaly; the image of the Devi was ultimately effective as the all-powerful mother of brotherhood. However, a definitive shift in the 'parenthood' of the Khalsa was slowly coming to the fore; Ratan Singh Bhangu's *Panth Prakash* instead sanctioned Mata Sahib Devan and Guru Gobind Singh as the mother and father of the Khalsa.[29]

The development of Sahib Devan as the mother of the Khalsa as opposed to the Goddess Devi was likely to have been influenced by Bhangu's attempt to establish for his British audience the distinct nature of the Sikhs from the wider Hindu community. Devi as *Mata* of the Khalsa would have made this distinction highly untenable. For similar reasons Devi had also disappeared at the time of amrit preparation in the *Prem Sumarg*. This development culminated with the Singh Sabha reformers in the late nineteenth and early twentieth centuries: the Devi could have no place within the worldview the Tat Khalsa was valiantly attempting to contour, particularly in light of Singh Sabha objectives to *conclusively* establish Sikh distinctiveness from the wider Hindu community. Earlier claims regarding Guru Gobind Singh's homage to the Goddess were met by calls for pragmatism. According to one writer: '[W]ho out of the bedlam would ever believe that the Great Guru approached a goddess for help in founding a religion inculcating the worship of none else but God, and condemning that of even Durga whom the Guru is alleged to have addressed, adored and worshipped?'[30]

Albeit inconsistently, attempts to establish distinct 'Sikh' patterns of nomenclature for women continued. In fact, Singh Sabha claims of females' unobstructed inclusivity in terms of ritual signification and distinctiveness within the order of the Khalsa necessitated novel versions of historiography. Max Arthur Macauliffe, the celebrated British historian was particularly obliging in this regard. Determined to by-pass the opprobrium of the Sikhs he relied heavily upon interpretations from prominent individuals within the Singh Sabha movement such as Bhai Kahn Singh of Nabha. He thus ensured that his writings were met with the approval of these new leaders of the Sikh community. Drafts of his work were also submitted to a special committee established by the Khalsa Diwan of Amritsar. Notwithstanding the magnitude of Macauliffe's achievements, his work can best be understood as 'the product of compromises and a composite of documents rather than the work of a single person.'[31] As a result of this censure, and, by-passing all early historical sources, the third wife of Guru Gobind Singh, Sahib Devan is presented as having first been baptized by Guru Gobind Singh and subsequently renamed 'Sahib Kaur'.[32] What is most fascinating about this palpable Singh Sabha influence upon his work is that Macauliffe had asserted earlier that that Guru Gobind Singh did *not* give directives for women with respect to the founding of the Khalsa order.[33]

Re-defining the Sikh Code of Conduct in the Twentieth Century

Given the variety of claims, doctrines, and attitudes in the development of the Sikh tradition, a prominent group of Singh Sabha reformers also took issue with the existing Sikh codes of conduct stemming from the eighteenth and nineteenth centuries. The discrepant injunctions found within these codes were deemed as having been tainted by the ever-pervasive Hindu tradition. The objectives of this small group of notables were primarily focused on eliminating the diversity of practices among the Sikhs by formulating an undefiled Sikh code that concurred with the reformed worldview of the early twentieth century.[34] They also addressed the performance of life-cycle rituals, an aspect that earlier codes had neglected.[35] In 1915, a prescriptive manual known as the *Gurmat Prakas* was produced which delineated an amended and 'correct' order of *rahit* for Sikhs.[36] The *Gurmat Parkas* was highly specific about the ways and means of naming procedures; they were to be carried out ten days after the birth of the child with the assistance of Sikh sacred scriptures. The signifier 'Singh' was exclusively associated with Sikh baptismal rites. Significantly, the document did *not* attend to the increasingly persistent voices that were advocating a unified and distinctive form of nomenclature for Sikh females; the *Gurmat Prakas* was silent about 'Kaur' as a 'Sikh' epithet.[37] Moreover, it evidently rejected the name 'Devi' for Sikh women who were being baptized into the Khalsa order as sanctioned by the *Prem Sumarg*.[38] Further, the 'mother' of the Khalsa was designated as Sahib Devan *not* Sahib Kaur in spite of the latter usage becoming increasingly widespread among Singh Sabha narratives and reports.[39] Evidently a consensus was not possible in this regard even among the tightly knit fraternity that constituted the leadership of the Singh Sabha movement.[40] Although drafted in 1910, the *Gurmat Prakas* only came to be issued in its final form in 1915. Even after five years of deliberation, and possibly because of this lag in publication, the code was largely disregarded by the wider populace.[41]

This impasse necessitated another attempt in 1931 to conclusively delineate Sikh rahit, this time under the auspices of the Shiromani Gurdwara Parbandhak Committee (SGPC). The final result however only appeared in 1950 as the *Sikh Rahit Maryada*. By this time it was finally recognized as the definitive statement of conduct for Sikhs a position it has maintained to the present time. What had during the early years of the twentieth century remained an ill-defined, disjunctive, and even cryptic endorsement of Sikh nomenclature for females had by this time been transformed to the level of prescription for Sikh females and fundamental to their very identity. Upon a child's birth, boys were required to be given the suffix 'Singh' and girls the suffix 'Kaur'.[42]

As has already been noted this naming practice among the Sikhs in a *culturally* significant manner had long been adopted, at least among a portion of the populace. Here however the appellation 'Kaur' as a specific Sikh *symbol* was for the first time officially sanctioned. Mata Sahib *Kaur* too was by this time firmly entrenched in the historiography of the Sikhs as the spiritual mother of the Khalsa Panth.[43] This later delineation of specified Sikh appellations to be given *at the time of birth* is indeed remarkable given its originality, at least at the level of explicit *rahit*. In the thirty-five year time period between the *Gurmat Parkas* and the *Sikh Rahit Maryada*, Bhai Kahn Singh of Nabha had published his monumental and highly influential *Gurushabad Ratanakar Mahan Kosh* also known simply as *Mahan Kosh*.[44] It definitively coincided the appellation 'Kaur' with *female initiation* into the Khalsa Panth. Kahn Singh's interpretation of the significance and application of the name 'Kaur' at the time of initiation was clearly rejected by 1950; the epithets 'Kaur' and 'Singh' henceforth came to be given at the time of birth instead.

The various applications of the signifier 'Kaur' are indicative of the heterogeneous nature of Sikhism in the nineteenth and twentieth centuries. They also point to the varied and fluctuating needs of a rapidly developing Sikh community during pivotal stages of its growth. The hard wrought distinctions between Sikhs and Hindus put in place through the process of reform spearheaded by the Singh Sabha movement were widely accepted by the 1950's. By the mid-twentieth century the appellation 'Kaur' had become *the* signifier of Sikh female collective identity. As such the application thereof came to be transferred to an even more fundamental platform than that of baptism, namely, the naming ritual occurring just days after a child's birth.

Previously, the conversion of a Muslim woman to Sikhism who had for years been married to a Sikh man was highly publicized by the press. Under the auspices of the radical Bhasaur Singh Sabha, her conversion necessarily included a name change. According to the *Khalsa Akhbar*:

[T]he Sri Guru Singh Sabha, Bhasaur, has administered the Gurmantra and holy *amrita* to a Muslim woman and ushered her into Sodhbans [the family of Guru Gobind Singh]. Her Sikh name is Kishan Kaur. A Sikh who had fallen by living with a Muslim woman has been baptized and renamed Ude Singh.[45]

By the mid-twentieth century however, public exhibition of Sikh distinctiveness through overt signifiers applied at the time of baptism was no longer necessary; infants were quietly furnished with by now widely accepted Sikh forms of nomenclature in the confines of their homes.

Needless to say, Singh Sabha initiatives intent on injecting new definitions, new applications, and an unheard of unanimity, to previously indistinct cultural practices, were immensely successful. Nonetheless, and perhaps surprisingly, it was only by the 1950s that they came to be officially ratified. As noted earlier, this end result was by no means accidental. For with the gradual authorization of specific Sikh naming practices for *both* males and females in the form of *rahit*, Sikh communal consciousness was inevitably heightened. By the mid-twentieth century the performance of these rituals, consistently communicated, reaffirmed, and rehearsed, had become securely established within the Sikh ritual drama.[46] Though speaking in a different context, the words of Carol Rosenberg nonetheless ring eerily true: 'Finally, however, the new order will establish its hegemony. The new wielders of power will move to suppress symbolic as well as literal disorder. The language of diversity will be muffled ... '[47]

Contemporary Scholars and the Rewriting of History

As has been shown, extant historical sources are unanimously varied with regard to both women's baptism into the order of the Khalsa as well as the application and implications of the term 'Kaur' among the Sikhs. Nonetheless, contemporary assumptions allow for scant contention in this regard. Khushwant Singh for example, in his ever-popular *A History of the Sikhs* unequivocally coincides the appellation 'Kaur' with that of 'Singh', adding that the surname Kaur is to be granted Sikh women at the time of baptism.[48] If one swings to the other side of the 'scholarly spectrum', W.H. McLeod who has almost single-handedly transformed the academic study of Sikhism through his near exhaustive scope of inquiry, has also failed to move beyond early twentieth century assumptions in this regard. This is indeed remarkable, given McLeod's meticulous research methodology and his resounding insistence on the need for a systematic reorganization and rigorous analysis of virtually all aspects of the Sikh tradition. With regard to the critique at hand, McLeod, in addressing Chaupa Singh's injunction against the utilization of half-names for those of the Khalsa brotherhood, inadvertently furthers the belief that the requisition encompassed women's naming practices as well; in essence he accords equal status to both 'Kaur' and 'Singh'.[49] Yet the *Chaupa Singh Rahit-nama* gives no indication of distinct nomenclature for Sikh females. Here McLeod is fortuitously furthering a redaction of Sikh history that is tinged by the Singh Sabha tendency to reinterpret historical sources in order to fit the Tat Khalsa agenda.

Nikki Singh takes this contemporary re-visioning of Sikh history one step further inasmuch as she contemplates both the rite of baptism for women and the signifier Kaur from an uncritical though professedly feminist perspective. Basing her insights wholly upon late Singh Sabha redactions of history Nikki Singh maintains that the signifier 'Kaur', female initiation into the Khalsa and the military symbolism are in and of themselves explicit and viable indicators of the inherent egalitarianism of the Sikh tradition. In her own words:

This baptism through steel was open to both men and women. Women were to wear the five emblems of the Khalsa, too. As men received the surname Singh, women received the surname Kaur, modified. Men and women no longer traced their lineage or occupation to the 'father'. As 'Singh' and 'Kaur', both were equal partners in the new family.[50]

In light of the indisputable contradictions and the immense variability within the tradition itself, Nikki Singh's attitude of certitude with regard to the historicity of her interpretation denotes the potency and longevity of Singh Sabha interpretations of Sikh history.

Grewal and Bal's critique regarding the methods and means of traditional historical analysis among Sikh scholars, particularly with regard to the scant sources addressing the creation of the Khalsa is highly applicable both to the issue of female baptism and the application of the appellation 'Kaur' among the Sikhs.

Most of the modern historians of Guru Gobind Singh have adopted the very simple method of selecting one and rejecting another detail from one of more of the chronicles. But once that selection is made the isolated point or passage is treated as literally true ... Now, it should be unwise on anyone's part to reject later tradition merely because it is much later to the events; and there is no doubt that traditions, as a valid form of evidence, can provide useful clues to past probabilities but later tradition cannot be accepted literally and it seldom leads to any certainties about the past.[51]

If we turn to positions taken by scholars addressing the inauguration of the Khalsa, baptism, and injunctions regarding nomenclature *as they pertain to women*, it becomes abundantly clear that the above noted critique is remarkably pertinent. The concurrence of even the most meticulous of scholars in the furtherance of untenable, inaccurate, and variegated claims in this regard is indicative of the indifference surrounding Sikh scholarship with regard to a systematic study of women's history. In this regard, modern scholarship has inadvertently failed to move beyond Singh Sabha renditions of history, particularly the highly modified version offered by Max Arthur Macauliffe, Kahn Singh of Nabha, and the ever prolific writer Bhai Vir Singh.

This tendency has long been recognized in a generalized sense in the academic study of Sikhism. The editors of *Sikh History and Religion in the Twentieth Century* note with considerable astuteness that Singh Sabha writers were ultimately successful in their attempts to redefine the Sikh tradition; in fact, by and large their interpretations came to acquire the status of implicit truth. Moreover, that status has continued to the present day. The editors continue with a warning: 'It is essential that we recognize the actual nature and extent of this influence and conditioning, if we are to comprehend the historical development of the Sikh tradition.'[52] Indeed, while for the most part scholars have taken this counsel to heart, close scrutiny and rigorous analysis of sources with regard to historiography as it pertains to women has been virtually non-existent. In short, in this regard scholars have done little to append to the contributions of the Singh Sabha reformers of the late nineteenth and early twentieth centuries. Historical questions regarding women within the Khalsa order have either been ignored, or, historians have simply furthered the highly biased outlook of the Singh Sabha reformers.[53]

The range of discrepant assumptions is indicative of the insignificance accorded not only to women's history, but also points to a pervasive unwillingness to engage in a careful analysis of the wider process of gender construction. For gender understood as a construct has significant consequences far beyond an awareness of the relationships between women and men. How and why the categories of male and female, subjective and collective have actively been constructed is crucial in coming to a more comprehensive understanding of the historical process. Analysis of the discursive structures in the formation of ritual identities from a gendered perspective allows for a more complex understanding of the mechanisms of inclusion and exclusion central to group identity formulation. Perhaps most important, the perspective of gender warrants an endorsement of historiography *beyond* the reiteration of rhetorical formulations, however imprecise, that served the purposes of a community in flux admirably well. More precisely, it allows for an understanding of how and why specific gender construction was fundamental to the very evolution of the Sikh community; this includes early configurations of identity, the process of Sikh adaptation to the colonial milieu, and the even more complex task of communal identity formation led by the Singh Sabha reformers.

Notes

1. W.H. McLeod, *The Chaupa Singh Rahit-nama* (Dunedin: University of Otago Press, 1987) pp. 35, 408.

With regard to injunctions against calling a Sikh by half his name, the Chaupa Singh, Daya Singh, and Mukti-nama of Bhai Sahib Singh versions of *rahit* are in agreement. See Gurpreet Kaur, 'Historical Analysis of Sikh Rahitnamas', Unpublished PhD Thesis (Amritsar: Department of History, Guru Nanak Dev University, 1988) p. 368.

2. See, 'kanwar' and 'kaur', R.L. Turner, *A Comparative Dictionary of the Indo-Aryan Languages* (London: Oxford University Press, 1966) p. 170.

The appellation 'Kanwar' also refers to females in the present day. The highly publicized case of Roop Kanwar who was burnt to death on her husband's funeral pyre in the village of Deorala, Rajasthan in 1987 attests to its contemporary usage. See Madhu Kishwar and Ruth Vanita, 'The Burning of Roop Kanwar', *Manushi* No. 42–3, 1987, pp. 15–25.

3. If we turn to the Adi Granth, Guru Nanak's 'Rag Asa' refers to 'Koer' in the context of Babur's conquest of the Punjab. The plight of the inhabitant, including *princes* is described [italics mine]. *Sri Guru Granth Sahib*, 4 Volumes (Patiala: Punjabi University, 1987) p. 417.

4. The woman referred to is Bijay Kaur. *Dasam Granth*, Volume Two, (Amritsar: Bhai Chatar Singh and Jeevan Singh Publishers, 1988) p. 1053.

5. Ganesh Das' *Char Bagh-i-Panjab*, completed in 1849 makes repeated references a number of both Sikh and Hindu males, largely of the Khatri caste who were given the name 'Kaur'. See J.S. Grewal, Indu Banga, trans. and eds, *Early Nineteenth Century Panjab*. From Ganesh Das' *Char Bagh-i-Panjab* (Amritsar: Guru Nanak University, 1975) p. 27.

6. While the concept under girding the actual process of 'rajputization' has been a pivotal aspect of my own thought processes regarding the origins and development of the name 'Kaur', I am grateful to Jeevan Deol for the feasible term 'rajputization' to better explicate this process. See Jeevan Deol, 'Rajputising the Guru? The Construction of Early Sikh Political Discourse'. Paper presented at South Asian Seminar, St. Anthony's College, Oxford, January 2000.

7. Syad Muhammad Latif, *History of the Panjab from the Remotest Antiquity to the Present Time* (New Delhi: Kalyani Publishers, 1994) p. 335, first published in 1889.

8. Widely known proverbs testify to the prevailing negative attitudes toward the Jat. In particular, Jats continued to be presented as crude and averse to education: 'What does a Jat know about dainties? He might as well be eating toad-stools'; 'A scythe has no sheath, a Jat has no learning'. Sir Herbert Risley, *The People of India*, W. Crooke, ed., second edition, (London: W. Thacker & Co., 1915) pp. 309–10.

9. Although the Jat Sikhs in particular had taken on traditional Rajput nomenclature, Rajputs themselves, highly fastidious in preserving their esteemed lineage retained their contempt toward the 'lowly' Jats. The Rajput Princess Brinda who married into the princely Jat Kapurthala family in the early twentieth century notes that other Rajputs were highly opposed to her marriage into Sikh royalty. The Kapurthala family on the other hand was elated by the match. See Brinda, *Maharani: The Story of an Indian Princess* (As told to Elaine Williams), (New York: Henry Hold and Company, 1954) pp. 1–39, 98.

10. Denzil Ibbetson, *Panjab Castes* (Delhi: Low Price Publications, 1993) pp. 100–1 (first published in 1916).

11. See for example, 'Genealogical Table', Latif, *History of the Punjab*, p. 335.

12. The majority of the women of the Guru lineage, including Guru Gobind Singh's first two wives, Sundri and Jito were given single names.

13. L. Janver, ed., *Dictionary of the Punjabi Language* (Delhi: Nirmal Pub. and Distributors, 1987) p. 109 (first published in 1854 by the Ludhiana Mission).

14. Bhai Maya Singh, *The Punjabi Dictionary* (Delhi: National Book Shop, 1992) (first published in 1895). The definition given by Maya Singh of Kaur is: 'a boy, a son, a child; the title of a prince, the younger son of a kin, Kumar.'

15. According to Rose the appellation 'Kaur' 'could hardly be borne by a man'. Rose, *The Glossary of the Tribes and Castes of the Punjab and North-West Frontier Province* (Patiala: Language Department, 1990) p. 551 (first published in 1883) .

16. Randhir Singh, ed., *Prem Sumarg Granth* (Jalandhar: New Book Company, 1965) p. 25 (first published in Amritsar, 1953).

17. L. Janver, *Dictionary of the Punjabi Language*, pp. 55–6.

18. Gilbert Lewis, *Day of Shining Red. An Essay on Understanding Ritual* (Cambridge: Cambridge University Press, 1988).

19. Ibid, p. 11.

20. Ibid.

21. Ibid., p. 167.

22. Names of prominent women among the Singh Sabha movement who collected funds for the victims of the Kangra Valley earthquake attest to this diversity. Of the ninety-nine names of women listed in the *Khalsa Advocate* less than half of the entries included the appellation 'Kaur'. The majority of women were reported as having only one name, or were noted as 'Singhni', or had two names other than the epithet 'Kaur'. This included names such as 'Dai' or 'Devi'. See *Khalsa Advocate*, May 6, 1905.

23. Ganda Singh, ed., *Bhagat Lakshman Singh*: *Autobiography* (Calcutta: Sikh Cultural Centre, 1965) pp. 110–11.

24. Bhai Vir Singh, *Sundri*, trans. Gobind Singh Mansukhani (New Delhi: Bhai Vir Singh Sahitya Sadan, 1988) p. 26.

25. Kahn Singh Nabha, *Ham Hindu Nahin*, [We Are Not Hindus], Amritsar, 1914, pp. 4–9, first published by Khalsa Press, 1899, reproduced in part in McLeod, *Textual Sources for the Study of Sikhism* (Chicago: University of Chicago Press, 1990) pp. 134–6.

26. Shamsher Singh Ashok, ed., *Gurbilas Patshahi 10*, (Patiala: Punjabi University Press, 1967) p. 103, cited in Surjit Hans, *A Reconstruction of Sikh History from Sikh Literature* (Jalandhar: ABS Publishers, 1988) p. 267.

27. Sukha Singh, *Gurbilas Daswin Patshahi* (Lahore: Lala Ram Chand Manak Tahla, 1912) pp. 203, 596, cited in Surjit Singh Hans, 'Historical Analysis of Sikh Literature, 1500–1850', Unpublished PhD thesis (Amritsar: Department of History, Guru Nanak Dev University, 1980) p. 419, 427.

28. J.S. Grewal, *From Guru Nanak to Maharajah Ranjit Singh* (Amritsar: Department of History, Guru Nanak Dev University, 1982) pp. 79–80.

29. Ratan Singh Bhangu, *Prachin Panth Parkash*, Bhai Vir Singh, ed., (Amritsar: Khalsa Samachar, 1939) p. 1790.

30. *Khalsa Advocate*, August 19, 1916.

Here the writers invoke the opinions of Macauliffe in rejecting Guru Gobind Singh's worship of Durga.

31. N.G. Barrier, 'Trumpp and Macauliffe: Western Students of Sikh History and Religion', Fauja Singh, ed., *Historians and Historiography of the Sikhs* (New Delhi: Oriental Publishers & Distributors, 1978) pp. 176–7.

32. See Max Arthur Macauliffe, *The Sikh Religion. Its Gurus, Sacred Writings and Authors*, Vol. V (Delhi: Low Price Publications, 1990) pp. 143–4 (first published in Oxford, 1909).

33. Proponents of the Singh Sabha reform movement who insisted that women were initiated as early as 1750, objected to Macauliffe's earlier observations. See Max Arthur Macauliffe, *Calcutta Review*, 1881, p. 162.

34. As noted earlier, Baba Khem Singh Bedi in the late nineteenth century had already produced a code of conduct, the *Sanskar Bagh* that was highly influential among his large following; this compilation was however held suspect by the 'true' Tat Khalsa.

35. Harjot Oberoi notes that the earliest *rahit-namas* omitted reference to the rules of passage rites; these included birth, marriage and death rituals. The *Prem Sumarg* and *Sau Sakhian* both heavily relied upon by the earlier Namdhari reformers briefly mention rites of passage, but did little to elucidate these rituals. According to Oberoi it is probable that the specific attention to these rites indicate their later date of composition. See Oberoi, 'From Ritual to Counter-Ritual', Joseph T. O'Connell, Milton Israel, Willard G. Oxtaby, with visiting editors, W.H. McLeod and J.S. Grewal, eds, *Sikh History and Religion in the Twentieth Century* (Toronto: University of Toronto, Centre for South Asian Studies, 1988) p. 155.

36. The committee seeking amendments to the existing *rahit* initially met in 1910. It was not until 1915, after years of intense deliberation that a book of order known as *Gurmat Parkas* was completed. See Chief Khalsa Diwan, *Gurmat Parkas* (Amritsar: C.K.D., 1952) p. 11, (first published in 1915).

I am indebted to Harjot Oberoi for his translation efforts and insights into this document.

37. See *Gurmat Parkas*, pp. 16–17, 28.

38. Randhir Singh, ed., *Prem Sumarg Granth* (Jalandhar: New Book Company, 1965) p. 25 (first published in Amritsar, 1953).

39. *Gurmat Parkas*, pp. 26, 28.

See also Khazan Singh, *History and Philosophy of the Sikh Religion*, Part I (Lahore: Newal Kishore Press, 1914) pp. 165–6.

40. As noted earlier, attempts to re-write Sikh history, particularly women's history as it pertained to naming conventions were inconsistent. Vir Singh had clearly connected the appellation 'Kaur' with his heroine's baptismal rite, he nonetheless

maintained Sahib Devan's original name as the mother of the Khalsa. See Bhai Vir Singh, *Sundri*, p. 26.

Further, Vir Singh was the editor of Ratan Singh Bhangu's *Prachin Panth Parkash* cited above. He took considerable liberties in the editorial process; perhaps surprisingly, Sahib Devan continued to be identified as the mother of the Khalsa. Needless to say the shift from Sahib Devan to Sahib Kaur was by the end of the nineteenth and beginning of the twentieth century in its rudimentary stage and thus inconsistently endorsed.

41. See 'Sikh Sanskar Vidya', *Punjabi Bhain*, (July 1912), pp. 41–2, for information of how the new code of conduct was to be disseminated.

42. Dharam Parchar Committee, *The Sikh Reht Maryada*, [The Code of Sikh Conduct and Conventions] (Amritsar: Shiromani Gurdwara Parbandhak Committee, 1994) p. 25.

43. Ibid., p. 37.

44. See Kahn Singh Nabha, *Mahan Kosh*, (Patiala: Language Department, 1993) p. 352 (first published in 1930).

45. The *Khalsa Akhbar*, September 18, 1896, cited in Harbans Singh, 'The Bakapur Diwan and Babu Teja Singh of Bhasaur', *The Panjab Past and Present*, Vol. IX, Part II, (October 1975), p. 323.

46. Harjot S. Oberoi, 'From Ritual to Counter-Ritual', Joseph T, O'Connell, et al., eds, *Sikh History and Religion in the Twentieth Century*, p. 156.

47. Carrol Smith Rosenberg offers an apt summary of the final stage of hegemonic ritual identity construction in the context of the evangelical revival of the late 1800s in America.

Disorderly Conduct.Visions of Gender in Victorian America (New York: Alfred A. Knopt, 1985) p. 164.

48. Khushwant Singh, *A History of the Sikhs*, Volume I (Delhi: Oxford University Press, 1991) p. 83.

Although Singh cannot be specified as an academic scholar of Sikhism, his highly readable two-volume *History* continues to be widely utilized and cited by academics and non-academics alike.

49. McLeod, *The Chaupa Singh Rahit-nama*, p. 237, note # 349.

50. Nikky-Guninder Kaur Singh, *The Feminine Principle in the Sikh Vision of the Transcendent* (Cambridge: Cambridge University Press, 1993) p. 120.

51. Grewal and Bal, 'Appendix C', *Guru Gobind Singh* (Chandigarh: Panjab University Press, 1967) pp. 182–3.

52. Joseph T. O'Connell, et al, eds, 'Editor's Introduction', *Sikh History and Religion in the Twentieth Century*, p. 12.

53. J.S. Grewal's recent book, arguably one of the most highly respected of contemporary volumes on Sikh history does not even address the pivotal questions of female baptism and nomenclature in history. Whether this is due to a lack of interest, or, simply because the lack of authoritative sources on the subject is open to conjecture.

J.S. Grewal, *The Sikhs of Punjab*, The New Cambridge History of India (Cambridge: Cambridge University Press, 1990).

7

Authority, Politics, and Contemporary Sikhism
The Akal Takht, the SGPC, *Rahit Maryada*, and the Law

N. Gerald Barrier

'The office of jathedar was created by the Gurus with the express mandate of being Ultimate decision-maker for the Khalsa Panth.'

Gurmit Singh Aulakh

'The SGPC leaders are *manmat* ... brave men with empty stomachs ... The SGPC and the jathedars are betraying Sikhism for political purposes and without devoted concern for Sikh values and the panth.'

Teja Singh Bhasaur

At the beginning of the twenty-first century, Sikhs are not primarily concerned with religious doctrines or details relating to rituals and ceremonies. Discussion on overall themes and specific publications or authors remains lively, especially in journals and on the internet, but power and politics tend to underpin much public debate and action. Religious issues very often are politicized.

The centrality of the Guru Granth Sahib as the holy scripture for Sikhs and other basic doctrinal issues have been largely resolved over the last hundred years. Similarly, patterns of worship and matters surrounding rites of passage such as birth, marriage, and death have become routinized mainly through the activist programs of the Singh Sabhas and their intellectual successors. Instead, most public discussions, whether in conferences, journals or newspapers, highlight another set of issues that fuel bitter debate and sometimes violent confrontation. In many numbers of *The Sikh Bulletin*, *The Spokesman*, *The Sikh Review*, and particularly the now defunct *World Sikh News*, for example, editorials and individual Sikhs contest matters not theological but rather political in nature. The role of key institutions and leaders, control of gurdwaras and shrines, celebration of annual or special events (including the nature of the Sikh calendar itself), and the relationship between current beliefs and academic works or supplementary scriptures such as the *Dasam Granth*—all are political in the broad sense that they involve struggles over resources and legitimacy, and ultimately, authority among Sikhs.

These political battles have been fought for at least a century, a reflection of continuing insecurity over the perennial minority status of Sikhs and their attempts to deal with an increasingly complex world both at home in the Punjab and abroad. This paper highlights several areas of contention, the role and interconnectedness of the Akal Takht, the SGPC, the *rahit maryada*, and legal affairs and the courts. Attention is first paid to pre-independence patterns because in earlier deliberations within Singh Sabhas, the Chief Khalsa Diwan, and the nascent SGPC, decisions were made or avoided that help condition how Sikhs view the world today. The more extensive section then utilizes primarily tract and journalistic materials in exploring some of the arguments concerning the authority of the Akal Takht and the SGPC, efforts to either apply or amend the Sikh Rahit Maryada first promulgated in the 1940s, and the changing legal institutions and decisions to which Sikhs are forced to respond. Concluding comments discuss the interconnection of these major elements in contemporary Sikh discourse, and implications for Sikhs involved in public life.

The Emergence of Modern Sikh Institutions and Politics, 1849–1947

A century of British rule in the Punjab confronted Sikhs with numerous religious and political challenges. In general, Western ideas and missionary activities helped sharpen the self-identity, boundaries, and institutions of Punjab religious communities, leading to substantial internal struggle within groups and the creation of new associations defending specific traditions and attacking others. Similar to the Arya Samaj in terms of fervour and organizational skill, the first Singh Sabhas struggled to mobilize Sikhs against perceived threats and toward a positive programme that would strengthen Sikhism in the modern world. Two networks emerged within the movement, contesting divergent ideas about Sikh identity, religion, and tradition. Underlying much of the discourse and actual contest, however, was a struggle to emerge as the legitimate spokesman for Sikh interests. The dual questions of 'Who is a Sikh?' and 'Who Speaks for Sikhs?' were intertwined in most of the public activities in the last three decades of the nineteenth century.[1]

Authority and political power involved at least four major players, the British, the Lahore Singh Sabha, the Amritsar Singh Sabha, and the Arya Samaj. British authorities were dominant partners in the first encounters. They controlled resources and patronage, access to employment in the army, police and civil service, and the overall functioning of key Sikh shrines and related institutions. Complexity and ambiguity characterized the emerging British policy toward Sikhs and Sikhism. On the one hand, the foreign rulers attempted to solidify support from those seen as influential within the community. This involved continuation of existing *jagirs* and grants to the many shrines and gurdwaras sprinkling the Punjab, assisting the Rajas and leading Sikh families through grants, special educational facilities and incorporation into government and decision-making, and regularizing and expanding Sikh recruitment into the army. Jat Sikhs were viewed as especially important both as potential soldiers and rural yeomen who would give assistance to the British in times of prosperity. Such considerations influenced revenue policy, approaches to indebtedness among peasants and Sikh gentry, and colonization policy in the rich canal areas opened after 1900. Similarly, the British attempted to be seen as friends of Sikhism by making arrangements for Sikhs to participate in self-government experiments and by providing funds for preserving rare documents and translating the Guru Granth Sahib.[2]

On the other hand, confidential correspondence and bureaucratic decisions reflected a sense that Sikhs could be dangerous and somehow must be contained and controlled. This came out most clearly in policies relating to administration of the Golden Temple. British policies toward the finances, personnel, and traditions involved in the central Sikh institution shifted periodically, but one constant theme involved preventing any one group from using its legitimacy to enhance their position, and either anticipating controversial situations or dealing with sudden flare-ups as they occurred. As C.L. Tupper summarized in a note reviewing the recent history of the Golden Temple, the Government could not 'stand aloof and make no sign until the peace were broken, blood shed, and a spirit evoked of which no man could predict the consequences.'[3]

Either careful supervision or direct control of Temple matters was necessary since unlike a *laissez faire* approach toward 'effete and purely ceremonial worship such as that of the Hindus', such intervention had political implications for the 'high-spirited and excitable Khalsa'. The rise of the Kukas in the 1860s and the threatened return of Dalip Singh a decade later reinforced British suspicion of particular threats from aroused Sikhs. Even projects intended as supportive, such as the creation of Khalsa College, could evoke danger in terms of competing groups who made demands on the government. The government attempted to remain above such controversies, but its decisions created new arenas for conflict between Sikhs and among Punjab communities in general that occasioned growing concern over the revival of Sikh militancy.[4]

The Amritsar and Lahore Singh Sabhas, along with their networks of supporters in certain regions and families, vied with each other to speak for community needs and to be seen as leaders by the British. Labelled *sanatan* Sikhs, the Bedi family and its supporters in Amritsar emphasized education and modest social reform as the most relevant and less disturbing programmes. They accepted diverse traditions and local custom, and opposed those who challenged their authority and belief that Sikhs were Hindu. Also seeing Sikhism in danger, the *Tat Khalsa* group in Lahore had a different view of the past and what needed to be done. They argued for the primacy of *amritdharis* and *kesdharis* in public life (initiated and uninitiated Sikhs who maintained symbols including uncut hair), rejection of Hindu practice, eliminating popular cults and local custom, and strengthening Sikh cultural boundaries.[5]

The competing networks used traditional and new political methods to defend themselves and to weaken the other. The Amritsar group was successful in their campaign to have the new Khalsa College built in their neighbourhood and effectively worked with *mahants* and officials in numerous shrines and gurdwaras to build a base of support. The linkage between their policies and Sikh managers in the Golden Temple was dramatized by the 'excommunication' of a leading Lahore activist, Gurmukh Singh in April 1887. They also brought libel cases in court, and recruited several publicists and scholars to argue their position. The Lahore group fought back effectively in two public arenas. First, they gradually dominated the new print culture that linked Sikhs through journalism and tracts, thus winning over allies and undercutting opponents. Similarly, they developed fresh organizational strategies to publicize favourable events, and mobilize public opinion. Coordinated *diwans* and other meetings were held throughout central Punjab, linking like-minded Sikhs and demonstrating authority in controversial matters.

The Arya Samaj made the claim 'Sikhs are Hindus', a major component of their substantial propaganda, and often sided with the Amritsar Sikhs in attacking Lahore activists. Its founder, Dayanand Saraswati, and the Arya Samaj in general quickly came to be seen as an imminent danger to Sikhism. The resulting tract warfare was virulent, provocative, and persistent. The Arya Samaj intensified the antagonism by launching a *shuddhi* or cleansing programme, ostensibly aimed at Muslim converts but evolving in an anti-Sikh direction. Samajists regularly paraded new Sikh 'converts' and further offended the Tat Khalsa by shaving their hair in public. The Arya Samaj and the revivalist Hinduism that it represented became Public Enemy Number One for Sikhs who championed *Ham Hindu Nahin* (We are Not Hindu).[6]

In 1902, no Sikh institution or group could claim to represent Sikhs intellectually and in politics. Pro-Hindu and anti-Tat Khalsa forces controlled virtually all gurdwaras and shrines, including the Akal Takht and the Golden Temple, balanced somewhat by a Tat Khalsa network of Singh Sabhas that combined occasionally for meetings and on large issues but primarily worked on local matters and regional self-strengthening. At that juncture, a fresh assortment of leaders attempted to fashion a central organization that would coordinate Singh Sabha activities and hopefully unify the community. Led by Sundar Singh Majithia, the Chief Khalsa Diwan (CKD) gradually emerged as a spokesman for Sikhs in public life and mobilized financial and political support in dramatic fashion.[7]

The CKD's legitimacy rested upon its ability to build new institutions, to communicate a message that appealed to most if not all Sikhs, and to demonstrate concrete results. The CKD expanded earlier Singh Sabha programmes, spreading a network of well-trained *parcharaks*, or preacher activists, who gathered funds and attempted to strengthen local organizations. Much attention was paid to controlling those missionaries. All had to be *amritdhari*, commit themselves legally to CKD loyalty, and keep records. Founded in 1908, the Sikh Educational Conference provided a fresh opportunity to raise donations, work up enthusiasm for a range of issues (Punjabi, new schools, scholarships), and in general, to cement relations between the CKD and Sikhs throughout the world. At the same time, the Diwan dominated the print culture affecting Sikhs. Two newspapers, the Punjabi *Khalsa Samachar* and the English-language *Khalsa Advocate*, lauded CKD efforts and initiatives, as did a revitalized Khalsa Tract Society, and a new Sikh Handbill Committee.

Despite these accomplishments, the CKD's attempt to *expand* the Singh Sabha mission of defining Sikh identity and practice proved difficult if not impossible. Its leaders realized that consolidation of resources and overcoming divisions and rivalry meant balancing commitments with compromise and at times, orderly retreat. Some issues such as legitimizing Punjabi, creation and public acceptance of holidays, widening popularity for Sikh dietary requirements, and defending symbols (notably, the turban and *kirpan*) proved successful, others involving reform of gurdwaras and changing attitudes toward social problems including treatment of low caste Sikhs, were approached gingerly.[8]

The most pressing issue inherited from the Singh Sabha movement, addressing questions concerning tradition and everyday practice affecting all Sikhs, remained unresolved. One notable exception, the battle to legitimize a distinctly Sikh marriage ceremony (*anand* marriage), evoked tremendous resentment within the community and with outsiders, and demonstrated the difficulties of trying to move further. In that instance, CKD mobilization of over 400 organizations across the world built a groundswell of support, but the leader of the Diwan on the Imperial Legislative Council, Sundar Singh Majithia, still had to make concessions to pass the controversial bill in 1908. Anand marriages would be legitimate only for those Sikhs who preferred the ritual, thus serving as a permissive and not legally binding requirement for Sikhs.[9]

The firestorm of controversy over marriage practice foreshadowed the CKD's inability to win general Sikh acceptance of a general guide to Sikh life, a Rahit Maryada. Radical Tat Khalsa publicists such as Teja Singh Bhasaur resisted any attempt to compromise on issues involving ceremonies or the fundamental issue of 'Who is a Sikh'. His Panch Khalsa Diwan demanded a full public debate and an agreement that real Sikhs were *amritdhari* and should control all public institutions and rituals. Other Sikhs who still championed loose boundaries between the community and Hinduism also joined the debate, and as a result, a draft collection of decisions on ritual and Sikh identity published in 1915, *Gurmat Prakash: Bhag Sanskar*, surfaced briefly and then disappeared from public debate. Holding together a fragile coalition of disparate personalities and ideologies thus meant that the CKD either had to compromise or bury fundamental issues.[10]

If the Diwan had trouble consolidating the community, its ability to deliver a coherent programme and successes in the broader political system proved even more difficult. The British had their own agenda, which included maintaining control over the Golden Temple and Khalsa College to insure that radical, anti-government factions did not use those institutions to destabilize foreign rule. Many Sikhs expected the CKD to combat the rulers on these and related matters, which the central organization did within only marginal success. Diwan leaders felt that the future of the minority Sikh community rested upon strengthening of British patronage combined with improved influence over official decision-making. The CKD therefore protested loyalty while criticizing specific policies. Over time the Tat Khalsa overcame many British fears about its potential militancy, and worked out a collaborative arrangement with the Raj. The negotiations over the anand marriage bill reflected such initiatives. Similarly, when the British removed a stone wall around the Gurdwara Rikabganj in New Delhi in 1913, the Diwan successfully negotiated a compromise that cooled tempers somewhat but which only postponed a much more heated confrontation after the war.[11]

The Rikabganj affair demonstrated the vulnerability of the CKD's claim to represent Sikhs politically. Radicals in the canal colonies mounted sharp attacks both on the British and its 'toddy' supporter, moderate Sikhs. From 1913 onward, the Diwan came under constant fire over handling of issues such as the right to wear kirpans, Sikh claims concerning holidays and Punjabi in the schools, and most heatedly, Sikh demands for one-third of the seats in the Punjab legislative council under the proposed 1919 reforms. It is not surprising that in the heated environment of the 1919 disturbances, the Amritsar massacre, and the public confrontations over control of shrines and gurdwaras, the centrality of the CKD eroded quickly, to be replaced by an emerging political power, the Akali Dal and its partner, the Shiromani Gurdwara Parbandhak Committee (SGPC).[12]

By the end of the 1920s, the political and religious landscape of Sikhism had changed dramatically. The SGPC moved to consolidate its premier position by combining religious and political issues, buttressed in 1925 by the passage of the Sikh Gurdwaras Act. The Act also set up the legal parameters within which Sikh public figures operated, replacing informal procedures with specific requirements that became actionable in the courts.

Moreover, the four *takhts* or traditional centres of Sikh religious and temporal power played a fresh role in Sikh public life. In the past, the *granthis* and managers of the shrines had been used by the British and anti-Tat Khalsa forces to contest policies of first the Chief Khalsa Diwan and then Sikh militants. Now the leaders of the takhts coordinated with the SGPC and the Akali Dal. In particular, following the creation of the post of *jathedar* of the Akal Takht in 1920, Sikhs increasingly looked to the Takht to provide legitimacy and direction. Finally, the long-avoided issue of preparing and circulating a Sikh code received fresh attention and support from committees associated with the SGPC. Although the SGPC, the legal procedures and laws affecting Sikhs, the Akal Takht, and the Sikh Rahit Maryada only evolved slowly in a time of political chaos occasioned by British decolonization and partition, all four would become key elements in political discourse and action in the decades after independence.

The 1925 Sikh Gurdwaras Act was a victory for the Tat Khalsa and the SGPC as well as a document that would profoundly affect future Sikh public life. The heated debate leading to its enactment by the Punjab Legislative Assembly highlighted divisions among Sikhs, attacks from Hindus, and British determination to revolve governance issues once and for all. Many central passages were the result of compromise and negotiation. For example, Tat Khalsa's insistence that only *amritdhari* Sikhs could vote and be elected gave way to a deliberately vague definition of 'Who is a Sikh'. Anyone ' who professes the Sikh religion' is a Sikh, and if challenged, can legitimize his claim by declaring 'I solemnly affirm that I believe in the Guru Granth Sahib, that I believe in the Ten Gurus, and that I have no other religion.' The only reservations on being able to vote and be elected representatives under the Act were the requirements of being over twenty-one years of age, enrolled on electoral lists in the constituency, and not being a *patit* (fallen Sikh or a baptized Sikh who cut his hair or committed other grievous offences).[13]

As to the scope of the act, specific gurdwaras would be notified and added to a schedule at the end of the legislation, or added later by a specific process. A special Judicial Commission would be established to hear petitions and deal with matters concerning gurdwara administration, consisting of a President who was a Judge of the High Court, and two other members who were judges, barristers, or senior pleaders. The Punjab Government would fill all vacancies. Appeals from the special judiciary would be heard by the High Court as per normal judicial procedure. On the issue of governance, each notified gurdwara would have a committee of management. Supervising all gurdwaras would be a special board, with 120 elected members, representatives from the four takhts and the Darbar Sahib, Amritsar, twelve members from the Sikh states, and fourteen members resident in India, co-opted by the Board. Other details about meeting procedures and the ongoing role of an Executive Committee set up the framework for the operation of the Central Board.

The SGPC, which took over control under the new Act, already had been involved in gurdwara administration since its founding in late 1920. The organization had its own constitution, which required members to maintain the five Ks, and while the actual Gurdwara Act does not specify such a requirement for the Central Board, for all practical purposes *amritdharis* and *kesdharis* assumed total control of the SGPC. Another parallel and more ostensibly political party, the Shiromani Akali Dal, had operated largely under the guidance of the SGPC during the campaign to win control of the gurdwaras. After 1925, however, the Akali Dal successfully contested elections within the SGPC, and from that point onward, the statutory body's centrality within Sikh politics was ensured.[14] ·

At the same time, the Akal Takht took on new political prominence as part of the Tat Khalsa movement that had become dominant among Punjabi Sikhs. The SGPC appointed its head, or jathedar, who tended to coordinate decisions and policies with the governing body. Sikhs historically had great respect for the Akal Takht as a central institution in Sikh tradition, but now, the administrative muscle of the SGPC and the activist politics of the Akali Dal reinforced its edicts and importance.

One incident illustrating this fusion of religion and politics involved a long-time critic of the Chief Khalsa Diwan and now the Akali Dal, Teja Singh Bhasaur. The zealous leader of the Panch Khalsa Diwan always denounced any compromise on ritual or defining the nature of Sikhism. From his perspective, the only Sikhs were baptized Sikhs. His mission also included earlier themes prominent among the Tat Khalsa, most notably cleansing Sikhism of any *manmat* elements such as Hindu influence in doctrine or scriptures. Accordingly, in 1917, he had published new editions of the Guru Granth Sahib without separating the words and excluded the *ragmala* section allegedly written by a Muslim. This led to a fierce public battle, personal attacks, and finally a call for the four takhts and the Maharaja of Patiala to intervene. In May, the Akal Takht issued a *hukam-nama* instructing Teja Singh to come and explain his action. Teja Singh refused, claiming that the Takht and the Chief Khalsa Diwan were cowards and non-Sikh. Neither Patiala nor the Akal Takht pursued the matter at that time.[15]

In 1921, Teja Singh's persistent criticism of the SGPC, the Akalis, and Patiala precipitated another challenge. The Akalis sent a *jatha* to Bhasaur, seized the Diwan's treasury in collaboration with the Raja of Patiala, jailed Teja Singh for a year, and confiscated literature. When this failed to quiet Teja Singh, the SGPC finally acted decisively. Responding to his shrill claims that the takhts were mere political pawns in the hands of *manmat* politicians, and his demands for a fresh republication of the Granth without the ragmala, the Gurmat Rahuriti Subcommittee of the SGPC ordered that Teja Singh and his wife Niranjan Kaur be suspended from the panth. On August 1928, the four takhts issued hukam-namas that separated or 'excommunicated' the two from Sikhism and threatened retaliation against any Sikhs associating with them or their programme.[16]

Why the moves against Teja Singh in 1921 and 1928, and not earlier? While the details of the decision-making process are not completely clear, certainly shifting political power and concerns had much to do with the raid and the excommunication. In 1921, the Akalis were engaged in numerous campaigns against opponents, and while Teja Singh was not the usual target of *morchas* and direct action such as mahants controlling shrines, from one perspective, his challenge was more serious. A prominent leader with at least some zealous followers now attacked those who claimed to have the mantle of 'true Sikhism' and therefore must be stopped. Similarly, in 1927 and 1928, the SGPC had the power and authority lacked earlier by the Chief Khalsa Diwan and could use its influence to silence a perennial critic. Teja Singh labelled the 1925 Act a sell-out and the Akalis and the SGPC sycophants interested not in Sikhism but in their own fortunes. The excommunication did isolate Teja Singh until his death in 1933, but he remained a virulent critic of Akal Takht/SGPC machinations. Only after seventy-three years has he officially been rejoined to the Sikh Panth on 3 May 2001 following negotiations between his relatives and the Akal Takht.[17]

The incident did not derive from the SGPC's over-arching concern with religious controversy and clarifying doctrine. The SGPC and the Akali Dal were mostly involved in politics, and willing to compromise on doctrinal issues if necessary. In the early stages of the gurdwara movement, for example, the Akali Dal issued a flier that said for 'political' and not theological reasons, a broad definition of 'Who is a Sikh' should be accepted, including *sehajdharis*. Like their predecessor, the CKD, the Akalis accepted compromise and avoided decisive discussion of boundaries and ideology. All too aware of the minority status of Sikhs, they tended to make decisions that maximized the size and strength of the community by including sehajdharis and not insisting on radical Tat Khalsa programs as argued by zealots such as Teja Singh Bhasaur.[18]

A notable institutionalization of this approach to politics and religion occurred in the preparation and publication of a Sikh Code of Conduct, the Sikh Rahit Maryada. Although the issue had continued to be debated since the early twentieth century, apparently, leadership by intellectuals such as Professor Teja Singh and Kahn Singh Nabha and the willingness of a now secure SGPC to entertain potentially disruptive debate brought the matter once again to the pubic in October 1931. A *rahu-rit* (way of life) subcommittee of the SGPC conducted several meetings at the Akal Takht and prepared a detailed draft. Those involved were mainstream Sikh religious and cultural leaders. In addition to the earlier Tat Khalsa intellectuals such as Teja Singh, Kahn Singh, Vir Singh, and Gyani Sher Singh, numerous other writers and activists were involved including Hira Singh Dard (prominent in the Rikabganj affair and on the staff of the Akal Takht), and Gurmukh Singh Musafir (teacher, gurdwara reform leader, at one time jathedar of the Akal Takht and General Secretary of the SGPC). The rough draft then was circulated to organizations and individuals, and after a year of refinement was delivered to the SGPC for approval. Four years later, in the fall of 1936, the All India Sikh Mission Board and the SGPC accepted the draft. The matter then lay dormant until the SGPC's Committee on Religious Matters made recommendations about additions and deletions in January 1945, which the SGPC again accepted a month later. The role of the Sikh public, the decision-making process, and final editing of the maryada remains problematic and unclear. A published version finally circulated in 1950, and almost 300,000 copies in English and Punjabi have been printed subsequently.[19]

Perhaps correspondence in Sikh newspapers of the period will highlight some of the controversies and adjustments that went into the final document, but apparently it evoked far less public clamour than earlier. Except for a handful of key passages and some notable omissions, the Sikh Rahit Maryada systematized most of the existing practices relating to rites of passage, the form and details of worship, and in general, important boundaries and guides to daily living. On the whole, the Rahit Maryada was a distinctly Tat Khalsa work grounded in an understanding of Sikh tradition as totally separate from Hinduism and with values that attempted to transcend Punjabi culture. Some earlier controversies over a Sikh calendar, rules affecting women, and matters relating to administration of institutions or the use of authority by special committees or individuals were not addressed. Specific non-Sikh actions and tanakhah (penance) were outlined, as were simple procedures for remedying transgressions. Major issues could be resolved by a *gurmata* decided by a Shiromani Jatha selected by the Panth or a representative gathering of the Guru Panth. The only reference to final authority was a concluding line, 'decisions of the local congregation can be appealed before Sri Akal Takht Sahib.'

The Rahit Maryada begins with a definition of a Sikh, one that incorporates earlier Chief Khalsa Diwan views as well as that in the 1925 Gurdwara Act: 'Any man or woman who has faith in One God, the Ten Guru Sahibs (From Sri Guru Nanak Dev Ji to Sri Guru Gobind Singh Sahib), Sri Guru Granth Sahib and the *Bani* and Teachings of the Ten Guru Sahibs; has faith in the *Amrit* of the Tenth King; and does not believe in any other religion, is a Sikh.' The definition does not draw sharp boundaries and leaves open interpretation as to superior claims by *amritdhari* or initiated Sikhs. As scholars have noted, the choice of the phrase '*nisacha rakhda*' (to believe in) can be interpreted as requiring baptism or affirming the value of such an action without actually experiencing *amrit*. Other parts of the maryada contain similar ambiguity, for example with reference to anand marriage requirements and funerals. Finally, initiated Sikhs (full-fledged Singhs, *tiar-bar-tiar singh*) alone constitute the Panth.

The Fusion of Religion and Politics in Modern Sikh Institutions, 1947 to the Present

The first decades after independence in 1947 brought periods of relative security and prosperity to Sikhs in the Punjab. Despite the persistence of internal political conflict and the difficulties inherent in remaining a minority, Sikhs managed to negotiate a reorganization of the Punjab in which they theoretically were a majority. In fact, coalition politics and the rise and fall of Akali popularity threatened Sikh dominance in the political system. Also, many problems remained unaddressed or unresolved, both economic and political.

During the period, the SGPC continued its control over key Sikh resources and also worked closely with the Akali Dal. A few amendments to the 1925 Gurdwara Act such as reserving seats for Sikh scheduled castes and including terms avoided earlier (sehajdhari, kesdhari, and amritdhari) did not evoke substantial public outcry or affect the legitimacy of the SGPC. The Akal Takht continued to be seen as a final adjudicator of major issues, both religious and political, although its power was exerted infrequently, often through calling important leaders to the Takht and with occasional hukam-namas that tended to be seen as just and popular. The Sikh Rahit Maryada became a reference for detailed ritual, and probably less so in the areas most affecting Sikh social life such as equality of women, approaches to the lower caste Sikh issue, and caste/marriage arrangements.[20]

Two major legal issues emerged, one at the beginning and a second at the end of the period, that eventually engaged Sikh leaders and the public in general in substantial debate over how Sikh traditions and customs fit into the changing world of Indian politics. The first arose from how Sikhs were perceived and treated in the first years after 1947. In the Constituent Assembly and later in the early 1950s, Sikhs continually lost in their efforts to strengthen their status electorally and to have the Punjab reorganized along linguistic lines. They remained a minority, and one increasingly viewed as under attack from the old enemy, the Arya Samaj and now a Hindu-dominated Congress. The place of Punjabi in universities and colleges, and within administrative circles, seemed to be under siege, as were boundaries between Sikhs and Hindus that appeared to have been made permanent by Tat Khalsa actions.[21]

Linked to the political losses were the decisions of the Constituent Assembly about legal matters relating to the Sikh religion. Following extensive debate and hostile criticism from Sikh delegates, Article 25 of the constitution concerning social welfare and reforms incorporated a definition of Hindu that includes Sikhs, Jains, and Buddhists. The relevant statutes do not provide for consultation with representatives of Sikhs before decisions are made affecting access to religious institutions or changes in personal law. Although earlier court decisions in the Punjab tended to use similar criteria in evaluating cases except when local and codified customary law pertained, this came to be seen as a major defeat for separate Sikh identity and the Tat Khalsa cause. Subsequent acts perpetuated Sikhs being identified as Hindus, as for example in Hindu Marriage Act, 1955, the Hindu Minority and Guardianship Act, and other laws on adoption and succession. In fact, the legislation tended to build on existing practice, and the operation of the various acts created little disturbance within the Sikh public in general.

The institutionalization of a new legal paradigm linking Hindus and Sikhs, however, created an issue that could become part of a heated political struggle in the future.[22]

The second legal precedent grew out of the pesky relationship between Delhi Gurdwaras and the SGPC. Prior to the 1925 Act, local managers of the thirteen historical gurdwaras in Delhi gave control of their institutions to the SGPC, and after 1925, a separate Delhi Gurdwara Prabandhak Committee supervised the local shrines, considerably influenced by the SGPC through elections and nominations. After partition, local administration became tattered and at times the cause of substantial violence. The constitution of the local governing body was unstable, with nominations followed by elections, and sometimes anarchy. In May 1971, the President of India appointed a five member Board to evaluate the situation, and despite SGPC resistance, the Delhi Sikh Gurdwaras Act (Act 82 of 1971) was passed. The Act provided for a Committee of forty-six members including four ex officio (the jathedars of the takhts), and some nominees. The SGPC expected to exert continuing influence over the shrines, but that varied with time and issue. The DGPC created a second major political arena for Sikhs, one with direct influence on the Indian government due to its proximity.[23]

Besides reinforcing SGPC anxiety about its inability to control all gurdwaras and Sikh resources, the 1971 Act served as a political and ideological milestone for Sikhs. The Act placed the control of Delhi gurdwaras totally in the hands of amritdhari Sikhs, who alone were eligible for positions on the Committee. Moreover, only Sikhs with unshorn hair could vote. The legislation therefore institutionalized the Tat Khalsa view concerning which Sikhs should dominate public life, and served as a stimulus for re-evaluating the issue among Sikhs in the Punjab.

Events in the Punjab after the late 1970s evoked a massive outcry and militant action over the nature of Sikhism and its survival. The often dormant issues of the role of the SGPC in providing leadership about doctrine and strategy, the place of the Akal Takht in politics and as an ultimate decision-making institution, the constraints and application of the Sikh Maryada in determining conflict resolution and legitimacy, and earlier legal boundaries—all came together in dramatic fashion and became central to the ways Sikhs thought and acted. In a time of renewed insecurity and fears of attack, Sikhs in the Punjab revisited old controversies and mixed religion and politics in an explosive brew.

The SGPC and the Akali Dal became enmeshed in the increasingly violent atmosphere affected by assassinations, the cry for Khalistan, and the fundamentalist challenges from Sant Jarnail Singh Bhindranwale and his associates in the Damdami Taksal. The raid on the Golden Temple, in June 1984, Operation Bluestar, boomeranged on the Indian government, and initiated a Sikh revulsion and militancy that polarized Punjab politics and made impossible normal political processes. The November attacks on the Sikhs in Delhi, and elsewhere, left a festering scar that remains until today. The Akali Dal splintered, and the SGPC quickly became marginalized as a centre of authority. In their places were new Dharmic Committees, youth organizations, and a bewildering assortment of terrorist and militant factions that vied with each other to control Sikh public space and ideology. Gurcharan Singh Tohra managed to keep a semblance of control over the SGPC, but just barely, and Parkash Singh Badal and his group in the Akali Dal survived severe attacks from the Akali Chief Minister Barnala and militants.[24]

Over a decade later, a combination of police oppression and a growing reluctance of Punjabi Sikhs to support militants and their causes helped pave the way for a return toward normalcy. The damage to the SGPC's reputation, however, had been severe. Its overtly political role and its vacillating policies had damaged an institution that many termed 'the Parliament of the Sikhs'. In the last two years, the factional infighting and the often ugly misuse of power has raised serious questions as to whether the institution has strayed from its once proud leadership, and, instead of addressing problems facing Sikhs, has itself become a major obstacle for advancement of the community.[25]

A similar questioning has occurred with reference to the institution that most Sikhs approach with reverence and great respect, the Akal Takht. In fact, since the late 1970s, the leadership of the Akal Takht and the politics of the SGPC have become intertwined, as the jathedars of the Takht have either chosen to pursue or been pushed into increasingly activist and controversial directions. Jathedars came and went in the 1980s and 1990s, issuing hukam-namas against opponents at the behest of particular interests. Different militant factions in essence appointed the leadership of the takhts, held them accountable for specific policies and messages, and then discarded them when political currents changed. The actions and edicts of jathedars Jasbir Singh Rode, Darshan Singh Ragi, and Professor Manjit Singh are well known and have been documented and criticized in various public gatherings.[26] Since 1998, in a period of relative political calm in the Punjab, however, the political role of the jathedars of the Akal Takht and other takhts has produced an astounding series of conflicts and 'hukam-nama wars' that continue almost unabated.

In the last two years, for example, the Akal Takht has excommunicated other jathedars, prominent politicians, and even the President of the SGPC.[27] In turn, Akal Takht jathedars have been denounced publicly and thrown out of office because of involvement with factions within the SGPC that lost out in power struggles. Exposés about misuse of funds and authority are common, and serious criminal charges have been levelled against prominent leaders of the takhts as well as the former head of the SGPC. Factions within the Golden Temple and among the jathedars of the five takhts regularly battle, and charge each other with graft and dishonesty. Jathedars from at least two takhts have been banned from attending particular religious meetings. An issue such as the attempt to modernize the Sikh calendar on the basis of solar dates (the *Nanakshahi* Calendar) rather than the traditional *Bikrami* format has become a political football, with the SGPC and the government accepting the new calendar and then being blocked by an Akal Takht edict. Competing Akali and jathedar factions held separate celebrations celebrating the birth of the Khalsa. Alignments shift, and hukam-namas are being rescinded.[28]

Two key elements stand out in these events. First, the SGPC and the Akal Takht are involved in an ugly and very public fight for supremacy, for political and ideological dominance, for the legitimacy to control resources and discourse. Over the last two decades, the jathedar of the Akal Takht has attempted at various times and in various ways to demonstrate independence from the SGPC. Hukam-namas and other directives are seen as means of bolstering primacy in particular areas, such as the calendar or supposed defense of maryada, or as acts of self-defence. Support groups have been cultivated, either in the form of public groups (institutes, intellectuals) or through relatively new associations such as *Sant Samajes* and the World Sikh Council. Tactics include establishing a new constitutional or public legitimacy for the Akal Takht as the supreme authority within Sikhism, as well as demonstrating a disdain for and distance from the raw politics within the SGPC.[29]

The SGPC has attempted to bolster its image and to expand its influence through a series of actions that limit the Akal Takht and highlight its own supremacy. For example, there have been initiatives to control publications relating to Sikhism, including printing of the Granth but beyond that, to any work that is judged 'unpanthic' or dangerous. Similarly, the SGPC wants its religious advisory committees to screen appeals and issues addressed to the Akal Takht, thus at the same time avoiding potential controversy and exerting control.[30] The SGPC had an advantage in the contest because of its legal position, its close ties to the Badal-controlled Punjab government and by inference, the central authorities. Most recently, the power and prestige of the SGPC probably has been enhanced by the recent declaration that Sikhs are a minority, and therefore all SGPC-run institutions can reserve at least 50 per cent of all places for Sikhs. Similarly, a central ordinance officially naming Damdama Sahib as a fifth takht removed any possible legal challenges and strengthened the hand of the SGPC in inter-jathedar squabbles.[31]

Second, both the SGPC and the Akal Takht share a vision of Sikhism once again under attack, this time either from divisive elements within the panth or through ill-fated alliances with the BJP and the arch-enemy now replacing the Arya Samaj as a foe, the RSS. In such an atmosphere, interpretations of religious doctrine and political strategy have become fused. A perennial issue about who is *patit* is given prominence again, with select SGPC members being charged with having patits, or fallen Sikhs, within their families or interacting with excommunicated Sikhs or others judged unfit. The disputes over the relationship between the Dasam Granth and the Guru Granth Sahib that were fought over a century ago again reappear, with charges of plots and counterplots.

In this context of conflict and political manoeuvring, the Sikh Rahit Maryada and the courts and laws affecting Sikh public life and institutions have received new attention and have become part of many publicized disputes. One of the most frequent charges is that a faction or individual is acting against maryada, tradition, or more specifically, against the rahit promulgated by the SGPC. The Jathedar of the Damdama Takht, for example, frequently criticizes other jathedars or members of the SGPC for participating in manmat or non-Gursikh practices.[32] Refusal to accept hukam-namas or even recension of hukam-namas automatically invokes charges of being against maryada. A more basic issue involves whether the jathedar of the Akal Takht can issue a hukam-nama by himself, or even outside the precincts of the Golden Temple such as in a phone booth, or whether the action has to result from unanimous decisions of all jathedars, or the calling of a special convention or *sarbat khalsa*. Similarly, the maryada or accepted tradition about how many *granthis* and jathedars constitute a legitimate quorum for edicts or major decisions evokes harsh charges and cries of illegitimacy. Major splits have emerged as to how tradition supports one or another position.[33]

The problem is that the Sikh Rahit Maryada does not really address procedures or institutional issues. Assumptions about correct panthic action therefore either must be extrapolated from the document or more usually, based upon some rather vague reference to earlier traditions. Even when the SGPC rahit maryada is specific about rituals and texts, variations and other approaches can be found among other groups or individuals affiliated with institutions such as the Damdama Takhsal. These differences generally are understood and tolerated except in instances where they can be brought up in the form of charges or being labelled 'un-Sikh'. Most recently, for example, some groups in the Akal Takht and SGPC opposed recitations and discussions at Damdama Sahib on the basis that they went against rahit maryada. Such incidents have led Sikhs in the Punjab and other parts of India to question the applicability of the SGPC document and even the need to re-examine its assumptions and language in light of contemporary issues.[34]

The 1925 Gurdwara Act, which legitimizes and creates the legal framework in which the SGPC must operate, has itself become an important element in the struggle for power. The Judicial Commission has increasingly to deal with petitions, charges, and demands for interpretation of statutes and practice. In early 1999, for example, the Punjab government led by Badal, the SGPC, the Commission, and the Punjab and Haryana High Courts addressed a series of challenges as to the legitimacy of new appointments to the judiciary body that eliminated a Badal opponent, Kashmira Singh Patti. Each stage in the process whereby Badal supporters gained control of the SGPC produced more court cases and challenges. At a final stage, Tohra attempted to disenfranchise ten pro-Badal members of the SGPC Executive Committee on the grounds that they were patit, having rejected hukam-namas from the Akal Takht and denigrated Sikhs. The Commission generally refused to get involved in most of the charges and manoeuvres, but almost every month, the High Courts had to evaluate one or more issues.[35]

Since the Gurdwara Act establishes the ground rules for election and electors, it was inevitable that competing Sikh factions would attempt to amend the legislation or create a new Act that would strengthen their base.

Complicating the discussion has been the effects of the Punjab Re-organisation Act 1966, which gave the SGPC 'inter-state' status (Haryana, Chandigarh, and Punjab) and authorized the central government to modify the 1925 Act as needed. Several modifications in 1995 and 1998 modified the Act, and vested control of elections and related SGPC matters in the hands of a Gurdwara Election Commission selected by the Centre.

Four issues run through the various drafts and committee reports (1978, 1985–6, and 1999–2000).[36] First, who will control gurdwaras under the new arrangements, and how will that leadership be chosen? There have been different models and approaches, but certainly the SGPC does not want to lose its premiere position. Conversely, political opponents would like to see a diminishing of SGPC power. Second, what would be the scope of the Act, to include all Gurdwaras in the Punjab or for that matter, throughout India? Some have suggested worldwide authority over gurdwara administration. Third, who votes and who is eligible? Pressure has built for modelling the wording of 'Who is a Sikh' along the lines of the Delhi Act, ensuring a kesdhari electorate and an amritdhari control over decision-making. That position, however, has met resistance from several quarters, and possibly could create divisions that would weaken Sikh political effectiveness. The compromises in the earlier definition of Sikh identity reflected at least in part, the realization that ambiguity in wording could be beneficial, a point not lost on many observers of the new legislative initiatives. Moreover, recommended voting changes include eliminating special representatives from the Scheduled Caste group (and guaranteed seats for women), again, issues evoking strong reactions. Finally, where would the Akal Takht and other centres of authority fit into the system? Could the jathedar or jathedars be guaranteed permanent posts with either specified or unlimited powers to guide not only religious but political decisions?[37]

Some activists argue that Sikhs should not focus only on gurdwara administration but force a debate over the troublesome legal definition of Sikhs as Hindus in particular acts and in the constitution.[38] Seminars and articles suggest that Sikhs have a unique perspective on God and personal law that requires separate legislation. Matters of dress, symbols, equality of the sexes, dietary code, and other items could be spelled out and then made actionable in the courts. This would protect Sikhs from Hindu intrusions and also strengthen Sikh identity. Opponents to such initiatives argue that the courts generally recognize the separate nature of Sikhism (and in fact, most recently, have made the Guru Granth Sahib a 'juristic person' that can hold and use property). A leading Sikh legal authority, Kashmir Singh of Guru Nanak Dev University, notes that in fact, the Hindu Marriage Act essentially is a secular law based largely on English jurisdiction, which with continuing amendment, 'suits every modern and progressive Indian'. Conversely, the creation of a separate Sikh personal law would open a 'Pandora's box', offering every faction and competing group an opportunity to fight and try to dominate decision-making.[39]

Heated arguments over the nature of the SGPC, the role of the Akal Takht in modern Sikh life, the applicability and interpretation of Rahit Maryada, and legal decisions and legislation affecting Sikh identity, all have implications for Sikhs living outside India. By the 1970s, Sikhs had major centres in North America, England, Asia, and other areas. Most institutions and issues tended to be localized and parochial. Disputes did occur over control of gurdwaras and related matters, but constitutions and bylaws required by Western law tended to set boundaries on disputes and offered judicial redress only in the most extreme cases. Local customs evolved in terms of congregational practice, and while rituals and some aspects of daily life had some connections with the Sikh Rahit Maryada, these tended to be mediated through granthis or visiting religious leaders and singing groups from the Punjab. The SGPC and the Akal Takht seemed far away and not a major concern in daily life.[40]

Then the turmoil in Punjab political and religious life in the late 70s took hold among Sikhs in North America and the UK, and a wave of activism swept away old elites, helped destabilize gurdwara politics, and raised urgent calls of 'Sikhism in danger'. In a definitive and insightful study, Darshan Singh Tatla has provided a clear record of the stages of Sikh political mobilization in the diaspora. Demonstrating that specific individuals and organizations already were planting the seeds of a call for a Sikh homeland, he then traces the instantaneous repercussions of Operation Blue Star. Many Sikhs quit cutting their hair, joined for the first time in mass protests, and provided resources for militant organizations both in the Punjab and abroad. In North America, new youth and radical organizations moved to dominate the print culture with new journals and a flood of inflammatory tracts. The resulting radicalization of diaspora politics in turn raised new questions about who speaks for Sikhism, what are the links between religion and politics, the need for a Sikh independent state, and ultimately, the source of authority for doctrines and specific programmes.[41]

In the decade after 1984, the inability of the SGPC and the Akalis to maintain control of central institutions and to focus community issues evoked strong criticism from supporters of the militants and Khalistan, as well as moderates opposing sustained violent confrontation. The *World Sikh News* and the World Sikh Organization, for example, sharply criticized veteran Punjab politicians for specific decisions and selfishness in time of panthic peril. Like the CKD earlier, in a time of protracted crisis, the SGPC proved unable to maintain its position as spokesman for Sikhs, neither could the diverse and changing groups and organizations that attempted to take its place, either in the Punjab or abroad. Again, Tatla and others have emphasized the way ideological and personal conflict have undercut the new committees and networks, and either hastened their demise or limited their effectiveness.[42]

Recently, the very public and ugly power struggles within the SGPC have done little to return the organization to favour abroad. SGPC officials still tour and receive accolades, but there has been little talk recently of associating local organizations and gurdwaras with or under SGPC authority. To the contrary, more attention has been paid either to the creation of an effective World Sikh Council as a central institution, or rather establishing either regional or national gurdwara associations that can help deal with local problems and focus community concerns.[43]

The Akal Takht, especially its vacillating leadership and ineffectiveness in the decade after Operation Bluestar, came under heavy attack from several quarters. Sikhs tended to separate questionable actions of jathedars from their continuing respect for the Akal Takht and the other four takhts as centres of panthic authority. Respect for the institution of the takhts remains high, but the events of the last few years have raised serious concerns about the role of the Akal Takht and Golden Temple authorities within the politics and religious life of Sikhs abroad. Jathedar Manjit Singh intervened occasionally in local affairs in North America, usually at the call of militants or Sikhs arguing for *amritdhari* dominance in public life. He also became involved in organized attacks on scholars whose work was seen by some as undercutting Sikh institutions and traditions. This weakened or destroyed several Sikh Chairs and studies programmes, as well as exacerbating divisions among local Sikhs in Vancouver, Toronto, and Michigan.[44]

Under his successor, Ranjit Singh, however, the Akal Takht became more active both in the Punjab and in North America, with hukam-namas on various subjects and a string of excommunications. The politicization of the *langar* customs in several British Columbia gurdwaras, growing out of power struggles between radical and moderate factions, led to the Akal Takht's now notorious hukam-nama against use of chairs, and a subsequent excommunication of key British Columbia Sikh leaders. This stirred the already volatile situation and contributed to assassination and armed conflict. Ranjit Singh's former record of violent action and his continued insistence, even in a Canadian Broadcast interview, about the legitimacy of violence in the name of the Gurus eventually led to a US State Department ban on planned tours of the US, and an increasingly vocal criticism of the misuse of Akal Takht power.[45] If anything, the events over the last year have further raised questions about the degree to which the Akal Takht should be involved in diaspora affairs and how hukam-namas should be viewed. There is also concern over the independence and qualifications of jathedars. Nevertheless, the authority of the Akal Takht still remains one option in attempts to resolve local conflicts, with a few new gurdwaras or some older ones now adopting fresh bylaws that specifically mention the Akal Takht as having ultimate power in doctrinal or political matters.[46]

The Sikh Rahit Maryada has become even more central in the daily life and disputes among diaspora Sikhs. Leaving aside the langar issue and occasional disputes over who can lead services and speak on subjects going beyond religion, the last two decades of tumult have intensified attention to symbols and the always tenuous relationship between the Sikhs who shave their hair and who may or may not maintain some of the other five Ks, and the Sikhs either kesdhari or actually baptized. Again, the problem is that the SGPC's rahit maryada does not present clear guidelines or definitions on Sikh identity. Some therefore want to modernize or change the document, questioning whether it really resulted from a legitimate process of open debate, or whether diaspora intellectuals should engage now in that debate.

Who is the adjudicator of issues regarding control of institutions, and even the role of maryada and the Akal Takht in local affairs? Increasingly in North America at least, the courts or complimentary judicial bodies have made decisions affecting gurdwara politics and broader matters such as the legitimacy of wearing turbans and kirpans in public or within specific settings or organizations such as the military and police. The laws vary from state to state, and among countries, and so the defining of what is a legitimate and required religious symbol has been sporadic and reflects local procedures.

The right to wear a kirpan has been fought out in numerous settings, with a variety of results. One case in Ohio, for example, resulted in an appeal victory for the kirpan as a religious symbol. The appeal court wrote a stinging indictment of the local judge who insensitively rejected the kirpan as part of a religious duty and labelled it merely a weapon. In Ohio more recently, however, a local granthi was seized by traffic police and hauled off to jail over the same matter, with little regard to statute law.[47] In a notable series of cases in California, Yuba City school authorities and local Sikhs finally worked out a compromise about the length and location of kirpans among Sikh students, but further south in the Los Angeles area, a compromise proved impossible, and Sikh youth stayed out of school a year before finally an agreement permitted 'safe' kirpans that clearly could not be used for violent purposes. These cases in the US grew out of 'freedom of religion' statutes in American law.[48]

In Canada, however, the kirpan issue involved not a case of religious freedom but rather human rights statutes that often are heard by special panels rather than the courts. In one recent and highly publicized case, for example, a Sikh was prevented from flying on a particular airline while wearing a kirpan. Other airlines had worked out procedures for such situations, but the one in question had a rigid security plan in operation. After days of testimony that seemed to support the kirpan as a vital religious symbol, the panel decided against the defendant, acknowledging that the kirpan in fact had religious symbolism and probably would not be used as a weapon, but affirming that the airline had a right to set up guidelines since there were no all-Canada agreements or statutes on the matter. The panel urged further discussion and either legislation or a definite plan supported by all Canadian airlines.[49]

The turban also attracted Canadian national attention as to whether Mounties could wear turbans rather than the traditional hat associated with the police uniform. Following years of negotiation, the government and the Royal Canadian Mounted Police agreed that Sikh police could wear turbans, but then an interest group challenged the decision and forced legal hearings. After protracted debate, turbans finally were permitted in 1994. Cases in the US have not been as dramatic or confrontational, but occasionally a shopkeeper or restaurant owner challenges Sikhs working or dining with turbans. Local statutes and a general understanding of religious symbols (especially when they are considered non-lethal) usually have meant a victory for Sikhs in those cases, sometimes with large cash settlements.[50]

American Sikhs have been very effective in educating the public on such matters and also building political networks at the local, state and national level.

Partisan interpretations of maryada are entangled in specific cases. One of the most frequent relates to Sikh views of equality and the nature of the panth. Should amritdhari Sikhs automatically become leaders in local institutions and have a dominant role in rituals and even administrative decisions? Often when earlier loosely constructed constitutions and bylaws are questioned, the issue of maryada becomes part of the legal argument. If Sikhs are egalitarian, and when bylaws give preference to those making large contributions or other commitments of *sewa* (service), cannot the general Sikh congregation assert its will despite existing procedures? Is there a standard Sikh congregational practice, and if so, what are the principles? The courts tend to avoid deciding such doctrinal issues, and often instruct litigants to accept mediation or settle such matters outside the official legal arenas. If decisions are rendered, they tend to deny claims that a congregation has the right to seize control despite existing bylaws, but rather, rules and procedures must be followed until amended in an orderly fashion.

One case in particular has brought together claims about the role of the SGPC and the Akal Takht, the prominence of Sikh maryada, and legal precedent. In Fairfax, Virginia, the Sikh Foundation of Virginia had operated since 1979 under a constitution and bylaws. The General Body, or congregation, contributed dues and held annual elections in March, around Baisakhi. Trustees guided the operation of the Foundation and the Fairfax Gurdwara, composed primarily of Sikhs who met requirements of substantial financial contributions to the organization. By 1990, more Sikhs moved into the Northern Virginia area, and there emerged a struggle over who would control the Foundation and how its resources would be used, including politics and support for Khalistan. Such a confrontation was typical of many confrontations in other gurdwaras across the country, involving a combination of factions, personalities, ideology, and political programme. A key event in Virginia involved the presence of a former jathedar of the Akal Takht, Darshan Singh Ragi, at a ceremony, where individuals critical of his refusal to support the most radical Punjab Sikhs physically attacked him. Faced with an attempted takeover, the Trustees went through the normal election procedures, and on March 28, 1993, a group of militants including Sikhs brought in for the purpose, broke up the meeting, threatened violence, and took over the gurdwara. Under court order, the factions met, and there was an attack on leaders of the Foundation, for which subsequently criminal charges were filed with convictions for assault.[51]

As often happens, the courts set up a fact-finding procedure, in this case, a commissioner to hear the arguments and evaluate opposing views. In the process, the group of militants declared that the court had no right to intervene because Sikhism was hierarchical/connectional like the Catholic Church, and therefore fell outside Virginia law. The group earlier controlling the Foundation argued that Sikhism always was congregational. The commissioner then proceeded to hear arguments, not on the facts, but on the nature of Sikh religion and institutions.

The hearings involved basic Sikh concepts of authority and the nature of local institutions. The first argument was that according to Sikh tradition, maryada, Sikhism is egalitarian, and therefore when a majority decides an issue (a resolution or gurmata), these override legal precedent. Another approach involved a group of five amritdhari Sikhs who constituted a *panj piare*, a committee to resolve issues. The visitors decided that requiring contributions for positions of leadership were against Sikh rahit, and that bylaws on membership requiring dues breached the maryada. The trustees rejected the report, but the recommendations that meditation be established, and that only kesdharis and amritdharis should lead the congregation, focused attention on the requirements of the Sikh Rahit Maryada and opened up new issues. The Commissioner, John J. Karcha, therefore broadened the discussion.

To complicate matters, at that juncture the Akal Takht became involved. The granthi of the gurdwara, Kuldeep Singh, wrote to Manjit Singh in 1993 and shared details on the controversy. The Jathedar asked for more information and became part of the decision-making process. After an exchange of letters and a meeting with a representative group of militants, the Jathedar declared that the case must be withdrawn from the courts and settled according to Panthic mores. He went on to assert amritdhari dominance, and that he should approve any further management board constituted in the future. To the surprise of many Sikhs, the leaders of the Foundation thanked the Jathedar for his suggestions, and then went on to say that he had no authority to intervene in local decisions, especially when they were constituted under local laws. They called on the Jathedar to reconsider, and warned of dire consequences if the intervention became a precedent implicating Sikhs across the world.[52]

A series of hearings in the summer of 1994 highlighted the stark difference of opinion within modern Sikhism. One group argued that the Sikh religion was similar to the Catholic Church, with the Pope (jathedar) at the top, and with all property belonging to the panth, and with a common creed, the Sikh Rahit Maryada. The opposition argued that Sikhism always had been congregational with no set rules or a single source of authority. Those supporting the hierarchical model argued that the SGPC had authority over Sikhs throughout the world, and that the Akal Takht required submission from all Sikhs. Sikhs throughout the country joined in the debate, with heated letters, public meetings, and representations. At issue was the nature of a document, the Rahit Maryada, written forty years earlier in the Punjab and now applied to a diaspora situation, and the ability and the legitimacy of the jathedar of the Akal Takht to make final decisions for the Panth, even at the local level involving factions and politics.

The court ultimately decided that the gurdwaras were congregational and that authority rested with those who followed the bylaws and constitution, in this case, those Trustees originally running the Foundation. Manjit Singh withdrew from the matter, and did not pursue the matter directly because of his dwindling political base, and much criticism of his decisions including the Fairfax intervention. However, he did get in one final salvo. Those who lost the contest set up their own separate Gurdwara and wrote a constitution that made the Sikh Rahit Maryada central to daily life. In addition, amritdharis were to control the organization, and the Akal Takht would have complete authority to intervene in local disputes instead of court cases. Manjit Singh responded to the new constitution by proclaiming it a model for real Sikh organizations, one that would prevent needless legal confrontation and resolve conflict in a panthic fashion according to maryada.[53]

Implications for Authority among
Sikhs and the Role of the Diaspora

The Fairfax conflict is only one in a series of incidents that have brought gurdwara disputes and underlying questions about authority and tradition into the courts. Sometimes the cases reflect ignorance of historical debates and lack of clarity regarding institutions and codes. They also reveal the willingness of Sikhs to manipulate symbols and arguments to buttress their specific agendas. In a recent confrontation in Michigan, for example, some of the arguments heard during the Fairfax proceedings began to emerge at the deposition stage. Before the courts had a final and probably lengthy hearing on local politics and the relevance of religious belief and authority, a settlement was reached, and the Akal Takht and maryada did not have to be debated in open proceedings.[54] Similarly, at a critical stage in the legal struggle involving control of several Vancouver gurdwaras, the court was asked to rule that several moderate members of Executive Committees should be removed as, due to their excommunication over langar, they ceased to be bona fide Sikhs. The judge overruled this strategy and instead of turning the gurdwaras back over to the pro-Akal Takht, radical group, ordered court-supervised elections that resulted in moderate victories.[55]

Such public encounters probably will not serve as future models for diaspora Sikhs caught up in local politics and confrontation. Everyone seems to be tired of incessant legal battles that embarrass and divert Sikh resources from more meaningful programmes. Clearly, the courts have rejected direct or implied intervention of outside forces in legal matters based on existing constitutions and legal precedent. Unless Sikhs purposely rewrite their constitutions to include a specific role for the Akal Takht or an interpretation of rahit maryada that expressly relates the SGPC document to actual procedures within the organization, congregational attitudes and bylaws will pertain. More importantly, the debates evoked by events among Sikh leaders in the Punjab and intellectual currents among Sikhs in North America point to a new direction in grappling with identity, authority and politics.

First, the rapid evolution of a worldwide communication system involving print, internet, and television means that interested Sikhs now have an abundance of information that reflects the divergent opinions on any given issue. No one argument based on a reading of history or the cry of 'Sikhism in danger' can dominate public opinion. Tours of politicians or the influence of *Sants*, who have become increasingly involved in Punjab and diaspora politics, will of course continue to influence local congregations, as will openly partisan sources such as issue-driven websites (for example, Khalistan.com or Burning Punjab). The literally thousands of sites relating to Sikhism raise the spectre of how one differentiates evidence and arguments. Major sources of timely and factual information, however, help give perspective to the partisan elements in the print culture. For example, a consistent forum for differing opinion, *The Sikh Review*, offers monthly correspondence and articles that address specifics and options, as do Sikh or Indian newspapers in North America and the UK. Probably most importantly, the availability of the *Tribune* and Indian news reports on the internet guarantee a fact-based analysis of long-term trends and specific incidents. In June of this year, for example, the manoeuvres behind the refusal of the SGPC to address details about 'Who is a Sikh', the referral of the matter to the central Minorities Commission, and the public recriminations were highlighted in Punjab, and Indian newspapers that reach many Sikhs across the globe.[56] The almost immediate news coverage of how Sikh politicians, both within and outside key Sikh institutions in the Punjab, cloak their public use or misuse of power with claims of religious legitimacy has intensified cynicism among readers and generated fresh approaches to modern Sikhism.

This coincides with a growing maturity and routinization of debate among Sikhs, especially in the United States. Most Sikhs remain content with local arrangements and with their personal understanding of the faith. They also are less likely to be driven in one direction or another by fiery claims or rhetoric, particularly as long as events in the Punjab move in more normal, routine patterns. The practicality of an affluent, well-educated, and public-minded Sikh community is a dominant factor in many diaspora settings. Too, concern with family and continuity of belief and culture is having a moderating effect. Interviews and meetings with Sikh youth indicate discontent over fights and court cases, of claims of religious authority and excommunication. They and their elders want to present a positive image of Sikhism in their new homelands. Sikhs tend to see themselves as American or Canadian Sikhs even though their connections to the Punjab have been reinforced by a marked resurgence of Punjabi culture and pride.[57]

Sikhs outside the Punjab are asserting their independence and leadership in addressing the many issues unresolved in the Singh Sabha and more recent Punjab movements. Some of the most exciting developments in terms of relating tradition to a rapidly changing world has emerged in the Sikh diaspora. Discussions include setting up regional or national organizations that can help deal with conflict and resolve issues. While such initiatives are potentially explosive, running the risk of setting up new arenas in which factions can fight and attempt to gain control, they do underline the unwillingness of Sikhs to accept unquestioned mandates and claims from the Akal Takht, the SGPC, and the Akali party. Within the last two months, efforts have been made to set up a new International Singh Sabha association that may serve as a conduit for discussion and help set priorities for Sikh groups and institutions.[58]

Scholars and academic institutions can assist in this process by continuing to study documents and historical events, and perhaps more important, by providing opportunities for serious interaction between academics and the Sikh public. For example, Sikhs are most concerned with issues of local governance. A university or a programme linked to a Sikh Chair could hold a conference that brings together representatives from a wide range of gurdwaras, not to set up a new organization but rather to talk, compare notes, discuss local conditions, specifics about bylaws, voting procedures (and alternative means of selection such as rotation), and related matters. Sikhs themselves can and should reach decisions on such critical matters and then find effective ways to implement them.

Underlying new initiatives and discussions is the realization that authority in Sikhism comes not from institutions that often are battlefields but instead, from within Sikhs themselves. In essence, Sikhs do not need external forces defining their faith and practice, the Guru Granth Sahib combined with common sense application of ideas will suffice. If the experience of the last century shows anything, it points to the pitfalls of over defining or strengthening boundaries that cause confrontation and schism. In this new century, the Sikhs in the diaspora have the potential of providing the intellectual leadership for modern Sikhism, and if they play a major role in the process of rethinking authority, politics, and tradition, the Sikh faith will continue to prosper as the newest and most vital of the world's religions.

Notes

1. The most recent and detailed treatment is Harjot Singh Oberoi, *The Construction of Religious Boundaries* (Delhi: Oxford University Press, 1994). Issues and sources summarized in N.G. Barrier, *The Sikhs and their Literature* (Delhi: Manohar, 1969). Also, survey of recent issues and trends in N. Gerald Barrier, 'The Singh Sabhas and the Evolution of Modern Sikhism, 1875–1925', in Robert Baird, ed., *Religion in Modern India* (3rd rev. ed. Delhi: Manohar,1995), pp. 192–223.

2. The British and the Sikhs are discussed in books by Oberoi and Barrier, as well Ian Talbot, *Punjab and the Raj, 1849–1947* (Delhi: Manohar, 1988). Some of the recent studies Tony Ballantyne, 'Resisting the "Boa Constrictor" of Hinduism: the Khalsa and the Raj', *International Journal of Punjab Studies* 6:2, 1999, pp. 195–216; Brian Caton, 'Sikh Identity Formation and the British Rural Idea, 1880–1930', in Pashaura Singh and N.G. Barrier eds, *Sikh Identity* (Delhi: Manohar, 1999), pp. 175–94; Ian Kerr, 'British Actions Towards the Sikhs and the Golden Temple in

the Last Half of the 19th Century', in Parm Bakhshish Singh, et al. eds, *Temple Golden* (Patiala: Punjabi University, 1999, pp. 87–99, and a critique by Nader Singh, pp. 100–8. Also very relevant are other Kerr articles cited in the Golden Temple piece.

3. C.L. Tupper note in 'The Golden Temple or Darbar Sahib at Amritsar', Punjab Government Home Confidential File A, Printed Notes, Printed March 14, 1890.

4. The Kuka and Dalip Singh incidents are reviewed in Oberoi, *Construction*, and Barrier, *Sikhs*. On the overall political strategy of the British and Sikhs, 'Sikh Politics in British Punjab Prior to the Gurdwara Reform Movement', in Joseph O'Connell ed., *Sikh History and Religion in the 20th Century* (Toronto: University of Toronto South Asia Monographs, 1988), pp. 159–90. Also see the Ballantyne essay in this volume.

5. Background on programmes, communications and conflict in Oberoi and Barrier volumes. For more recent discussion of issues, Barrier, 'The Formulation and Transmission of Sikh Tradition', in Pashaura Singh and Barrier eds, *Transmission of Sikh Heritage in the Diaspora* (Delhi: Manohar, 1996), and relevant articles on key leaders and Singh Sabha institutions in Harbans Singh ed., *The Encyclopaedia of Sikhism* 4v. (Patiala: Punjabi University, 1995–8).

6. The key work on the Arya Samaj remains Kenneth Jones, *Arya Dharm* (Berkeley: University of California Press, 1976), and two seminal articles: 'The Arya Samaj in British India', in Baird ed., *Religion in Modern India*, pp. 26–54; 'Ham Hindu Nahin: Arya-Sikh Relations, 1877–1905', in *Journal of Asian Studies*, 32 no. 3 (May 1973). On the Sikh response, J.S. Grewal, 'Nabha's *Ham Hindu Nahin*', in Pashaura Singh, *Sikh Identity*, pp. 231–51.

7. On the CKD and its cultural and political role, Surjit Singh Narang, *Sikh Politics* (Jalandher: Punjab Development Society, 1998). Also, Barrier, 'Competing Visions of Sikh Religion and Politics: The Chief Khalsa Diwan and the Panch Khalsa Diwan, 1902–1928', in *South Asia* 23 no. 2 (2000), pp. 33–62. I currently am completing a volume that evaluates the history of the CKD and its formative role within modern Sikhism.

8. Political strategies and results evaluated in Barrier, 'Competing Visions', and 'Sikh Politics'. On Tat Khalsa criticism of the CKD, Lal Singh, *Kalmi Tasvir* (Chandigarh: n.p., 1965) and Lal Singh, *Itihas Panch Khalsa Diwan* (Bhasaur: Panch Khalsa Diwan, 1967).

9. On the debate and the Act, Barrier, 'Competing Visions', pp. 43–5. On the controversies and criticism, reports in *Khalsa Samachar*, September–October 1909, and especially Sewa Ram Singh letter, *Khalsa Advocate*, September 5, 1909.

10. PKD challenge reviewed in Barrier, 'Competing Visions', pp. 48–56. I appreciate Hew McLeod's noting that the *Gurmat Prakash* was reprinted by the CKD as late as the early 1950s.

11. On the incident, Harjot Obeori, 'From Gurdwara Rikabganj to the Viceregal Palace', *Panjab Past and Present* 14, pp. 182–98. Also, Barrier, 'Competing Visions', pp. 45–8. British political ambivalence toward the Tat Khalsa and the CKD reflected in Petrie's secret CID report, 'Memorandum on Recent Developments in Sikh Politics, 1911', reprinted in *Panjab Past and Present* 4 (1970), pp. 300–79. Also detailed assessment of Sikh political strategy in Rajiv Kapur, *Sikh Separatism* (London: Allen and Unwin, 1986), pp. 47–104.

12. In addition to Kapur's analysis, the contemporary book by Teja Singh, *Gurdwara Reform Movement and Sikh Awakening* (Jullundur: Desh Bhagat Yadgar Committee, 1922). Also, Sukhmani Bal, *Politics of the Central Sikh League* (Delhi: Books and Books, 1990); Mohinder Singh, *The Akali Movement* (Delhi: Macmillan India, 1978); Richard G Fox, *Lions of the Punjab* (Berkeley: University of California, 1985).

13. Although a detailed analysis of the issues and events surrounding the passage of the 1925 bill remains unwritten, a useful overview is in Kapur, *Sikh Separatism*, pp. 183–91. Also, Mohinder Singh, *Akali*, pp. 126–36. The text and important related documents including selections from debates is in M.L. Ahluwalia, *A History of Sikh Politics and Gurdwara Reforms* (New Delhi: Ashoka, 1990). For detailed analysis of the legislation and its subsequent implementation, Kashmir Singh, *Law of Religious Institutions—Sikh Gurdwaras* (Amritsar: Guru Nanak Dev University, 1989); Surjit Singh Gandhi, *Perspectives on Sikh Gurdwaras Legislation* (Delhi: Atlantic, 1993).

14. For an overview on Akali politics, K.L. Tuteja, *Sikh Politics* (Kurukshetra: Vishal, 1984), and essays in Paul Wallace, Surendra Chopra eds, *Political Dynamics and Crisis in Punjab* (Amritsar: Guru Nanak Dev University, 1998).

15. Documents in *Kalmi Tasvir* and *Itihas Panch Khalsa Diwan*. Analysis of the major incidents and implications in Barrier, 'Competing Visions', pp. 59–61.

16. *Shiromani Gurdwara Parbandhak Committee Ailan 82* (1928); also hukam-nama reproduced in Harjinder Singh Dilgeer, *The Akal Takht* (Jullundur: Punjabi Book Company, 1980), pp. 71–2.

17. *Tribune*, May 5, 2001. Unless otherwise noted, *Tribune* reports and editorials are from the extensive articles found on its website, TribuneIndia.Com. The family gave an unconditional apology for challenging 'Gurbani' and offered a donation of Rs 101 to the Akal Takht.

18. SGPC document, *Sikh Kaun Hai* (Amritsar, 1920). This also is clear from the secret negotiations and public rhetoric leading to the 1925 Gurdwara Act. Background in Kapur, and documents in Ahluwalia.

19. Discussion of issues and evolving nature of the document are in articles by D.S. Chahal, 'Who is a Sikh', *The Sikh Review* 42 (May 1994), pp. 21–33; 'Gurdwara Act—Definition of a Sikh', *Understanding Sikhism—The Research Journal* 2, no. 1(2000), pp. 43–6, and other correspondence and notes in the journal. Also

especially useful are the extensive comments in Chahal's website documents on Rahit Maryada and Sikh Identity. Also, seminars and correspondence among groups of Sikh intellectuals, including the Institute of Sikh Studies, Chandigarh. There are several editions in circulation, with various translations from Panjabi. One English version is *Sikh Reht Maryada: The Code of Sikh Conduct and Conventions* (Amritsar: Dharma Parchar Committee, SGPC, 1994). Also background on rahit-namas and the rahit in several volumes by W.H. McLeod, especially *Who is a Sikh?* (Oxford: Clarendon Press, 1989). McLeod's latest work on rahit will be the standard guide to the literature. *Sikhs of the Khalsa: A History of the Khalsa Rahit* (New Delhi: Oxford University Press, 2003).

20. Background on amendments and implications in Kashmir Singh, *Law*, and Surjit Singh Gandhi, *Perspectives*. Also essays in Kharak Singh, *On Gurdwara Legislation* (Chandigarh: Institute of Sikh Studies, 1998).

21. The language issue surveyed in Baldev Raj Nayar, *Minority Politics in the Punjab* (Princeton: Princeton University Press, 1966). Detailed treatment, based on an interesting assortment of sources, is in Sangat Singh, *The Sikhs in History* (New York: author published, 1995). Also important are the overviews by Paul R. Brass, *Language, Religion and Politics in North India* (London: Cambridge University Press, 1974), and J.S.Grewal, *The Sikhs of the Punjab* (Cambridge: Cambridge University Press,1990).

22. For a fundamental study of the politics behind the Indian constitution, with numerous references to religious issues and the Sikhs, Granville Austin, *The Indian Constitution* (New Delhi: Oxford University Press, rep. 1999). The dynamics of Sikh politics, and the contributions of Ambedkar and Nehru, are explored in Sangat Singh, *Sikhs*, pp. 213–81. Also recent debate on Hindu-Sikh legal connections in Kharak Singh ed., *On Sikh Personal Law* (Chandigarh: Institute of Sikh Studies, 1998).

23. On the politics underlying Delhi legislation, Jitender Kaur, *The Politics of Sikhs* (New Delhi: National Book Organisation, 1986). Legal issues reviewed in Kashmir Singh, *Law*.

24. Among the dozens of scholarly and polemical volumes on this period, noteworthy surveys include the books by J.S. Grewal and Sangat Singh. Also, critical essays in J.S. Grewal, Indu Banga eds, *Punjab in Prosperity and Violence 1947–1997* (Chandigarh: Institute of Punjab Studies,1998), Harish Puri, et al., eds, *Terrorism in Punjab* (Delhi: Har Anand, 1999), and Wallace, Chopra, *Political Dynamics*. Important documents with background are in Gurmit Singh, *History of Sikh Struggles* 4v. (New Delhi: Atlantic,1990–2).

25. For example, a stream of articles in *The Sikh Review*, *The Sikh Bulletin*, *The Spokesman*, and surveys conducted periodically by the *Tribune* staff. Over 2,000 *Tribune* articles have dealt with the SGPC since 1998, and many of those deal with factions, politics, and at times, either criminal or 'unSikh' action (however defined by opponents).

26. Details about adverse reactions in meetings and by organizations, documented regularly in the *Tribune* since 1998. Illustrated by articles in *Tribune*, January 8, 1999; January 11, 2001; *The Sikh Review* (November 1998, pp. 59–71).Also, conferences on the Akal Takht, such as an earlier one, Jasbir Singh Ahluwalia, H.S. Dilgir, *Sri Akal Takht* (Chandigarh: Guru Gobind Singh Foundation, 1994). Every number of the *Spokesman* over the last two years has had articles critical of the jathedars of the Takhts, and in general, loose procedures and political ploys.

27. The *Tribune* index has over 300 references to excommunications, with three times that many citations on hukam-namas. Their political nature was examined at length in *Tribune* and *Spokesman* surveys and editorials. Overview and background on specific cases in *Tribune*, February 19, 2000; March 14, 2000; February 28, 2000.

28. The *Tribune* regularly documents the specific disputes. For example, articles September 30–October 15, 2000. Similarly, *The Sikh Bulletin* and the *Spokesman* carry correspondence on the calendar issue, events leading to and subsequent to the Khalsa celebrations, and the struggle over an appropriate Sikh calendar. A useful survey on the calendar dispute is in articles and correspondence, *Understanding Sikhism*, 1999–2001(for example, v.2,#1, pp. 48–51).

29. Overview in *India Today*, September 14, 1998; articles in *Sikh Review*, December 1995; *Tribune*, May 29, 2000, and an article titled 'Hukamnamas, a Record of Sorts in Three Years', *Tribune*, October 26, 2000. In addition to attempting to limit criticism and participation from other takhts, and also public discussion of issues such as its authority, and controversial matters relating to the World Sikh Council, the Akal Takht has an activist policy gauged to extend its authority over publications and accepted practices such as holding anand marriages in hotels.

30. On the Dharm Parcharak committee and new Itihas boards, *Tribune* January 7, 2001; April 1, 2001 October 4, 2000; May 5, 2001. Both Bibi Jagir Kaur and her successor, Talwandi, have argued against the Akal Takht becoming a dictatorship, and Kaur in particular issued a series of warnings against individuals claiming to fashion Sikh doctrine while lacking any real understanding of tradition. *Tribune*, April 2, 2000. Also controversies between the SGPC and the Akal Takht on the severity of penalties in cases affecting local Amritsar publishers, and limits placed on discussion of the Akal Takht by scholarly conferences. *Tribune*, September 14, 1998.

31. *Tribune*, April 3, 2001; January 16,18, 2001, and discussions in May 1999 concerning official recognition of Damdama Sahib as the fifth takht. These and similar issues are reviewed monthly in *The Spokesman*.

32. For example, news in *Tribune*, June 13, January 10, 2001.The earlier excommunication of takht jathedars and the refusal of all five jathedars to meet together continues to create public spectacle and also raises calls about not following 'maryada'. Some of the most informed reviews of events and criticism of leadership actions are in *The Spokesman*, for example, December 2000, pp. 29–32.

33. Such issues are raised frequently in correspondence, articles in *The Sikh Review*, and in websites constructed by groups monitoring for 'heresy' and misdeeds of Sikh rulers. For example, criticism of the practices such as Akhand Paths by email (for a fee), and other initiatives by the SGPC and the Akal Takht, *Tribune*, January 27, March 15, 2000. Also the explicit criticisms of authority and need for broader consensus rather than Akal Takht edicts, in the Guru Gobind Singh Foundation seminar, *Sri Akal Takht*.

34. Articles in the *Tribune*, May–June, 2001. See for example, articles on May 18, June 21, June 23, 2001. Also editorials and correspondence in the *Spokesman* and *The Sikh Bulletin*, c. September 2000–June 2001, and a summary article by Gobind Thukral in the *Tribune*, February 13, 1999. On the current manufacture of 'maryada', the recent decision by the Akal Takht that any extra printed pages of religious texts, and particularly the Guru Granth Sahib, should be deposited at designated Gurdwaras. *The Hindu*, May 11, 1998. *The Spokesman* sees the maryada disputes as political manouevring and in some cases, influence of Brahmanical forces misusing tradition to undercut gur-bani and the SGPC rahit maryada. January 2001, pp. 7–8.

35. For example, articles in the *Tribune*, January 3, 1999; February 2, 1999; February 25, 1999. On the hukam-nama and pro-Badal forces in the SGPC, *Tribune*, December 31, 1999.

The Courts and the Commission constantly have been dragged into the politics of the SGPC, the World Sikh Council, and at times, decisions made by the Akali Dal and Badal. While trying to avoid adjudicating issues such as textbooks and interpretation of tradition and history, petitions and claims invariably find their way into the agendas of courts at every level.

36. The earlier discussions on the revision of the Gurdwaras act are reviewed in Kashmir Singh, *Law*; Kashmir Singh, *Sikh Gurdwaras Legislation* (Amritsar: Singh Brothers, 1991); Surjit Singh Gandhi, *Perspectives*. I appreciate his advice and clarification of issues for this essay. Also, extensive coverage in the *Spokesman* and the *Tribune*. The latest attempts to formulate a new act reviewed in *Tribune*, March 20–9, 2001.

37. Thukral essay in the *Tribune*, February 13, 1999. Also, a series of articles on the Gurdwara Act in *The Spokesman*.

38. Seminar proceedings, Kharak Singh, *On Sikh Personal Law*; also Harbinder Pal Singh article, 'Sikh Personal Law and Constitution', *The Sikh Review*, May 1997, pp. 38–44.

39. Kharak Singh, *On Sikh Personal Law*, p. 70. On the Supreme Court decision concerning the Granth as a 'juristic person', *Tribune*, August 3,4, 2000. Also overview and implications in *Understanding Sikhism* 2, no.2 (2000), pp. 24–8 (article by Kashmir Singh).

40. The interaction of local Sikh and host cultures, and the rich variety of responses of Sikhs to new challenges outside Punjab, are reflected in numerous monographs and articles. Some issues summarized in the articles, N.G. Barrier and Verne Dusenbery eds, *The Sikh Diaspora* (Delhi: Manohar,1989), Pashaura Singh and N.G. Barrier eds, *The Transmission of Sikh Heritage in the Diaspora* (Delhi: Manohar, 1996), and Pashaura Singh, N.G. Barrier, *Sikh Identity*. Most recently, Darshan Singh Tatla has reviewed history and issues, especially in the UK and North America, in *The Sikh Diaspora* (Seattle: University of Washington Press, 1999).

41. Darshan Singh Tatla, *Sikh Diaspora*, pp. 113–208.

42. Overview in N.G. Barrier, 'Controversy among North American Sikhs', *International Journal of Punjab Studies* 6, no.2 (1999), pp. 217–40. Also, Arthur Helweg, 'Sikh Politics in India', Barrier and Dusenbery, *Sikh Diaspora*, pp. 305–36; Shinder Thandi, 'The Punjabi Diaspora in the UK and the Punjab Crisis', Pashaura Singh and Barrier, *Transmission*, pp. 227–52. The sources and underlying issues reviewed in Darshan Singh Tatla, *Sikhs in North America* (Westport, CT: Greenwood Press, 1991).

43. Discussion in *The Sikh Bulletin* and a variety of letters of articles in *The Sikh Review* 2000–1, from North American Sikhs, on alternative approaches to authority and organization.

44. The politics underlying the various Sikh chairs surveyed in Joseph O'Connell, 'The Fate of Sikh Studies in North America', in Pashaura Singh, Barrier, *Transmission*, pp. 269–88.

45. Correspondence with Hardev Singh Shergill, and documents supplied to the US State Department, including tapes from Canadian Broadcasting Corporation with Jathedar Ranjit Singh. Also articles in *India West*, January 29, 1999, February 19, 1999. The Vancouver controversies and the ban on the Jathedar's travel to the US and Canada are covered in a variety of stories, including those in *India Abroad*, *India Today*, and meetings reviewed in *The Sikh Bulletin*. For example, Gurcharan Singh article, 'Sanctity of Hukamnama and Lunacy in Vancouver', in *The Sikh Review* (November 1998), pp. 59–71.

46. Draft constitution of a Gurdwara set up after the Fairfax Gurdwara case, and the letter from the jathedar of the Akal Takht lauding its emphasis on amritdhari control and submission to the Akal Takht. Ranjit Singh to Surinder Singh Hansra, August 20, 1998. Deposition Exhibit in Fairfax proceedings.

47. Documents from the Ohio court proceedings and a file of clippings and report records (including Order December 3, 1999, Municipal Court), which Ranbir Singh Sandhu graciously supplied from his own archives.

48. Detailed account of kirpan issue in California and Canada, John Spellman, 1996 Michigan Conference on Sikh Identity, unpublished paper. Also, Vinay Lal, 'Sikh Kirpan in California Schools', in Mohinder Singh ed., *Sikh Forms and Symbols* (Delhi: Manohar, 2000), pp. 108–41.

49. Depositions, evidence, and final ruling, Kirpan case. I appreciate Hew McLeod's providing me with the relevant documents. McLeod was a major expert witness supporting the position that the kirpan for an amritdhari Sikh is a vital symbol.

50. Background on the turban case in Narindar Singh, *Canadian Sikhs*, pp. 137–40; Tatla, *Sikh Diaspora*, pp. 99–102.

51. Review of the case in Barrier, 'The Fairfax, Virginia Gurdwara Case and Sikh Identity', in Pashaura Singh and Barrier, *Sikh Identity*, pp. 365–78. The major responses to the case, and the ensuing controversies, can be found in the editorials and letters in *Sikh World News*, 1993–4. In the depositions, a former jathedar of the Akal Takht, Darshan Singh, questioned the wisdom and basis for Manjit Singh's intervention.

52. Letter and response in the *World Sikh News*, April 29, May 27, 1994.

53. 'There is no super congregational body controlling its action.' Emphasizing the independent nature of the local gurdwara, John Karcha referred the matter to the Circuit Judge, who almost immediately ruled in favor of the legitimacy of the earlier administration. Fourth Report of the Commissioner in Chancery, Circuit Court of Fairfax County, 16 July 1996.

54. Depositions and final rulings in the Sikh Society of Michigan, Inc. v Sikh Center of Michigan, Ind., et al., Oakland County Circuit Court Case 96-535016-CZ. I served as an expert witness in both the Fairfax and Michigan cases.

55. Correspondence with the court and lawyers representing the moderate group attempting to maintain control of the gurdwaras. I served as an expert witness in part of the proceedings.

56. *Tribune, The Sikh Bulletin*, and the *Spokesman* articles. Also a series of letters, comments and communiques on Khalistan net and Sikhe.net.

57. These and similar issues are discussed in I.J. Singh, *The Sikh Way: A Pilgrim's Progress* (Guelph: Centennial Foundation, 2001). Also the reflections of local community response in articles in *Sikh Identity* and *Transmission*. Van Dusenbery's arguments about the variation and complexity of Sikh experience outside the Punjab, are especially relevant in his earlier publications on Sikhs in Singapore and Australia. Variations in rahit are reviewed in Pashaura Singh, 'Observing the Khalsa Rahit in North America,' in Pashaura Singh and Barrier, *Transmission*, pp. 149–76.

58. Recent issues of *The Sikh Bulletin* and correspondence with Hardev Singh Shergill.

8

Ethnic Dynamics within a Transnational Framework
The Case of the Sikh Diaspora

Arthur W. Helweg

Introduction

The Sikhs are a mobile people who have a history of surviving in a variety of contexts. In the Punjab, their homeland, they ruled for a brief period. For the most part, however, whether in the Punjab or outside it, they have, for much of their history, been objects of discrimination, subjugation, and rule. There are times in Punjab history that the slaughter of Sikhs was so great that chroniclers of that period describe rivers of Sikh blood flowing through the land. (Ibbetson 1883)

The Sikh experience is not limited to the Punjab. About 10 per cent of this sixteen million-strong community comprise the sikh diaspora. About one million Sikhs are divided between Great Britain, Canada, and the United States. Much of the remaining diaspora population is to be found in remote and urban areas of Australia, Burma, Cambodia, China, East Africa, Fiji, Kenya, Malaya, New Zealand, the Philippines, Singapore, Thailand, and Uganda (Helweg 1979: 6; Singh, Iqbal 1986: 3; Tatla 1999: 11). In fact, the story is often told that when Neil Armstrong landed on the moon, a Sikh farmer passed him as the Sardar was ploughing the ground.

The question immediately arises: How does one understand a people who have lived and survived in such a variety of situations and environments? This is an issue that the field of migration studies has been wrestling with for decades.

Migration Studies

Traditionally, migration studies has concentrated on four broad topics: (1) causes of population shifts; (2) social-psychological concerns of immigrant adaptation; (3) social problems caused by immigration; and (4) the nature and dynamics of migrant groups and individual social networks. The vast majority of these studies have used a model which only considered the adaptation of the immigrant societies to the host communities (Barth 1969, Bryce-Laporte 1980, Glazer and Moynihan 1975, Jackson 1969, Jansen 1970, Kasdan 1970, and Shaw 1975).

In the last three decades there has been an explosion in globalization, that is, an increased efficiency in worldwide communications, transportation, and economic integration into the world system (Robbins 1996:345–6). Globalization has resulted in changes in migrant behaviour, causing scholars to rethink old models. For example, the concept of leaving the old country for a new one is being replaced with the migrants residing in a locality, and still being part of, and managing affairs, in both the place of origin and the locality in which they presently reside. Also, as a result of the Civil Rights Movement in the US, scholars are paying greater attention to issues of political economy. It has quickly become evident to researchers studying population movements that ongoing interactions are taking place that transcend political, geographical, and social boundaries as well as geographical and social distances.

In the 1970s and early 1980s, the ongoing influence of the sending and/or home society began to be considered in the analysis of immigrant behaviour (Gmelch 1980: 135–7, Hendricks 1974, Jeffrey 1976, and Helweg 1978, 1979, 1986). Nancy and Theodore Graves (1974) argued that three social arenas must be considered to comprehend the behaviour of expatriates: (1) the sending community; (2) the migrant group; and (3) the receiving society, for, a three-way diachronic process is continually taking place.

A transnational perspective became prominent in the 1990s. Often using network analysis, scholars in migration studies have been in the forefront of issues like deterritorialized identity, cultural productions, and social practices.

Much of the scholarship on transnational migration has concentrated on both the political, economic and social conditions that promote transnational formation and the material and social capital that cross national boundaries. Less attention has been paid to production, recognition and character of those cultural items that also cross national borders (Pessar 1999:58).

By 'transnational' we mean:

the process by which immigrants build social fields that link together their country of origin and their country of settlement (Schiller 1992: 1).[1]

Thus transmigrants, are individuals who:

... develop and maintain multiple relations family, economic, social organizational, religious and political, that span borders (Schiller, Basch, Blanc-Szanton 1992, 2).

Because of their survival in such varied circumstances and their migratory tradition, the Sikhs are a good community to study so as to better understand migrant behaviour. One framework that I find helpful in understanding the complexities of migrant and Sikh actions is field theory. As will be shown below, field theory enables the researcher to manage the complexities of human actions as they are in the actual life situation.

In field theory, according to Kurt Lewin (Cartwright 1952), the researcher identifies the field of enquiry and then analyses the forces influencing the behavioural process. As the following analysis will show, this is an ideal methodology to use in studying transmigrants, because the framework is holistic, and therefore, many of the issues that were formerly treated as separate processes are placed in a proper context. In other words, the broader approach conforms more to the actual situation of recent immigrants because it can consider ongoing interaction, with other relevant communities and institutions besides host and origin.

Consequently, to analyse Sikh migrant behaviour the scholar first establishes the field of enquiry and then works out the relevant force fields within the field. Contrary to some who take an extreme transnational or world system frame work, everything on the globe does not impact on everything else. The researcher has to identify the relevant forces.[2]

I will seek to demonstrate that there are certain key processes that the migrant or migrant community experience. Also, the identity of an individual or group, like the Sikhs in England, changes in response to the forces exerted by their place of origin, their new abode and possibly elsewhere. Also changes in identity respond to the changing nature and composition of the migrant community (Helweg 1986b).

The Sikhs in England

The Sikhs are a community highly respected for their aggressive, innovative, and militaristic behavior. Many scholars agree with E.J.B. Rose (1969: 52) when he writes, 'the Sikhs are perhaps the most mobile and versatile people in the whole of India.' When the British annexed Punjab in 1849, they recognized the militaristic qualities of the Sikhs, classified them as a martial race and incorporated them into the Indian Army. Sikh experiences in the military acquainted them with opportunities throughout the Empire, and they took advantage of these by emigrating to regions of opportunity.

In 1947 when the Sikh homeland, the Punjab, was partitioned between India and Pakistan, many were left destitute, as non-Muslims in the area allotted to Pakistan had to leave for India. As a result, the resources of India's Punjab were severely taxed. When news of opportunities abroad, especially in England, reached those in India through friends, relatives and travel agents, many decided to emigrate (Helweg 1986: 24).[3]

Gravesend, Kent, the community of focus for this study, is located on the outskirts of London's industrial sector. Like other port cities in England, it had a few Indians living there intermittently for many years previous to the Sikh influx. Its paper, cable, rubber, printing, cement, engineering, shipbuilding, and ancillary enterprises made for an attractive industrial region for immigrants. South Asians now number over 7,000 with seventy per cent being Sikhs.[4] By 1980, the Sikh community in Gravesend was losing its categorization as an immigrant community for forty-five per cent of its members were born in England.

Punjab, their homeland is the most prosperous region in India.(Singh, Iqbal 1986: 118, Wallace 1986: 369–72). The village of Jandiali, Punjab, from which many of Gravesend's Sikhs emigrated to Britain, is a Sikh community located halfway between the cities of Jullundur and Ludhiana. This village has sent over two-thirds of its 1,608 inhabitants to England. Other emigrants are scattered around in the north Indian states of Rajasthan and Uttar Pradesh. Still more are in New Zealand, Australia, Canada, the Philippines, and the United States. Since 1972, labour opportunities have developed in Dubai, Iran, and other Middle Eastern countries. While most Jats went to England, the bulk of Chamar males and specialist castes gained economic enhancement in the oil rich countries (Helweg 1986: 213).

The Transnational Dynamics of
Sikhs in Gravesend

As one observes the Sikhs in England over the last three decades, five of many possible processes become evident. I use the term process because what is being described is neither a phase, where one unit has to precede another, nor do the processes have to follow a set order. Also, these units are not mutually exclusive.

The five of many possible processes are 'Decision-making', 'Freedom', 'Conflict', 'Settlement', (Helweg 1986b) and 'Nationalism', (Tatla 1999). These processes are not mutually exclusive nor is a set order predetermined.

Decision-making Process

When the question is posed as to why people migrate, the overwhelming answer is: 'For the money.' Also, when models like game theory are used, the assumption is that choosing whether to stay or leave is an individual decision. As I will show below, both positions are too simplistic and do not do justice to the decision-making process of emigrating or immigrating. As I see it, the force fields of enquiry for deciding who stays and who leaves, are the social situation at the sending and receiving ends of the migration stream, the open and closed channels of travel, and the selection and interpretation of information.

For example, in 1965, Jagdev Singh Grewal's family sponsored him to leave Punjab and settle in England. The family land was not producing enough to feed all three brothers and their families, so emigration was an option chosen to alleviate potential disaster. Jagdev was chosen because he was well-educated, conversant in English, and considered most likely to succeed. It was assumed that after he established himself he would help the other members of the family by either helping them emigrate, or by sending remittances back to Punjab. In other words, the economic situation required the Grewal family to take action to ensure survival and the decision to send Jagdev to England was a family decision, not an individual decision on Jagdev's part. In fact, when one considers the immigration to the States at the turn of the century, either the peasants entering from Eastern Europe were not as poor as often thought or they had financial backing, which means that the decision to leave was not an individual one. Also, emigration was not a new mode of behaviour for Sikhs in the Punjab. Jagdev and his family had many friends and relatives abroad. Emigration was an established pattern of behaviour. Without the economic situation, the tradition of emigration, and relatives providing support, people like Jagdev would have never emigrated.

Information flow is another force field in the Decision-making Process. Sikh villagers had mixed perceptions about the British. They respected the rule of the Raj and the preference they received to enter military service. They had a 'colonial mentality' developed where subjects regard their colonizers or past colonizers as prestigious—even when the colonized sought independence from them (Fanon 1963). On the other hand, Westerners were considered dirty and immoral. Besides Britain did not side with Sikhs in India, Canada, and the United States when they experienced discrimination in those countries. The dissatisfaction that developed resulted in revolutionary movements like the Ghadar Party[5] (Khushwant Singh 1966: 168–92), and a few Jandialians participated in the movement.

In 1947, the partition of the Punjab resulted in slaughter and destruction. The states resources were severely taxed. Meanwhile, the situation on the receiving end encouraged migration to Britain. There were acquaintances, from the area, in the UK around Jandiali, and they had been encouraging friends and relatives to enter Britain. Thus, the situation in England was conducive for Jagdev to emigrate. When the pros and cors were weighed, Jagdev and his family agreed that England should still be his destination. Also, the channels of migration were more open to Britain at this time than any other country. Britain had a policy of open entry to all members of the Commonwealth. The United States was restricting entrants from Asia and Africa and the 'White Australia Policy', which also prohibited the permanent entry of Asians and Africans, was still in effect.

The information transmitted between the sending and receiving groups is frequently inaccurate, stereotypical, and exaggerated, especially in the early days. Also, if the truth is transmitted, it may not be believed if it counters existing stereotypes. Information from English exaggerated the prosperity and opportunities abroad without considering deficiencies. One letter illustrates the nature of the information being sent back to Jandiali.

My job in Gravesend is very easy. I go to work at 8 a.m. and push the green button to make the machine go. I sit in my chair until mid-morning, when I push the red button to stop the machine and take a half-hour tea break. After tea, I return and push the green button to make the machine go and sit in my chair until lunch. At lunchtime I push the red button to stop the machine, take an hour off until 1 p.m.

When I return I push the green button again to make the machine go. At tea-time in the afternoon, the red button is pushed to stop the machine and we take a half-hour off for tea, and then again I push the green button to start the machine until it is time to go home at 5 p.m. Then, I push the red button and stop the machine. For this I make Rs 1800 a month.[6]

To a villager averaging Rs 200 a month, if he had a successful harvest, England was paradise. The few Indians who had been in England impressed the villagers. When emigrants visited home, they wore new clothes, bought prior to leaving the UK for India, and spent money on relatives and friends in Jandiali as if their assets were inexhaustible. Those emigrants returning, especially in the 1950s, were reported in the press and their claimed successes abroad were greatly boasted. A clerk in the post office was referred to as a 'postal official', a sweeper at Bowater Scott Paper Company was an 'employee at Bowaters', a typist for the local borough council was a 'member of the borough civil service'. Later on, the tales of travel agents and smugglers who wanted client fees further supported the myth of England as a paradise. The emigrant's position in England may have been lowly, but in Jandiali, he was a 'bara sahib', an important person whose emigration not only increased his esteem but also that of his kin group. The tales of wealth and success in Britain were compatible with the esteem villagers had for the British. They had seen the power of the Raj and recalled lavish parades as well as the grand life style of British in India who had lived in opulent houses, belonged to exclusive clubs, had numerous servants and travelled in entourages.

Last, the doors for entry into Britain were open while entry into the US, Australia, and Canada were being closed. Consequently, after the situation in England was considered, along with the available channels and information, Britain was chosen as the destination for Jagdev Singh Grewal.

Capsule Summary of Decision-making Process

The *situation* is that emigration is being considered. The *Field of Enquiry* is the English community and the potential area of emigration. The *Force Fields* include: (1) the situation at both ends of the migration stream; (2) the channels open for the migration stream and; (3) the nature, composition, and believability of information; (4) decision-making procedure for potential emigration. Their *identity* has not changed but the potential emigrant sees his social rank becoming higher.

Freedom Process

The situation of Gravesend was typical of most migrant communities in that the men arrived first and sponsored their wives and children later. As a result, the migrant community was initially composed primarily of males whose goal was to make a lot of money and return to their homeland with a fortune. Communications with those in their place of origin emphasized success as a result of the money sent back—negative information was neither transmitted nor believed.

Sikhs during this time relied heavily on the advice of friends and relatives. The Sikh community in Gravesend came about when Bhuta Singh founded an employment service and provided labourers to build an oil refinery near Gravesend on the Isle of Grain. He recruited Indian labourers who originated from his village. The word spread concerning his employment agency. Many Sikhs responded, and, for a fee, he provided jobs, housing, and took care of bureaucratic requirements. One of these early labourers was Bhajan Singh of Jandiali. Bhajan Singh encouraged and helped his village mates to migrate to Gravesend and take advantage of the opportunities. Being a sponsor gave him prestige at home and in England.

Since they considered England a temporary abode, men worked insatiably hard, often logging 90 hours a week. They wanted to earn money fast, and when they learned that the white English did not like to work on weekends, they filled weekend vacancies. Their concern was not with how much money they earned per hour, but how much was acquired totally.

The men lived in crowded conditions—thirty or more men to a three-bedroom house. Men slept in shifts, and when one left for work, another took his cot. Their social centre was the Pub, where they quenched their thirst with a glass of beer or ale. The arrangements were meagre, but it was temporary and there was the promise of greater prosperity and power upon returning to Punjab.

Men were so busy making their fortune that caste rules were overlooked, and proud high caste men performed demeaning jobs which involved cleaning latrines and sweeping cigarette butts—work they would never do in the Punjab. If they had to work beside a low caste individual, it was tolerated as they only wanted money and enhancement of social position in their home society. For expediency, many Sikhs discarded their turbans and shaved their beards because employers hesitated to hire a man with long hair, which might get caught in machinery. For these Punjabi males in

England, their primary goal was making money and enhancing their *mann* or *izzat*,[7] prestige, in India.

The Sikh immigrants in England remained apart from their English hosts, and the English ignored them as well. More important in the minds of those in England, Jandialians judged success abroad according to the wealth one sent back or displayed in the village. If a male earned in England and sent money back to his family and relatives, his kin group was proud. In summary, they were relatively free of social prohibitions of either the British or their homeland. The British host society did not care as long as the Sikhs remained apart and confined to their allotted space and the community in the Punjab did not question behaviour in England as long as remittances flowed back.

Capsule Summary of Freedom Process

The *situation* is the early years of an immigrant community where norms of the host or sending community, for what ever reason, are not being applied. The *Field of enquiry* is the immigrant community; communication with sending and host societies is minimal. The *Force Field* is the immigrant's quest for making money with the goal of returning to the home region when wealthy enough. Their *identity* is still with their place of origin, but they feel their social ranking is higher.

Conflict Process

The Conflict Process results when the Immigrants have to deal with irreconcilable cultural dictates demanded of them by the cultural clashes of the sending and host communities. Their goal may still be to return to their land of origin but conflicting social control mechanisms are being established with the arrival of wives and children.

By 1960, the Gravesend–Jandali migrant group realized immigration restrictions would be imposed by 1962. With the threat of controls, men brought in their wives, children and friends. Although their plan may have been to still return to the Punjab, the arrival of family members resulted in village norms being imposed on a population that had lived in freedom of certain restrictive norms. The result was aptly described by one Gravesend Sikh who stated: 'We have one foot in England and one foot in India and it hurts in the middle.'

The 'hurt in the middle' became a reality with the arrival of wives, children, and village mates for the males could no longer behave as they pleased. They came under close scrutiny of their home village. Punjabi women abroad wrote home and portrayed the true nature of life in Britain. Since it was their responsibility to guard family honour for both their husband and natal family, they pressurized their spouses to adhere to village norms. Parents wanted to set a good example for their children. The increased communication with India made everyone doubly careful and conscious of their behaviour, for their goal was to be highly respected in Jandiali, where they planned to resettle.

The ramifications of this new situation were that Sikhs in Gravesend were caught between conflicting cultural demands. For example, Sikhs had learned that trimming their hair and beards increased their marketability in jobs while in England. Such actions often broke the hearts of their parents in the Punjab, for religious dictates maintained that unshorn hair was crucial to spirituality and masculinity. The Gravesend Sikh male was torn between his desire for a good job in England by compromising on Sikh beliefs, and causing parental anguish or setting a bad example for his children.

As a result, the Sikhs in Gravesend raised ethnic boundary between them and the English.[8] They worked to instil their cultural heritage and pride into the second generation and to keep their children from absorbing the host culture and becoming 'Brown British'. Therefore, the migrants continued their interest in their place of origin, reacting to elections and politics in India as if it directly affected them. Immigrant vernacular newspapers described riots, elections, and political figures in detail. There was a dichotomy. On the one hand Gravesend Sikhs did not want their children to become British, yet, they were unwilling to give up the good life and wealth of England. The longer they stayed the more they wondered whether they had made a wise decision. They could see their second generation already resisting Asian culture and emulating some British norms.

The Gravesend Sikhs countered Western influence by strictness, holding language classes in the Gurdwara and conducting instruction on Punjabi and Sikh culture. The elders also downgraded English norms and tried to stop their offspring from interacting with the whites.

The influence from India continued to be strong. Gravesend Sikhs preferred spouses for their children from India. They desired arranged marriages with those of rural background because of the high regard villagers were supposed to have for the elderly. For those with a daughter, they could keep her home if married to a boy from India for the village lad was loyal and beholden to his wife's family for sponsoring him. Since these boys seldom had kin support in England, they were at the mercy of their wife's family. Thus they shifted the balance of power in favor of the female and her family.

A few returned to India but life there was difficult. They neither had knowledge nor business experience in the Punjab and quickly lost their fortunes. Others were unhappy without English amenities. It may not have been any one thing in particular, but life in the village, especially for women, was difficult. Having savoured privacy in Gravesend, females preferred England where they were the mistresses of their house without having to yield to a mother-in-law. Teenagers returning to the village had their share of hard times. Young boys found their Punjabi inadequate and part-time jobs for youth in Punjab were limited and frowned upon by elders. Thus boys became bored. Girls, because of their chaperoned and restricted life in England, did not face the same problems to the same degree as boys. Youngsters were unhappy and wanted to return to their British ways of life.

The casual visitor to Jandiali in 1970 saw new multi-storied farm house outside the village. A few England returnees on holiday were visible around the village. Being an England returnee, however, began to lose its former charm and prestige. It was no longer enough to be an English migrant or have a son or relative in Britain. Now, the emigrant had to have a decent job and display proper behaviour in England.

Emigrants not only sent capital to Jandiali, they also communicated innovative ideas and modern agricultural technology. Relatives and friends abroad continually sent different varieties of seeds and information concerning innovative farm techniques. Sikh Jats tried these new methods and if successful, they implemented them.

In Jandiali, emigrants continued to play an active role in village affairs, even though they resided in England. A group of emigrants donated money to build the new village place of worship to fulfill Bhuta Singh's dream of having a Gurdwara in Jandiali with a tower so high that one could see Phagwara, which was three miles away, from its top. The *zaildar's* or headman's group resisted the new construction but the emigrant faction won. The poorer Jat element had initially emigrated to England from Jandiali to make money but an additional consequence was that they had power to influence village affairs.

The year 1970 brought with it the plight of the Kenyan Asians who were being expelled from Kenya. Many were Sikhs but not Jats. They were generally wealthier and established in professions or business. They tended to separate themselves from the Jats of village origin. Yet, they were also Sikhs and were able to impose their conservatism on the Jat element, which caused greater cultural conflict in the Sikh community.

Summary Capsule of Conflict Process

The *situations* when sending and host communities impose conflicting norms on the immigrant community. The *Field of Enquiry* includes the immigrant community, the host society, the sending area and in this particular case, the Kenyan Asians. The *Force Fields* are those cultural tenets that imposed tension on the immigrant group. Their *identity* is still with their village of origin but to have esteem there they must be successful in England, which means to some, compromising one's beliefs such as cutting your hair.

Settlement Process

The Settlement Process is when the immigrant community realize that they are a permanent part of their new abode—returning is not a viable option. In other words, they have changed from an immigrant community to a minority group. England had initiated restrictive legislation concerning immigration so that ongoing communication with kinsmen in India decreased. Meanwhile Britain's cities in 1981 exploded in racial violence and Gravesend was not immune to those influences.

The result of all this is that Sikh immigrants may have called themselves 'Sikhs', but what was meant by that differed according to place of origin, sect membership, and generation. Divisions along these lines were rising in the community. Sikhs in England did not necessarily identify with India. They were a group of their own. The village in India was no longer their evaluator. Those in England saw themselves as above their village counterparts, as those in India perceived of themselves as more pure and superior to the emigrants. Those in England developed their own life style. However, discriminatory practices and violence increased and the Sikhs in England, like other minorities, resented such treatment. Thus the negative attitude toward the English host community increased. Even in the village, reference group behaviour was evident as those who had emigrant affiliations accentuated their distinctiveness from the others. They formed their own political group and used their assets to control village politics.

The ramifications of this changed identity were many. When the Festival of India was held in Britain in 1981, some South Asians held a 'Counter Festival' which emphasized Indian immigrant culture. As one boy stated,

'We are not white British nor are we lackeys of the Indian government, we have our own culture to communicate.' Yet, when India won the World Cup in cricket, the Sikh immigrants cheered and sweets were distributed to passing motorists as they traversed Southall, the Indian community in London.

Sikhs, like other Asians, began to align with West Indians and other minorities in Great Britain. As a result their attitudes changed. They saw affirmative action as a right, due to the exploitation of their country by the British—a shift from the earlier years when they saw themselves as guests in the country which belonged to the white English. The Sikhs in England began taking a greater pride in militant responses to white violence and discrimination. Their purpose in life included fighting for their rights in their abode. They were not English but they were not of India either. They had developed a new ethnicity that was neither British nor Indian, but their own creation.

This new identity did not necessarily prohibit individuals of the Sikh diaspora from buying land and investing in India. Some hoped their children would take over the family acreage. Others had a prosperous business or businesses. But leaving England permanently was not a consideration.

Capsule Summary of Settlement Process

The *situation* is that the immigrant community realizes that returning to their homeland is for most not a viable option. The *Field of Enquiry* is the immigrant community, the English host society, the sending community and other South Asian groups like the Kenyan Asians, the major *force field* is the Indian and Sikh migrant communities developing their own *identity* that is separate from the other Asian communities as well as separate from their counterparts in India. They are NRIs (Non-Resident Indians) or England Returned.

Nationalism Process

The Sikhs had established an ethnic unity shortly after the death of Guru Gobind Singh. They had a language, Gurmukhi, which was a derivation of Punjabi, a language going back to ancient times. They claimed a homeland, Punjab, an area they once ruled. They had a history that traced them back to the beginning of time. As Khazan Singh (1914a, 1914b) argued, Sikhism was not a new religion but a return to ancient and purer ways. Sikhs had a mythology about themselves as soldier-saints with a strong tradition of martyrdom. They wore distinctive symbols that set them apart. Last, they had a culture with an agreed upon set of values, meanings, and beliefs. Thus, with a common homeland, language, history, culture, and mythology, the worldwide Sikh diaspora was united in an ethnicity that tied its members to a community which had its origins from the beginning of time. Membership gave meaning to the lives of its adherents by providing an ancient tradition on which to build so that those who followed would have a better life.

When India was granted independence in 1947, the Sikhs cast their lot with Nehru and the Congress Party rather than press for their own independent homeland.[9] However, the later Sikh quest for independent nationhood was a direct result of actions by the government of India. Largely due to the policies of the central government and Prime Minister Indira Gandhi, the Sikhs and other people of the Punjab did not feel they were being treated fairly. The quota for Sikhs in the military was reduced and unemployment was high in the Punjab. Also, political manoeuvring by the Congress Party promoted lawlessness and gangsterism. One result was Operation Bluestar–the code-name for the invasion of the Sikh sacred Golden Temple in Amritsar by the Indian Army on June 3, 1984. This was a major blow to all Sikhs, a community that had provided a contingent in India's armed forces far in excess of their numbers and sacrificed proportionately much more during the history of India than any other community.

When anti-Sikh rioters were unleashed after two Sikh bodyguards assassinated Mrs Gandhi, Sikhs in India and abroad found themselves alienated from their homeland. Thus diaspora Sikhs were prominent in providing support for the separatist movement of Khalistan.

England may have been their home, but having an independent homeland was perceived as crucial for the survival of Sikhism and thus a common goal for all Sikhs in England as well as Sikhs of the diaspora in general (Mahmood 1996: 155–74 and Singh, N. 1994: 133–55). The Sikhs had all the ingredients to form a nation except the capability of obtaining and maintaining political control of their homeland.

As of times of old when the Mughals ruled, oppression of the Sikhs had come from Delhi. History was repeating itself. In spite of the massive monetary contributions by the Sikh diaspora, and the pressure they put on their governments, especially in Canada, the United States, and the United Kingdom to aid and recognize the Sikh government in exile, the insurgency came to an end.

Capsule Summary of Nationalism Process
The *Field of Enquiry* includes all Sikh and Asian Indian communities world wide. The primary *Field Force* is the actions of the Indian government.

Conclusions

Of course, the goals of a scholar influence the framework used in analysing migrant behaviour. Field Theory is one of many possible approaches. In this particular study, the processes outlined above are not mutually exclusive. However, they tend to follow the same general order in the United States and Canada (Bains and Johnston 1995, La Brack 1988, Singh, Narindar 1994, and Tatla 1999) as outlined above. Also, each process revealed the changing nature and impact of the different force fields which resulted in the changing identity of the Sikhs in the diaspora. As the community in Gravesend illustrates, there was a shift from identification with village of origin to being a separate entity.

No group stands alone, because of interactional relationships with other groups and forces. The response of Sikhs to the desecration of their holiest shrine forged a unity of Sikhs in the diaspora with each other as well as those in Punjab. Differences that had existed were overlooked or minimized to work for the common cause of Khalistan. This situation also shows how one individual, such as Mrs Gandhi or one institution, like parts of the government of India, can cause sudden shifts in a peoples' identity. The influence that a force has is also determined by the self-concept that a people have about themselves. When the Sikhs in England saw themselves as villagers, the force of village culture was much stronger than when they perceived of themselves an independent entity.

Last, with the current emphasis on globalization it can be difficult to isolate or determine relevant factors in influencing migrant behaviour. Field theory frameworks make the understanding of behaviour more manageable by helping to isolate the relevant forces impinging on the situation.

Notes

1. Arjun Appadurai (1990, 1996) has also studied and developed a framework for understanding global cultural flows and their impact on people socially embedded in a locale and habituated to a specific set of identities and practices.

2. In the situation of the Sikhs, there may be more than three communities involved. For example, Sikhs who lived in East Africa, moved to Britain, shifted to

Canada and finally settled in the United States have many more influences than just the sending, receiving, and migrant groups. In their case the unit of analysis involves many societies.

3. It should be kept in mind that the Sikhs were not the only people from South Asia going to the United Kingdom. Pakistanis, Bangladeshis, Gujaratis, Muslims, and Hindus all were part of the UK/South Asia migration stream.

4. These numbers are an under-representation of the South Asian contingent because the census only identified ethnic groups by place of birth, thus the actual figure will be forty per cent higher.

5. The Party was a revolutionary movement that functioned between 1902 and 1915.

6. It is interesting to note that the same process took and takes place in the United States among immigrants. Known as the 'American Letters', immigrants glorify life in America to the extent that people visiting expect life to be much more lavish than what they find.

7. *Mann* is the Punjabi word for *izzat* which refer to the communal evaluation of a family. It was a cultural goal to work so that the kin group was held in high esteem by the comunity (Helweg 1986: 12–21).

8. This is not to imply that the English did not do their part to maintain social separation. The point is that there was a conscious endeavour among Gravesend Sikhs to create distinctions between them and the English host society.

9. This is a controversial point for, whether the Sikh negotiators realized it or not, the British were willing to grant them a homeland with political independence. Such demands were never made by the Sikh representatives.

References

Appadurai, Arjun, 1990. 'A Disjunction and Difference in the Global Economy', *Public Culture*. 2 (2: 1–24).

———— 1996 'A Sovereignty Without Territoriality: Notes for a Postnational Geography', *The Geography of Identity*, edited by Patricia Yager, Ann Arbor: University of Michigan Press.

Bains, Tara Singh and Hugh Johnston, 1995. *The Four Quarters of the Night: The Life Journey of an Emigrant Sikh*, Montreal & Kingston, London, Buffalo: McGill Queen's University Press.

Barth, Fredrik, 1969. Introduction, *In Ethnic Groups and Boundaries: The Social Organization of Cultural Difference*. Edited by Fredrik Barth. Boston: Little Brown.

Bryce-Laporte, Roy Simon, ed., 1980. *Sourcebook on the New Immigration: Implications for the United States and the International Community*. New Brunswick, New Jersey: Transaction Books.

Cartwright, Dorwin, 1952. *Field Theory in the Social Sciences: Selected Theoretical Papers by Kurt Lewin*, London: Tavistock Publications.

Fanon, Frantz, 1964. *The Wretched of the Earth*, New York: Grove Press.

Glazer, Nathan and Daniel P. Moynihan, 1975. *Ethnicity: Theory and Experience*, Cambridge: Harvard University Press.

Gmelch, George, 1980. 'Return Migration' In *Annual Review of Anthropology* Vol. 9, Palo Alto: Annual Reviews Inc.

Graves, Nancy B. and Theodore Graves, 1974. 'Return Migration' *Annual Review of Anthropology*, Vol. 3, Palo Annual Reviews Inc.

Helweg, Arthur, 1986a. *Sikhs in England, Second Edition*, New Delhi: Oxford University Press.

_____ 1986b. 'Indians in England: A Study of the Interactional Relationships of Sending, Receiving and Migrant Societies' *Studies in Migration: Internal and International Migration in India*, Edited by M.S.A. Rao. Delhi: Manohar.

_____ 1979. *Sikhs in England: The Development of a Migrant Community*, New Delhi: Oxford University Press.

_____ 1978. 'Punjabi Farmers: Twenty Years in England', *India International Centre Quarterly*. 5:1.

Hendricks, Glen, 1974. *The Dominican Diaspora*, New York: Teachers College Press.

Ibbetson, Sir Daniel, 1883. *Punjab Castes*, Patiala: Languages Department of Punjab (Reprinted in 1970).

Jackson, J.A., ed., 1969. *Migration*, Cambridge: Cambridge University Press.

Jansen, Clifford, ed., 1970. *Readings in the Sociology of Migration*, London: Pergamon Press.

Jeffrey, Patricia, 1976. *Migrants and Refugees: Muslim and Christian Families in Bristol*, Cambridge: Cambridge University Press.

Kasdan, Leonard, 1970. Introduction, *Migration and Anthropology*, Robert F. Spencer, general editor, Seattle: American Ethnological Society and the University of Washington Press.

Mahmood, Cynthia Keppley, 1996. *Fighting for Faith and Nation: Dialogues with Sikh Militants*, Philadelphia: University of Pennsylvania Press.

Pessar, Patricia, 1999. 'The Role of Gender Households, and Social Networks in the Migration Process: A Review and Appraisal', *The Handbook of International Migration: The American Experience*, edited by Charles Hirschman, Philip Kasinitz, and Josh DeWind, New York: Russell Sage Foundation.

Robins, Kevin, 1996. Globalization, In *The Social Science Encyclopaedia, Second Edition*, edited by Adam Kuper & Jessica Kuper, London: Routledge.

Rose, E.J.B., 1969. *Colour and Citizenship: A Report on British Race Relations*, London: Oxford University Press.

Schiller, Nina Glick, 1999. 'Transmigrants and Nation-States: Something Old and Something New in the US Immigrant Experience', *The Handbook of International Migration: The American Experience*, edited by Charles Hirschman, Philip Kasinitz and Joseph DeWind, New York: Russell Sage Foundation.

——, Linda Basch, and Cristina Bland-Szanton, 1992. *Towards a Transnational Perspective on Migration: Race, Class, Ethnicity and Nationalism Reconsidered*, New York: The New York Academy of Sciences.

Shaw, R. Paul, 1979. *Migration: Theory and Fact*, Philadelphia: Regional Science Research Institute.

Singh, Iqbal, 1986. *Punjab Under Siege: A Critical Analysis*, New York: Allen, McMillan and Enderson.

Singh, Khazan, 1914a. *History of the Sikh Religion*, Chandigarh: Department of Languages, Punjab.

—— 1914b. *Philosophy of the Sikh Religion*, Chandigarh: Department of Languages, Punjab.

Singh, Khushwant, 1966. *A History of the Sikhs, Volume 2: 1839–1964*. London: Oxford University Press.

—— 1963. *A History of the Sikhs, Volume 1: 1469–1839*. London: Oxford University Press.

Singh, Narindar, 1994. *Canadian Sikhs: History, Religion, and Culture of Sikh in North America*, Ottwa: Canadian Sikh Studies Institute.

Tatla, Darshan Singh, 1999. *The Sikh Diaspora: The Search for Statehood*, Seattle: The University of Washington Press.

9

Writing Prejudice
The Image of Sikhs in
Bharati Mukherjee's Writings

Darshan S. Tatla[1]

Introduction

In June 1984, the Sikhs of Punjab attracted much publicity in the western media. As the Indian army invaded into the Sikhs' holiest shrine, the Golden Temple, Amritsar, TV stations brought pictures of fighting in progress and the devastation it caused to the sacred complex of buildings. Analysts predicted a blood bath ahead; within four months, the Indian Prime Minister, Indira Gandhi, was shot dead, followed by an unprecedented massacre of Sikhs in India's capital. This set the scene for further violence, including Sikh insurgency lasting for a decade, suppressed largely through extreme repression by the security forces. The convulsions, since then, within the Sikh community, both in the Punjab and among the Sikh diaspora, have given rise to many contested narratives about the sequence of events leading to such bloodshed. Journalistic and scholarly literature around 1984 events is extensive ranging from official statements, commissioned reports, dissertations and learned articles.[2] The Sikh diaspora's vigorous participation in the ensuing struggle led to many kinds of narratives describing their role and vision. The Sikh history, politics, its traditions, and culture, were the subject of much heated debate in this volatile atmosphere. During this period, a new genre of writings also surfaced; a fictional characterization of Sikhs' role in the post-1984 Punjab. This literature has as yet found little notice.[3]

This paper examines Mukherjee's portrayal of diaspora Sikhs' role in the Punjab, focusing on two such accounts: a non-fictional book *The Sorrow and the Terror: the Haunting Legacy of the Air India Tragedy* is shared with her husband, Clark Blaise. It is a scathing investigation of how some Canadian Sikhs plotted a conspiracy and almost got away with it. Mukherjee's fictional writings, a story in her *Middleman* collection, and a major novel, *Jasmine*, are examined as literary extension of the investigative work. Mukherjee's portrayal of Sikhism and Sikh characters, it is argued, leads to a negative image of the community. The paper concludes with brief comments on the role of fiction in imagining minority characters. Bharati Mukherjee—an 'American citizen of Bengali-Indian origin' as she prefers to describe herself is a 'Distinguished Professor of Literature at the University of California, Berkeley'.[4]

Mukherjee's writings have received many accolades. She rejects minority writers' major concern with the preservation of cultural identities. Her works have found much discussion not least due to her enthusiastic support for the 'American dream' and its 'melting pot' philosophy. She has outlined her literary agenda; it, 'begins by acknowledging that America has transformed me. It does not end until I show how I [and the hundreds of thousands like me] have transformed America'.[5] Complimented for challenging predominant concerns of minority discourse to remember and recover marginalized histories in the face of racism and denigration, her writings, instead, 'celebrate cultural dislocation as a positive virtue' free from the old constricting cultural foundations. Her works are about 'broken identities and discarded languages' and chronicle the 'exile of fractured lives, caught up in a cross-cultural metamorphosis'. Her works are seen as a new departure from minority writers' pre-occupation with the retrieval of histories and lives facing the hegemonic discourse of host society.[6]

However, this paper suggests a more moderate interpretation of Mukherjee's two works locating them into a new genre of writings by Hindu intellectuals dealing with the contradictions of India's cultural plurality. As an upper class Bengali Brahmin, Mukherjee's American neo-nationalist ideology challenging migrants' exclusivity can be understood from an Indian context and background. After setting a highly integrative nationalist agenda for post-colonial India, its predominantly Hindu elite has aggressively propagated an overarching Indian identity while the state has faced various ethno-nationalist claims.[7] Mukherjee's American neo-nationalism, her condemnation of the 'cultural baggage' of immigrants, and their 'exclusive reproduction in the first world', it is argued, arises partially from her understanding of the old world, and of India's multiethnic experiment in particular, where several minorities have graduated from seeking 'special position' to 'nationalist struggles' threatening its fragile unity. Thus, her creative works can be seen as part of a shared 'burden' of an emerging and somewhat aggressive Hindu elite, while taking an intellectually consistent position between the adopted country and homeland.

The Prose: Air India Tragedy

Written after a year's intensive research and with a noble mission as the authors point out in the introduction, *The Sorrow and Terror: the Haunting Legacy of Air India Tragedy* was spurred by the agony of traumatized relatives whose dear ones had died in the crash. Published in 1987, at the height of violence in the Punjab, when daily shoot-outs between Sikh militant groups and security forces were reported in the western media, this is investigative journalism at its best with two literary authors chartering a major air tragedy.[8] The authors set out to find the real reasons for the tragic event in which most victims, 'were Canadian citizens', while, 'both India and Canada were trying to wash their hands off the incident'.

Setting the theme, the authors tell us they have a 'political point of view' but this ignores larger forces such as the involvement of CIA, Indo-US relations, the Pakistan factor or the Soviet–Afghan triangle. Instead, they want to paint the human side of the tragedy, treating the event as 'fundamentally an immigration tragedy with terrorist overtones'. Their approach is highlighted through numerous interviews with crash victims' relatives scattered across North American cities, from Toronto, and Montreal to Vancouver, and Detroit. The authors travelled to Ireland, and obtained information by scanning official and unofficial documents, Coroners' reports, proceedings of an Indian official inquiry, the Kirpal Commission, transcripts of terrorists' trials, bail hearings, and interrogations in Duncan, British Columbia; Brooklyn, New York; Hamilton, Ontario; Montreal, Quebec, and elsewhere. The book draws upon taped interviews with family members, Irish hospital workers, 'volatile Khalistanis', and Sikh leaders across North America. Piecing together evidence from conflicting information for the biggest act of terrorism in Canadian history, the authors have performed a necessary and daunting task.

The study commences with a 'background' chapter on Sikhism. It reminds the readers that Sikhs are not terrorists and objects to such headlines as 'Sikh bomb suspected' linking them with terrorist acts. In the charged atmosphere of Sikh–Canadian relations, when the general impression about Sikhs was as 'violent people', the authors offered a salutary caution. Moreover, 'all Khalistanis are Sikhs but not all Sikhs are Khalistanis'. The Five Ks are seen to be part of the Sikh attire of a religious tradition which is a fusion of Bhakti and Sufi elements, tied to Punjab's geography. Gradually the faith was transformed into a militant army as conflict arose between Mughal rulers of the region, and emperors Jehangir and Aurangzeb who attempted 'to destroy the faith, root and branch'. Thus began the final phase of early Sikh history, an almost constant series of battles, murders, and intrigue, ending with the founding of the Khalsa by Guru Gobind–the pure and the militant army of the faithful. The authors conclude that the Khalsa in ordinary times has always meant the Sikh community, has now 'come to mean those dedicated to the political agenda of Khalistan'. And surprisingly, add further:

a Sikh who is baptised into the faith today is most assuredly following the priestly leadership of a militant Khalistani [p. xxv].

Further abandoning the cautious approach, readers are then told, 'perhaps no great injustice is done if the western reader simply thinks of Sikhism as a religion like Christianity or Islam with a noble theology, a saintly founder and a confusing set of mutually exclusive teachings. Humble and arrogant, persecuted and aggressive, militant and pacifist' [p. xxv]. Readers are told about differences of politics and opinions within the community. Thus Sikhs raised with the notion that all of India is their home, and that secular education, travel, and self-improvement are their birthright feel that Khalistan is a medieval farce, an invitation to join the seventeenth century ['and become the Palestinians of India', as one successful Toronto Sikh businessman put it] at a time when Punjab is the wealthiest and most progressive state in India [xxviii]. Finally, 'it is important to retain that sense of basic warmth and trust and to stress the difference between Khalistanis, the supporters of Sikh independence, of the exacting of "blood for blood" revenge against India or against Hindus or even against dissenters within their own community, and the 15 million Sikhs in India and now around the world who constitute the community of believers' [xxviii]. Then follows some elaboration of the term Khalistan; how in 1971 Jagjit Singh Chohan brought it into public arena with an eerie drama of setting up embassies in western countries, circulation of Khalistani currency notes, maps, and passports. Though Chohan's efforts invited ridicule from most

Sikhs, the authors somehow still assert that, 'Khalistan movement was already in place in the 1970s' among the Sikh diaspora, and in 1982–3 it was 'resurrected by money' when newspapers were floated with free swinging libellous editorials. Chohan's efforts were 'only rescued by Bhindranwale and the Golden Temple invasion … since then, he has struggled to control the forces it so enthusiastically released'.

The new fundamentalism inspired by Bhindranwale places absolute emphasis on the maintenance of five Ks as 'to have been born in a Sikh family, but not to maintain the external forms of the religion is to show contempt for the Khalsa' p. xxvii]. Without elaborating the political scene of the Punjab and its manipulation by the Central government, readers are informed that the rise of Bhindranwale was 'facilitated through official patronage' to weaken the Akalis by Indira Gandhi, the Indian Prime Minister. This introduction is brought to close with further reminders of warm relations between Sikhs and Hindus, the latter often visiting a gurdwara, with indeed many families giving a son to 'Sikhism'. Also, most Hindus, without thinking too deeply about it, consider Sikhism as one of many variants of Hinduism and, 'the constitution of India even considers a shaven, unturbanned Sikh a Hindu' [xxvii].

After this prologue, the main text is divided into five sections. The first chronicles significant events from October 31, 1984 to June 23, 1985— the day of the Air India tragedy. On October 31, 1984, some Sikhs in New York led by Gurpartap Singh Birk were celebrating the murder of Indian prime minister, Indira Gandhi, who was shot dead by her Sikh bodyguards. They did not know the massacre of Sikhs in India's capital was also beginning. The next reference is to November 8 when Birk and three other Sikhs begin training at Frank Camper's centre under surveillance by the Federal Bureau of Investigation [FBI]. Camper's training outfit lures would-be mercenaries, vigilantes, white supremacists, and survivalists and became a trap for some Khalistanis mainly due to their naïveté. A meeting of the World Sikh Organization is noted in December. The next entry is January 6, 1985 with reference to Birk's diary, planning to bomb India's strategic sites including the Homi Bhabha Atomic Centre. On May 4, Birk and another Sikh are arrested by FBI and charged. On May 12, Lata Mangeshkar, the legendary Indian film singer has a concert in Toronto in aid of a charity, where irate Sikh leaders negotiate with the police authorities not to disturb it seeking certain 'conditions'. The Indian high commission asks for extra security on May 13. On June 4, Inderjit Singh Reyat explodes a bomb in a jungle outside Duncan, BC while Royal Canadian Mounted Police [RCMP] men watch. June is the 'memorial month' and 'spectacular vengeance has been promised' [pp. 14–15].

From here, the narrative is about a Sikh cell deciding on an action plan. The reader is taken through an imagined scenario by this cell. The cell has decided to bomb an Air India plane. The dates available for this are 8th, 15th, 22nd and the 29th. The flight on the 8th is cancelled, 15th is too soon, so the 22nd is fixed. The routes of AI flight 182 are checked, its arrival at Toronto, then to Montreal, London, Delhi, and Bombay. Another flight, Canadian Pacific, is also considered a possible target. [Canadian Pacific connects at Tokyo to Air India flight to Bangkok]. A bomb timed for its departure at Tokyo, is also under consideration. This terrorist cell now nominate a particular Singh for a specific job; while one confirms ticket availability, another arranges to change the names of booked passengers, and yet another confirms and pays for the tickets. There is concern about the waiting list status at Montreal airport, and a more literate Sikh with fluency in English is sent to streamline the passage. On June 22, 1985, both Singhs are at the check points; one in Vancouver for the CP flight leaving for Tokyo's Narita airport, another at Montreal for the AI flight leaving for London and going from there to Delhi. Both get their luggage checked but do not board the plane. On June 23, as both planes are on the sea, the readers are told that celebrations are in progress at Sikh temple, Malton. This assertion is based on the evidence of a pizza deliverer who remembers distinctly the party mood and later identifies one of the suspects from a mug shot. This imaginary scenario ends there.

The second section of the book narrates in detail the aftermath of the Air India flight 182. As the tragic news spread, first fifteen relatives arrived at Cork airport on June 26. Indian ambassador Kiran Joshi and Razia, his Muslim wife, a physician, swung into action with whatever resources they had, calling more personnel from London. At Cork, the care and sympathy of Irish police, doctors and nuns are described in contrast to the Canadian officials' detached attitude. The hectic search for bodies led to the recovery of 131 persons, while 198 bodies could not be retrieved, lying deep in the sea. Grief-stricken relatives, parents, husbands or wives, identified the remains of 132 bodies scrupulously lined up in a large hall. Sharks competed with Irish divers in their pursuit for the remaining bodies still under the sea. The Hindu relatives' belief in fate provided great consolation, as Irish and Canadian officials noted with some relief. The authors condemn squarely the Canadian Prime Minister, Brian Mulroney's call to his Indian counterpart, Rajiv Gandhi, with his condolence message 'for its characteristic neglect of remorse', and worse still, the Federal Minister of Transport, Dan Mazankowski' criticism of Air India for failing to take adequate precautions against three suspect bags in Montreal. This official attitude was almost 'rubbing salt into the wounds' and caused intense pain as it absolved Canada of its responsibility for the disaster.

In section three, the chronicle shifts to the victims' relatives and the text is accompanied by some photos. The first interview is with Prakash Bedi in Toronto, a forty-five year engineer working for American Motors. Sobbing, he narrates, how he lost his wife and two children in the crash. He blames three concerned countries, India, Canada, and the US, who have done nothing to remember the victims of terrorism. He laments the absence of official ceremonies and that it is left to relatives to grieve in temples and ethnic societies. He calls for the construction of a commemorative building. Until last June, he had no revulsion for the Sikhs. Born in the Punjab with common Sikh relatives he has lived in Detroit where they were regular visitors to the local gurdwara and Hindu temple. A few incidents did alert him to a Hindu–Sikh divide in the first five months of 1985. One particular incident he remembers well when he and his young son were ignored by *langar* servers, who heaped 'blessed food only on the plates of turbaned men', and especially 'of men re-baptised into Khalsa', the 'men known for their loyalty to the Khalistan movement' [p. 91]. Each time langar servers walked deliberately, slow, unseeing, past the conspicuously empty plates of Prakash Bedi and his nine year old son [p. 92]. Humiliated thus, they stopped going to the gurdwara. Now he regrets as he might have seen Air India posters on the gurdwara walls, and heard the rumours of boycott and the sabotage. He also remembers a *nihang*, as the last person on the flight carrying a huge picnic hamper. Was he sneaking a bomb onto the plane? He felt so at that time and told the Royal Canadian Mounted Police about it. Another relative, Sam Swaminathan, an engineer, lost his entire family—his wife, a fifteen year old son, two young daughters, a brother-in-law and sister-in-law. They were on their way to India to perform the last rites for Mrs Swaminathan's father. From Detroit, he now derives consolation from reading the *Gita*. Another couple who lost two daughters, Shyamala Jean and Krithika Nicola, are similarly chronicled; their daughters were upcoming dancers of Bharatanatyam. A further chapter charts the grieving couple, Raju and Meena Sarangi who lost an artist daughter, as they almost forced her to go on holidays despite her protests. They have donated a fellowship in her memory at the Ontario College of Art. There is also the anguished story of Vijaya Thampi from Bombay who lost his wife and now looks after their six year old daughter. During the interview he says, 'I can't pardon the men who did it, I know there are good Sikhs, of course, but I tell you, I feel not too thrilled to see a turbaned guy. I hope I don't ever find myself in a situation where a Sikh needs my help, because I may not be able to give it' [p. 132].

The next section is devoted to investigations carried out by various government agencies starting with the discovery of the black box. The British were excluded from the investigations having annoyed India with comments on Bhabha Centre's incompetence.[9] From the last communication recorded in the plane's cockpit, Canadian and British investigators feel inconclusive, while India's Bhabha scientists find the bomb theory was positive proof of a bomb and go on to suggest its impact. Piecing together pathological evidence, different authorities provide conflicting assessments [pp. 137–42].

Meanwhile, the Indian authorities rapidly released the names of wanted men. From the passengers list, it is found that L. Singh and M. Singh were two persons who did not board the plane. Their fare was paid by the same person and this pointed towards a Sikh conspiracy. Canadian agencies, RCMP and CSIS, mounted an investigation on an unprecedented scale to catch them. The solid evidence of a bomb in CP baggage while being transferred at Narita airport provided precise details of a AM/FM stereo tuner, a Sanyo model FMT 611K with its serial number. This lead eventually helped police to arrest Inderjit Singh Reyat in December 1986, whose cheque paid for this tuner in Duncan, BC. The police case rested on Japanese evidence of the serial number of a tuner used allegedly for a bomb by Inderjit Reyat. With the RCMP testimony supported by an informer, a former member of the cell, Reyat was jailed for ten years [and later re-charged with larger conspiracy in October 2000].

Along the way, the authors reveal some interesting details, such as the Sikh co-pilot, Bhinder's friendship with Jagdev Singh Nijjar—a publisher of a Khalistani paper in Toronto. The cockpit recordings show Bhinder as quite a 'fanatic' as he warns his assistant pilot about female crews' greed for liquor. Bhinder also had dinner with Nijjar on the night before and he carried two plain wrapped parcels on his private trolley into the plane. The RCMP took this friendship at face value. The authors find Nijjar's 'militant' brother working in Ecuador for the Khalistani cause. At this point, the authors remind us that rumours are competing with hard news within the community, and that 'we have entered the world of half truths; Reyat would not even acknowledge knowing Parmar, and who had never heard of Rajiv Gandhi then the prime minister of India' [p. 44]. This section also discusses some peripheral issues, such as role of foreign powers. Many such reports from the Indian press are dismissed as 'unreliable', citing such a distortion by the Soviet/Indian media in reporting American UN ambassador, Jeanne Kirkpatrick's, imaginary speech. India's attitude towards the west is also noted especially after the Rajiv–Reagan meeting in 1985 which led to tight surveillance and more restrictive refugee applications, noting how Gurpartap Singh Birk's lawyer accused the judge of changing his tunes to please the new Indo-US political alliance.

The authors conclude their investigation by identifying four persons as the main culprits. One man who became informer in March 1986, regaled the police with the startling claim of knowing the man who financed the conspiracy. The authors do not reveal the real name of the financier, but it is a remarkable investigative feat that the person they met and interviewed was almost certainly Ripduman Singh Malik, a prominent Sikh of BC who was arrested in October 2000 and charged for the same crime as authors have alleged in the book. The authors just call him *sardar*, describing his involvement in several community projects, including a bank, a school, and some welfare schemes. During the interview, authors find out that the *sardar* is annoyed with 'impure' Sikhs, signalling that this is a story 'of a crusader's hatred of infidels'. When *sardar* says 'I am isolated', authors conclude that 'it is the isolation of the self-appointed prophet' [p. 167]. The authors also implicate another man, presumably Ajaib Singh Bagri—a pamphleteer who thrust several Khalistan mementos and dollar currency notes into their hands.

The study dismisses rival conspiracy theories. Thus Zuhair Kashmeri and Brian MacAndrew's claim that the bomb was most probably planted by Indian intelligence agencies to shatter the Canadian Sikh campaign is rejected as based on a minor point; that India released the names of suspicious persons ahead of Canadian authorities.[10] The authors then ask, with increasing frustration, why the RCMP did not bring a case against the Sikh cell to which their evidence clearly pointed. The authors feel the legal requirements for a convincing prosecution should be dispensed with by making changes in the requisite laws. The authors remind the cost of the investigations stands at $60 million dollars, and rising—the largest Canadian criminal case that remains unresolved.[11]

On Canada's Role in the Tragedy

The Canadian government is repeatedly taken to task as readers are reminded that Air India was above all, 'a Canadian tragedy'. They ask 'why Canada— a tolerant, comfortably stuffy state hosted the worst terrorist act of modern times?' [p. 203]. Despite repeated warnings, 'why the terrorist cells were allowed to develop and play their politics' in Canada? The authors point out that grieving families question the governments not reviewing slanderous broadcasts and libellous editorials in Canada's Punjabi language media. The authors assert that 'even death threats and assaults were not followed up'. If in 1983 and 1984, Khalistanis operating in Canada were told that they were under close surveillance and not exempt from accountability, the tragedy perhaps could have been avoided [p. 201]. The authors attribute government inactivity to complacency and multiculturalism. Complacency, or the Canadian myth of instinctive goodness—which says 'it cannot happen here'—encouraged slackness at airports regarding security. This was the attitude behind misplaced condolences in Prime Minister Mulroney's call to Indian premier, Rajiv Gandhi after the crash: 'it is theirs, not ours, and it is a terrible pity. It still has not happened here'. The incident was still called a tragedy for the 'Indo-Canadian community' even as an opposition MP objected to its misleading use. However, the authors note with dismay, that Canada's uneasy balance between authoritarianism and liberal democracy is upset only when the threats to its stability are perceived as a challenge to mainstream society. Only after the tragedy of Air India did the Canadian foreign secretary, Joe Clark sign an Indo-Canadian treaty in Delhi to suppress Sikh terrorism, and the government ended its moratorium over deportation of Sikhs who had unsuccessfully claimed refugee status after the invasion of the Golden Temple.

The authors see the policy of multiculturalism as a major culprit. This policy, authors say, is an expedient: 'a Canadian invention towards "them", a way to deal with non-English, non-French, "ethnics" and "visible minorities"'. Multiculturalism, the authors assert, as contrasted with American 'melting pot'; 'rewards their resistant diversity, not their ability to assimilate'. However, they come up with just one example of this charge of 'rewards' at work in the Indo-Canadian community: the Federal Ministry of Multiculturalism funds specifically 'Punjabi' dances at a generically 'Indian' function. 'No one objects to that, except when "Punjabi" becomes "Sikh" and Sikh becomes "Khalistani"' [p. 200]. Furthermore, 'the nuance seems subtle to outsiders, but not to Indians, and not to the videotapes who use the footage, complete with Khalistani flags and slogans, as evidence of Canadian approval for Khalistan' [p. 200]. Moreover, often the work of CSIS and RCMP clashes with that of Ministry of Multiculturalism, as the latter in fact might be paying for the legal appeals of certain individuals under police scrutiny or funding of the projects of a 'cultural' nature that police take to be dangerously political. Mukherjee and Blaise remind their readers about the bigger players in the wider picture, when some twenty years earlier, President de Gaulle of France used the Canadian stage to declare 'vive le Quebec libre' at the opening of Expo '67. Of course Canada is no stranger to secessionist movements. The most important was one in 1976 in Quebec when the election of Rene Levesque which was allowed 'to go to referendum and sputter out peacefully'. Just six years earlier, Pierre Trudeau had placed the entire country under martial law following a single political kidnapping by the banned FLQ [Front de liberation du Quebec] [p. 200].

The authors advance a second major argument to see the tragedy as an outcome of Canada's immigration policies. From the mid-sixties, the East Indian community, till then predominantly comprising the Sikh working class, and West Coast focused, became Hindu, professional, and Ontario-oriented. This new group quickly established itself in medicine, professions, teachers and entrepreneurs, emerged as the most successful immigrant group, a 'model community' with high profiles and incomes. This successful group comprised most of the passengers of AI flight 182. Thus the Sikh community never grew in the explosive, variegated fashion that later characterized the southern European, or Indians, Chinese and West Indians of the present day. Thus, the authors conclude, Air India 182 was not just a jumbo on its way to India when tragedy struck:

it was also a symbol of Canadian immigration policies, failed and successful. The two communities of Indian immigrants met that morning off the coast of Ireland; the financially successful and professionally assimilated Canadian suburbanites in the plane, and the unilingual, desperate Canadians on the ground ... two sides of the immigration drama one unintelligible without the other [p. 205]

Concluding this section, the authors predict, 'bitterness between the communities of Indian born Canadians particularly between Sikhs and Hindus, for a long time.... As with victims of the Holocaust or their children confronting a German or his children, it may take a generation or more before the two communities can speak again' [p. 205].

Portrait of a Canadian [Sikh] Terrorist

The last section summarizes the authors' thesis about the Air India disaster. Starting with an accusatory sub-title, 'portrait of a Canadian terrorist', Mukherjee and Blaise advance what seems an extraordinary hypothesis about Canadian Sikhs' involvement in terrorism. The authors are at pain to connect the tragedy with the country's past and recent immigration policies towards the Sikhs. They argue that the Khalistani movement is essentially ground in the community of first generation unassimilated Punjabi immigrants. A profile of Khalistani campaigners is provided by dividing them into two main groups; romantically inclined native born Canadians; and unemployed immigrants. While the first group only provides money, the second group forms its manpower. Then a history of Punjabi immigration to Canada is outlined to confirm this simple if somewhat inelegant proposition. Canada experimented with an open door policy during 1969 and 1973, which resulted in the admission of a staggering number of uneducated, ill-equipped, and technologically unemployable Sikhs from the Punjab. Their life style contrasts sharply with the peculiar nature of Sikh-Canadian life, which began at the turn of the century, with its alternative turn of abuse and tolerance, its heavy representation in lumber and trucking industries, its low-profile marginality—the results of generations of racial quotas and non-citizenship [the right to vote granted only in 1949] leading to its gurdwara based culture and comparative indifference to professional and higher education [p. 205]. These Sikhs have:

... remained untouched by Canadian experience .... They work in Sikh-run shops, live in shabby, near-dormitory conditions, without hope of gaining rewarding employment. Lacking English or skills, mainstream Canadian society has bypassed them. In case of married Sikhs ... their children are beyond their control or influence, while their daughters refuse to marry the groom of their father's choice. They are also under pressure to send money to marry off sisters and to provide for aged parents .... Indeed, there is no real Punjab for them to return to ... the poor but proud Jat Sikh males thus *time-bombs, ripe for conversion* [p. 177, emphasis added].

This argument about 'alienated, frustrated and unemployed Sikh immigrants as raw materials of Khalistan' is stretched to an extraordinary length. It is asserted that the conditions of unemployed Sikh youth in Vancouver or Toronto were hopeless until the Khalistan cause came along. The authors argue, that if persuasive orators in the community could successfully appeal to the code of *izzat* and convince such under-educated and unemployed Sikh youth that:

their honour, their dignity, their manhood, their women's virtue are all in their hands and that second thoughts are a sign of weakness, that any opponent is the agent of devil and death given or death received in the defence of the Khalsa is noble service, and finally, that lies and denial are justified in the higher services of the faith, then the leaders have created the nucleus of an armed cult [p. 177].

For such disillusioned, disoriented Sikh youth, 'who would not visit a community centre, the only place they felt themselves vaguely important is the gurdwara'. This experience is generated from a single viewpoint. Here, the Sikh youth sees a leader like, 'Talvinder Parmar entering the temple ... as if he owns it and no one has the courage to oppose him'. 'The old Canadians are toothless', he notes, 'never too concerned about covering the head, taking off shoes, they were too busy making it in Canada, proud of their contracts with mainstream businessmen and politicians ... their children are in universities, doing well, marrying outside the Khalsa'. This youth sees, for the first time in his life, that 'he is a better Sikh ... has kept his hair, his purity'. Then the authors draw a general conclusion: 'Khalistan appeals to the dreams of revenge of any embittered alienated ethnicity'. In a pure Sikh state, the Sikh youth would be somebody, '... for the first time since he's been in Canada, Khalistan makes him feel he belongs somewhere'. Thus concludes the last sentence as the authors began this chapter: with a heading—'Portrait of a Terrorist', Canada in the 1980s [p. 175].

Mukherjee and Blaise go on to elaborate why such Sikh minds are capable of terrorism. They have seen, in many Khalistani homes in North America, full colour pictures of the Delhi riots, with the still-smouldering bodies of Sikh men thrown off trains. 'It is upsetting game-room decor' and it is 'strange to encounter the posters again in the foyers of Sikh gurdwaras'. Yet there it is, the call to *shaheedi* [martyrdom] [p. 185]. Even professionals are not immune from this syndrome. One such Sikh professional on WSO from New York is quoted: for six days a week I work for Reagan, seventh for Khalistan'. They cite critics within the community who feel, 'Khalistanis are incapable of rational thought and live in their own world where violence is confused with righteousness where past crimes of Hindus ... are used to justify retribution' [p. 161]. As a proof of Khalistanis' glee in killing others, the authors remind us that 'it is known that cell members were celebrating in a Sikh temple in Malton on early morning of 23 June' [p. 161].

If these were not sufficient reasons for readers to see many turbaned Sikhs as violent persons and leading a violent campaign for Khalistan, in the next chapter the analysis shifts to the Punjab. Mukherjee and Blaise underline here how Sikhism has an almost in-built tendency towards violence. This is primarily, authors argue, due to the fear of re-absorption into Hinduism, so the issue becomes one of 'purity versus pollution' of the faith [p. 183]. Whatever observers may make of the situation, the authors speak on behalf of the Sikhs, for whom, 'it is primarily an internal Punjabi civil war fought among classes and generations of believers to determine the shape of their future' in which 'traditionalists want to keep the world still, immune from radical changes unable 'to understand the changed world' [p. 184]. Such men obviously, 'have failed to take advantage of the progress' and modernization which for them, threatens, 'purity' while conversion from below adds to the 'pollution'. Ultimately the authors locate the logic of violence in the debasement of Sikh religious tradition;

Sikhism, like many religions, is based on superior versions of love and harmony. In its time and place, it was superior to the visions and practices around it. But like all religions, Islam and Christianity particularly, it has an intolerant streak, that corrupts its vision and lends itself to the opposite interpretation of its original intentions. We all know by now, because we have nearly lived through the twentieth century, the inevitable destination of religious movements that turn political. We know from western history the fate in store for any mass movement that prides itself on purity alone and has no core of beliefs but vengeance, no code of behaviour except an unbending obedient to ritual observance [p. 216].

The Fiction

After this investigative feat, with many accusatory notes against Canadian Sikhs and Sikhism, let us now turn to Mukherjee's fiction' which provides more material in assessing her real and imaginary Sikh characters. Indeed, it will become apparent that her fictional characters take shape and draw much sustenance from the investigative work discussed above.

The Management of Grief: *A Story*

In *Middleman and Other Stories*, the last story is, 'The management of grief'.[12] While the title obviously taunts the modern welfare state's personnel, such as social workers and other staff, who are mobilized in an emergency to counsel the victims of a traumatic event, its characters are directly borrowed from the author's experience with grieving families discussed in *Sorrow and Terror*. Indeed, so close is the borrowing, that after reading interviews in the above book, even the names of affected families seem familiar. The story revolves around Mrs Shaila Bhave, an Indian immigrant in Toronto who has lost her husband Vikram and two teenaged sons, Vinod and Mithun in the Air India crash. Her friend, Kusum, has lost her husband, Satish, and a daughter. Another friend, Dr Ranganathan from Montreal has lost his entire family.

The story begins in a Toronto suburb, when Mrs Bhave finds herself surrounded by small Indian community from her neighbourhood who all share the news of the Air India tragedy. Dr Sharma—the treasurer of the Indo-Canada Society—is with his wife, Kusum and several others. They discuss the news concerning the air crash and the young boys keep chanting 'it is Sikh bomb'. The men, though 'not using the word', 'bow their heads in agreement' [p. 180]. While discussing the tragic news, they are also informed by Kusum's daughter, Pam, that a reporter is on the way to meet them.

Another visitor, Judith Templeton, a social worker, from the provincial government contacts them. From 'multiculturalism'? Mrs Bhave asks; Templeton replies, 'partially', but obviously, her mandate is much bigger. Templeton tells Mrs Bhave, 'I have been told you knew many of the people on the flight ... perhaps if you'd agree to help us to reach the others ... ?' [p. 182] Four days later, Mrs Bhave, Kusum, and Dr Ranganathan are in Ireland to find the last remains of their dear ones to take them to India for final rites. Mrs Bhave narrates events there in the first person. 'The Irish are not shy, they rush to me and give me hugs and some are crying' and 'I cannot imagine reactions like that on the streets of Toronto'. 'They carry flowers even for passing them to any Indian they see' [p. 187]. A policeman calls her to match the photo of her son, Vinod, but this turns out to be someone else. Underneath the sea, sharks are lurking, perhaps devouring the 'remains of her son'. Eventually, from Ireland, most relatives go to India. Kusum and Bhave are on the same flight to Bombay. Bhave meets her aged parents and once again becomes the only child of rich parents. Friend and relatives come to pay their respects, among them some Sikhs, and seeing them, 'inwardly, involuntarily I cringe' ... 'my parents are progressive people, they do not blame communities for a few individuals' [p. 189].

Mrs Bhave returns to Toronto and Templeton is again at the door 'with her theories of grief management'. These progress from 'rejection, depression, and acceptance to eventual reconstitution'. She seeks Bhave's help to reach an elderly Sikh couple whose sons have also died in the crash. The couple had joined their Toronto-based sons only a few weeks earlier and are unfamiliar with life there. But the Sikh couple is very distrustful, especially of Templeton, who tried twice taking another interpreter and offering them air fare to Ireland and carrying some bank forms for power of attorney. But the couple refused to sign anything, fearing that money they receive will end the company's or country's obligation to them. That, they think, is like 'selling their sons for two airline tickets' for a place they have never seen. Mrs Bhave offers to go with Templeton but warns: 'they are Sikh. They will not open up to me a Hindu woman'. Then what she wants to add is;

as much as I try not to, I stiffen at the sight of beards and turbans. I remember a time when we all trusted each other in this new country, it was only the new country we were worried about. [p. 193]

Templeton and Bhave meet the old Sikh couple who refuse to listen to the reason. The old man remains defiant in his 'peasant' way and spurns any help. The old Sikh lady asks why 'no one else gets *angrezi* [white] visitors'. Mrs Bhave tries to soothe her by saying the government wants to help them, but they remain adamant, thinking the government is after their money and tell the visitors, 'not to worry, we are honourable people'. The old man knows how the government takes peoples' money and says, 'we are accustomed to that'. [p. 194]

Mrs Bhave gets on with her life as a widow. She sets up a trust with the help of her husband's old lawyer, and plans to support a charity. By selling her large house and buying a small apartment downtown, she saves enough money. Kusum has settled to an ascetic's life at Hardwar singing *bhajans* in tranquillity. Pam, after an unsuccessful career in California, opens a department store in Vancouver selling cosmetics. Dr Ranganathan has moved to an academic post at Texas where he vows not to tell anyone of his personal loss. The story ends as Mrs Bhave takes a walk in the park, murmuring and hearing voices from her lost family, who say, 'your time has come, go be brave'.

The story presents a measured contrast between the Sikh couple and other relatives [Hindus] of the air crash. While the latter are busy re-constituting their lives, contributing even amidst their tragedy towards the welfare of their adopted country, the Sikh couple remains unapproachable and 'alienated' from the surrounding world. Their 'peasant' ways and self-defined 'honour' makes them suspicious of others. While the skills and religious heritage of the Hindu professionals provide them with new hope in the face of tragedy, the Sikh couple's dogmatic attitude ensures an enclosed world. From this somewhat eerie portrait juxtaposing a peasant Sikh couple against Hindu professionals, the next step almost seems logical: plotting the trajectory of a Punjabi Hindu girl in the United States fleeing a feudal Punjab, driven out by Sikh terrorists. Thus, *Jasmine*, seems almost necessary and, as we shall see, below, crucial events in the heroine's life are influenced by the killers is the 'Khalsa Lions'.

Jasmine: *A Novel*

Mukherjee's novel *Jasmine*, revolves around Jyoti, a Hindu girl from Hasanpur village in the Jalandhar district of Indian Punjab.[13] Born in 1965, she is the fifth daughter of nine children. Written in the first person, it is Jyoti who carries the narrative. She tells the readers that her father was a refugee from Lahore and had settled in Hasanpur owning thirty acres of land tilled rather reluctantly by her brothers, Arvind-prar and Hari-prar. The partition of Punjab had left a deep mark on her father, who still maintained authority but lacked position, and who 'lived in a 'bunker'; his shattered mind admiring all things 'Lahori', women, music, *ghazals*, who always tuned to Pakistani broadcasts to hear authentic Punjabi. He 'would not even speak Hindi', as he associated this language with Gandhi, 'responsible for partition'.

Jyoti's education ends at high school when her father turns down her teacher's plea, [a Sikh], to let her go to college. The teacher was impressed by Jyoti's English compositions and her interest in his library containing books from the British Council library, some with USIS stickers. Jyoti even read *Shane*, a thin volume about an American college but she could not cope with more wordy British books such as *Great Expectations* and *Jane Eyre*. The setting of Jyoti's household is fascinatingly described; her four sisters are married off to greedy drunken husbands. Her brothers have enrolled for technical diplomas in the nearby Jalandhar city. They have set their sights at Bahrain or Qatar or somewhere, after their cousins who had emigrated to the Middle East and remitted loads of money. Jyoti grows up doing household chores, her only novelty watching an American film on TV, 'Seven Village Girls Find Seven Boys to Marry', dubbed in Hindi. She learns something of America through letters sent by her teacher's nephew from California. Jyoti's father dies suddenly gored by a bull. The land is eventually sold to a Sikh, 'Vancouver Singh'—a Canada returnee who sports a funny yellow raincoat and boots. With money from the sale of land, her brothers open a scooter repair shop in the city.

Enter the Khalsa Lions

By this time, Punjab's descent into anarchy is signalled by the appearance of Sikh boys' gangs, the 'Khalsa Lions'. They threaten the Sikh teacher; a pamphlet accuses him of being a 'bad Sikh'. The narrative informs us that 'Khalsa means pure'. As lions of purity, the gang dressed in 'white shirts, and pyjamas and indigo turbans' and all of them toted heavy *kirpans* on bandoliers. They had money to zigzag through the bazaar on scooters. Like Arvind and Hari, the new 'Khalsa Lions' are farmers' sons. The money for scooters came from smuggling liquor and guns across the border with Pakistan. One day, 'Khalsa Lions' throw stones and fruits at the teacher. In no time, Vancouver Singh's farm becomes a hot bed of Sikh terrorists where bombs are made with money earned from smuggled goods across the border, an acceptable profession for young men.

One of the 'Khalsa Lions' is Sukhwinder, or Sukhi for short, a class fellow of Jyoti's brothers. Sukhi has obviously changed completely after meeting Bhindranwale and is now a zealot. He calls for purifying the Sikh faith and is determined to carry out his master's instructions. He wore his beard 'the way the Khalsa lions did, long and stiffly combed out over his chest'. Sukhi had 'unforgiving eyes', and on one occasion, when Jyoti brought him a glass of water and sweet tea, he didn't drink either, as if 'drinking anything in our impure, infidel home would contaminate him' [p. 64]. Her brothers and Sukhi have a long night of boisterous political arguments. Jyoti hears the flat and authoritative voice of Sukhi:

the Khalsa, the Pure-Bodied and the Pure-Hearted, must have their sovereign state, Khalistan, the Land of the Pure. The Impure must be eliminated. [p. 65]

When her brothers laughed and asked, 'are you going to kill your brothers in the village?' Sukhi replies,

'You must leave, then leave or be killed. Renounce all filth and idolatry. Do not eat meat, smoke tobacco, or drink alcohol or cut your hair. Wear a turban, and then you will be welcome'. Asking what else they should do, Sukhi orders, 'keep your whorish women off the streets'. [p. 65]

Jyoti expects a fight but her brothers must have been in a good mood. They ask where Sukhi got these views; 'I have visited Sant Bhindranwale in the Golden Temple'. The brothers retort 'the Sant is an idiot' [p. 65]. Later, her brothers are joined by another fellow, Prakash—Jyoti's future husband. The newcomer becomes animated and calls Sukhi a 'fool'. Sukhwinder does not tire, his voice becomes louder and he start calling all Hindu men rapists, and declaims: 'the sari is the sign of the prostitute', and 'Hindus are bent upon the genocide of the Sikh nation. Only Pakistan protects us'. The new man, Prakash, keeps arguing:

Sukhi, there is no Hindu state, there is no Sikh state! India is for everyone ... Have you forgotten what the Muslims did to Sikhs in partition? What the Moguls did to your own ten gurus? Have you forgotten what emperor Aurangzeb did, what Emperor Jehangir did? [p. 66]

While Jyoti falls in love with Prakash's voice, Sukhi peevishly replies, 'They were Moguls, not Muslims'. Prakash asks, 'Not Muslims, Sukhi? I don't think they worshipped Jesus Christ?' Sukhi says, 'They were Afghan slaves, not true Pakistanis. True Pakistanis are Punjabis, like us. If they were cruel to Sikhs, it's because of Hindu influence on them. Many of them had Hindu mothers and Hindu concubines who taught them to kill Sikhs. Pakistanis were Hindus who saw the light of the true god and converted. So were Sikhs. Only bloodsucker banyas and untouchable monkeys remained Hindu'. Prakash snaps back saying,

what absolute rubbish you speak. You've lost your mind. Don't talk nonsense about the light of the true God. They had to convert or have their heads chopped off'. [p. 66]

Then Prakash warns her brothers saying, 'this man is a danger to us and himself'. Sukhwinder does some sabre-rattling and leaves on his scooter. Jyoti is soon married to Prakash Vijh, who calls her Jasmine. Prakash opens a repairing shop for old toasters, radios, and VCRs 'imported' by expatriates. He has also contacted his one-time professor Devinder Vadhera in America who promises him admission to Florida's International Institute of Technology. This is, in fact, a racket operated by several Indian agents to bring in illegal students for fees, as Jasmine learns later in her American odyssey. As she starts enjoying her blessed married life, the Khalsa Lions appear on the scene. One day, when Prakash takes her to a shop to buy her a new sari, the Khalsa Lions strike. Two of them, including Sukhwinder— he was clean shaven now, and the next moments happen so quickly that Jyoti remembers only in flashes. Obviously Sukhi placed a VCR with a bomb inside and fired at it while shouting, 'prostitutes, whores'. The bomb kills Prakash instantly while Jyoti survives to recognize her husband's dead body.

Jyoti's mother tells her how the scooter 'boys' chased the Sikh teacher. They first knocked his turban off, holding his beard and his exposed white hair in his hands. He pleads, 'I am a good Sikh, why are you doing this to me?' [p. 85]. The boys pull out his ceremonial comb, while his students watch in stunned disbelief. A gang leader chops at the hair in great clumps and then frees his rolled up beard and chops it off. Spinning him around until he staggers and falls, they shoot him, emptying over thirty bullets in his body.

Journey to America

As a widow, Jasmine hates Punjab's 'feudalistic' society 'where the old and new is fighting'. She is determined to follow her late husband's advice to try America. Her brother manages to obtain her passport and visa by falsifying papers including her date of birth, making her nineteen. Describing her journey among refugees, mercenaries, guest workers, outcastes, and deportees, she flies in a Boeing 747 taking her first to Sudan—where her co-passenger, a Filipino, shifts to Bahrain. Then onwards to Europe, Hamburg, and Amsterdam where she is ferried on a human cargo ship, to Paramaribo, and from hence to the States. She sleeps in the tiered bunks of *Gulf Shuttle*, the boat anchored off the shores of Florida. The ship's captain, 'Half-Face' is a Vietnam veteran assisted by Kingland, a Caribbean who hands Jasmine a penknife which she would surely need in dangerous times ahead. Passengers are loaded into a waiting truck in the dark, while the uncertain Jasmine is picked up by the captain, Half-Face, eyeing her with lust for a night of passion. Booking into his usual hotel, he throws open her suitcase, throwing Prakash's suit and her Ganpati across the room. He rapes her, but she manages to hide in the toilet, slashing her tongue in anger. She returns to thrust the penknife in the sleeping Half-Face's chest furiously.

Clutching Ganpati, she burns her suitcase and runs from the hotel and walks three miles east of Fowler Key, Florida. She is rescued by a kind Quaker lady, Lillian Gordon who takes her home where she joins three other Kanjoban women refugees. Lillian asks, 'are we talking India here? Punjab? are you Sikh?' Jasmine replies, 'no Hindu [p. 130]. A doctor sews back her severed tongue. After recuperating for a week, she gets on a Greyhound bus to reach Professor Vadhera in, Queens, New York. Lillian lends her $100 and the address of her daughter Kate Goldstein. Lillian is later prosecuted for keeping undocumented persons and 'exploiting' them for domestic labour, and jailed for contempt of the court. Lillian sent her and the others $20 every Christmas through her daughter.

Professor Vadhera turns out to be a human hair trader, married to a Patiala girl, Nirmala, living with his arguing and grumbling parents, among neighbouring Punjabis with the daily routine of watching old Indian videos. While Vadhera promises her to buy a green card from middlemen, Jasmine decides to leave them. Lillian's daughter, Kate arranges a job to look after Duff, an adopted daughter of Taylor and Wylie Heyes, at Columbia University.

Wylie offers her a separate room but Jasmine is unused to such mothering conventions, and insists on sleeping in Duff's room. Jasmine has a new name, Jase, and her job is 'caregiver' earning $95 dollars a week, an unheard-of luxury. Living in Claremont Ave, just by the side of Barnard College, Jasmine also enrols at Columbia University for some courses. Looking after Duff, she chalks out a routine: a visit to museums, a stroll in the park followed by nightly stories. She even finds a part-time job in the Mathematics department answering phones. The university's Indian Languages department engages her as a Punjabi reader and she is complimented for her perfect Doaba accent by the tutor working on a linguistic atlas of Punjab [p. 180]. She is courted by another academic studying land reforms in the Punjab funded through the Ford Foundation. However, as she learns fast, in America, nothing lasts. Taylor and Wylie, both in their late 30s, have a precarious relationship. Soon, Wylie falls out with Taylor and moves in with Stuart Eschelan—an economist who has a smattering of Hindi learnt in Delhi. They go to Paris for a fortnight. Never sure of the American code of love, she develops affection for Taylor when he thanks her for support without which 'he would have gone crazy'. Between Taylor and Jasmine, unspoken feelings blossom into love.

The Khalsa Lion Strikes Again

But at this crucial moment in her life, the 'Khalsa Lion' appears on the scene again. The incident provides a crucial break in the story. On a Sunday morning, Taylor and Jase are strolling in the park and Duff runs up to a hot dog vendor. Prompted by Duff, Jasmine looks at the dark-skinned vendor, recognises Sukhi and runs back, hysterical and shivering. Taylor manages to drag her out of the park to the bottom of Riverside Drive. Jasmine tells Taylor: 'that was the man who killed my husband'. Shaken, Taylor urges her to call the police. Jasmine then narrates her full story and reveals the fact that she is illegal [pp. 188–9]. Taylor assures her, 'New York's huge. We can move downtown, go to Jersey ...' But Jasmine insists, 'this isn't your battle. He'd kill you, or Duff, to get at me', and decides to try her luck in Iowa. While taking this painful decision, as a Hindu, she is comforted by her belief in a pre-ordained life and recalls, 'in all my life, I have never dithered. God's plans have always seemed clearly laid out' [p. 189].

Wylie had told Jasmine about some connections in Iowa, where she applies for a nurse's job. Waiting at the reception, she meets Mrs Ripplemeyer—a volunteer on that particular Wednesday who offers her a better bargain. She asks her son, Bud, to employ her. Jasmine changed to Jase. She now becomes Jane—a live-in partner for Bud—a middle-aged banker turned farmer. His household, besides his mother, consists of an adopted young Vietnamese refugee boy, Du. Bud had just divorced Karin. Jane and his ex-wife Karin get on quite well, even though Karin is still in love with her former husband. While Bud operates a bank and farms in Baden, Iowa, Jane handles all the household chores quite well. As she becomes pregnant, Bud asks her to marry him. But fate has many other tricks to play in Jasmine. Harlan Kroener shoots Bud over a loan dispute and paralyses him. Du, his adopted son decides to leave for Los Angeles where he discovers a sister and other relatives.

Finally, Jasmine receives a letter from Professor Taylor from Columbia saying he is coming up to Baden to take her to California for a new life. 'Greedy with wants and reckless from hope' [p. 241], she is ready for further adventure and risk as 'the frontier is pushing indoors through uncaulked windows'. So the novel finishes [or begins] for Jyoti—a Punjabi rural Hindu girl, through her many destinations and transformations in the new world.

On Mukherjee's Sikh Characters

The role of fiction in portraying [and distorting] a community's image is as old as fiction's history. The Jews, the Irish, and indeed all communities have been subject to such prejudices. Although literary works are not as calculated as the rational strategies of secret services of modern states to destroy 'perceived enemies', be they individuals or a minority, literary ridicule contributes to an atmosphere that accompanies or indeed precedes such witch-hunting. While literary prejudice in itself is rarely life-threatening, its negative images constitute a more subtle defence of a majority or a state's mistreatment of a minority. From the 1980s Sikhs, due to their ill-fated campaign for Punjab autonomy, have increasingly been condemned as 'communalists', 'separatists', and finally as 'terrorists'. Much encouraged by Indian official proclamations of 'Sikh terrorism' in the aftermath of events in the Golden Temple, this state sponsored propaganda found corroboration through several channels. Among them, the Indian media, provincial presses, weeklies and journals played their dubious roles. A new source, in the form of fictional narratives, with Sikh characters, emerged in due course of time, of which Mukherjee's *Jasmine* is just one.[14]

Mukherjee's fiction and non-fictional writings, it is suggested by the above reading, contributes to a stereotyped image of Sikhs. In her non-fictional work there are clear passages of this nature; in her fiction, a Sikh character is intentionally portrayed in this way. Moved by 'shared remorse' in undertaking the Air India tragedy investigation, the authors' investigative oeuvre leads them far beyond its limits of identifying persons and their motives. Indeed, right from the introduction, the authors indulge in many worrying generalizations. It is, of course, unquestionable that Sikhs or whoever bombed the plane, should be tried and sentenced, and every sane person sympathizes with the victims of the crash and their relatives. But the wholesale and crude generalizations offered in the book through which a religious tradition along with the majority of followers are condemned are hardly justified.

A distorted portrayal of Sikhism and of those waging a struggle for an independent Sikh homeland is attempted through two stages. First it is asserted, [all] baptized Sikhs are committed to Khalistan and they are prone to violence. The Sikh faith is itself seen to be deficient in coping with the modern world. While noble at its point of origin, it has degenerated into 'rituals and purposelessness'. Moreover, the allusion to Canadian Sikhs' alleged disputes over 'purity' and 'pollution' and their use of ritualistic vocabulary are played up to the sensitivities of the western audience. With already hostile images circulating about Khomeini's *fatwas* and the rise of 'Islamic fundamentalists' in the Western media, it was easy to extend this analogy towards 'menace' of Sikh fundamentalism. Making the usually false dichotomy between moderates and fundamentalists, the authors try to deflect and belittle the Sikhs' hurt, due to the desecration of their most sacred shrine in Amritsar, in the following words:

Many thinkers, then, would see the sources of Sikh fundamentalism in the internal struggle of traditionalists [that is, Punjabi-speaking landowners] as they strive to maintain control of a world they no longer understand. And they recruit their supporters among the lost, embittered and alienated young men who have failed to take advantage of Punjab's rapid development. Moderates see the invasion of the Golden Temple as an irrelevance—at best, a convenient Khalistani recruitment tool that was made available by Mrs Gandhi's stupid blunder at the very moment when

Khalistani agitation was dying down from its violent excesses. For them, the Golden Temple invasion was the Reichstag Fire of the Khalistani movement. They *needed* it, desperately. If it had not happened, it would have been invented .... The *khalsa* turned violent. [p. 184]

One has to read this paragraph aloud to see the gross perversion in the last sentence; '*if it had not happened, it would have been invented*'. Moreover, by creating the impression that Khalsa Sikhs are prone to violence in her non-fictional work, Mukherjee creates exactly such a character, Sukhi, in her fiction, *Jasmine,* who provides crucial breaks in the heroine's life. Sukhi is a member of the 'Khalsa Lions' who are mindless, trigger-happy men without an iota of humanity. The crude portrayal of a Sikh as a terrorist and a member of the Khalsa is obviously meant to invite scorn and hatred. The author is surely aware that the Khalsa is a common term used for the Sikh community.[15] The Khalsa men and women of 'martial traditions' is a popular self-image cultivated by the community through various narratives stretching back to the eighteenth century. The Sikh recruitment into regimental armies under the British rule, also gave rise to the idea of Sikhs as 'brave' men and they were bracketed as a 'martial race'. Although particular individuals have gained sustenance from such a self-image, and in fact, Sikhs as a group gained favour in terms of armed forces recruitment during the British rule in the aftermath of mutiny of 1857, when the army was reorganized along the 'martial races' theory, this self-serving image only cloaks a far more sinister reality: that of a vulnerable community from the eighteenth century to the contemporary time, allowing a brief period of Sikh hegemony under Ranjit Singh, the one-eyed 'Lion of the Punjab'. Thus the manipulation and impregnation of a resonant term with a particular favourable self-image of the community can be seen as a literary device adding to prejudiced and stereotyped image. Mukherjee's 'Khalsa Lions' in *Jasmine* are skilfully created to invite hatred from a western reader.

Second, Blaise and Mukherjee categorize Canadian Sikhs as unadaptable and illiterate, and castigate Canada repeatedly for allowing the immigration of such unskilled people in the early 1970s. Let us see if these people deserve such labels. In the 1960s, Sikhs peasants were pioneering the agrarian revolution in the Punjab by adopting new technology and intensive farming methods. It was from a rapidly developing Punjab economy and society that Canada drew young men fresh from schools or colleges who took advantage of its immigration laws in the 1970s. Do they deserve the contemptuous portrait of 'unadaptable and illiterates'? Dividing Sikhs into turbaned and unturbaned, the former are docketed as uneducated, unemployed, and without hope. For them, Khalistan means being 'powerful' in the community. In this respect a fallacious distinction is made between more integrated early Sikh migrants and alienated Punjabi youth of later years. The authors then contradict their arguments by reminding the reader that professionals have also joined in the protests. In a sense, however, nothing has changed after eighty years. Sikhs are still manual workers, perhaps, 'living in self-enclosed world in the west', while Hindus are professionals, progressive, and contributing to their host society in a productive exchange. Canadian authorities are also castigated for observing legal niceties: 'while a number of Sikhs who actually planted the bombs roam freely'. Essentially, Sikhs, in general, are being blamed before the due process of law could find those who are guilty.

This is, indeed, a new imagining of the Sikh persona; from fierce patriotic warriors of India to separatists and terrorists bent upon destroying India. The Khalsa's imputed 'bravery' has now become a liability due to the appearance of Sikh nationalism in contemporary India. Faced with an ethnic strife in several provinces with Kashmiris, Nagas, and Sikhs' questioning India's unity, Indian creative writers face a new challenge in writing fiction about the post-colonial Indian situation. Concerned with the future of India, a typical reaction of the Hindu elite has been to project ethnic demands as nothing more than terrorism. This transformation of a community's image, defines a new contour of a 'concerned' Indian intellectual's agenda. Mukherjee's non-fiction and fictional characterization of Sikhs, it can be suggested, are part of a new genre of Indian literary writings; largely a product of diaspora writers—with some hesitation one adds a further adjective, of Hindu background. This genre projects non-Hindus in specific ways. Added to Muslim characters, Sikhs find themselves characterized as backward looking, emotional, prone to violence and finally, terrorists. Such cross-cultural imaginative writings form an integral element of the Indian literary past, in which portrayal of 'others' were offered by Hindus, Muslim, and other minority writers. An explanation in terms of past interaction between Bengalis and Sikhs can also be offered. Historically, Sikhs and Bengalis had much closer ties despite the physical distance between the two provinces. From the Ghadar rebellion in 1914–15 against the British rule in India to the Naxalite insurrection for proletarian revolution in the late 1960s, the Bengali elite has guided some Sikh activists. In this exchange, some stereotyped images have also surfaced: Bengalis admired Sikh peasants' 'bravado'; the latter were in awe of 'intellectual foresight' of the former. Thus, Tarknath Das, a Bengali exile in America in the first decade of twentieth century organized night classes for the benefit of Sikh workers of British Columbia and Washington. Through education and 'guidance' he wanted to stir lumber-mill workers' revolutionary 'zeal'.[16] Mukherjee's caricature of North American Sikhs, in a sense, echoes a continuity, with added flavour and vehemence.

What is new is its transportation to the diaspora setting. This is the space of Mukherjee's intellectual trajectory, where her creative fiction and other writings might be located. Her imagined and real Sikhs reveal her as someone not only grappling with India's multi-ethnic heritage but also trying to take an intellectually consistent position between America's 'melting pot' and Canada's 'multiculturalism'.[17] To question the Department of Multiculturaism for funding of cultural diversity is one thing, but to assert that such a policy was primarily responsible for such a disaster as Air India tragedy is to let imagination run wild. Can anyone seriously believe that tiny amounts sanctioned for various [mostly symbolic] ethnic community projects amount to consolidation or worse ethnic separatism?[18]

Such small pieces of prejudice have a cumulative effect on the public mind and could lead to serious policy implications. Thus, as the Air India plane crashed into the sea, the slandering of the Canadian Sikhs began. In the lengthy process of Canadian security forces trying to arrest the culprits, the image of Sikhs suffered so much that according to a scholar, court cases involving Sikhs were leading to prejudicial outcomes:

Regrettably, there have been several criminal cases affecting Sikhs in Canada in which investigating or prosecuting officials have been found to have compromised the integrity and credibility of their work ... This repeated violation of the normal guidelines in the case of Sikh defendants has alienated many Sikhs and undermined confidence in Canadian investigative and judicial agencies ....[19]

Matters were not restricted to law and order cases only. An academic chair for Sikh Studies funded by various Canadian Sikh organizations was kept in abeyance, and reluctantly sanctioned at the University of British Columbia in 1988, fearing India's displeasure over such a gesture to the Sikh community.[20] Applications from Sikh refugees were routinely turned down. As a small boat load of Sikh refugees arrived in Canadian waters in July 1987, a more restrictive immigration bill was pushed hastily through the parliament.[21] In this anti-Sikh wave of public opinion, Canada's foreign secretary concluded an extradition treaty with India to deal with 'Sikh terrorists' operating on Canadian soil. The foreign secretary later sought the boycott of several Canadian Sikh organizations, lumping the so-called moderate World Sikh Organization with more militant Babbar Khalsa and others. The official advice about boycott led to a vigorous debate in the parliament where members pointed out double standards being applied in the case of Sikhs compared with other diaspora communities of Ukrainians, Lithuanians, Latvians, Armenians and Jews involved in similar campaigns.[22] It seems quite a feat on the part of two creative writers to write approvingly of Canada's revoking of stay for Sikh refugees after the signing of Indo-Canadian Treaty, paying little attention to its human rights implications and ignoring India's appalling record of torture, extrajudicial killings and violence against dissidents, militants and minorities.

Of course, *Jasmine* lends itself to many interpretations. It represents images of cultural alienation and fragmentation, 'freed from the dignities of the old culture'. Writing in the diaspora and for a new diverse audience, it is perhaps inevitable such post-modernist literature alludes to metaphors, bizarre images, and epochal transmutations through time and space. After all, how is one to rationalize, write, and make sense of the amazing multi-ethnic mix of New York suburbs, or the new ethnography of California? But such ventures exact their price. In the post-modernist era of novel writing, probably it would be unwise to complain about the elementary descriptive errors found in *Jasmine*, such as the colour of militant Sikhs' turbans [saffron not indigo], use of vehicles by them [motorcycles not scooters], the location of Hasanpur, a village mentioned near the border, [the Jalandhar district boundary does not extend to Indo-Pakistan border], the reason why Jyoti's father was against the use of Hindi by [attributed as an option—most Punjabi Hindus speak Punjabi—though preferring Hindi and Sanskrit], the allusion to Kali [a Hindu goddess much revered figure in Bengali Hinduism but hardly among Punjabi Hindus. Perhaps for a concerned Hindu intellectual, many Hinduisms ultimately ought to 'speak the same language']. Nor should one question the stretch of imagination in Jyoti's life, the violence done to her character by her multiple transformations. Equally unrealistic are the doctored dialogues between Sukhi and Jyoti's brothers and her late husband. Even some interviews in the factual air conspiracy book seem incredible for instance, Prakash Bedi's account of the gurdwara langar where he and his son were not served food [people sitting alongside would have found that totally objectionable and said so]. Perhaps these odd statements and broken selves are essential to post-modernist constructions that defy logic and common sense. Besides destroying the personality of its heroine Jyoti, *Jasmine* also constructs a Sikh character as the 'other'. The diverse constituency of critics and readers of such fiction might be bamboozled by the writers' dexterity but the creation of the 'other' emerges as almost a plot and is embedded in old-fashioned prejudices. It is as hurtful if not more for its post-modernist deviousness. Mukherjee's creation of particular images of Sikhs as contemptible and hateful characters in her fiction and non-fiction works raises some serious questions about the role of fiction in generating prejudice against a vulnerable minority.

Notes

1. The paper was presented at a seminar at the Centre for South Asian Studies, Coventry University. I am grateful to Ian Talbot, Gurharpal Singh and N.G. Barrier for comments. Needless to say, views presented are my own.

2. For a review of titles on the post-1984 Punjab crisis, see D.S. Tatla and Ian Talbot, *The Punjab*, Oxford: Clio 1994.

3. Apart from an admirable notice on Ondaatje's *The English Patient,* see Nikky-Guninder Kaur Singh, 'The Mirror and the Sikh: the transformation of Ondaatje's Kip', in Shackle, c. et al. [eds], *Sikh Religion, Culture and Ethnicity*, Curzon, 2001, 118–41. The portrayal of Sikhs by non-Sikhs has been a much debated point for almost a century. Armed with western education, the new Sikh intelligentsia questioned writings of Arya Samajis, Punjabi Muslims, and Christian missionaries, including some commentaries by English administrators. This interrogation of non-Sikhs' works has continued to the contemporary period. While much of this debate has included serious critiques, a small fringe among Sikhs has reacted more sharply to such writings. In the 1990s, this fringe scored some success as it managed to manipulate the institution of Akal Takht to 'rein in' such scholars and 'control' the Sikh diaspora's interpretations of the *rahit.*

4. Among her writings, her novels are: *Leave it to me* [1997?] *The Holder of the World,* [1993] *Jasmine* [1989], *The Tiger's Daughter* [1971]; collections of short stories are: *Darkness* [1985], *Middleman and other Stories* [1988]; non-fiction works both written in collaboration with Clark Blaise—a fellow writer and her husband: *Days and Nights in Calcutta* [1977], *The Sorrow and the Terror: Air India Tragedy* [1988], She is also author of *Critical Fictions: The Politics of Imaginative Writing* [1991]. Detailed bibliography of her works, biography, interviews and related critical articles can be downloaded from website: *Women Writers of the Color: Voices from the Gaps: Bharati Mukherjee.*

5. *American Dreamer,* January/February 1997. This article was first published in Bart Schneider [ed.] *Race: An Anthology in the First Person,* New York: Clarkson Potter: 1997.

6. See for example, Gail Ching-Liang Low, 'In a free state: postcolonialism and postmodernism in Bharati Mukherjee's fiction', *Women: A Cultural Review,* vol. 4, no. 1, pp. 8–18. Carman Wickeramagamage, 'Relocation as Positive Act: The Immigrant Experience in Bharati Mukherjee's Novels', *Diaspora,* vol. 2, no. 2, pp. 169–99.

7. This agenda can be identified through Hindu intellectuals' writings on the British colonial discourse, the debate on Indian historiography, and on such diverse topics as the American intentions and hegemony in South Asia. On the emergence of Hindu diaspora, and its attempts at reconstruction of a unified Indian heritage, see Vertovec [2000].

8. Clark Blaise and Bharati Mukherjee, *The Sorrow and the Terror: The Haunting Legacy of the Air India Tragedy,* Penguin Books Canada Limited, 1987 and published by Penguin Books, 1988. References herein refer to the paperback edition, 1988, with an introduction [ix–xxix], p. 219.

9. What disturbed Britain, Canada, and indeed several other countries who were interested in the causes of explosion was the Indian government's swift decision to strictly limit access to the 'black box' discovered after frantic efforts by international teams of navigation experts. Britain complained that the Bhabha Atomic Research Centre in India did not have the equipment or the expertise to analyse the tapes and other material found. See part 4, chapters 1–3., pp. 137–62.

10. Zuhair Kashmeri and Brian McAndrew, *The Soft Target: How Indian Intelligence Service Penetrated Canada.* Toronto: James Lorimer, 1989. The two journalists at *The Globe and Mail,* as its authors have argued that the Indian government agencies were responsible for the bombing of Air India flight 182 The inordinate delay by Canadian authorities to conclude their investigations has also led to suspicion by many Sikhs who feel that any eventual trial will be witch-hunting of the Sikhs.

11. On June 5, 2001, the Crown Counsel filed a new indictment against Ripduman Singh Malik, Ajaib Singh Bagri, and Inderjit Singh Reyat. They are jointly charged for murder, conspiracy to commit, murder and attempted murder of the passengers and crew of an Air India flight. They are being tried by the Supreme Court of British Columbia.

12. *The Middleman and Other Stories,* London: Virago Press, 1990, p. 197. All page references are to this edition.

13. *Jasmine.* London: Virago Press, 1991. All page references are from this edition.

14. For a sample of such writing, see Partap Sharma, *The Days of the Turban*, London: Bodley Head, 1986. Malony K. Dhar, *Bitter harvest; a saga of the Punjab*, Delhi: Ajanta, 1996.

15. While addressing a Sikh congregation, a speaker would usually begin with '*piyare Khalsa ji*' [dear members of the Sikh community].

16. Also see, Himadri Banerjee, 'Bengali Perception of the Sikhs: The Nineteenth and Twentieth Centuries', in Joseph O' Connell, Milton Israel, and W.G. Oxotby [eds] *Sikh History and Religion in the Twentieth Century*. University of Toronto Press, 110–33. Bharati Mukherjee, as a trustee of Tarknath Das Foundation at Columbia University, will not be unaware of Tarknath's warm contacts with the Sikhs in British Columbia in the first decade of the twentieth century.

17. On Mukherjee's American neo-nationalism see, Brewster, Anne, 'A Critique of Bharati Mukherjee's Neo-Nationalism', *SPAN: Journal of the South Pacific Association for Literature and Language Studies*, vol. 34–5 (1992–3).

18. Except, of course, during a debate in the Indian parliament where over indulgence shown to overseas Sikhs was strongly condemned. An Indian MP blamed Canada for funding Sikh separatism to the tune of millions of dollars. See Tatla [1999:157, 264]

19. Joseph O' Connell, 'Postscript: the view from Toronto', in Joseph O' Connell, Milton Israel, and W.G. Oxotby [eds] *Sikh History and Religion in the Twentieth Century*, University of Toronto Press, p. 444. Also see D.S. Tatla, *The Sikh Diaspora*, London: UCL Press, 1999, p. 134.

20. See Tatla [1999: 271].

21. See Tatla [1999: 172–9]. For an excellent study comparing different reception accorded to Tamil and Sikh refugees by Canadian authorities, see S.G. Hyder, *The Dialectic of Crisis*, University of Calgary, M.A. thesis, 1991.

22. See Tatla [1999: 165–79] for a summary of the debate in the Canadian Parliament.

Bio-bibliographic
Notes on Contributors

Tony Ballantyne (PhD Cambridge) is Assistant Professor of History at the University of Illinois at Urbana-Champaign. He is the author of *Orientalism and Race: Aryanism in the British Empire* (Palgrave-Macmillan, 2001) and is currently working on a monograph tentatively entitled *Entangled Histories: Sikhism, Colonialism and Diaspora*.

N. Gerald Barrier is Professor of History and a Middlebush Chair in the Social Sciences, University of Missouri, Columbia. His primary focus has been modern Sikh history (nineteenth to twentieth century), with particular focus on the 1880–1925 period (Singh Sabhas, Chief Khalsa Diwan). In addition to writing or editing nine books on the Sikhs and the Punjab, he has written over thirty scholarly articles on the region. His most recent interests include final preparation of a book on *Sikhism in the Modern World*, which will trace the interaction of religion and politics in Sikh institutions from the Chief Khalsa Diwan period to the present, and completing a total revision of his *Sikhs and their Literature* (this will cover most major themes, issues, reflected in Sikh books and articles, and include an annotated and union-listed guide to over 4000 titles and approximately 250 newspapers).

Louis E. Fenech is Associate Professor of South Asian and Sikh History at the University of Northern Iowa. He is the author of number of works on martyrdom and Sikhism including *Martyrdom in the Sikh Tradition: Playing the 'Game of Love'* (OUP, 2000) and 'Martyrdom and the Execution of Guru Arjan in contemporary Sikh Sources' in the *Journal of the American Oriental Society* (2001). He has also recently published 'Contested Nationalism; Negotiated Terrains: The Way Sikh Remember Udham Singh "Sahid" (1899–1940)' in *Modern Asian Studies* (2002). He is currently writing a book entitled 'Symbolic Capital and Colonialism in 18th–20th century India: Bhai Nand Lal Goya and the Sikh religion'.

Arthur W. Helweg is a Professor of Anthropology, Western Michigan University. He has done anthropological research regarding development in India and Pakistan. He has also done extensive research on Indians in the diaspora, especially Sikhs in Britain and Asian Indians in the United States. He has over 140 publications which include: *Sikhs in England* (New Delhi: Oxford University Press, 2nd ed. 1986), *An Immigrant Success Story* (Philadelphia: University of Pennsylvania Press; London: C. Hurst; and New Delhi: Oxford University Press) and, *Punjab in Perspective* (East Lansing, MI: Asian Studies Center of Michigan State University, 1987), which he edited with Surjit Dulai. His book, *An Immigrant Success Story* was awarded the Theodore Saloutos Award for the best book on immigration history published in 1990. Professor Helweg has done field research in India, Australia, Canada, England, Romania, and the United States. He has also consulted for the United States Agency for International Development and the United States Office of Education. He has also been awarded research grants from the Fulbright-Hays Program of the US Office of Education, US State Department, Smithsonian Institution, and Institute for Indian Studies.

DORIS R. JAKOBSH is an instructor of Religion and Culture at Wilfred Laurier University/University of Waterloo, Waterloo (Ontario), Canada. She was educated at the University of Waterloo, Harvard University and the University of British Columbia. She also spent one year in the Punjab, India, conducting research on the Sikhs and colonial history. Dr Jakobsh teaches courses in World Religions, Indian Religions, Sikhism, and Asian History. Her area of specialization is gender construction in Sikhism. Her forthcoming book, published by Oxford University Press, is entitled *Relocating Gender in Sikh History: Transformation, Meaning and Identity.*

W.H. (HEW) MCLEOD is a New Zealander who taught for nine years in the Punjab and there developed a life-long interest in the Sikhs. He returned to New Zealand in 1971 to teach History at the University of Otago and since then has paid frequent visits to the Punjab. Almost all of his books and published articles concern Sikh history, religion, and sociology. The books include *Guru Nanak and the Sikh Religion* (1968), *The Evolution of the Sikh Community* (1976), *Early Sikh Tradition* (1980), and *Who is a Sikh?* (1989), all of them published by the Clarendon Press in Oxford and re-published by the Oxford University Press in India, both singly and as a single omnibus volume (1999). OUP in New Delhi produced *Exploring Sikhism* (2000), a collection of his previously-published articles, and in December 2002 released his *Sikhs of the Khalsa: A History of the Khalsa*

Rahit. Professor McLeod retired in 1997 and has since been an Emeritus Professor of the University of Otago. He is a Fellow of the Royal Society of New Zealand.

ROBIN RINEHART is Associate Professor of Religion at Lafayette College, Easton, PA. Author of *One Lifetime, Many Lives: The Experience of Modern Hindu Hagiography* (Oxford University Press, 1999), her research focuses on religious literature of the Punjab and interactions among different religious traditions.

NIKKY-GUNINDER KAUR SINGH is Professor and Chair of the Department of Religious Studies at Colby College. Her interests focus on poetics and feminist issues. Nikky Singh has published extensively in the field of Sikhism, including *The Name of My Beloved: Verses of the Sikh Gurus* (Translations from Sikh Sacred Literature. San Francisco: HarperCollins 1995; and Delhi: Penguin, 2001), *The Feminine Principle in the Sikh Vision of the Transcendent* (Cambridge: Cambridge University Press, 1993), *Sikhism: World Religions* (New York: Facts on File, 1993; translated into Japanese: Tokyo, 1994), and *Physics and Metaphysics of the Guru Granth* (Delhi: Sterling Publishers, 1981; Delhi: Manohar, 1995).

PASHAURA SINGH occupies the position of Sikh Studies at the University of Michigan, Ann Arbor. His most recent publications include *The Guru Granth Sahib: Canon, Meaning and Authority* (Oxford University Press, 2000) and *The Bhagats of the Guru Granth Sahib: Sikh Self-Definition and the Bhagat Bani* (Oxford University Press, 2003). He has co-edited with N. Gerald Barrier two volumes, *The Transmission of Sikh Heritage in the Diaspora* (Manohar, 1996) and *Sikh Identity: Continuity and Change* (Manohar, 1999). He is currently working on a monograph entitled *Life and Work of Guru Arjan.* As the chief architect of four major international conferences in the area of Sikh Studies, he organized the present conference in September 2001 from which this book derives.

DARSHAN SINGH TATLA is a Visiting Fellow in the Department of Sociology and Anthropology at the Punjabi University, Patiala. His recent works include *Sikhs in North America* (New York: Greenwood, 1991), and *The Sikh Diaspora: Search for Statehood* (London, UCL Press, 1999).